Building English Skills

Orange Level

Building English Skills   Purple Level

Building English Skills   Yellow Level

Building English Skills   Blue Level

Building English Skills   Orange Level

Building English Skills   Green Level

Building English Skills   Red Level

Building English Skills

Orange Level

Prepared by the Staff of
The Writing Improvement Project

McDougal, Littell & Company
Evanston, Illinois

Staff of THE WRITING IMPROVEMENT PROJECT

J. A. Christensen, East High School, Salt Lake City, Utah

Stephen G. Ham, New Trier Township High School East, Winnetka, Illinois

Marilyn V. Kemp, Chairperson, English Department, New Trier Township High School East, Winnetka, Illinois

Joy Littell, Editorial Director, McDougal, Littell & Company

Robert J. Lumsden, Evanston Township High School, Evanston, Illinois (Yellow and Purple Levels)

Patricia Phelan, Chairperson, English Department, Hale Jr. High School, San Diego, California

William A. Seabright, Director of Design, McDougal, Littell & Company

Agnes Stein, English Department, Bloomfield College, Bloomfield, New Jersey

Marcia Baldwin Whipps, East High School, Salt Lake City, Utah

The Staff wishes to thank the more than 1500 students who contributed samples of their writing for analysis.

Acknowledgments: See page 262.

Grateful acknowledgment is made to The New Yorker for "Humoresque" by Fred Moeckel; copyright © 1962 by the New Yorker Magazine, Inc.

ISBN: 0-88343-459-8

Chapters 1, 8, 9, and the Handbook contain, in revised form, some materials that appeared originally in English Arts and Skills, grade 9, by Ronald J. Wilkins et al, copyright © 1965, 1961 by The Macmillan Company. Used by arrangement.

Contents

The page numbers for the Handbook (the second half of this book) appear in red.

Handbook

The page numbers for the Handbook (the second half of this book) appear in red.

8.0 Adjective and Adverb Usage 162

9.0 Verb Usage 172

10.0 Capitalization 186

11.0 End Marks and Commas 197

12.0 The Semicolon, the Colon, the Dash, and Parentheses   211

13.0 The Apostrophe   219

14.0 Quotations   227

15.0 Spelling 233

16.0 The Plurals of Nouns 247

17.0 Good Manuscript Form 252

SPECIAL FEATURES OF THIS TEXT

The Composition Chapters (First half of text)

Vocabulary Development. Chapter 1 emphasizes *learning word meanings from context, inferring word meanings, multiple meanings,* and *the precise use of words.* An adequate vocabulary, and the ability to use synonyms precisely, are prerequisites to good writing.

Using the Senses. Chapter 2 revitalizes an awareness of the five senses as a way of enriching writing.

The Paragraph. Chapters 3 and 4 comprise an intensive study of the paragraph. Chapter 3 provides guided opportunities to write expository paragraphs developed by various methods: using facts or statistics, using specific examples, using an incident or an anecdote, and using comparison or contrast. Chapter 4 treats in detail the descriptive paragraph and the narrative paragraph. Both chapters provide a wealth of first-rate models, along with helpful analysis.

The Composition. Chapter 5 provides a clear, workable blueprint for an expository composition. Chapter 6 deals with descriptive, explanatory, and narrative compositions.

Writing Letters. Chapter 7 provides help in writing informal letters. It also presents the proper forms for business letters and discusses various types of letters such as requests for information, letters of order, and letters of complaint.

Sentence Improvement. Chapter 8 provides an intensive program for sentence improvement based on a study of over 3000 student themes. This program is based on the belief that *the important problems of writing begin at the level of the sentence.* Some of these problems involve errors in grammar, but many of them are problems of meaning and sense. In each book, a chapter is devoted to those sentences which, though grammatically correct, are nonetheless unsatisfactory. In this book, for example, Chapter 8 deals with empty sentences, the circular sentences that say nothing (pages 188-192); it also deals with overloaded sentences, the sentences that contain too many ideas (pages 196-198).

The Handbook (Second half of text)

The Handbook is arranged in 17 numbered sections, as follows:

Grammar. Sections 1-4 provide a thorough treatment of traditional grammar in a contemporary setting. Section 5 is an optional chapter on modern grammar.

Usage. Sections 6-9 deal with problems of usage.

Capitalization, Punctuation, Spelling, and Manuscript Form. Sections 10-17 deal with the mechanics of writing.

Special Features of the Handbook. The Handbook has some distinct advantages over other available handbooks:

1. The typographic arrangement is clear and attractive. Type and open space have been used to set off definitions and examples so as to make them easy to find and easy to read.

2. Since each topic is a short phrase (printed in red) rather than a rule, it is easy to locate.

3. Within each topic, there is a full explanation of each concept, followed by examples, and where appropriate, by the definition or generalization printed in boldface type.

Chapter 1

Building Your Vocabulary

Do you know why your English book begins with a chapter on building your vocabulary? It begins this way because your success in school will depend to a great extent on your knowledge of words. Words are tools you will use in reading, writing, speaking, and listening. They are the tools you will use in mastering other subjects—history, science, foreign languages, and so on.

Scientific studies have shown that the larger your vocabulary is, the greater your chances are for success in school and in later life. If you take your study of this chapter seriously, you will indeed enlarge your vocabulary. But far more important, you will acquire the *power* to add constantly to your supply of words.

This chapter will show you how to unlock the meanings of unfamiliar words by seeing how they are used in the sentences in which they appear. It will also show you how to use the dictionary to find the exact word you are looking for.

With a large vocabulary at your command, you will be able to master your school subjects more quickly and easily. You will also be able to express your thoughts and feelings more precisely.

Part 1

Learning Word Meanings from Context

During your study of this chapter, you will learn several useful ways of finding out the meanings of unfamiliar words. The meaning of a word is determined by the *context* in which it is used. The **context** of a word is the sentence or group of sentences in which the word appears. Frequently, the context of a passage will help you determine the meaning of an unfamiliar word.

From books or television programs you know that when a detective is called to the scene of a crime, he first examines the surrounding territory for evidence which might help in solving the crime. In much the same way, you can often learn the meaning of an unfamiliar word by careful examination of the "surrounding territory"—the *context* in which the word is used. This examination will frequently give you some clue to help you unlock the meaning of the unknown word.

There are several types of context clues which can help you discover the meaning of an unfamiliar word. The most common types are these:

1. Definition or restatement
2. Example
3. Comparison
4. Contrast

Once you have learned to use these clues, you can easily unlock the meanings of many unfamiliar words.

Definition or Restatement

Sometimes a writer will reveal the meaning of a word by defining it for you. This type of clue is the easiest to detect. Study the following example:

The boys declared the long climb up the steep cliff a *grueling* experience—one that left them utterly exhausted.

According to the dictionary, *grueling* is defined as "very tiring, exhausting." Notice that the phrase which follows the dash is practically the same as the definition taken from the dictionary.
Here is another example:

Howard Hughes spent the last few years of his life *secluded* in well-guarded hotel suites, shut off from personal contact with even his closest business associates.

Even if you do not know the word *secluded*, the context of the passage points to the words "shut off from." One dictionary definition for this work is "barred or shut off from the view of or relations with others." Thus the context provides a definition of the word *secluded*.

The most obvious context clue in this category is the **appositive,** a restatement of the same idea in other words. Here is an example of this type of restatement:

The directors of the Bay City Zoo have announced the purchase of a pair of *quetsals*, crested birds native to Central America.

Without the appositive phrase "crested birds native to Central America," you might not know whether quetsals were animals or vending machines.
Here is another example of an appositive:

Uncle Ivan is very fond of *kohlrabi*, a garden vegetable related to the cabbage.

For persons unfamiliar with kohlrabi, the appositive phrase "a garden vegetable related to the cabbage" provides the context clue essential to unlocking the meaning of the word.
By skillful use of the context clue of Definition or Restatement, you will be able to unlock the meanings of many unfamiliar words quickly and easily.

Example

Another way in which context can help unlock the meaning of an unfamiliar word is by giving one or more examples. When several examples are cited, they achieve a "snowball" effect; that is, they pile up in such a way that with a little thought you can make a fairly accurate guess at the meaning of the unfamiliar word. In this type of clue, watch for certain "key" words which will help you unlock the meaning of the unfamiliar word.

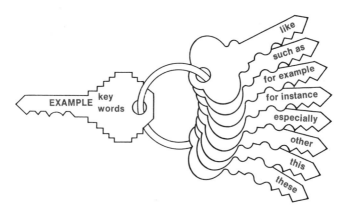

Be alert for key words in the following example:

A small museum near Vicksburg, Mississippi, contains some excellent examples of Civil War *memorabilia*, such as flags, cannonballs, maps, guns, photographs, and both Union and Confederate uniforms.

In this example, several clues help you determine the meaning of *memorabilia*: the word *examples*, the key words *such as*, and the list of examples all help you understand the meaning of memorabilia—a collection of things worth remembering.

Here is another example:

The reading teacher must be prepared to deal with *dyslexia* and other types of reading problems.

The skillful reader can use the key word *other* to help unlock the meaning of dyslexia—a type of reading problem.

Comparison

A third very effective type of context clue is comparison. In this type of clue, the writer compares the unfamiliar word with other, more familiar, words. By paying close attention to these comparisons, you can unlock the meaning of many unfamiliar words.

Certain key words can help you determine the meaning of an unfamiliar word when you use the comparison context clue:

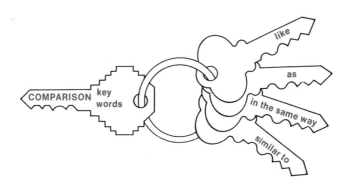

Note how the use of a key word in the following example helps you understand the meaning of the word *dromedary*.

> The *dromedary*, like all desert animals, can go for long periods of time without drinking water.

Even if the context does not fully reveal that the dromedary is a type of camel, the word *like* helps to point out the dromedary as a type of desert animal. By comparing the unfamiliar word to something more familiar, the writer gives you a key to help unlock the meaning of the unfamiliar word.

Contrast

By contrasting an unfamiliar word with something with which you are familiar, the writer of a passage gives you a valuable type of context clue. Here again, certain key words will help you determine the meaning of the unknown word:

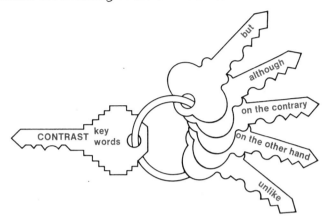

The contrast in the following example helps to make clearer the meaning of the word *archaeologist*:

> The *archaeologist*, unlike many other students of ancient history, actually digs in the earth to uncover remains left by former civilizations.

Two context clues help you understand the word *archaeologist* in the example above. The word *unlike* tells the reader that the archaeologist is being contrasted with something else. The word *other* gives a very helpful clue by telling the reader that the archaeologist is a student of ancient history who searches in a unique way for knowledge of the past. Sometimes more than one context clue will be given in a particular sentence.

Exercises
Learning Word Meanings from Context

A. The sentences on the next page contain words with which you may be unfamiliar. Using the context clues which you have just studied, select the *best* meaning for the italicized word in each passage. Write down the letter which you think represents the correct response. After the letter, tell which context clue (or clues) you used in determining the meaning of the italicized word.

1. Several *lustrous* objects added to the brightness of the room, especially the glimmering chrome sculpture, the gleaming crystal chandelier, and the sparkling silver doorknobs.

   A. stolen   C. shining
   B. expensive   D. handmade

2. I was simply *petrified* from fright; I couldn't move a muscle.

   A. panicked   C. thrilled
   B. paralyzed   D. scared

3. Some nations have unwisely *exploited* their colonies, taking as much wealth out of them as they could.

   A. taken advantage of   C. destroyed
   B. enslaved   D. bought and sold

4. Of course this narrative is *fictitious*; it has no basis in fact.

   A. colorful   C. important
   B. changeable   D. imaginary

5. The story was too *somber*; I prefer something with a more cheerful setting.

   A. sleepy   C. lengthy
   B. sad   D. noisy

6. Paul's *scrupulous* attention to detail, such as dotting every *i*, crossing every *t*, and forming every letter perfectly, makes his handwriting a pleasure to read.

   A. careless   C. very careful
   B. left-handed   D. occasional

7. SALT for Strategic Arms Limitation Talks and NATO for North Atlantic Treaty Organization are examples of *acronyms*.

   A. governmental agencies
   B. important business organizations
   C. words formed from the first letters of other words
   D. words borrowed from foreign languages.

8. Although the cheerleaders maintained their customary *exuberance*, the spectators silently mourned the team's tenth consecutive loss.

A. high spirits   C. appearance
B. embarrassment   D. routine

9. The works of two *prolific* authors, Agatha Christie and William Shakespeare, fill several shelves in most libraries.

A. poor   C. internationally famous
B. producing many works   D. lucky

10. The sign beside the beautiful fountain in Rome contained the warning *aqua non potable*. Those who failed to heed this *admonition* became sick from drinking the water.

A. invitation   C. sign
B. information   D. warning

B. Read the following passage very carefully. Copy the underlined words on a sheet of paper. After each word, write your idea of the meaning of the word. Check your meaning with a dictionary. (You may want to review the types of context clues before you begin this exercise.)

Shortly after the *Golden Clipper* left Pago Pago, several of the crew members became ill with <u>enterocolitis</u>. Since all of the men who suffered from this severe intestinal disorder had eaten at the same seaside cafe, the ship's doctor <u>surmised</u> that the seamen had <u>contracted</u> this disease by eating <u>tainted</u> fish.

The government of the Philippines, however, fearing the spread of a <u>contagion</u>, refused to let the ship dock in Manila Bay. Instead, the entire crew was transferred to a <u>lazaretto</u> floating three miles offshore. A staff of doctors and nurses cared for those who were ill and carefully observed the other crew members for any signs of the <u>malady</u>. When no new cases developed after three days, the Philippine doctors ruled out any possibility of a <u>contagion</u>. The ailing seamen were then transferred to a hospital in Manila, and the others were permitted to return to the *Golden Clipper* and dock in Manila Bay.

C. Choose a feature article from a newspaper or a magazine. The article can be about fashion, sports, or any other subject. Read the article carefully. When you come across an unfamiliar word, write down the sentence in which it appears. Using the skills you have learned for unlocking the meanings of new words, write down the definition you have determined from the context clue. Be prepared to share with the class the context clue that helped you unlock the meaning of the word.

Part 2
Inferring Word Meanings

The context in which an unfamiliar word appears does not always provide clues as obvious as the ones in the examples you have just seen. Instead of stating directly the meaning of the word, the writer may just imply certain things. The reader must read between the lines to pick up clues. This process of reading between the lines in order to reach some conclusion is known as **inference.**

Most of the context clues you used in Part 1 were found in the same sentence with the unfamiliar word. When you are trying to **infer** the meaning of a word, you will frequently have to look elsewhere in the paragraph, or at the whole paragraph, for information that will help you. Among the various types of inference you may use when trying to infer the meaning of an unknown word are these:

1. Inference based on the main idea
2. Inference based on stated details
3. Inference based on cause and effect relationship
4. Inference based on implied comparison
5. Inference based on implied contrast

Study the following examples carefully. Try to use the suggested inference technique to determine the meaning of the underlined words.

Inference Based on the Main Idea

The main idea of the following paragraph centers around the meaning of *planned obsolescence*. No doubt, you know the meaning of *planned*, but you may not know the meaning of *obsolescence*.

> Much of the American economy is based on the principle of planned *obsolesence*. Recently various consumer groups have criticized manufacturers for turning out products which are designed to wear out in a short time, especially since the technology exists to make longer-lasting products. Criticism has also been directed at the American automobile industry for "brainwashing" the American consumer into believing that his year-old car is outdated as soon as the new models go on sale.

From the main idea of this paragraph, you can infer that oblescence means:

A. investment   C. high prices
B. uselessness or outdatedness   D. patriotism

Inference Based on Stated Details

The various details in the following paragraph help you infer the meaning of *impromptu:*

> It was an intensely hot summer Sunday. Most of the neighbors were indoors with air conditioners and color TVs going full blast. Suddenly, there was a power failure. After about a half hour, most houses had lost their pleasing coolness and people began to drift outdoors in search of a gentle breeze. Before long, everyone was sharing soda, lemonade and iced tea. Food began to appear, someone fetched picnic tables, and an *impromptu* block party developed. All around me, people were getting acquainted, and no one seemed to care that the power was still off. Nor did the spirit of the party die with the

end of the evening. We have since organized a block softball team and a number of charity projects. Ever since that power failure, our neighborhood has been a more pleasant place to live.—PETER PAGE

From the details stated in this paragraph, you can infer that *impromptu* means:

  A. done without previous preparation C. exciting
  B. carefully planned and organized D. wooden

Inference Based on Cause and Effect Relationship

You read the following passage earlier to determine by context the meaning of *admonition*. As you read the passage this time, note that the effect or outcome of a particular action is stated. See if you can correctly infer the meaning of the phrase, *aqua non potable*.

> The sign beside the beautiful fountain in Rome carried the warning *aqua non potable*. Those who failed to heed this admonition became sick from drinking the water.

The cause and effect relationship in this passage leads you to infer that the Italian phrase means:

  A. keep off the grass C. water for horses only
  B. no swimming D. undrinkable water

Inference Based on Implied Comparison

From the implied comparisons in the following passage, try to infer the meaning of *amalgam*:

> Sonia's pleasing personality is an *amalgam* of the most desirable traits of the other members of her family. She has her father's cheerfulness, her mother's sense of humor, and her sister's calmness.

From the comparisons in this passage, you can infer that *amalgam* means:

A. combination C. mockery
B. denial D. delight

Inference Based on Implied Contrast

The contrasts in the following passage should enable you to infer the meaning of *transformation:*

> Sophia took a hard look at him; an astounding *transformation* had taken place. No longer did he appear lackluster or even middle-aged. His expression sparkled, his clean-shaven face was flooded with color; he had shifted his shoulders about until his coat fitted him the way the tailor had meant it to; he bristled with a youthful zest and energy. . . . But most important for her were his eyes, now bright, clear, knowledgeable, the lids opened wide to let in all the sights the world had to bestow upon an eager and penetrating mind. —IRVING STONE

The best meaning for *transformation* in this passage is:

A. accident C. movement
B. change D. sin

Exercise
Inferring Word Meanings

Read each of the following passages in its entirety. Then reread the passage, paying particular attention to the italicized word or words. Based on your understanding of the passage, try to infer the meaning of each of the italicized words. Write down your inference and check it with a dictionary.

1

Many politicians are masters at the art of *circumlocution.* This fact is often best illustrated in press conferences. In response to a controversial question posed by a reporter, some politicians can talk for several minutes without ever really answering the question.

2

Most Americans would find it difficult to adapt to the *ascetic* lifestyle of a monk. Garage door openers, dishwashers, garbage disposers, stereos, and color televisions—the luxuries which many pampered Americans consider necessities—are all absent from the life of a Franciscan monk.

3

The sudden collapse of the Brennan Dam sent a *torrent* of devastation into the St. Thomas Valley. Within a matter of hours, however, numerous organizations and individuals met the *exigency* of the situation with food, clothing, shelter, and medical help for the survivors.

4

A true *gastronome*, like Julia Child, is probably unimpressed by the billions of hamburgers sold by fast food, carry-out restaurants. Better known as "The French Chef," Mrs. Child is the author of a number of books on French cooking. For her, the art of cooking rests more in the quality than in the quantity of the final product.

5

The immediate destruction of the earthquake was much less than the destruction caused by the *ensuing holocaust*. The earthquake ruptured both gas and water lines throughout the city. Without a water supply the firemen were unable to combat the numerous fires started by the broken gas lines.

6

The Better Business Bureau is investigating a new product that claims to cure practically every type of human ailment. It claims to bring immediate relief for arthritis, headaches, colds, vitamin deficiency, low vitality, backache, and sleeplessness. Because of the *preposterous* claims of the new medicine, the suspicions of the medical profession have been aroused.

Part 3

The Multiple Meanings of Words

Most of your vocabulary development in school thus far has probably involved learning the meaning and spelling of each new word. For many words, this plan is acceptable, but for many other words it does not go far enough. Assigning *the* meaning to a word often ignores the numerous additional meanings of that word.

Before you read the next section, write down on a piece of paper a definition for the word *court*. Now compare your definition with the uses of that word in the following sentences.

1. Helen and Alice are going to the tennis *court* for a game this afternoon at three.
2. The strolling players set up their stage in the inner *court* of the castle.
3. The Queen and her *court* attended the New Year's Ball.
4. The judge asked the *court* to consider the evidence carefully.
5. Some politicians do everything in their power to *court* the favor of those whose patronage they desire.
6. The reigning king usually held *court* on the first day of the month, to receive the petitions of his subjects.
7. Did you hear the story of the man who was too shy to *court* the woman he loved?
8. Some persons are foolish enough to *court* danger.
9. Our home is on a very short street known as Canterbury *Court*.

Did your definition of *court* fit any of the sentences? If not, share with the class a sentence using *court* to fit your definition. From these examples, you will see the necessity of being aware of the multiple meanings of a word.

Webster's New World Dictionary lists 13 different meanings for the word *court*. The multiple meanings of words need not pose a problem for you if you remember what was said in Part 1 of this chapter: The context of a word determines its meaning.

Dictionary Entry for <u>Court</u>

court (kort) **n.** [OFr. < LL. < L. *cohors:* see COHORT] **1.** an uncovered space wholly or partly surrounded by buildings or walls **2.** a short street, often closed at one end **3.** *a)* an area for playing any of several ball games [a tennis *court*] *b)* a part of such an area ☆**4.** a motel: in full, **motor court 5.** *a)* the palace of a sovereign *b)* the family, advisers, etc. of a sovereign, as a group *c)* a sovereign and his councilors as a governing body *d)* any formal gathering held by a sovereign **6.** attention paid to someone in order to get something **7.** courtship; wooing **8.** *a)* a person or persons appointed to examine and decide law cases, make investigations, etc.; judge or judges *b)* a place where trials are held, investigations made, etc. *c)* an assembly or meeting of the judge or judges, the lawyers, and the jury in a law court —**vt. 1.** to pay attention to (a person) in order to get something **2.** to try to get the love of; woo **3.** to try to get; seek [to *court* favor] **4.** to make oneself open to [to *court* insults] —**vi.** to woo —**adj.** of or fit for a court —**out of court** without a trial —**pay court to** to court, as for favor or love —**court′er n.**

word used as a noun ─

word used as a verb (transitive) ─

word used as a verb (intransitive) ─

word used as an adjective ─

8 meanings of *court,* used as a noun.

4 meanings of *court,* used as a verb.

1 meaning of *court,* used as an adjective.

Exercises
Words with Multiple Meanings

A. Just as the word *court* has multiple meanings, each of the words in the following list can be used in several different ways. Write at least five sentences for each of the following words, making sure that each sentence illustrates a different meaning for the word.

note	light
round	ring

B. The word *key* may be used correctly by the persons indicated below. Look up the different meanings in the dictionary and show the use of each in an original sentence.

1. a locksmith
2. a typist
3. a singing teacher
4. a person solving a puzzle
5. a piano tuner
6. a composer of songs
7. a student of the geography of Florida
8. a student studying pronunciations in the dictionary
9. a mathematics teacher

C. Give the meaning of the word *square* in the following sentences, taking the precaution of checking with the dictionary in cases where you are not quite sure.

1. A band concert is to be held in the village *square* tomorrow evening.
2. On Monday we can *square* our accounts.
3. Carpenters use *squares* to test right angles.
4. We are going to learn to find the *square root* of numbers.
5. He *squared* the surface with a straightedge.
6. The sergeant told the recruits to *square* their shoulders.
7. What is the formula for the area of a *square?*

D. The following sentences contain phrases using forms of the word *book.* Explain the meaning of the italicized phrases.

1. Even though his team lost the final game, the coach admitted that the referees had called the fouls *by the book.*
2. Miss Schwartz has *kept books* for the Acme Paving Company for forty-three years.
3. The officer *booked* the man for suspicion of burglary.
4. The candidate said he wanted to make *an open book* of his family finances.

Part 4

Gaining Precision in the Use of Words

Precision is one of the marks of power. The concert singer who is exactly "on pitch," the archer who hits the "bull's-eye," the sky diver who lands directly "on target"—all display a precision which marks superior skill.

Precision in the use of words is essential to achieving word power. Precise use of synonyms and antonyms distinguishes the person with a powerful vocabulary from the person with an ordinary vocabulary.

Synonyms

Synonyms are words that have similar meanings. They do not usually mean *exactly* the same thing. Each one has a meaning slightly different from the others. You should have as many synonyms as possible in your vocabulary so that you can say exactly what you want to say and understand exactly what you read and hear.

Let's see how synonyms work. If a neighbor asked you if you were a *pupil* in East High School, would you say "Yes"? If he suggested that your ten-year-old brother was a *student* at Jefferson Elementary School, would he be right? If he called you a *scholar*, would he be using the correct word?

Note how the dictionary sets you right about these three words:

1. The word *pupil* applies to a child in school, or to someone studying privately with a teacher.

   EXAMPLES:

   Ruthmarie is a *pupil* of the famous singer, Carlo Amato.
   Bobby is a *pupil* at Jefferson Elementary School.

2. The word *student* applies to someone attending a high school, a college, or university.

   EXAMPLES:

   Several hundred high school *students* attended the rally.
   I am a first-year student at East High.
   Cousin Bob is a third-year *student* at the State University.

3. The word *scholar* is reserved for a learned person who is an authority in some field, or to a student who has a scholarship.

   EXAMPLES:

   Uncle Andrew is a Biblical *scholar*.
   Charles is a Fulbright *scholar*.

You can see from these examples that you might feel somewhat insulted if someone said you were a *pupil* at East High. You would probably prefer to be called a *student*. At the same time, you will realize that you probably should not be called a *scholar*. This is exactly what is meant by precision in the use of words. The more careful you are in the choice of synonyms, the more effective will be your use of the language.

A good dictionary is a valuable tool for developing precision in the use of synonyms. Most dictionaries contain **synonymies,** listings of synonyms explaining their differences or shades of meaning. The careful use of the synonymy sections of your dictionary is very important, especially since there are very few absolute synonyms in English.

Examine the synonymy entered in *Webster's New World Dictionary* following the word *brave:*

Dictionary Entry for Brave

brave (brāv) **adj.** [Fr. < It. *bravo*, brave, fine, orig., wild, savage < L. *barbarus*, BARBAROUS] **1.** not afraid; having courage; valiant **2.** fine; splendid [a *brave* new world] —**n.** **1.** any brave man **2.** a N. American Indian warrior —**vt. braved, brav′ing 1.** to face with courage [they *braved* the storm] **2.** to defy; dare —**brave′ly adv.** —**brave′ness n.**

SYN.—**brave** is the general term that implies fearlessness in meeting danger or difficulty; **courageous** suggests readiness to deal firmly with any dangerous situation because of self-discipline and strong convictions; **bold** stresses a daring nature, whether shown by courage, insolence, or defiance; **audacious** suggests reckless boldness; **valiant** emphasizes a heroic quality in the courage shown; **intrepid** implies absolute fearlessness in facing something new or unknown; **plucky** is usually used of someone who continues fighting even though at a disadvantage —**ANT. craven, cowardly**

synonymy

To the casual user of the language, the words *brave, courageous, bold, audacious, valiant, intrepid,* and *plucky* are interchangeable. To the precise user of the language, they are not. Each synonym carries a meaning not present in the other six words.

A precise user of the language might speak of a *brave* warrior, a *courageous* pioneer, a *bold* robber, an *audacious* plan, a *valiant* knight, an *intrepid* explorer, and a *plucky* youngster.

Synonyms add variety and color to our language. The use of the same words over and over is the mark of a poor writer or speaker. You may have some words in your vocabulary which you tend to overuse. Certain words, particularly colloquial expressions, are overused to such an extent in daily conversation that they lose much of their impact. In your speaking and writing, make a conscious effort to avoid such repetition.

The Thesaurus. The thesaurus is a reference book which can be an invaluable help to the writer. It is a storehouse of synonyms and word usage. Your clarity and your effectiveness in writing are dependent upon accurate word choice, and a thesaurus can help you find the exact word you need.

Here is an entry from *Roget's Thesaurus:*

DANGER.—I. *Nouns.* **danger,** chance, hazard, insecurity, jeopardy, peril, unsafety, risk, pitfall, endangerment; storm brewing, clouds gathering, clouds on the horizon; crisis.
dangerousness, riskiness, touch and go, unsafety, treachery; venturousness, etc. (see *Adjectives*).
[*dangerous person*] **menace,** threat, serpent, viper; dangerous woman, *femme fatale* (*F.*).
II. *Verbs.* **endanger,** expose to danger, hazard, jeopardize, peril, imperil, risk, speculate with, venture, compromise.
[*accept danger*] **risk,** hazard, venture, adventure, dare, stake, set at hazard, speculate.
III. *Adjectives.* **dangerous,** chancy, risky, ticklish, touch-and-go, venturous, venturesome, adventurous, adventuresome, speculative; hazardous, perilous, parlous, precarious, insecure, jeopardous, critical, queasy, unsafe, ugly, treacherous, serpentine, viperous.
See also CHANCE, FEAR, THREAT, WARNING.
Antonyms—See PROTECTION.

Antonyms

Antonyms are words that mean the opposite of each other. *Summer—winter, night—day, near—far, happy—sad* are examples of antonyms. Knowing how to use antonyms well will make your speech and writing more colorful and more precise. The correct use of antonyms will aid you greatly when you need to present a contrast.

Exercises
Gaining Precision in the Use of Words

A. Note the monotonous effect of the overuse of the word *fantastic* in the following paragraph:

> The Homecoming dance was a *fantastic* affair. The decorations committee did a *fantastic* job. The band, Jimmy and the Junior Beatles, was really *fantastic*. The hungry students consumed all of the *fantastic* refreshments. Everyone agreed that this was the most *fantastic* dance ever held at Jefferson High School. other words beside fantastic.

Rewrite this paragraph, substituting words for the overused word *fantastic*. The rewritten paragraph should be not only more colorful than the one printed above, but it should also give the reader a more precise picture of what the dance was actually like.

After you have rewritten the paragraph, check your words against the dictionary or thesaurus. Are there any words you would now use instead of the ones you chose yourself?

B. Study the following synonymy from *Webster's New World Dictionary* given after the word *estimate*. Write a sentence for each of these four words—*estimate, appraise, evaluate,* and *rate*—to illustrate the different shades of meaning of each word.

es·ti·mate (es'tə mat'; *for n.* -mit) **vt. -mat'ed, -mat'ing** [< L. pp. of *aestimare:* see ESTEEM] **1.** to form an opinion about [to *estimate* the merits of a movie] **2.** to make a general but careful guess about (size, value, cost, etc.) [he *estimated* the size of the crowd to be 300] **—vi.** to make an estimate **—n.** **1.** a general calculation of size, value, etc.; esp., an approximate figuring of the probable cost of a piece of work made by a person undertaking to do the work **2.** an opinion or judgment [this is a good book in my *estimate*] **—es'ti·ma'tive adj. —es'ti·ma·tor n.**

SYN.—**estimate** refers generally to the forming of a personal opinion or judgment; **appraise** implies the intention of giving an accurate or expert judgment, as of value or worth [to *appraise* a new house]; **evaluate** also connotes an attempt at an exact judgment, but rarely with reference to value in terms of money [let us *evaluate* the evidence]; **rate** implies the comparing of one person or thing with another or others as to value, quality, etc. [he is *rated* the best in his field]—see also **SYN.** at CALCULATE

answer, explain if needed

C. Answer the following. Use your dictionary if necessary.

1. Could the same person be *uninterested* and *disinterested* in the same project at the same time?

2. Could a person be *healthy* in an *unhealthful* climate? Explain.

3. If someone said you were a *bore*, would you be happy about it? If he said you were a *boor*, would you feel better or worse?

4. Explain the difference between *flash, glitter,* and *sparkle.* Use each in an original sentence.

5. If a person has an *irritable* disposition, he is easily annoyed. If he has an *irascible* disposition, what is his trouble?

6. Can you be *happy* without being *cheerful?* Could you be *cheerful* without being *happy?*

7. *Neat, tidy, trim* are often used interchangeably, but each word implies something different from the others. Use each in an original sentence that will make the distinctions clear.

8. Could you be *eager* without being *anxious?* Explain.

9. You would not object to being told you were *curious.* How would you feel if someone told you you were *inquisitive?*

10. If certain facts were *obvious,* would they also be *apparent?* Under what circumstances would you use *evident?*

D. Answer the following. Use your dictionary if necessary.

1. If a person is *unscrupulous,* would you care to deal with him? What word would you use to designate the opposite trait?

2. *Niggardly* persons have few friends. What quality would they have to cultivate to change the situation?

3. If a person were *illiterate,* would he necessarily have to be *uncultured?* Explain. Give two words opposite in meaning.

4. You attend a student rally; nothing much is accomplished. A classmate says the meeting was *unorganized;* another says it was *disorganized.* Which term is correct? Explain.

5. If you found a classroom door marked "Atypical," what type of student would you expect to find entering it?

6. You find the word *abridged* on the cover of a novel you are about to read. Would you expect a complete telling of the story as the author wrote it?

7. If you were told that doing a certain thing would be a

disservice to the school, would you persist in doing it? Give a reason for your answer.

8. What type of person is a *malcontent?* What word would you use to indicate someone of opposite disposition?

9. What is the difference between being *asocial* and *antisocial?*

10. What is the difference in meaning between the following: *illegal* and *illegible.* Use each in a sentence.

E. Write down two synonyms for each of the words given below. (Use a dictionary or thesaurus if necessary.) Use each synonym in an original sentence that clearly shows the difference in meaning.

1.	fear	6.	hesitate	11.	oblivious
2.	lazy	7.	spite	12.	deplore
3.	guard	8.	injure	13.	observe
4.	scoff	9.	scanty	14.	noticeable
5.	scold	10.	hateful	15.	error

2 more

F. Think of an antonym for each of the following words and use the antonym you choose in a sentence. As you discuss the sentences in class, you will notice that different students have chosen different antonyms for the same word. This illustrates that the antonym of one word may have several of its own synonyms.

1.	overpass	6.	extraordinary
2.	arrival	7.	lenient
3.	immovable	8.	huge
4.	difficult	9.	poverty
5.	defective	10.	vivid

use other word in sentence.

G. Find in your local newspaper or your favorite magazine five pairs of synonyms and five pairs of antonyms. Be prepared to tell the class why these words have been used correctly.

Summary

In this chapter you have learned and practiced four ways of building your vocabulary.

Sometimes the *context* of a passage will help reveal the meaning of a word:

   a.   by defining the word for you,
   b.   by giving one or more examples,
   c.   by comparing the word with other more familiar words, or
   d.   by contrasting the word with something with which you are familiar.

A second way to determine the meaning of a word is to make an *inference* based on the general sense of the passage. This requires "reading between the lines."

A third way to build your vocabulary is to learn the multiple meanings and uses of words you already know.

A fourth way to build your vocabulary is to increase your knowledge of synonyms and antonyms and to use them precisely.

Review Exercises

A. Using the techniques of context clues or inference which you studied in Parts 1 and 2 of this chapter, try to determine the meaning of each italicized word in the following sentences. Write down your understanding of the word. Consult a dictionary to see if your definition fits one of the dictionary definitions.

   1. One of the pitiful characters of Greek legend is Cassandra. She possessed the ability to foretell future events, but her *fatidic* statements were never believed.

   2. Spring *freshets* often wash out many bridges in mountainous regions.

   3. Even a brief conversation with Professor MacAllister reveals the extent of his *erudition*. His *voracious* reading over a period of more than sixty years has enabled him to speak knowledgeably on topics ranging from Shakespeare's sonnets to nuclear power.

   4. After nearly two generations of bloodshed and death, the war-weary residents welcomed the peace treaty and looked forward to *halcyon* days.

5. Among the *witticisms* of the late Senator Everett Dirksen is his often-quoted comment about the *mushrooming* federal budget: "A billion here and a billion there and the first thing you know, it adds up to real money."

6. Joyce prefers the glamorous excitement of a high fashion model to the *mundane* routine of a suburban housewife.

7. Most doctors object to spending time with *hypochondriacs* when they could be devoting more time to patients who really are sick.

8. His writings are much too *verbose*; he fills a whole page with what could better be said in a single sentence.

9. Palm trees are *indigenous* to tropical and subtropical climates.

10. Mrs. Haverford's doctors were quite pleased with the progress she made following her surgery. Soon she was able to resume her normal activities. Both Mrs. Haverford and her doctors were amazed and disappointed when a *recrudescence* of the ailment forced her return to the hospital.

B. Each of the following passages contains several words which may be unfamiliar to you. Read each passage in its entirety. Then reread the passage, paying particular attention to the italicized words. Based on your understanding of each word as it is used in the passage, write your own definition for that word. Check your definitions with a dictionary.

1

Dressed in *funereal* attire, friends and relatives gathered at the mortuary to *commiserate* with the *bereaved* young widow. The minister's *eulogy* praised the heroism of her husband, who died after rescuing three children from their burning apartment. Over 100 of his fellow firemen joined the *cortege* to the cemetery.

2

The winner of the Olympic *decathlon* is often *dubbed* "The World's Greatest Athlete." The *recipient* of the gold medal not only must possess the *dexterity* which enables him to perform well in each event, but he also must have the *stamina* to endure all ten events.

3

Most people are familiar with the *diurnal* animals of the forests, such as squirrels, chipmunks, and most birds. An afternoon walk on a *sylvan* path will reveal many of these animals engaged in their normal, daily activities. The *nocturnal* creatures, such as owls, bats, and opossums, are much less familiar since most people do not *frequent* their *habitats* at night.

Chapter 2

Using the Senses in Writing

Have you ever thought about yourself as a fantastic receiver of information, one who uses sight, hearing, touch, taste and smell all at one time? Without any conscious effort on your part, all of these senses are operating right now. Your senses bring you knowledge about your world, enabling you to be alive to all the excitement of living today.

When you were a very young child, experiencing the world for the first time, you had a heightened sensitivity to every sensory impression. Your world was newly fresh and exciting every moment. As you grow older, you tend to take your senses for granted because they operate as automatically as breathing. You need to recapture the rich enjoyment of coming alive to your senses in order to sharpen your perceptions and add new dimensions to your writing.

One of the best ways to collect your sensory data is to record your ideas, observations and experiments in a journal or diary. This collection of impressions will be a rich treasure house of material from which to draw as you continue to write. The pages that follow will examine your five senses, one at a time, though of course they are always working together.

Part 1

The Sense of Sight

Everything visible in the world can be seen by your eyes. There is a difference, however, between merely looking at a thing and really seeing it. Here is what one writer has discovered:

TO LOOK AT ANY THING

To look at any thing,
If you would know that thing,
You must look at it long:
To look at this green and say
"I have seen spring in these
Woods," will not do—you must
Be the thing you see:
You must be the dark snakes of
Stems and ferny plumes of leaves,
You must enter in
To the small silences between
The leaves,
You must take your time
And touch the very peace
They issue from.

JOHN MOFFITT

The writer is telling you that to really see any one thing is to see it with all your senses. You, in fact, must *become* that thing and enter into the core of it. You must experience a new awareness of the thing so that you can transmit its essence to your reader.

Here is a sight question to consider in order to see how observant you are right now. Record the answer in your journal.

What colors were used in painting your classroom? Suppose your classroom is painted yellow. Is it *warm* yellow? *streaked* yellow? *almost* yellow? Is it a *loud* yellow? a *singing* yellow? a *lemon* yellow? Each of these "yellows" creates an entirely different image for your readers, forcing them to bring their own senses into play. A sense of sharing exists between you and your readers as you help them recreate your experience.

Exercise
Testing Your Sight Observations

Record your answers to the questions below in your journal. Make your observations as specific and interesting as possible so you can use them later in your writing.

1. What color are your teacher's eyes?
2. What kinds of things are on the walls of your classroom?
3. Are there any clouds in the sky? Describe them.
4. What colors and shapes are the pens and pencils you have with you right now?
5. What color clothes was your mother or your father wearing this morning when you left home?
6. Which way does the front door at your house swing when it opens? Describe the door.

Training in Seeing

You are already a kind of expert at observing the world with your eyes, from noticing the color when you pick out your favorite shirt to noticing the subtle facial expressions on a person's face that invite a particular response from you. Expert as you are, here are some suggestions for training your sight to be even sharper.

1. On a piece of paper, draw a floor plan of a room at home, putting in all of the major pieces of furniture and the color of each. Share your plan with another person in class. Now take the floor plan home with you and check your sense of sight. Make any necessary corrections or additions to the plan, being partic-

ularly specific about color. Bring it back to class tomorrow and be prepared to tell a group what you discovered.

2. Select a small object near you—something on your desk, on the floor, or on the wall. Study it carefully for a short time. Then move so that you can no longer see it. Write a detailed description of the object, including size, color, shape, texture, and any unusual characteristics. In describing its size, for example, don't be content with saying it's two inches long. Try to bring the other senses into play. Is it the size of a walnut? the size of a matchbox? the size of a toothpick? When you feel you have included all possible details, turn back to see how well your description fits. Share your writing with another person by reading your description of the object without naming it. See if this person can recognize what you are describing.

3. Sit down in a familiar place in a room at home or at school, or outside if you wish. Write down everything you can see without turning or moving your circle of vision. Notice all the things you usually see in this spot; then concentrate on finding something you did not expect to see here. Describe it as specifically as you can, allowing your other senses to affect what you see. Share your experience with someone in class.

4. Stretch your sense of sight by careful observation on your way to or from school. Going your same familiar way, find ten things of interest that you never noticed before. Be prepared to write out this list of new "sights" to share with the rest of the class.

Here is a list of "sight" words to help you make your descriptions more vivid, more exact. Study the words and try to determine in what way each of the related words is different. Add your own words to the list and record them in your journal.

Colors

red

pink
salmon
rose
coral
raspberry
strawberry
tomato
currant
cherry
crimson
cardinal
vermillion
carmine
flame
ruby
garnet
wine
blood
maroon
burgundy

blue

sky
sapphire
azure
delft
porcelain
wedgewood

turquoise
aqua
aquamarine
violet
peacock
cobalt
royal
navy
steel

yellow

beige
buff
straw
peach
apricot
butter
buttercup
lemon
chartreuse
citron
canary
chrome
gold
topaz
ochre
saffron
sulphur
mustard
butterscotch
orange
tangerine

persimmon

green

celery
mint
apple
lime
kelly
emerald
olive
pistachio
chartreuse

white

snow
milky
marble
cream
ivory
oyster
pearl
silver
platinum

purple

lavender
amethyst
lilac
orchid
mauve

plum
mulberry
pansy
fuchsia
magenta

black

jet
ebony
licorice

gray

ashen
dove
steel

brown

sandy
almond
amber
tawny
hazel
cinnamon
nutmeg
chocolate
coffee
copper
rust
ginger

Sight Words

bronze	zip	loiter	crinkled
walnut	ram	stray	flared
mahogany	speed	slink	oval
	chase	stalk	conical
colorless	hurl	edge	cylindrical
rainbow	swat	sneak	tubular
	flick	stagger	hollow
	whisk	lope	rotund
Movements	rip	canter	chubby
	shove	waddle	portly
fast	swerve	drag	fat
	smash	sway	swollen
hurry	drop	soar	lumpy
run	plummet	lift	clustered
scamper	bounce	drift	padded
skip	dive	droop	tufted
scramble	swoop	heave	topheavy
dart	plunge		pendulous
spring	swing		jutting
spin	fly	**Shapes**	irregular
sprint	sail		proportioned
stride		flat	angular
streak	**slow**	round	triangular
propel		domed	rectangular
trot	creep	curved	hexagonal
gallop	crawl	wavy	octagonal
drive	plod	scrolled	square
dash	slouch	globular	pyramidical
bolt	lumber	rolled	tapering
careen	tiptoe	scalloped	branching
rush	bend	ruffled	twiggy
race	amble	frilled	split
zoom	saunter	crimped	broken

Sight Words

spindly	transparent	pretty	pale
skinny	translucent	heavy	pasty
thin	opaque	flat	sickly
wiry	muddy	stout	small
shapely	grimy	wide	tiny
winged	young	rigid	miniature
shapeless	drab	narrow	timid
	dingy	overloaded	shy
	dull	congested	fearful
Appearance	dark	cluttered	apprehensive
	dismal	crowded	tearful
dotted	rotted	jammed	nervous
freckled	old	packed	frightened
spotted	used	squeezed	terrified
blotched	worn	bruised	hysterical
wrinkled	untidy	tied	wild
patterned	shabby	stretched	bold
mottled	messy	tall	dramatic
flowery	chintzy	erect	tantalizing
striped	cheap	lean	irresistible
bright	ugly	slender	exhuberant
clear	ramshackle	supple	energetic
shiny	tired	lithe	animated
glowing	exhausted	lively	perky
glossy	arid	muscular	attractive
shimmering	awkward	sturdy	arrogant
fluid	crooked	robust	flamboyant
sparkling	loose	stolid	expansive
iridescent	curved	hardy	imposing
glassy	straight	strong	regal
flashy	orderly	healthy	stately
glazed	formal	frail	elegant
sheer	crisp	fragile	statuesque

large	dazzling	vivid	tidy
huge	opulent	flushed	handsome
immense	jeweled	fiery	pleasant
massive	lacy	blazing	sunny
gigantic	lavish	verdant	calm
showy	exotic	fresh	serene
decorative	gorgeous	clean	unruffled
distinctive	radiant	scrubbed	nerveless

Exercises
Using "Sight" Words in Your Writing

Now that you have stretched your sight experiences, here is a chance to practice using specific details in order to help your reader "see" as clearly as you do what you are describing.

A. Here are ten things you might see every day. Write a sentence describing each one. Try to select sight words that are exactly right to describe what you see. Record the sentences in your journal.

a shoe	a stone
the sidewalk	a dog or cat
the sky	a slice of bread
someone's hair	a button
a leaf	a piece of soap

B. Here is a paragraph that recreates a vivid sight impression.

She first saw him that Sunday as he walked down the long steps in clear view from her ledge of rock across the river. Between them was a transparent pool in the mountain pass.

Every rock on the bottom shimmered in green-gold helicoid light. Comfortable, conscious of the rock's heat on her stomach through her bathing suit, she watched him down the path, his white shirt flashing through the trees with the motion of his walking. Bronze skin, a tall leanness, eyes blue as the sky, hair brown in the shade and copper in the sun and wavy as the sea. She was sure, thinking of it later, that if there had been the trace of a limp in his walk, she would have noticed it and known who he was. But she watched him walk the entire way, conscious only of his beauty.—KATIE LETCHER LYLE

Make a list of all the color words in the paragraph. Next, make a list of all the words or phrases that create action or movement. What part of the description does not appeal to the sense of sight? To what other sense does it appeal?

c. You have stretched your sight experiences, studied a list of sight words, written sentences, and looked carefully at a paragraph that recreates a sight experience. You are now ready to write your own paragraph. You may use any of the subjects in Exercise A, any ideas from your journal, or any subjects from the following list. You may also use an entirely new idea.

your room	outside the window
the kitchen	a puddle of water
a dream	a quiet or a busy scene

Part 2
The Sense of Hearing

Have you ever temporarily lost your sense of hearing, perhaps from an ear infection or a bad cold? Only at such times are you likely to be aware of how much you depend on this particular sense as you move through your day, from the alarm clock on waking up, through the sounds of traffic as you cross the street, to the greetings of friends at school and even your mother's call for dinner in the evening. Here are some hearing questions to help you tune in to this sense right now. Record your ideas in your journal.

1. Close your eyes and listen for one minute. List the sounds that you were able to hear in the classroom.

2. Right now, pick out a sound that you never heard before in this time and place. Describe it.

3. List the usual sounds at the beginning and end of a period in this class. List the same beginning and ending sounds for another class, to compare them.

4. List all of the sounds that you can remember hearing in the cafeteria or lunch room.

5. List the sounds you are so used to at home that you do not ordinarily notice them.

6. List all of the sounds you like to hear; then list all of the sounds you hate to hear.

7. Stop up your ears for one minute and concentrate on the kinds of sounds that come to you. Try chewing, humming, shaking your head to see what different kinds of sounds and tones you hear. Describe them.

8. List all of the musical sounds you know.

9. List all of the sounds that you associate with one particular sport you play.

Training in Listening

In order to increase your sensitivity to sounds, you may sometimes need to close your eyes and concentrate only on listening, without your sense of sight to distract you. It is possible to develop more acute hearing, to notice more with your ears than you did before. Mothers often have unusual hearing where their children are concerned. You probably have better than average ability to detect slight changes in tone of voice that might indicate changes in mood and personality in your parents or friends. Careful listening to sounds can add a rich new dimension to your life and to your writing. Here are some suggestions for training your ears to hear even more. Record your responses in your journal.

1. Take a pad and pencil, or your journal, to bed with you tonight. After you are comfortably settled in the dark room, listen carefully to every sound you can hear. Then turn on the light long enough to write down all of the sounds you were able to hear. Take this list with you to school in the morning so that you can share what you heard with someone else. Did this careful listening have any effect on how easy or difficult it was for you to go to sleep?

2. Listen to three conversations: one at school, one at a store or on the way home, and one at home. Listen particularly for the tone of voice the speakers use and ways in which this tone can affect the meaning of what is being said. Write up your findings from this "hearing" experiment by recreating one of the dialogues as well as you can remember it or by writing a new dialogue of your own. It is easier if you limit the characters in the dialogue to two people. In your writing indicate changes in tone of voice and the emotion you think each person is feeling. For example:

> Customer (loudly and angrily): That item is marked a dollar and nine cents.
>
> Cashier (bewildered): Isn't that what I charged you? It's right here on the sales slip.
>
> Customer (muttering, trying to save face): I guess you rang it up so fast I didn't see it.
>
> Cashier (hurt but well trained): I'm sorry, m'am.

Now that you are listening more carefully to the sounds in your world, you will want to develop greater skill in describing what you hear. On the next page is a list of "hearing" words to study. As you read each word, try to hear the sound each one conveys. Try to add more words to the list and record them in your journal.

Hearing Words

Loud Sounds

crash
thud
bump
thump
boom
thunder
bang
smash
explode
roar
scream
screech
shout
yell
whistle
whine
squawk
bark
bawl
bray
bluster
rage
blare
rumble
grate
slam
clap
stomp
stamp
noise
discord

jangle
rasp
clash
caterwaul
clamor
tumult
riot
racket
brawl
bedlam
pandemonium
hubbub
blatant
deafening
raucous
earsplitting
piercing
rowdy
disorderly

Soft Sounds

sigh
murmur
whisper
whir
rustle
twitter
patter
hum
mutter
snap

hiss
crackle
bleat
peep
buzz
zing
gurgle
swish
rush
chime
tinkle
clink
hush
still
speechless
mute
faint
inaudible
melody
resonance
harmony
musical

Speech Sounds

stutter
stammer
giggle
guffaw
laugh
sing
yell

scream
screech
snort
bellow
growl
chatter
murmur
whisper
whimper
talk
speak
drawl

Exercises
Using "Hearing" Words in Your Writing

A. Here are ten sounds you are familiar with. Spend a few minutes "hearing" the sounds in your mind. Write a sentence about each sound that describes it as vividly as you want your reader to hear it. Record the sentences in your journal.

the wind	a fire
feet walking	rain
a car starting	a door opening
opening a can of soda	turning on a faucet
a police car siren	a lawnmower

B. Here is a paragraph describing the terrifying shift of sounds in these children's world. As you read it, notice the strong contrast between words and phrases that bring to mind loud sounds and strong actions and those that bring to mind quiet sounds and silent images.

It was as if, in the midst of a film concerning an avalanche, a tornado, a hurricane, a volcanic eruption, something had, first, gone wrong with the sound apparatus, thus muffling and finally cutting off all noise, all of the blasts and repercussions and thunders, and then second, ripped the film from the projector and inserted in its place a peaceful tropical slide which did not move or tremor. The world ground to a standstill. The silence was so immense and unbelievable that you felt your ears had been stuffed or you had lost your hearing altogether. The children put their hands to their ears. They stood apart. The door slid back and the smell of the silent, waiting world came in to them. —RAY BRADBURY

Make two lists, one of the loud sounds and strong actions, and one of the quiet sounds and silent images in the paragraph. What, if anything, is different about the last sentence in the paragraph?

C. Now put all of your hearing experiences and practice together to write a paragraph in which sound plays an important part. Use an idea from your answers to these listening exercises, from the work on listening recorded in your journal, from one of the following starting ideas, or from a new idea.

1. I adjusted the ear plugs to protect my ears, dove into the water, and all of a sudden . . .

2. As I was listening to the radio with my headset on, the strangest thing happened.

3. Without warning, all sound suddenly disappeared. It had become a strange new world in which I did not fit.

4. Take an ordinary sound that is familiar to you. Exaggerate this single sound in your writing until it becomes sinister or exciting and takes on a new meaning.

5. Contrast two completely different sounds, or a particular sound and quiet.

6. Describe an event by sound words only, leaving until the last sentence of the paragraph the final clue as to what you are describing.

Part 3
The Sense of Touch

With sight and hearing you respond to things around you, objects seen and sounds heard. Your other three senses are much more personal and intimate. Touch is the most intimate of the senses because it brings an immediate sensation. Your brain records a response. Taste requires contact for its functioning, and smell functions when you are close enough to an object for your nose to recognize an odor, or when the odor is overwhelmingly strong. Each of your five senses has an important part to play in your life.

Sudden loss of any sense produces fear and dislocation for most people. If you can remember a time when you were sick, or for some reason temporarily lost the use of one of your senses, you can probably remember how uncomfortable it was, how hard it was to deal with a new and unfamiliar world. The more you use and enjoy all of your senses, the more you fully experience life and the world around you.

The rest of this chapter contains questions and exercises that will help you survey your experiences with touch, taste and smell. Record your responses to these senses in your journal. Your collection of sensory data will furnish you with many good ideas for writing as you go along. Let's begin with the senses of touch.

1. List all of the objects you can touch while you are seated in your chair right now.

2. Describe your physical sensations now. Are you cold, hot, warm, cool, comfortable? How do you know?

3. List any rough objects in the classroom, then any smooth ones.

4. What noticeable physical habits do you have? Do you bite your nails? cross your legs when seated? talk with your hands? run your hand through your hair? If you can't think of any for yourself, list some that you observe in another person in the classroom.

5. List some things that are cold to the touch; hot to the touch; rough; smooth; wet.

Training in Touching

1. While in a car or on a bus, tune in to your sense of touch. Apply all of your nerves to reporting how your body responds to the ride and write up your experience. Here are some questions to consider: Am I comfortable? How do my stomach, my arms, my legs feel? How fast are we going and how can I tell? What is the temperature like? Is there a window open? Is anyone sitting near enough to touch me? Which of my senses is least able to operate fully in this situation?

2. Search around the room, in your pockets or purse for any two objects that have very different textures. Have these near you so that you can write a description that contrasts the way they feel to your touch.

Following is a list of touch words. Study it and write down an object that you think belongs with each word. Add more words and objects to the list and record them in your journal.

cool	slippery	silky	gritty
cold	spongy	satiny	sandy
icy	mushy	velvety	rough
lukewarm	oily	smooth	sharp
tepid	waxy	soft	thick
warm	fleshy	wooly	pulpy
hot	rubbery	furry	dry
steamy	tough	feathery	dull
sticky	crisp	fuzzy	thin
damp	elastic	hairy	fragile
wet	leathery	prickly	tender

Exercises
Using "Touch" Words in Your Writing

A. Write sentences describing how each of these ten things feels. Try to make the reader feel the same thing you are feeling. Record your sentences in your journal.

a piece of cotton	a blanket
an apple	a sunburn
a dry leaf	the bark of a tree
an ice cube	ice skating or roller skating
a warm bath	a toothache

Would another person know what you were describing if the name of it were left out? Which of the above things requires you to reach out and touch or pick it up? Which of the things is something you experience as a sensation happening to you?

B. In the following paragraph notice words that are related to feeling, both inner feeling and outer sensations.

As he tried to make his inept way, the pain was with him, because every time he tried to inhale, the night air hit the holes in his teeth and attacked the open nerves. The street was hard and filled with sharp dark things and he didn't have shoes on to protect him. He was still in his pajamas, a helpless creep just like the stoop gang always said, staggering along with a cripple closing the gap behind him. Something jammed into his foot then, something that hurt enough to penetrate into his brain deeper than the air against the nerves. Babe hoped it wasn't the broken glass but only maybe a rock that would hurt like crazy but not lay his foot open to even more serious pain. —WILLIAM GOLDMAN

All of the sentences in the paragraph contribute to the image of a person desperate to get away, experiencing pain, stumbling on something sharp. Phrases like "pain was with him" and "attacked the open nerves" express his inner state. "Jammed into his foot," "hurt like crazy," "lay his foot open," "more serious pain" are specific descriptions that enable you to feel Babe's hurt with him as he struggles. Helpless images increase the sense of suspense: "a helpless creep," "staggering," "a cripple closing the gap." If you have ever had unpleasant trips to the dentist, you cringe with Babe when the air hits the open nerves in his teeth. If you have ever stepped on something sharp while going barefoot, you have experienced the jabbing thrust of pain.

C. Here is another paragraph that will give you an entirely new feeling about rain.

There were things that crawled on his skin. Things grew upon him in layers. Drops fell and touched other drops and they became streams that trickled over his body, and while these moved down his flesh, the small growths of the forest took root in his clothing. He felt the ivy cling and make a second garment over him; he felt the small flowers bud and open and petal away, and still the rain pattered on his body and on his head. In the luminous night—for the vegetation glowed in the darkness—he could see the other two men outlined, like logs that had fallen and taken upon themselves velvet coverings of grass and flowers. The rain hit his face. He covered his face with his hands. The rain hit his neck. He turned over on his stomach in the mud, on the rubbery plants, and the rain hit his back and hit his legs. —RAY BRADBURY

Pick out the words in the paragraph that are related to the sense of touch. Instead of a soft and gentle spring rain, something pleasant, this rain is a menace from which the men cannot escape. In every sentence of the paragraph you can "feel" the heavy, never-ceasing rain coming down on your body as you read.

D. Touch is the most intimate of the senses, bringing sensations of pleasure or pain. It is an immediate experience. Having sharpened this sense in practice and experience, write a paragraph emphasizing touch. Look over your notes and what you have recorded in your journal. Choose an object or experience to write about from this material or use one of the following suggestions. You may also develop a new idea.

diving into the water of a lake or pool	trudging through the snow on a cold day
walking along a beach or a road on a hot day	feeling mud or sand between your toes

Part 4
The Sense of Taste

1. List the things you like the taste of; then list the things you dislike the taste of.

2. Think of one taste you like or don't like. Describe what happened when you last experienced this taste.

3. Make a list of some things you have tasted and what quality of taste goes with each thing. For example: lemons—sour, candy—sweet.

4. Survey your family at home or some of your friends to see what tastes they like and don't like. Bring your results to school and compare them with those of a classmate.

Training in Tasting

Record the following experiences in your journal.

1. At dinner tonight plan to concentrate on your sense of taste. Sort out the flavor of each of the different things you eat. After dinner make a list of the foods you had. Beside each food write a short phrase that describes the flavor. Make some notes about your tastes in general. Do you like strong or mild flavors? Are there some foods you would eat hot but not cold, and vice versa?

2. Think for a minute about a taste you like very much and one you strongly dislike. Describe each taste, telling when you tasted it and what it was like.

Here is a list of taste words. As you think about each taste, try to recall your own taste experience with it. What things would you relate to each taste? Try to add more words of your own and record them in your journal.

Taste Words

---

oily	sugary	tangy	gingery
buttery	crisp	unripe	hot
salty	ripe	raw	burnt
bitter	bland	alkaline	overripe
bittersweet	tasteless	medicinal	spoiled
sweet	sour	fishy	rotten
hearty	vinegary	spicy	
mellow	fruity	peppery	

Exercises
Using "Taste" Words in Your Writing

A. The sense of taste differs in each person. Here are some things you may have tasted. Write a sentence for each one, trying to use exact words to describe how it tastes to you. Record the sentences in your journal.

a lemon drop	gum
a piece of toast	an egg
a blade of grass	a pencil
ice cream	medicine
an orange	Coke

Reread your sentences. Would every member of your family agree with your descriptions? Compare your sentences with those of someone sitting next to you. Where do you agree and disagree?

B. Read the following passage and notice all of the words that are related to the sense of taste.

> Ben tried not to look at them as he gouged them open with his thumbnail, their juices covering his hands. He debated about throwing the entrails away but at last did, thinking that other quail could be back for water in the morning.
> Ben looked at the raw, bloody thing in his fingers, the bones showing ghastly white in what was left of the sunset.
> Then, and with his eyes shut, gagging, he put it to his mouth and tore the flesh off with his teeth. Close to nausea, he did not chew at all, just swallowed the tough, slimy stuff, forcing his throat to accept it. —Robb White

In this passage some of the words describe the appearance of the quails as Ben tears them open. These visually descriptive words are all the more powerful because Ben is going to eat what he is holding. Words related to taste are "juices, entrails, raw, bloody, bones, gagging, mouth, flesh, tough, slimy stuff, throat." All of the words in the sentences help to create the impression of something horrible to eat.

C. Notice the difference in this paragraph which *appeals* to the sense of taste, especially the different kinds of foods included here.

> On Sunday mornings Momma served a breakfast that was geared to hold us quiet from 9:30 A.M. to 3 P.M. She fried thick pink slabs of home-cured ham and poured the grease over sliced red tomatoes. Eggs over easy, fried potatoes and onions, yellow hominy and crisp perch fried so hard we would pop them in our mouths and chew bones, fins and all. Her cathead biscuits were at least three inches in diameter and two inches thick. The trick to eating catheads was to get the butter on them before they got cold—then they were delicious. When, unluckily, they were allowed to get cold, they tended to a gooeyness, not unlike a wad of tired gum. —MAYA ANGELOU

Notice specific words that describe the food:

> ham—thick pink slabs, home-cured
> tomatoes—sliced red
> eggs—over easy
> potatoes—fried, and onions
> hominy—yellow
> perch—crisp, fried so hard. . . .
> biscuits—cathead, three inches in diameter, two inches thick,
>   delicious; when cold, gooey like a wad of tired gum

In addition, the writer speaks not just of "eating" the perch; but says, "we would *pop* them in our mouths." She contrasts eating biscuits hot and cold, two different experiences. You probably would have no difficulty choosing which meal in the two passages you would prefer to eat.

D. Do you think your tastes change with time? Are there some things you like now that you didn't before? After concentrating on tastes, you are ready to write a paragraph of your own in which you appeal to the sense of taste. Look over the ideas in your journal or try some of the following ideas.

1. Ask someone at home to give you something that is all right to eat, but not to tell you what it is. Close your eyes so that

you can concentrate only on the taste. In a paragraph, describe the experience and the taste. Keep the events in this experience in the order they happen.

2. What is your favorite taste? Can you remember the first time you tasted it? What was happening at the time? Where were you? Who was with you? In a paragraph, recreate the moment or create a brand new situation in which you would like to be tasting the same thing right now.

Part 5
The Sense of Smell

1. List your favorite smells; then list the smells you dislike.

2. Starting when you leave this room, begin to list everything you can smell. Be aware of how the smells change with place, time of day, temperature or other variables.

3. Choose a room at home or at school and describe all the different smells that are there when you walk in.

4. Think of an outdoor place where you like to be. List all the smells you can remember that are there. If this is a place you can go to on your way home today, check to see how well your nose "remembers."

5. Think of a past experience you have had that has a particular smell connected with it. List what you can remember about the place, such as the time of day, what happened, and the smells you remember.

Training in Smelling

1. It is difficult to train your sense of smell because you usually react only to strong odors, either pleasant or unpleasant. However, a change of surroundings can often help you develop this sense. Take a note pad or your journal with you and go through your house immediately after you come in from outside.

Go into two or three different rooms and take notes about all of the smells you encounter. Do these smells change in intensity with the temperature in the room? Bring your notes to class to discuss with someone else.

2. Make a "nose trip" to a store in your area—a drugstore, supermarket, department store, hardware or automobile supply store, greenhouse or florist. List all of the different odors you can smell there. Describe each odor carefully enough so that another person who was not there would be able to know what you are talking about. While you are in the store, make a list of the things you can recognize by their odor without using your eyes or hands to identify them. Compare your results with someone else's. It might be more interesting if you and another person did this in the same store and compared your findings.

Here is a list of smell words. As you study each word, try to recall your experience with the smell. Add your own words to the list and record them in your journal.

Smell Words

---

sweet	minty	acidy	sickly
scented	odorous	acrid	stagnant
fragrant	pungent	burnt	mouldy
aromatic	tempting	gaseous	musty
perfumed	spicy	reeking	mildewed
heady	savory	putrid	damp
fresh	sharp	rotten	dank
balmy	gamy	spoiled	stench
earthy	fishy	sour	
piney	briny	rancid	

Exercises
Using "Smell" Words in Your Writing

A. Write a sentence describing the smell of each of the things listed below. Be sure to identify the kind of flower or food or perfume. Record your sentences in your journal.

a fire	perfume
a flower	toothpaste
food cooking	cookies
wet coats	chalk
rain	popcorn

If the thing you are talking about were not named in the sentence, would your reader still know what you were describing?

B. Read the following paragraph that describes the smells of a small town. Notice all of the words related specifically to this sense. Can you find the two other words that are synonyms for smell?

> In my memory, Stamps is a place of light, shadow, sounds and entrancing odors. The earth smell was pungent, spiced with the odor of cattle manure, the yellowish acid of the ponds and rivers, the deep pots of greens and beans cooking for hours with smoked or cured pork. Flowers added their heavy aroma. And above all, the atmosphere was pressed down with the smell of old fears, and hates, and guilt. —MAYA ANGELOU

Did you notice the following:

    odors—entrancing
    earth smell—pungent
    cattle manure—spiced
    ponds and rivers—yellowish acid
    greens and beans—with smoked or cured pork
    flowers—heavy aroma

The writer also talks about "the smell of old fears, and hates, and guilt." These are experiences not usually related to smells. What do you think she is saying?

c. Concentrating especially on the sense of smell, write a paragraph using smell as a central idea. Use something from your notes in your journal, from the suggestions below, or a new idea of your own.

   1. Write the first paragraph of a story that opens with a particular smell. It could be any kind of story, even a mystery in which the smell plays an important part.

   2. In the paragraph by Ray Bradbury on page 39, the last line reads: "The door slid back and the smell of the silent, waiting world came in to them." Using this as your first sentence, write a paragraph describing the smells of that world.

Part 6
All of the Senses Working Together

You have spent a lot of time practicing the use of your five senses, concentrating on one at a time and sharpening each one. Now it's time for you to pull together all you have learned. Look over the work you have done thus far on your senses—your lists, notes, and all of the material in your journal. Find the writing that you most enjoyed doing, or the activities that were most satisfying to you. Before you write, study this example of sensory writing in which all of the senses are working together.

The evening is lovely.

True, it is not raining but still it is lovely. The puriri stands at the window motionless and shadowy, the forest mysterious and still, and between them the clearing, without the fox-gloves which have died down in the winter. Water voices drift up from the river, the tui lets fall an occasional note, his signature to the evening, while from the forest emanates an odor made up of all the winter decomposition and all the summer blooming; exotic, pungent . . . heady.

It is the enchanted moment when day faces night, a magic time which holds in itself a capacity for improbability unlikely in the daytime. The fire is still going in the stove with one overlong arm of wood beckoning from the firebox, while moths and other night-winged creatures make a freeway of the window. —SYLVIA ASHTON-WARNER

List the senses used here, with the words and phrases related to them. What one sense is missing? The writer speaks of enchantment, "magic," "improbability." What senses are involved here? What kind of mood does this passage create in the reader?

In the following paragraph, the effect is quite different. Notice, again, the senses to which the writer appeals.

The Family came for the wedding. In a great autumnal avalanche of maple, sycamore, oak, elm leaf they hissed and rustled, fell in a shower of horse chestnut, thumped like winter apples on the earth, with an overall scent of farewell-summer on the wind they made in their rushing. —RAY BRADBURY

All of the senses are involved here. You see and feel autumn leaves, taste the winter apples, smell autumn, hear the hissing and rustling. Notice the vivid action words: "avalanche, hissed and rustled, fell, shower, thumped, wind, rushing." If you read the paragraph aloud, the words themselves have a crackling, autumnal quality to them.

Exercise
All of the Senses Working Together

You are now ready to write about all of the senses working together. Reread John Moffitt's poem "To Look at Any Thing" on page 28. To experience any thing fully, the poet says, you must "Be the thing." If you are a fish, for example, you live in a watery world. Light and dark are shadowy, color is muted. You are cold blooded. You have scales, fins, a tail. Your eyes are on the sides of your head. You have to search for food. Dangers are of a different order. Time doesn't exist as humans know it.

Write a short composition in which you are something other than yourself. Put all your senses to work in your particular world. *Be the thing.*

Here are some suggestions to stir your imagination, but you can be anything else you wish.

a motorcycle	a pillow
a snake	a bird
a bee	an animal
a stone	a window
a rug	a fence
a tooth	a weed

Chapter 3

Writing Effective Paragraphs

Until now, you may have had difficulty organizing the ideas in your writing. This chapter will help you learn how to organize your ideas so that they will communicate clearly, and so that your reader will not have to hunt for what you are trying to say. It will also help you to learn *different* ways of organizing those ideas so that your paragraphs will have variety.

Part 1

What Is a Paragraph?

A paragraph is a group of closely related sentences dealing with a *single topic or idea*. Usually, one sentence, called the **topic sentence,** states the main idea of the paragraph. All the other sentences must be related to this topic sentence. These sentences further explain or support the main idea. If they are

not related to the main idea, you have only a series of disconnected sentences, not a paragraph.

Analysis 1

Study the following examples:

1

In the World of Tomorrow, aquanauts could wear diving
helmets that function like gills. Made of plastic or silicone
tubing, they would enable the aquanaut to breathe "oxygenated" water such as sea water which has oxygen dissolved
in it. Like fish, they will take in the oxygen through gills and
breathe out carbon dioxide, which diffuses out through the
gills. Experiments with mice, rats, and dogs have shown they
can breathe under water in oxygenated water up to eighteen
hours, so far, and tests are still continuing. —KENNETH K.
GOLDSTEIN

2

The wolverine may well rate as nature's most fearsome
fighter. In battle with an enemy, he is a twisting, slashing blur
of sheer fury that bewilders and terrifies an adversary. He has
been known to attack a 1,200-pound moose—a creature more
than 40 times his weight—and is capable of defending himself against an entire pack of wolves. Wolverines have killed
bears and mountain lions. —REED MILLARD

You can easily see that these are well-organized, well-written
paragraphs.

In example 1, the writer tells us, in the first sentence, that "In
the World of Tomorrow, aquanauts could wear diving helmets
that function like gills." In the remaining sentences, he explains
what these helmets will be made of, how they will function, and
what experiments are being done in relation to their use.

In example 2, the writer begins with the statement, "The wolverine may well rate as nature's most fearsome fighter." We may

assume, then, that the writer will give us more information about the wolverine; and he does not disappoint us. Every sentence gives a further description of the fighting abilities of that "fearsome fighter."

In both of these examples, we can see how all the ideas are tied together, or are related to each other.

Analysis 2

Now, study the following examples:

1

Indians cultivated and developed many plants that are very important in the world today. Some of them are white potatoes, sweet potatoes, corn, beans, tobacco, chocolate, peanuts, cotton, rubber, and gum. The log cabin was an adaptation of the Indian log or longhouse. Plants were also used for dyes, medicines, soap, clothes, shelter, and baskets.

2

A whale, one of the largest animals in the world, is killed by Russian and Japanese whale hunters every 17 minutes. This makes some people angry. Someday, whales might be like the dinosaur and disappear forever. People are showing their anger in many ways. One Japanese businessman says: "Many Japanese could not live without whale meat." Some people are writing letters to the Japanese Prime Minister, and others are asking people not to buy Japanese products. If this hurts Japanese business enough, the Japanese government may stop the whale hunting.

It is not difficult to see that these are not paragraphs. The writers have not taken the time to organize their ideas, and the result is merely a series of disconnected sentences.

In example 1, we assume, from the first sentence, that the paragraph will be about the cultivation and development of plants by the Indians. However, in sentence 3, we suddenly learn about log cabins, an idea that is not related to the others in the paragraph. This problem is easily solved by removing the third sentence so that we now read as follows:

> Indians cultivated and developed many plants that are important in the world today. Some of them are white potatoes, sweet potatoes, corn, beans, tobacco, chocolate, peanuts, cotton, rubber, and gum. Plants were also used for dyes, medicines, soap, clothes, shelter, and baskets.

In example 2, we have a different problem. Although all ideas seem to relate to the killing of whales, the sentences are so disorganized that we cannot be certain. Our problem here is to rearrange the sentences so that they *do* relate to each other in a logical way.

The first sentence in example 2 tells about killing whales. Let's begin our revision by listing together all the sentences that refer to whales, like this:

1. A whale, one of the largest animals in the world, is killed by Russian and Japanese whale hunters every 17 minutes.

2. Someday, whales might be like the dinosaur and disappear forever.

3. One Japanese businessman says: "Many Japanese could not live without whale meat."

Now, list all the sentences that refer to the attitude of the people, like this:

1. This makes some people angry.

2. People are showing their anger in many ways.

3. Some people are writing letters to the Japanese Prime Minister, and others are asking people not to buy Japanese products.

4. If this hurts Japanese business enough, the Japanese government may stop the whale hunting.

If we look at our first two sentences about killing whales, we can see that they are fairly close in their relationship. Sentence 1 tells us about the killing of whales. Sentence 2 suggests that if the killings continue, whales might someday disappear; so let's add "if this killing continues" after "Someday." Our paragraph now reads like this:

> A whale, one of the largest animals in the world, is killed by Russian and Japanese whale hunters every 17 minutes. Someday, if this killing continues, whales might be like the dinosaur and disappear forever.

If we add the third sentence, about the Japanese businessman, to these first two sentences, we can see that it does not relate to them. So let's remove that sentence completely. Then we'll add the four sentences about the people. We now have six sentences that read as follows:

> A whale, one of the largest animals in the world, is killed by Russian and Japanese whale hunters every 17 minutes. Someday, if this killing continues, whales might be like the dinosaur and disappear forever. This makes some people angry. People are showing their anger in several ways. Some people are writing letters to the Japanese Prime Minister, and others are asking people not to buy Japanese products. If this hurts Japanese business enough, the Japanese government may stop the whale hunting.

We finally have a paragraph, because all the ideas are related. We do, however, have one minor problem because of the weak repetition of ideas in the two sentences: "This makes some people angry. People are showing their anger in several ways." This may be solved by combining the sentences so they read: "This makes some people angry, and they are showing their anger in several ways."

Now, because we have revised carefully and put all our ideas neatly together in their proper places, we have good paragraphs, and our readers do not have to hunt for what we are trying to say.

Exercise
Making Groups of Sentences into Paragraphs

Study the following groups of sentences. Explain which of them are paragraphs, and which are merely groups of unrelated or disorganized ideas. Revise the latter by rearranging sentences, by dropping sentences, or by adding words and dropping words so that they become paragraphs.

1

Paula Murphy is known as the fastest woman in the world. She has raced over Ontario Speedway and Bonneville Salt Flats fast enough to leave Richard Petty far behind in the dust. She is slim, soft-spoken, friendly, and pretty. She has broken through speed records, broken down sex barriers, and broken her neck for racing. She is a female drag-strip racer.

2

The wind was blowing so hard it lifted the trees right out of the ground. Every bush and tree for miles around had been uprooted. There I was barebacked on my old horse, Dan. I was surprised that I was still riding my horse. My saddle, bridle, blanket, everything had been blown off. I had nothing on except my "Roebuck" pants. The dust was so thick you couldn't see a thing.

3

Daniel let the caterpillar go and just lay still for awhile. He had nothing to do, really. Across the street, a little girl was playing basketball. The air was still, and there was not a cloud in the sky. He got up and chased a dog across the street, and just watched things in general. He was waiting for his father to come home.

4

Indian people place a high value on mother earth and nature. Land is owned in common, and it is not fenced off in individual ownership. There is peace in being close to mother earth. The land, water, and animals—all things of nature—are used sparingly. They are used for a purpose. The Anglo people are just beginning to recognize this.

5

Jason thought about the robbery. He knew the man in the pawn shop had recognized him. The man would tell his mother, and she would beat him when he got home. The thought of her made him flinch. Why did he always go back to her? Why didn't he just run away? These were the thoughts that were gnawing into his mind. The golden radiance of the day had finally conquered the night.

6

The road was deserted as she'd been told it would be. The trees made a black arch bending in the rain. The sky was filled with dark, heavy thunderclouds. Suddenly, she saw an old woman and a child standing silently in the rain. The old woman held an end of her shawl around the child's shoulder. But the little girl still shivered in the cold. She had long, blonde hair.

7

Crazy Horse was dead. He was brave and good and wise. He never wanted anything but to save his people, and he fought the Wasichus only when they came to kill us in our own country. He was only thirty years old. They could not kill him in battle. They had to lie to him and kill him that way.

8

If parents respect, or even show an interest in the programs their teen-agers watch on TV, useful discussion can often be started. Nothing is more important to a 14-year-old than having his opinions listened to and respected. The types of things parents and their children will share on TV will change with age. Values and situations shown on television may be used as the basis for lively and productive discussions.

Part 2

The Length of the Paragraph

One problem you may have in regard to writing the paragraph is trying to decide just how long a paragraph should be. The solution to that problem is fairly simple. *A paragraph should be long enough to develop a single idea.*

If your paragraph is too short, your reader may feel cheated because he did not get all the information he needed to understand your idea clearly. Notice in the following paragraph, for example, how incomplete the information is.

> Almost anyone would have treated me better than Uncle Eldon did. From the first day, he worked me like his slave.

If we end the paragraph here, we are left with the question of exactly what "Uncle Eldon" did to the writer to make him work like a slave. In order to resolve this question, we must continue the paragraph with more specific detail, as in the following example:

> Almost anyone would have treated me better than Uncle Eldon did. From the first day, he worked me like his slave. I cut down trees. I sawed the fallen trees into logs. I dragged the logs to the house and cut them into kindling. Whenever the kindling pile was high, I was sent to clean the drafty old barn or to do other work in the cold.

By expanding the number of words—from 22 to 67—we have a more interesting paragraph, and one that communicates with greater clarity.

The Topic Sentence

Earlier in this chapter, we said, "A paragraph is a group of closely related sentences dealing with a single topic or idea. Usually, one sentence, called the *topic sentence*, states the main idea of the paragraph. All the other sentences must be related to this topic sentence."

In this section, you will be working specifically with topic sentences because, in order to write a good paragraph, you must be able to write a good topic sentence.

We have already said that a good topic sentence states the main idea of the paragraph. However, there is more than that involved.

A good topic sentence is like a contract between you and your reader. In your topic sentence you are saying, in effect, "Look, I have this idea I want to explain to you." And the reader, honoring that contract, says, "All right, explain it to me." The rest of your paragraph, then—if you, yourself, hold to that contract—will explain the idea.

Let's look at some examples of topic sentences.

1. *Depending on where you plan to ski, reservations are sometimes a problem.*

2. *John Chewie was a farm laborer.*

3. *There has never been a generation so detached from their parents.*

Writer 1 has made a contract with us in which he says he is going to explain some information he has about getting reservations at ski lodges. Writer 2 says he wants to explain something about John Chewie, a farm laborer. Writer 3 says he wants to explain something about the detachment of young people from their parents. Let's see how well they held to their contracts through the remainder of their paragraphs.

1

Depending on where you plan to ski, reservations are sometimes a problem. The largest complexes, like Vail and Aspen, have plenty of rooms nearby, but just as many people are standing in line to fill them. Christmas week and much of February and March are especially hectic at *all* resorts. Many lodges take reservations for these periods as early as July. In any event, always call ahead well in advance of your intended trip.

The paragraph *does* go on to give an explanation of the author's opening statement, so here the contract is complete.

2

John Chewie was a farm laborer. He worked in the strawberry and vegetable crops, when there was work. Most of the time he was unemployed. Hands were more numerous than jobs. Like his neighbors, he hoed a hard row. He was a poor backwoods Indian.

Here, again, the remainder of the paragraph gives further explanation about John Chewie; so, again the contract is complete.

3

There has never been a generation so detached from their parents. The house is junky; the car is crummy; parents are "out of it." A kid who lacks money can live off his peers. Children used to love their parents, but not any more. One's heart bleeds for the poor parents.

In this paragraph the writer has not held to his contract. The remainder of the sentences are so loosely related to the topic sentence that we do not really understand the author's "explanation."

Exercise
Analyzing Paragraphs

Read the following examples carefully. Then decide in which statements the writers have kept their contracts with their readers, and in which they have not. Give reasons for your decisions.

1

My father has a peculiar habit. He is fond of sitting in the dark, alone. Sometimes I come home very late. The house is dark. I let myself in quietly because I do not want to disturb my mother. She is a light sleeper. I tiptoe into my room and undress in the dark. I go to the kitchen for a drink of water. My bare feet make no noise.

2

Day after day we cover up this bare human body. We hold ourselves in careful control lest our bodies cry out messages our minds are too careless to hide. We smile constantly, for a smile is a sign not only of humor or pleasure but it is also an apology, a sign of defense, or even an excuse.

3

Your grandmother could probably tell you what it was like to run a house on coal. Back then, she had a ton or so delivered down a chute into the basement. Each morning, she'd stoke up the furnace, then carry some more upstairs for the old black stove in the corner. Over the years, oil and natural gas have become the major household fuels.

4

When my little dog died, I was very sad. It was on Valentine's Day. My birthday is on Washington's Birthday. I cried a lot, but it didn't bring my little dog back. We buried him in a vacant lot down the street, and my dad made a tombstone for him. On my birthday, I got some new roller skates.

5

People have trouble deciding what I am. Indians mistake me for one of their own; in Chinatown they give me a menu written in Chinese; and once even a Japanese kid asked me if I was Korean. My ancestors are full-blooded Japanese, but I have had to get used to people thinking I'm something else.

6

The needs of our country have changed since its beginnings. When the first settlers arrived, they had to work very hard.

People don't have to work very hard anymore. The Pilgrims were able to increase their food supply and get protection from the cold. Machines do most of the work nowadays.

7

For the individual American, the main advantage of the metric system will be its simplicity. Instead of the fifty-five measurement units of the English system, the metric system has only three. These are meters, grams, and liters. For the comparison shopper in us all, the metric system will standardize product sizes, making it easier to judge value.

8

Leonard Bernstein was unmistakably a child prodigy. He never touched a piano until his Aunt Clara stored her battered upright in the family parlor when he was ten. He promptly revealed an almost miraculous affinity for the instrument. He went through piano lessons, and devoured the scores of symphonies and operas like so many comic books. At thirteen he composed a gigantic piano concerto.

Part 3
Working with Topic Sentences

The topic sentence usually occurs as the first sentence of the paragraph. As such, it performs two tasks:

1. It makes a general statement about what is to follow.
2. It controls and limits what can be discussed in the remainder of the paragraph.

Although there is some overlapping in these two tasks, we shall consider each one separately in order to understand how each works.

The Topic Sentence Makes a General Statement About What Is To Follow

In writing the topic sentence, we must make it broad enough so that it can be supported or developed, by specific detail, through the remainder of the paragraph. For this reason, we say the topic sentence makes a general statement, or is wider in its scope than the rest of the sentences in the paragraph.

In order to clarify this point, let's look at two good topic sentences that make such general statements:

1. *The city brought blessings, but it brought misery too.*

2. *A person can do something for peace without having to jump into politics.*

It is not difficult to see that these sentences contain very little *specific* information. They are well written and interesting, but the information is only enough to arouse our curiosity. If the ideas interest us at all, we find ourselves saying, "Don't stop there. What kinds of miseries are you talking about? What do you mean, I can do something for peace without jumping into politics? Tell me more."

The good writer will satisfy our curiosity by giving us specific details in the rest of the paragraph to explain the general statement in the topic sentence.

Let's see how the writers of our two topic sentences narrowed and explained their general statements through the remainder of their paragraphs.

1

The city brought blessings, but it brought misery too. Disease flourished in crowded streets because of inadequate plumbing and unsanitary water supplies of early cities. Economic privations came also, because when a man was laid off at a mine or mill he often had no farm to turn to for food. Crime increased and necessitated more laws and law enforcers, all costing more and more money. —D. S. HALACY

The writer first makes the general statement, "The city brought blessings, but it brought misery too." Then he gives us three specific supports for his statement. The city brought *disease*; it brought *economic privation*; and it brought *crime*.

2

> A *person can do something for peace without having to jump into politics.* Each person has inside him a basic decency and goodness. If he listens to it and acts on it, he is giving a great deal of what it is the world needs most. It is not complicated but it takes courage. It takes courage for a person to listen to his own goodness and act on it. —PABLO CASALS

In this paragraph, the method of explanation is somewhat different from that used in the first paragraph. The writer makes the general statement, "A person can do something for peace without having to jump into politics," as the previous two writers did. However, instead of giving us several supporting points of proof, he develops, or expands, his idea. He explains *what a person can do:* listen and act upon his decency and goodness; *why he can do it:* because he is basically decent and good; and *what is involved in doing it:* using his courage.

Exercises
Working with Topic Sentences

A. In the following paragraphs, the topic sentences have been removed, leaving only the supporting details. Read each of these paragraphs carefully; then, for each one, write a good topic sentence. Be.sure your sentence is a general statement that is broader than the details in the rest of the paragraph.

1

So many skiers go there during Christmas week that it's nearly impossible to bump shoulders with a resident. But Aspen's popularity is well earned. The slopes are magnificently groomed, the ski school is tops, and everyone in the world knows it.

2

All she saw from the front of the room was a little black boy who squirmed in his idiot's seat and made noises and poked the kids around him. I guess she couldn't see a kid who made noises because he wanted someone to know he was there.

3

At first his feet slipped but then they took hold. He charged low and hard with mouth opened up like a steam shovel. The lower jaw and the big teeth flashed as he crossed the pit bottom. The wildcat fell back from the heavy charge and rolled under the dog. In that second he raked his claws into the dog's stomach.

4

Make every move count. Take a lesson from the cat who so well represents potential energy. Notice how he moves, stretches, relaxes. He looks uninterested and almost lazy, but let the mouse run by and the cat pounces upon him with one swift, forceful movement. The cat wastes no energy. He can teach you a great deal about conservation.

5

It was already hot, and the grasshoppers began to fill the air. Still, it was early in the morning, and the birds sang out of the shadows. The long yellow grass on the mountain shone in the bright light, and a scissortail hied above the land.

6

One man killed a sturgeon by wading into the water with an ax. Using bayonets, Lewis and Clark's men once caught enough salmon to feed them. Indians caught big Southern catfish by diving into the water with any available red object for bait, seizing the fish as it approached and dragging it to shore.

7

The middle-aged person may still hold much of the political and economic power in this country but the admired figure is by and large the young person. Much of the commerce of our society is directed toward the youth market. The young person's needs are the first to be catered to by advertising. Art and to a certain extent music are dominated by youth. Even clothing and hair styles seem to be largely determined by their influence.

8

A presidential commission tells us we are a racist nation. Another presidential commission tells us we are the most violent nation in the world. An historian tells us the streets are less safe these days than during the Depression when millions were hungry and jobless.

B. Following is a list of topic sentences, each of which makes a general statement. Some of these statements require facts or opinions to complete them; others require observation or imagination. Choose at least two of these topic sentences. For each one you choose, write a paragraph in which you support or develop the topic sentence.

1. Autumn was advancing, and the sky was full of luminous clouds.
2. The Rolling Stones are a very successful rock group.
3. Mr. Nolan's grocery store had just been robbed.
4. The teacher thought I was a troublemaker.
5. Automobiles account for some sixty percent of all the air pollution in the United States.
6. A television addict is a person who can't turn the tube off.
7. Sometimes I feel lost in the crowd.
8. Today it is popular to talk about "returning to the good old days."
9. If you like me, I'll like you.
10. When I watch television, I know somebody's going to try to sell me something.

11. Why does my tongue always freeze at the wrong time?

12. The car wheezed, coughed, and sputtered, fouling the air with dirty black smoke.

13. In the world of make-believe, I can be anything I wish.

14. There are times when I have found people cold and thoughtless.

15. I fell in love with the sky.

The Topic Sentence Controls and Limits the Ideas That Can Be Discussed in the Remainder of the Paragraph

From your earlier study of the paragraph, particularly the manner in which the topic sentence functions as a "contract," you have learned how the topic sentence controls the remainder of the paragraph. We said that the topic sentence states the main idea, and that *all the other sentences must be related to this topic sentence*. Therefore, the topic sentence *controls* what the paragraph contains.

In *limiting* what can be discussed in the paragraph, the topic sentence serves a slightly different function.

We know that the topic sentence makes a general statement, a statement that is broader in scope than the rest of the paragraph. However, if this topic sentence is *too* general, the remainder of the paragraph will have to be either extremely long in order to give an adequate explanation of the idea, or it will have to contain nothing but more general statements.

To cover an idea adequately in a paragraph, the topic sentence must be limited or narrowed. As an example, let's study the following paragraph written by a student:

> Winter is a very cold season, but it is also very beautiful. The white, glistening snow on the ground, trees, and houses is a very eye-catching scene.

"Winter is a very cold season, but it is also very beautiful" is much too broad a topic sentence to be adequately supported in a paragraph. Indeed, we could write an entire composition on that subject. Because it is so broad, all the writer can do is give us another vague generality about the snow. Certainly this is not enough information to let us see why the writer thinks winter is cold but beautiful.

In order to communicate this idea more clearly, we must *narrow* the subject. We'll limit our paragraph to a *specific* winter's morning: "The winter morning was cold and still." Now we have limited our topic to a point where we can add some specific details to develop our idea, as in the following example:

> The winter morning was cold and still. The crust of the snow was like fragile glass and shattered with a loud noise as my feet broke through it. The icy air froze my nostrils and numbed my hands. Except for my footsteps, the world was silent, frozen to attention by winter's command.

By limiting the scope of our general statement and adding specific details, we can now let our reader visualize and understand what we are talking about.

Exercises
Working with Topic Sentences

A. Below, you will find a series of sentence pairs. In each pair, one topic sentence is too general; the other is properly limited in its scope. Decide which one is too broad and which one has been sufficiently limited to be covered in a paragraph.

1. a. Basketball has many interesting features.
   b. Basketball demands quick thinking and split-second timing.

2. a. James failed history because he spent too much time in dramatics.
   b. Extra-curricular activities are time-consuming.

3. a. Several old buildings on Mason Street should be torn down because they are in such bad condition.
   b. Old buildings should be torn down.

4. a. Mountains are beautiful.
   b. The Blue Ridge Mountains stretched before us like a scene from Cinerama.

5. a. Pets can be a nuisance.
   b. My cat, Siggy, is constantly getting into mischief.

6. a. Because he bought the cheapest one he could find, Joe's bicycle didn't last very long.
   b. People find that economy doesn't always pay.

7. a. Graduation from high school is very important.
   b. Without a high school diploma, it is almost impossible to get a good job.

8. a. People of all ages read comic books.
   b. My grandmother likes to read my *Super Comics*.

9. a. Reckless driving is a serious problem.
   b. Statistics show that most automobile accidents are caused by reckless driving.

10. a. Works of art are difficult to create.
    b. Oil painting takes time, effort, and patience.

B. Following is a list of broad topic sentences. Rewrite each one, limiting its scope. Then choose at least two of the sentences that interest you. Write a paragraph on each of them.

1. Automobiles are not as safe as they could be.
2. Soap operas have similar plots.
3. Many people are afraid of freedom of speech.
4. Travel is becoming faster—and noisier—all the time.
5. The pedestrian isn't always right.
6. The Presidency of the United States is a difficult job.
7. You couldn't find a more interesting neighborhood than mine.
8. Smoking is dangerous to a person's health.
9. Horses are interesting animals.
10. Growing vegetables is good therapy.
11. Most television programs are alike.
12. The fashion magazines are showing wild clothes.
13. Teenagers don't like discipline.

14. San Francisco is a historic city.
15. Vacations are fun.

C. Study the following list of subjects. Write a *broad* topic sentence and a *limited* topic sentence for each subject on the list.

EXAMPLE:

SUBJECT: Stamp Collecting.
BROAD: Stamp collecting is a fascinating hobby.
LIMITED: A beautiful stamp from Japan started me on my hobby of stamp collecting.

1. Things I Fear
2. Television Advertising
3. The Fight for Women's Rights
4. The Decay of Our Cities
5. The Future Is Ours
6. Snobs
7. Photography
8. Pollution
9. War
10. Loneliness
11. Phonograph Records
12. Racial Prejudices
13. Classrooms
14. Politics
15. Projects Started but Never Finished

Part 4
Developing the Complete Paragraph

Once you have decided upon—and properly limited—your topic sentence, your next step in writing is to develop the idea in that sentence into a well organized paragraph. You do this by adding several more sentences that give additional information. There are several ways of doing this:

1. by using facts or statistics
2. by using specific examples
3. by using an incident or an anecdote
4. by using comparisons or contrasts

Using Facts or Statistics

In order to understand how topic sentences may be developed by the use of facts or statistics, let's look at the following example:

> The federal government is at last becoming involved in planning our cities of tomorrow, and increasing sums of tax money are being made available for planning and developing new towns, for encouraging alternative growth centers, and for aiding in urban renewal projects. Approximately two billion dollars a year is being spent in this manner by the government, mostly as "revenue sharing" with the states, cities, and counties. While this seems a large amount, it should be remembered that estimates of the total cost to make room for additional Americans by the year 2000 are something like three *trillion* dollars! —D. S. HALACY

The writer begins with a general topic sentence concerning the involvement of the government in city planning, narrows this to a statement concerning the amount of money currently being spent, and finally moves to the most important statement: "estimates of the total cost to make room for additional Americans by the year 2000 are something like three *trillion* dollars!" He has therefore moved from the least important fact to the most important fact.

This method is the usual one for organizing the information within a paragraph. The writer moves from a general topic sentence to a series of narrow statements, ending with the most important statement. In this way the writer can build his ideas to a climax, or emphasize a particular point.

Let's look at another example:

Italy has contributed more immigrants to the United States than any other country except Germany. Over five million Italians came to this country between 1820 and 1963. Large-scale immigration began in 1880, and almost four million Italian immigrants arrived in the present century. —JOHN F. KENNEDY

Here again, you can see the same arrangement. The author has moved from the general topic sentence concerning Italian immigrants to the statement concerning the immigrations between 1820 to 1963, then to the final important statement concerning immigration to the present century.

Exercises
Developing a Paragraph by Using Facts or Statistics

A. Following is a series of "scrambled" paragraphs. The sentences are all out of order. Rewrite each paragraph, placing the sentences in proper relation to each other.

1

The lake is becoming strangled by lack of oxygen. Industries fill Lake Erie with fifteen billion gallons of waste. Weeds are the only form of life which survives.

2

On May 7 of this year the Census Bureau reported that the number of poor people in the nation increased last year for the first time in a decade. And this is before taxes. Another seven million white families earn between $5,000 and $7,000 a year, just above the welfare level. Two-thirds of the total are white.

3

They tended to gravitate to the farming communities. By 1963, almost 130,000 Czechs had migrated to this country. They also formed enclaves in cities, principally in Chicago, Cleveland, and New York. It is one of these homesteads that is portrayed by novelist Willa Cather in *My Antonia.*

4

People no longer touched each other. Wars, riots, and revolutions flourished. By the early 1990's the old morality had crumbled. Conversations were icily polite. Neighbor mistrusted neighbor. The old certitudes had vanished.

5

In the average home the television is turned on some five hours and forty-five minutes a day. The average male viewer, between his second and sixty-fifth year, will watch television for over 3000 entire days—roughly nine full years of his life. (More than 25 percent have two or more sets.) There are 60 million homes in the United States and over 95 percent of them are equipped with a television set.

6

The pearls grow around the grains of sand. In addition, they are interesting because pearls often grow inside their shells. After a few years these oysters produce a very valuable crop of pearls. Oysters make very good food. In Japan, pearls are grown by placing single grains of sand inside the shells of young oysters.

7

It can make a person very ill. It can damage cells in the body. We know that LSD does great damage to the body. Also, it makes people do dangerous things, sometimes resulting in death. This is caused by damage to cells in the brain. It can also cause some people to have a nervous breakdown.

8

Many of their songs were very old. During the pioneer days, families enjoyed doing things together. Square dances were also held and the whole family went to the dance together. They read stories by the fire. They liked to sing and listen to music together.

B. Following is a list of general topics, each one of which lends itself to paragraph development through the use of facts or statistics.

Choose three of the topics that interest you and do some research into them. Narrow the scope of each topic into a strong topic sentence that can be adequately developed in a paragraph. Then develop each topic, moving from the least important facts to the most important facts, into a paragraph.

1. Television violence and the American society
2. The fight for women's rights
3. Atoms for peace
4. Advertising and the American way of life
5. The search for new forms of energy
6. Scholarships for college
7. Movies and censorship
8. The pollution of our oceans
9. Native Americans work for equality
10. A city of tomorrow
11. The values of a high school education
12. New developments in space exploration
13. Changes in today's education
14. The fight against seal-hunting
15. Noise pollution in our cities

Using Specific Examples

Sometimes the topic sentence will consist of a general "truth" or general idea that is best supported through the use of specific examples. Let's look at the following paragraph:

> The biggest corporations have become too powerful and too rich, and are not accountable to anyone. General Motors' annual revenues last year (1970), 18.8 billion dollars, were larger than the budgets of 100 countries in the world. Chase Manhattan Bank has 25 billion dollars in assets. Standard Oil has 19 billion dollars in assets. —J. NEWFIELD AND J. GREENFIELD

The writer begins with the general statement: "The biggest corporations have become too powerful and too rich, and are not accountable to anyone." He then supports this statement with three specific examples:

1. In 1970, General Motors had revenues of 18.8 billion dollars.
2. Chase Manhattan Bank has 25 billion dollars in assets.
3. Standard Oil has 19 billion dollars in assets.

The following example uses a similar technique:

> Dozens of enterprising businessmen made American life richer, safer, and more comfortable. Gail Borden invented condensed milk, a healthy, safe product, in a time (1859) when fresh milk was often dangerous. Willis Carrier named his 1902 invention "air conditioning." Clarence Birdseye discovered frozen foods, and Aaron Montgomery Ward brought the department store to the most isolated farm through the innovation of the mail order catalog. —K. S. KNODT

In this example, the writer also states a general idea: "Dozens of enterprising businessmen made American life richer, safer, and more comfortable." He then supports that statement with four examples:

1. Gail Borden's invention of condensed milk,
2. Willis Carrier's invention of air conditioning,
3. Clarence Birdseye's discovery of frozen foods,
4. Aaron Montgomery Ward's innovation of the mail order catalog.

Exercise
Developing a Paragraph by Using Specific Examples

Here is a list of general topic sentences. Choose three of them, and develop them into paragraphs through the use of specific examples.

1. Women can succeed in a "man's" world.
2. Science fiction can help us accept the "future shock" of tomorrow.
3. Even great leaders can fail in something.

4. One is often surprised by the intelligence of animals.
5. Some comics have a place in today's education.
6. A winner may sometimes have to overcome a severe handicap in order to win.
7. "Beautiful" women are not always born beautiful.
8. Some people become expert at escaping punishment.
9. Frozen foods have made modern cooking a pleasure.
10. Today's automobiles are more efficient in saving gas.
11. People too often decide that a person accused of a crime is guilty before the case is tried.
12. Some movies portray excessive violence.
13. Environmentalists have helped to halt pollution.
14. Americans don't always win.
15. The minor characters in a book are often remembered most.

Using an Incident or an Anecdote

The incident or anecdote can add a personal touch to almost any form of writing, although it is usually limited to the writing of inspirational pieces and "self-help" articles. The writer draws from his personal experiences to explain or clarify his ideas. The strength of this type of development lies in the fact that the incident or anecdote, if well chosen, can drive a point home very sharply and imprint the idea very clearly on the reader's mind.

Children have taught me much of what I know about love. To them love is nothing fancy, but very real—a feeling to be taken seriously. "If you love somebody," a six-year-old boy named Charlie once told me, "you help him put his boots on when they get stuck." —LESLIE KENTON

The writer could have developed the topic sentence with the addition of several more impersonal statements, but notice how the paragraph comes "alive," is more memorable, with the inclusion of that simple little personal experience.

Writing a paragraph that uses an incident or anecdote is pleasing because it focuses upon you, the writer, personally. You are drawing from your own unique store of experiences to clarify an idea you have, and you are doing this by telling us about something you have done, have heard, or have felt—as in the following example:

> I think that one of the reasons I became a writer was because once, when I was driving home with my parents, they let me keep a date with a rainbow. There had been a heavy summer storm, when suddenly I screamed, "Stop the car! I must write a poem about that beautiful rainbow!" My father pulled up at the side of the road and off I went into the drizzle and the sunshine, while they waited. It was one of those special moments that change you, make you more than you've been. It is an experience in saying "Yes!" to life—and that's really what spontaneity and joy are all about. —EDA LESHAN

Here, again, the writer could have gone on to explain, with facts and examples, how she came to be a writer. But how much more clearly we understand her reasons from her one simple anecdote.

Exercise
Developing a Paragraph by Using an Incident or an Anecdote

Here is a list of topic sentences, each one of which may be developed by an incident or an anecdote. Choose two of the sentences that interest you. Then, drawing from your personal experiences, develop each of the sentences into a paragraph.

1. A kind friend can help you forget your troubles.
2. Sometimes a bad experience can turn out to be funny after all.
3. An angry word can ruin your day.
4. It usually pays to be on time.
5. Experience is sometimes a tough teacher.
6. You don't have to travel to find adventure.
7. Sometimes you have to learn to say "No!"

8. Baby-sitting is not the world's easiest job.
9. You have to be taught to hate.
10. A kind teacher can help you to know yourself.
11. There are some things you can't learn from books.
12. A good laugh can sometimes be "good medicine."
13. A pet can teach you how to love.
14. Popularity isn't always that important.
15. You don't have to join a team to learn sportsmanship.
16. Sometimes a girl can win where a boy can't.
17. Repairing a _____ can teach you patience.
18. Hero-worship sometimes pays off.
19. There are times when you have to forgive.
20. Sometimes "best" friends aren't.

Using Comparisons or Contrasts

In developing a topic sentence by comparisons or contrasts, you will also be using facts, examples, or incidents. The important point to remember here, however, is that you are explaining the *differences or similarities* in the facts or ideas.

Using Comparisons. Let's look at some examples of comparison first:

> Both President Lincoln and President Kennedy were attacked suddenly by an assassin on a Friday, and each in the presence of his wife. Each man was shot in the head; in each instance, crowds of people watched the shooting. Lincoln's secretary, named Kennedy, had advised him not to go to the theater where the attack occurred. Kennedy's secretary, named Lincoln, had advised him not to go to Dallas where the attack occurred.

The writer's purpose in this paragraph is quite clear. She is pointing out the similarities in the deaths of President Lincoln and President Kennedy by *listing specific points of comparison.*

You, as a person, are constantly learning by comparison. You compare the flavor of the hamburgers at McDonald's with the flavor of the hamburgers in the school cafeteria; Jean's ability as a basketball player with Lynn's; Joe's personality with David's; Mr. McFarlane's teaching ability with Mr. Becker's. As a result of this continuous experience in comparing, you should have little difficulty in applying this technique to your writing.

Let's look at another example:

> Although some may appreciate a five-speed's trappings, most will discover this animal combines the worst of a three- and a ten-speed. The typical five-speed is built on the same heavy frame as the three-speed, often has the same wide saddle and upright handlebars, but has the five-speed gear cluster and changer bolted on in back. For two extra gears of dubious value, you pay almost as much as you would for a low-priced ten-speed, but pedal around as much weight as you would on a three-speed. —S. MARSHALL

By comparing the five-speed bike with the three-speed and ten-speed bikes, the writer is able to point up the disadvantages of the five-speed. He has carefully chosen his points to illustrate his purpose, leaving out all other unnecessary points of comparison.

Using Contrasts. Now, let's look at some examples of contrast. Remember that in using this method of development, we are concerned with emphasizing *differences*.

> Although Henry Chatillon and Tête Rouge were the same age, that is, about thirty, they were very different. Henry was twice as large, and fully six times as strong as Tête Rouge. Henry's face was roughened by winds and storms; Tête Rouge's was bloated by sherry-cobblers and brandy-toddy. Henry had led a life of hardship and privation; Tête Rouge never had a whim which he would not gratify at the first moment he was able. Henry, moreover, was the most disinterested man I ever saw; while Tête Rouge cared for nobody but himself. —FRANCIS PARKMAN

The personalities of the two men in this paragraph become much clearer and more vividly alive because of the contrasts which the author has pointed out to us.

In the following example, notice how the writer contrasts the life of the peasant in the Old World with his life in America.

> In America bread never came without complications. The peasant, new to the means of earning his livelihood, added to the difficulties in making ends meet through inability to use efficiently whatever money came to his hands. At home, only the improvident were incapable of nurturing their families out of their own farms and gardens. But in America every crumb was paid for. The unfamiliar process of shopping led to countless losses and often induced the immigrant, whatever the cost, to deal with peddlers, as in the Old World.
> —Kirsten E. A. Borg

Exercises
Developing a Paragraph by Using Comparisons or Contrasts

A. Following is a list of topics that may be developed through comparison. Choose two topics that interest you, and write a paragraph of comparison on each. You may need to do research on some of the topics.

1. A novel and a movie based upon the same novel.
2. Two of your close friends.
3. A garden and a part of a forest.
4. Rock music and jazz.
5. A boxer and a dancer.
6. Modern dress and dress in the 1920's.
7. The singing style of two popular singers.
8. Ice-skating and roller-skating.
9. Your neighborhood and one in a nearby town or city.
10. An American city and a European city.

B. Following is a list of topics that may be developed through contrast. Choose two topics that interest you, and write a paragraph of contrast on each. You may need to do some research on some of these topics.

1. Popular music of the 1940's and the popular music of today.
2. Riding a bicycle and riding a motorcycle.
3. A country street before and after a snowstorm.
4. A cat and a dog as pets.
5. Advertising on radio and advertising on TV.
6. Two of your close friends.
7. Bathing suits in the 1920's and the bathing suits of today.
8. Eating an apple and eating a peach.
9. Airplane travel today and in the 1950's.
10. Mountain skiing and cross-country skiing.

Chapter 4

Types of Paragraphs

Having learned several different ways of organizing paragraphs, you are now ready to work with types of paragraphs:

1. Descriptive
2. Explanatory
3. Narrative

Part 1

The Descriptive Paragraph

Choosing Words and Details Carefully

In writing good descriptive paragraphs, you must decide what your focus is and what impression you want to create. You must then choose your words carefully and select precise details, in order to paint a word picture that appeals to your reader's senses. Note, in the following example, how the writer appeals to your visual sense.

The village was a fairly typical one, consisting of small shacks with walls built out of the jagged off-cuts from the sawmill, and whitewashed. Each stood in its own little patch of ground, surrounded by a bamboo fence, and these gardens were sometimes filled with a strange variety of old tins, kettles, and broken barrels, each brimming over with flowers. Wide ditches full of muddy water separated these "gardens" from the road and were spanned at each front gate by a small, rickety bridge of roughly nailed branches. —GERALD DURRELL

When the writer of this paragraph decided to describe the village he had seen, he had to decide exactly what aspect he wanted his reader to see. After he had decided to describe only the houses and gardens, he had to sort out the details, keeping only those that created a vivid impression of the houses and gardens and eliminating those that were weak or unrelated to his specific view. Notice how precisely the writer has selected his details so that we might visualize what he is describing.

Ways of Organizing a Descriptive Paragraph

To help your reader follow your description, the details, particularly in visual description, should usually follow some logical order of organization. You may describe your scene from side to side, from bottom to top (or the reverse), or from near to far (or the reverse). You may use other methods of organization, provided you include key words to indicate to your reader that you are changing directions.

Let's examine some descriptive paragraphs in which the writers have used specific methods of organization. Notice how the writers have used space words and phrases to help the reader move from one place or thing to another.

1. FROM SIDE TO SIDE.

The set is magnificent. The left half of the stage, in itself the complete width of a large Western stage, depicts a hillside in cherryblossom time with, in the foreground, a garden and

thatched entrance gateway. The gateway is free-standing—
the fence omitted as superfluous. On the right-hand side is a
villa raised off the ground in the traditional manner. Both
outside and interior are visible. —WIM SWAAN

Notice the use of the words "left half of the stage," "in the foreground," and "On the right-hand side"—all of which lead us
from one side of the scene to the other.

2. FROM BOTTOM TO TOP (OR THE REVERSE).

Two more white faces stand out in my memory, a pair of
nurses I saw from time to time in the clinic. They wore white
shoes, white hose, and white dresses. Above their bleached
faces their foreheads had been shaved halfway back over their
scalp's curve to make a sharp widow's peak where starched
black hair began to arch upward, reminding me of a cobra's
hood. Their lips were gone. Their brows were plucked. They
were always together, a pair of reptilian kabuki creatures at
loose in the camp hospital. —JEANNE WAKATSUKI HOUSTON
and JAMES D. HOUSTON

The line of organization here is from bottom to top. The writers
first make a general statement about *white faces*. They then
lead us upward from shoes, to hose, to dresses, to focus finally
on those faces.

3. FROM NEAR TO FAR (OR THE REVERSE).

We drove past a barbed-wire fence, through a gate, and into
an open space where trunks and sacks and packages had been
dumped from the baggage trucks that drove out ahead of us.
I could see a few tents set up, the first rows of black barracks,
and beyond them, blurred by sand, rows of barracks that
seemed to spread for miles across this plain. —JEANNE
WAKATSUKI HOUSTON and JAMES D. HOUSTON

Here the writers begin with a description of the scene nearest to
them, then lead our attention to "a few tents," beyond this to
"the first rows of black barracks," and "beyond them . . . rows
of barracks that seemed to spread for miles across this plain."

We mentioned earlier that you may use other methods of organization than these three provided you indicate to your reader that you are changing directions. Read the following example and notice how the writer, in the words we have underlined, indicates this change of direction.

> Our first camp in Glen Canyon, just below the junction, is almost unimaginably beautiful—a sandstone ledge <u>below</u> two arched caves, with clean cliffs <u>soaring</u> <u>up</u> <u>behind</u> and a long green sandbar <u>across</u> the river. Just <u>below</u> us is the masked entrance of Hidden Passage Canyon, which at sunup glows softly red, its outthrust masking wall throwing a strong shadow <u>against</u> the cliff. <u>Beyond</u> this masking wall is the kind of canyon that is almost commonplace here, but that anywhere else would be a wonder. —WALLACE STEGNER

Using Space Words and Phrases

When a writer wants to tell how things look or how things are arranged, he uses space words and phrases. These words and phrases help the reader to follow the writer's view as he moves from one place or thing to another.

DIRECTION

left	through	between
right	into	beyond
above	ahead	among
below	behind	in front of
center	across	in back of
up	toward	forward
down	against	backward
past	around	parallel

DISTANCE

foreground	close to	far
background	next to	long
halfway	leading to	short

beyond	in the center of	twenty feet
distant	approximately	about ten miles
away from	near	twenty kilometers

AREA OR SPACE

outside	field	room
inside	hillside	stairway
interior	acre	stage
exterior	hut	alley
lawn	villa	street
garden	mansion	road
courtyard	closet	narrow
park	hall	wide

Describing a Person

Describing a person is different from describing a place or a thing. The writer must strive to capture the essence of a person. If the writer merely lists the physical characteristics of a person, the description will probably result in the following:

> The woman was elderly. She was short and had bent shoulders. Her hair was white and her eyes were brown. She wore tennis shoes and an old gray sweater.

This description sounds like a police report on a missing person. It is merely a dull list of physical statistics and reveals nothing about the essence of the woman. Notice the difference in the following description of the same woman.

> A woman with shorn white hair is standing at the kitchen window. She is wearing tennis shoes and a shapeless gray sweater over a summery calico dress. She is small and sprightly, like a bantam hen; but, due to a long youthful illness, her shoulders are pitifully hunched. Her face is remarkable—not unlike Lincoln's, craggy like that, and tinted by sun and wind; but it is delicate too, finely boned, and her eyes are sherry colored and timid. —TRUMAN CAPOTE

This description makes the woman come alive for the reader. It reveals her personality, her character and her outlook on life. She becomes an interesting human being, not merely a statistical report.

Here is another description, this time of a young boy. Try to determine how the writer has made his description so colorful and interesting.

> When Wheldon first arrived at our school, he was carrying a natty little briefcase and wore a pink spotted tie and short trousers. His long, thin face was as white as a sheet in a TV ad, and his eyes were so watery behind his huge spectacles that gazing into them was like looking out of the portholes of a sinking ship. He had collapsed shoulders almost meeting under his chin, and his hair looked as if each separate strand had been carefully glued into place, ready for church. He reminded you of a cheerful but undernourished sheep. —Peter Jones

Notice the descriptive words: "natty," "collapsed," "undernourished sheep." Can you find the similes and metaphors that make this description so humorous? From the physical description, try to explain in your own words what kind of boy Wheldon is.

Exercise
Writing Descriptive Paragraphs

Following are two lists of topics that may be developed into descriptive paragraphs. Choose one topic from each list. Decide which method of organization is best suited for your topic from the first list. Decide exactly what you wish to reveal about the person from the second list. Then write a paragraph on each.

List 1

1. An interesting building in your home town
2. The waiting area in an airport or train depot
3. A machine shop or car repair garage
4. The street on which you live
5. The check-out counter of a store

6. A doctor's or dentist's waiting room
7. A busy street
8. A scene in nature

LIST 2

1. An interesting woman you have known
2. An interesting man you have known
3. A grandparent
4. A brother or sister
5. An entertainer
6. The host on a TV show
7. A friend
8. Your first impression of someone

Appealing to the Senses

Thus far, our examples have appealed to the sense of sight. Descriptive paragraphs may also appeal to the other senses, either individually or in combination.

SOUND:

Through the window next to her chair she heard the household noises as sounds on a distant stage. There was Father's pipe clacking against the ashtray, and the rustle of his newspaper. There was a small boy throwing books onto a chair, and the cookie jar thudding onto tile. —ROSEMARIE BODEN-HEIMER

TASTE:

Alvah absently drew out his radnip and crunched off a bite of it. The taste was faintly unpleasant, like that of old protein paste or the wrong variety of culture cheese but he chewed and swallowed it. —DAMON KNIGHT

TOUCH:

The pain spread slowly outward from the inner depths until the whole stomach reverberated. It was like the wild clanging of a bell. Or like a thousand bells which jangled simultaneously at every breath he breathed and every throb of his pulse, rocking his whole being. The lieutenant could no longer stop himself from moaning. —Yukio Mishima

SMELL:

The filthy streets are seldom cleaned. The inaccessible alleys and rear yards are never touched, and in the hot summer months the stench of rotting things will mark these places. Here and there an unwitting newcomer tries the disastrous experiment of keeping a goat, adding thereby to the distinctive flavor of his neighborhood.

COMBINATION:

Early morning is a time of magic in Cannery Row. In the gray time after the light has come and before the sun has risen, the Row seems to hang suspended out of time in a silvery light. The street lights go out, and the weeds are a brilliant green. The corrugated iron of the canneries glows with the pearly lucence of platinum or old pewter. No automobiles are running then. The street is silent of progress and business. And the rush and drag of the waves can be heard as they splash in among the piles of the canneries. It is a time of great peace, a deserted time, a little era of rest. —John Steinbeck

Exercises
Using the Senses in Describing

A. Write a short paragraph in which you describe the *sound* of one of the following:

1. A jet landing
2. A motorcycle in the distance
3. Eating potato chips
4. A cricket
5. A police siren

6. A dog barking
7. A clock ticking in an empty room
8. A baby crying
9. Traffic on a city street
10. A "rock" group

B. Write a short paragraph in which you describe the *taste* of one of the following:

1. An onion
2. Root beer
3. Raw celery
4. Buttermilk
5. A lemon
6. A fresh strawberry
7. A pickle
8. Rose petals
9. Fresh mushrooms
10. Vanilla ice-cream

C. Write a short paragraph in which you describe the *feeling to the touch* of one of the following:

1. Walking barefooted on a sandy beach
2. Snow down your back
3. Sandpaper
4. A cold shower on a hot day
5. Walking barefooted on wet grass
6. A city street on a hot day
7. Burning your finger
8. Walking in the rain
9. Petting a dog or cat
10. Drinking ice water

D. Write a short paragraph in which you describe the *smell* of one of the following:

1. Frying fish
2. A carnation

3. A dentist's office
4. A stale garbage can
5. Ripe apples
6. Frying hamburgers
7. A school gymnasium
8. A laundromat
9. Stale cigarette smoke in a closed room
10. A city street on a hot day

E. Write a short paragraph in which you use a *combination of senses* to describe one of the following:

1. Chalk scratching on the blackboard
2. A cut finger
3. Eating a raw carrot
4. A rainy afternoon
5. A jet flying overhead
6. An old lady at her first football game
7. A classroom
8. A man crying
9. Riding a motorcycle
10. A bouquet of roses

F. Select one of the following statements as the topic sentence for a paragraph. Write a short descriptive paragraph in which you create a single sensory impression.

1. The scene before me was one of total dreariness.
2. Have you ever lain awake at night while everything about you was strange, silent, and still as death?
3. The room was bright with color.
4. The street was a carnival of activity.
5. The delicious smells made my mouth water.
6. The dress was as crazy as the wearer.
7. I had never seen him so angry.
8. He was trying to make lunch for the children.
9. He had been burning incense in the room.
10. The room was an absolute mess.

Part 2
The Explanatory Paragraph

The explanatory paragraph does just what its name implies—
it explains. This is not a difficult form in which to write because
every day of our lives we are asked to explain something. A friend
who was absent wants us to explain the English or the math assignment. Mother wants to know why we were late coming home
from school. Our history teacher asks for an explanation of the
events leading to Civil Rights legislation. A stranger wants to
know the quickest way to the airport.

Ways of Developing an Explanatory Paragraph

In each of these situations we are drawing upon our own store
of knowledge and offering information—an explanation. To be
meaningful, an explanation must be clear, accurate, and well-
organized. Therefore, the explanatory paragraph uses any of the
techniques previously discussed under "Developing the Complete Paragraph" (Chapter 3). It can use *facts or statistics, specific examples, an incident or an anecdote,* and *comparisons or
contrasts.* Much of this study, therefore, will be in the form of a
review.

Let's look at some further examples of these methods for developing the explanatory paragraph.

FACTS:

You'll find long-distance bus travel efficient as well as
economical. Intercity buses are faster than cars or trains and
not much slower than planes for distances of 300 miles or
fewer, if you count the time you spend getting to and from
the airport. The bus lines guarantee you a seat without an
advance reservation, and bus schedules tend to be weather-
proof. Hence, you won't get "bumped" because a reservations

clerk overbooked, and you won't land in Baltimore when you set out for New York.

EXAMPLES:

Faced with rising food costs, several of the nation's self-supporting zoos have hit upon a cagey scheme to enlist community assistance in feeding their hungry boarders. At the Gladys Porter Zoo in Brownsville, Texas, patrons are invited to join the "Take a Lion to Lunch Bunch." As zoo officials are careful to explain, patrons are not required to take one of the big cats to a drive-in for burgers and fries. They are merely asked to pick up the tab for the cost of feeding an animal at the zoo for a day, week or month. Lunch for a lion comes to $4.72, but you can treat a gorilla for $2.01, and it costs only 17 cents a day to play host to a boa constrictor. —WOMAN'S DAY

INCIDENT:

In Chicago, Mary Ann Slovaki was driving home about ten o'clock one night when the radiator hose in her car broke. The mishap occurred on one of the city's most crime-ridden streets, but she didn't even have to roll down her window to ask for help. A request over her CB radio brought three immediate responses—one of them from the police. —T. E. DEIKER

COMPARISONS OR CONTRASTS

Unlike as Whittier and Franklin were in many respects, they were alike in others. Both had sympathy with the lowly which comes of early similar experiences. Both learned a handicraft, for Franklin set type and worked a printing-press, and Whittier made slippers. To both of them literature was a means, rather than an end in itself. Verse to Whittier, and prose to Franklin, was a weapon to be used in the good fight.

Giving Instructions

In its simplest and most practical form, the explanatory paragraph is used to give instructions:

> The SONY Cassette is provided with a convenient safety device to prevent accidental erasure of valuable recording. The small tabs located at the rear of the cassette will activate the safety device when these tabs are broken out. To protect side 'A' recordings, break out the tab of side 'A', and to protect side 'B', break out the tab on side 'B'. When the cassette is installed with these tabs broken out, the Record Button can not be depressed.

The easiest way to organize explanatory material—particularly that which gives instructions—is to do it in *chronological order*; that is, first things first:

> The quickest way to the airport from here is by the freeway. Go three blocks north to 9th Street, then turn left, and go three blocks west. That will take you to Michigan Avenue where you'll see the on-ramp to the Westbound Freeway. Stay on the freeway until you see the "Airport Exit" sign about eight miles west of town.

> A hot door means danger! If the door is not hot, it may be carefully opened about an inch. Care must be taken to avoid a back draft or explosion when fresh air from the room meets the fire outside. Brace a foot against the bottom of the door and open it about one inch. If you feel extreme pressure against the door or feel an in-rush of heat and fire, close the door at once. There is too much heat on the outside for you to leave by the door. If there is no pressure and you feel no great amount of heat, then open the door wide enough to look into the hall. If you see smoke but no fire and do not feel extreme heat, you may proceed rapidly through the hall and to the outside.

The writers of each of these paragraphs have placed their ideas in clear, chronological order. One point follows the other, simply and logically.

Exercises
Writing Explanatory Paragraphs

A. Complete one of the following:

1. A new wrist watch you have had for only a short time has already stopped running three times. You have decided to send the watch back to the company for a refund. Write a one-paragraph letter to the company explaining why you are returning the watch.

2. You have just read a help-wanted ad for a job that interests you. Write a one-paragraph letter to the company, explaining why you are qualified for the job.

3. Write a paragraph explaining why you like, or don't like, something.

4. Read the following poem. Write a paragraph explaining what the poem means to you.

   SELF EXPRESSION

   Mother has caught her head
   in the bubble-gum machine
   looking for her purple leotard.
   Her black one she's saving
   for funerals, she said.
   Now if someone will answer her ad
   and return her feather boa
   constrictor, maybe she will stop
   sharpening her fingers
   and begin to cook again.

   ANN DARR

5. Write a paragraph in which you explain how to look up information in the Yellow Pages of the telephone directory.

6. Write a paragraph to a friend explaining how to operate a CB radio.

7. Write a paragraph explaining how to repair a flat bicycle tire.

8. Write a paragraph explaining how to hem a skirt.

9. On page 102 is a section of a road map. Imagine that you live in Sioux Falls, and that you have a friend who lives west of you, in Pierre. Write a paragraph explaining to your friend the best way to get from his city to yours.

10. Refer again to the road map on page 102. Imagine that you and your family live in Fargo, and that you are planning a weekend holiday in Coleharbor. Write a paragraph explaining to your driver the best way to get from Fargo to Coleharbor.

B. Write an explanatory paragraph, using the appropriate method of organization, on two of the following topics. Narrow your topic sentence so that you can develop your explanation adequately in a paragraph.

1. The major cause of pollution in America
2. Why I favor/do not favor gun control.
3. The quality of consumer goods in America is growing worse/ better.
4. Buying a good bicycle
5. The major points of interest in my home town
6. What to look for in a good TV show
7. A failure-proof method for making fudge brownies
8. The results of TV violence
9. Our next step in space exploration
10. _____ is a good book because _____.
11. Smoking *is* dangerous to your health.
12. What is the *real* purpose of prison?
13. The bad effects of drug abuse
14. The strangest animal I ever knew
15. Movies should/should not be rated.
16. One way to improve our schools
17. Sometimes you have to learn to live with loneliness.
18. Do people really fall for advertising gimmicks?
19. Let's put a stop to noise pollution.
20. The best way to study for a test
21. What is it that makes him/her a unique individual?

22. What is a "hero"?
23. We don't always see what we think we see.
24. A funny incident at the beach/at camp/in the bleachers
25. Growing up with the "boob tube"
26. The times are still changing.
27. Happiness comes from within.
28. How to build a camp fire
29. Learning to read *is* important.
30. You have to learn to love.

Part 3
The Narrative Paragraph

The narrative paragraph is the simplest and most natural form of writing. It may be based upon fact, upon the imagination, or a combination or both.

The narrative paragraph is the telling of events: "Once upon a time, long, long ago, there lived . . ."; "Last night while I was watching television . . ."; "A funny thing happened to me on the way to school this morning." The events in a narrative paragraph are usually told in **chronological order,** the order in which they occurred in time.

Using Time Words and Phrases

You can help your reader follow the order of time or the passing of time in your narrative by using time words and phrases such as the following:

A Point in Time

one month	next year	at midnight
two days	yesterday	tonight
tomorrow	last week	at this moment

ORDER OF TIME

next	soon	immediately afterward
then	instantly	the next day
later	momentarily	the following Friday

PERIODS OF TIME

for a moment	during the day
for an hour	after a week

ACTIONS REPEATED IN TIME

once	seldom	occasionally
twice	sometimes	frequently

A BREAK IN TIME

at the same time	meanwhile	before this happened

In the following paragraph note the time words and phrases that help you follow the events as they occurred.

> *Soon* the biggest of the boys poised himself, shot down into the water, and did not come up. The others stood about, watching. *After a long time* the boy came up on the other side of a big dark rock, letting the air out of his lungs in a sputtering gasp and a shout of triumph. *Immediately,* the rest of them dived in. *One moment,* the morning seemed full of chattering boys; *the next,* the air and the surface of the water were empty, but through the heavy blue, dark shapes could be seen moving and groping. —DORIS LESSING

Here are two more narrative paragraphs. Notice how they set a scene and tell a kind of story. Can you find any time words or phrases? How important are they to your understanding of the events in the paragraph?

> Once upon a time, not so very many years ago, there lived in a small town called Smiles, Pennsylvania, a little boy

named Benjamin Thurlow Ballou. He had no brothers and no no sisters. He lived all alone with his mother, his father, and his doggie. His mother, who was a college graduate, was named Mummy. His father, who was a television repairman, was named Daddy. And his doggie, who was an Airedale, was named Sid. —Edwin O'Connor

It is four o'clock in the morning on the Mexican border. The lights of the Border Station flicker on the deserted streets. A truck parks in a dark alleyway. The driver lights a cigarette and waits. Hundreds of people with small bundles move noiselessly past the yawning border guards. The driver spits contemptuously at the ragged ones. These are his human cargo. —Stan Steiner

The Topic Sentence in the Narrative Paragraph

Because narrative paragraphs are not always constructed like other kinds of paragraphs, you may find that they do not always have a topic sentence.

The expert had arrived and was going to take care of everything. I floated toward the back of the theater a hundred pounds lighter in spirit. For the first time in longer than I could remember, I knew the cool pleasure of watching a rehearsal without having to be in charge. —Phillip Lopate

For our present study, however, it would be well for you to practice writing narrative paragraphs *with* topic sentences. Note the following examples:

I *spent the day wandering aimlessly through the bright streets.* The noisy penny arcades with their gaggle-giggle of sailors and children and the games of chance were tempting, but after walking through one of them it was obvious that I could only win more chances and no money. I went to the library and used a part of my day reading science fiction, and

in its marble washroom I changed my bandage. —MAYA
ANGELOU

*It was always at dusk that my mother's loneliness came
home to me most.* Painfully alert to every shift in the light at
her window, she would suddenly confess her fatigue by removing her pince-nez, and then wearily pushing aside the great
mound of fabrics on her machine, would stare at the street as
if to warm herself in the last of the sun. "How sad it is!" I
once heard her say, "It grips me! It grips me!" Twilight was
the bottommost part of the day, the chillest and loneliest
time for her. —ALFRED KAZIN

Exercises
Writing Narrative Paragraphs

A. Following is a list of topic sentences written by professional
writers. Choose one that interests you. Then, using your imagination,
develop that sentence into a narrative paragraph.

1. Imagine, if you can, a small room, hexagonal in shape, like
the cell of a bee.
2. The little fellow was lying on the bare hospital cot, arms
rigidly straight and teeth clenched tightly together.
3. The darkness of night overtook the dog when he had limped
only about ten miles from the burning village.
4. Turner Tippett sauntered down Broadway with an expansive
smile on his face and a roll of greenbacks in his hand.
5. One of the strangest relationships in the world is that
between father and son.
6. "You ought to be ashamed of yourself," said his mother,
and Fred Kramer had no doubt that he should
7. I was prepared to dislike Max Kelada even before I knew him.
8. Conradin was ten years old, and the doctor had pronounced
his professional opinion that the boy could not live another
five years.
9. The year was 2081 and everybody was finally equal.
10. His right name was Frank X. Farrell, and I guess the "X"
stood for "Excuse me."

B. Following is a list of topics, each of which may be developed into a narrative paragraph. Choose a topic that interests you and, drawing from your own experience, write a narrative paragraph based on that subject. If none of these topics interests you, you may develop one of your own.

Don't waste time with unnecessary details; begin your "story" immediately. Try to make it sad, happy, serious—but always as interesting as possible.

1. I Learn To Ride a Bicycle
2. My First Experience As a Baby-sitter
3. A Trick That Back-Fired
4. My First Date
5. The Day My Pet Died
6. How I Encountered Ecology
7. The Night I Tried To Cook Dinner
8. A Frightening Experience
9. The Diary of a Dog
10. Hitch-Hiking's Not for Me
11. The Results of My Little White Lie
12. I Learned To Fight My Own Battles
13. My First Trip to the City/Country
14. We Lost the Game
15. My First Night Alone
16. I Fought for My Rights
17. We Moved to a New Neighborhood
18. A Day at the Fair or the Speedway
19. Strange Sounds Were Coming from Somewhere
20. I Met a Famous Person

Chapter 5

Writing a Composition

By now you are familiar with the paragraph and the various ways it may be organized. The next step in writing is the longer composition.

A single paragraph rarely stands by itself. It is usually a unit within a longer composition. In this chapter you will study several ways in which paragraphs may be joined together to form the longer composition.

Part 1

What Is a Composition?

Our definition of the composition is only slightly different from that of the paragraph. In defining the paragraph, we said, "A paragraph is a group of closely-related sentences dealing with a *single topic or idea.* Usually, one sentence, called the *topic sentence,* states the main idea of the paragraph. All the other sentences must be related to this topic sentence. These sentences further explain or support the main idea."

A **composition** is a group of closely related *paragraphs* dealing with a *single topic or idea*. Usually, one paragraph, called the *thesis paragraph*, states the main idea of the composition. All the other paragraphs must be related to this thesis paragraph. These other paragraphs further explain or support the main idea.

In order to see how little difference there is between the organization of the paragraph and the organization of the composition, let's compare the two.

A PARAGRAPH

Physical differences alone can affect perception. Boys and girls actually see and hear things in a slightly different way. Boys hear low tones better and high tones more poorly than do girls. Visually, females of all ages are more aware of their surroundings than are males. Females find it harder to ignore details and pick out one thing in a scene.

A COMPOSITION

WHISTLING THROUGH GRASS

Going out into the fields and meadows is supposed to be relaxing, but the true show-off never misses an opportunity. A classic pastoral attention-grabber is whistling through a blade of grass. Many of you probably know how to do this, while more of you have doubtless seen and heard it performed. For those of you who have somehow missed the boat, here's all there is to it.

But first, *when* do you whistle through grass? Our opinion is that you wait until it's very quiet, when the only sounds you hear are the sweet chirping of crickets and the melodic strains of birds in the trees. Then you pluck a blade, place it between your hands, and blow. The crickets and birds will fall at your feet, deeply in awe.

Pick a blade of grass around six inches long. Hold it between your thumb and index finger. With your other hand, pull the blade tight against the thumb holding it. Keep the edge of the blade facing you. The point is to have as narrow a surface as possible close to your mouth. Place your left thumb against your right thumb. Your hands come together in two places: at the thumb's first knuckles and at the ball of the hand below each thumb. Make sure to lock the blade in at these points; keep the blade as rigid as possible.

Now blow steadily, not too strong, not too weak. Practice until you get a smooth, confident sound. Once you master this trick, you'll never forget it. It's like swimming and riding a bicycle. —Ferrell and Eisenberg

The topic sentence in the first example, the single paragraph, tells us that the paragraph is going to be about physical differences affecting perception. The rest of the sentences explain that idea.

The thesis paragraph of the composition tells us that the composition is going to be about whistling through grass. The rest of the paragraphs explain that idea. You will also notice that each paragraph within the composition begins with a topic sentence that tells us what the paragraph will be about.

Part 2

Deciding on a Subject

"What shall I write about?" is the first, and perhaps the most difficult question a writer asks when faced with writing a composition. In answering this question, the writer must ask himself two more questions: "What am I interested in?" and "What do I know about?"

If you yourself have little interest in a subject, you will have a difficult time creating interest on the part of your reader. If you have little knowledge of your subject and try writing "off the top of your head," your writing will have little value to your reader. You must be interested in your subject, and you must know something about it.

In making your final decision as to what to write about, you should also consider the two most important sources of information available to you: (1) yourself, and (2) others.

Yourself as a Subject

Some of you may ask, "Why should I write about me?" Using yourself as the subject for a composition may seem a bit unusual, but the answer to the question is very simple.

You should write about yourself because you are an individual. You are unique. There is no other person in the world just like you. No one looks the same; no one acts the same; no one thinks the same. No one else in the world has lived a life exactly like yours or has had experiences exactly like yours. In some ways other people may be somewhat similar to you, but there is always a difference. And it is this difference that makes you interesting and unique.

As an example, study the following composition. Notice how the student who wrote it drew from his own "uniqueness," from his own experiences, to explain what "growing up" meant to him.

UNDERSTANDING OF A SORT

On a hill I stood and whispered to the far sea. I was ten, not really much younger than I am now, though almost a decade separates that little boy I was from the bigger boy I am. Understanding of a sort has come between us—or perhaps it is a loss of understanding.

The sea was bluer then, I think. Ten years ago the little boy thought that seas are blue because the water is blue—all the way to the bottom. Now the bigger boy knows that seas are blue because they reflect the sky. And the bigger boy wishes that the little boy had never found out.

The tide is coming in. Tides, the bigger boy has been told, come in because of the magnetism of the moon. The little boy thought the tide comes in because on the shore a good water mother calls it to her arms. Lying on the hill, the little boy used to wait and try to hear her call. But she always called so softly that he never could hear her. If ever he had heard her, he planned to run down the hill to the beach and hunt until he found her in one of the coves. She would have room in her arms, he was sure, for him as well as for the sea.

When the little boy, ten years ago, stood on the hill and watched the sea, he stood in another land, apart from the country of drab people and dingy towns. They did not exist for him. But the years have brought a growing in the towns and people about him. The vines of reality climbed over him and after a while he became part of them. Now they are forever with him.

The bigger boy I am cries again to be the little boy I was; but the voice comes back to me as a hollow echo, thwarted by the wall of understanding that the years have built between us. But there—the water mother is calling in the sea. I think I almost hear her.

In this recollection, you can easily see that your own experiences, your own thoughts, your own feelings provide an almost endless source of subjects for interesting compositions.

Exercise
Yourself as a Subject

In order to stimulate your thinking in regard to yourself as the subject for a composition, study the following suggestions for topics. After you have studied them, draw from your own experiences and make a list of at least ten topics of your own. If any of the topics listed here interest you, you may add them to your list. *Keep your list for future reference.*

1. My Fondest Dream
2. My Family at the Dinner Table
3. My Own Pet Prejudice
4. Thoughts on Growing Up
5. Souvenirs I Have Collected

6. My Kid Sister/Brother
7. The Day I Learned Fear
8. Things I Can't Do Without
9. My Nicest Compliment—I Think
10. The Worst Party I Ever Attended
11. I Thought He/She Was My Best Friend
12. My Dog Taught Me a Lesson
13. I Live in a World of Me
14. My First Fight
15. The Nerve of Some People
16. I Went Out for the Team and Lost/Won
17. How Music Affects My Imagination
18. My First Date Was Almost My Last
19. I Made the Same Mistake Again
20. A Person I Learned to Like/Dislike

Others as a Subject

From what you have read, you know that good writing depends on how much a writer knows about a subject. Because no writer wants to spend all his time writing about himself, and because it is impossible to learn everything from first-hand experience, the writer must often turn to other sources of information.

In going beyond himself for subjects to write about, the writer may use many different sources. He may interview someone who has had a unique experience or who has become an authority in a certain area. He may study various types of current research. He makes use of the entire field of published material, gaining his information however and wherever he may.

In gathering his information, the writer studies as much as possible, collects as much information as possible so that he knows more about the subject than the average individual does. It is because he has gained an above-average understanding of his subject that he is able to write with interest and knowledge. He knows what he is talking about. In the following example, the author writes with authority about *sumo*, the Japanese art of wrestling.

SUMO TOURNAMENTS

A special type of Japanese wrestling is called *sumo*. Sumo is probably Japan's oldest sport. It began hundreds of years ago as a part of a Shinto religious ceremony. Some Shinto shrines had special buildings built for sumo matches, held to honor the gods. In the year 858, it is said, the two sons of the emperor wrestled to see who would succeed to the throne.

Today sumo is so popular that tournaments are held every year in the large cities. Thousands go to the huge stadiums to watch the matches. Others view them on television. The sumo wrestlers are tall and heavy, sometimes weighing 300 pounds. Each wrestler wears only a ring about his waist and a loin cloth. The place where they perform is a circle that measures 15 feet across.

Before the wrestlers begin a match they throw salt into the ring to drive away the evil spirits. Then they step out and practice balancing exercises. After this more salt is thrown, and there are more exercises. Finally they are ready and the referee flips his fan.

The wrestlers charge at each other. Each tries to lift or push the other out of the ring. If any part of the wrestler's body except his feet touch the ground, or if one wrestler steps out of the ring, the match is over. The whole contest takes no longer than about one minute.

There are usually about 15 matches in one afternoon. The tournament continues for several days until all the wrestlers have been in the ring. The winner is called a grand champion. No one in Japan is more admired than a Sumo Grand Champion. —Lee W. Farnsworth

There is one important note of caution here: If the writer takes information from another source, even if it is only an original idea from some other book or from some other person, *he does not copy the material word-for-word and claim it as his own.* While a writer sometimes *quotes* the words or an idea of another person to explain or prove a point, *he always gives credit to the originator of the quotation or the idea.* A good writer never takes credit for someone else's work.

Exercises
Others as a Subject

A. In order to stimulate your thinking in regard to sources of information other than yourself, study the following examples. After you have studied these examples, make a list of ten topics of your own. If any of the topics listed here interest you, you may add them to your list. *Keep your list for future reference.*

1. The Art of Sky Diving
2. Current Developments in the Women's Movement
3. Contributions of the Chicanos to America
4. The History of "Rock"
5. Ecology: Its Development as a Social Force
6. The Japanese Game of Go
7. Photography as an Art
8. Is There Really a Generation Gap?
9. The Growth of Violence in America
10. Soccer: A New Sport for the U.S.
11. Animals, Birds, and Reptiles: The Endangered Species
12. Local Superstitions Still Live
13. The History of Advertising
14. New Experiments in Energy
15. Are We Approaching a New Ice Age?
16. The Japanese Tea Ceremony
17. Is There Really Danger in Aerosols?
18. Experiments in Nuclear Fission
19. What Makes a Hero?
20. The History of Civil Rights in America
21. The Modern Olympic Games
22. School Athletics: Are They Still Important?
23. Planning New Cities for the Future
24. Growing Old in America
25. The Arts in America: Are They Still Important?

B. Study your list of topics carefully. Decide on one topic that interests you most, one which you would like to know more about. It is possible that you already have some opinions about some of these topics, but at the moment our emphasis is upon gaining more information, not merely giving opinions.

After you have decided on your topic, spend some time in your school library, in your public library, or with some authority on the subject—any source of information available to you. At the moment, your purpose is to see how much information is available on the subject.

As you find books, articles, or sources of information you might use, write the name of the book or article, the author's name, and the call number on a 3 × 5 card so you will not have to look up this information again. You might also jot down a sentence or two as to what the book or article is about.

Suppose, for example, you have decided to write a composition on American music. You find a book which you think might be interesting and helpful, so you write down the following information on a card:

Call Number 780
EL 78N

The National Music of America and Its Sources. Title

Louis C. Elson Author

Covers the history of American music from Puritan times to 1889. Emphasis is on patriotic music. Comment

By doing this, you will not have to waste time going back through the card catalog if you decide later that this is a book you'd like to study.

Part 3
Narrowing the Subject

One important procedure in writing the paragraph was to narrow an idea so that it could be treated adequately and satisfactorily within the limits of the paragraph. The same holds true in writing the composition.

As an example, suppose we consider the subject "The History of Music in America." It is not difficult to see that our subject is so broad that it could fill an entire book. Even if we narrowed the subject to "Music in Twentieth-Century America," we still have too broad a subject. As a subject for a composition, we must choose one very small segment of "The History of Music in America" to write about. By doing so, we increase the number of possibilities for composition topics immensely.

GENERAL TOPIC: The History of Music in America

SPECIFIC TOPICS: Who Really Wrote "Yankee Doodle"?
Francis Scott Key and "The Star
Spangled Banner"
W. C. Handy: The Father of Jazz
Scott Joplin and Ragtime
Louis Armstrong: Jazz Musician
Elvis Presley and the Rise of "Rock"

Of course, many many more specific topics could be added to the list.

Let's look at another example. Suppose our general topic is "The Contributions of Japanese-Americans to American Society." Again, we have numerous possibilities suggested for specific topics.

GENERAL TOPIC: The Contributions of Japanese-Americans
to American Society

SPECIFIC TOPICS: Daniel K. Inouye: Soldier and Statesman
Seiji Ozawa: A New Breed of Symphony
Conductor

Dr. S. I. Hayakawa: World Authority
in Semantics
Minoru Yamasaki: Distinguished
American Architect
Dr. Hideyo Noguchi: World-Famous
Bacteriologist

By choosing one of these specific topics, we can now cover the material in a short composition, as in the following example concerning Senator Daniel K. Inouye.

DANIEL K. INOUYE: SOLDIER, STATESMAN

Hawaii has given us the first Japanese-American representative to Congress—Daniel Ken Inouye, now a U.S. Senator.

Daniel Inouye was born of Japanese parents in Honolulu in 1924. During World War II he fought with the 442nd Regimental Combat Team and received the Distinguished Service Cross. When he returned to Hawaii, he became an attorney, entered local politics, and served in the territorial legislature. When Hawaii became a state, he was elected as its first representative to Congress.

The House was very still on August 23, 1959. It was about to see the swearing in, not only of the first congressman from Hawaii, but of the first Japanese-American in either House of Congress.

"Raise your right hand and repeat after me," said Speaker Sam Rayburn.

The hush deepened as the young congressman raised not his right hand but his left hand and repeated the oath of office. Congressman Inouye had no right arm. He had lost it in combat in World War II.

Because of his excellent record as a representative, Daniel Inouye was elected to the U.S. Senate in 1962, where he has served ever since. In 1968 he was the keynote speaker at the Democratic National Convention.

—Dorothy and Joseph Dowdell

Exercise
Narrowing the Subject

In your last assignment, you chose a general topic for writing, and began to look up information about it. Now, you must narrow that topic to a point where you can cover it in a short composition. This will necessitate some reading on your part.

Look through the list of books that you made on your last assignment. Select two or three books that you think would be most interesting, and check the Table of Contents for possible specific topics.

Continuing with American music as an example, suppose we have on our list of books *A Short History of Music in America*. That sounds like a book we might use. We check the Table of Contents and find the following general headings:

I.	Before the Settlers
II.	Music in the Colonies
III.	First Native Composers
IV.	The Years of the Revolution
V.	The Turn of the Century to the 1830's
VI.	Continuing Growth in the Nineteenth Century to 1860
VII.	From the Civil War Through the 1880's
VIII.	Last Years of the Nineteenth Century
IX.	First Decade of the Twentieth Century
X.	The Second Decade and World War I
XI.	The Twenties
XII.	The Thirties
XIII.	American Folk Music
XIV.	The Forties
XV.	Music at the Half Century
XVI.	At the Bicentennial

It is not difficult to see that each of these headings is still too broad. We find, however, that the Table of Contents is broken down into even narrower topics. So we reread the Table of Contents, and under "The Second Decade and World War I" we discover a topic that catches our attention:

Early Jazz
　　Origins
　　Dixieland Jazz
　　Sources of Jazz

Here are at least three specific topics suggested by the Table of Contents in this book:

1. "The Origins of Early Jazz"
2. "Dixieland Jazz"
3. "The Sources of Jazz"

From your study of the Table of Contents of the books you have chosen, make a list of several specific topics related to your general topic. In some books the Table of Contents may not be broken down into narrower topics, but you should not have too much difficulty in deciding what the narrower topics could be.

Choose one specific topic from your list—one that is of particular interest to you—to serve as the basis for a composition.

Begin reading from your listed books in order to gain background information for the next steps in your work.

Part 4
Deciding on the Audience and the Purpose

You must decide for whom you are writing the composition, and your purpose for writing the composition, before you begin to write.

1. **A good writer always keeps his audience in mind.** The reason for this is very simple. If you are writing for a child of seven or eight, your choice of words, the amount of information you use, and the amount of explanation you include will be quite different from what you would use if you were writing for your classmates. Your choice of words, the amount of information you use, and the amount of explanation you include for your class-

mates would also be quite different from what you would use if you were writing for adults.

The good writer also decides whether he is writing for an audience with some knowledge of the subject or for an audience which is quite unfamiliar with the subject.

In order to clarify this point, let's look at two paragraphs, both written on the same subject but written for two entirely different audiences.

MOHENJO DARO, AN ANCIENT CITY IN INDIA

From what was found in Mohenjo Daro we know that the people who lived there knew how to make bricks. With the bricks they made neat houses for themselves. They could plan cities, and keep them clean by laying drain-pipes to take away the dirty water. They built huge public baths for people to wash in, and broad streets for chariots and bullock-carts. They must have been clever craftsmen, because fine pots of clay and weapons made of copper and bronze have been found in the city. They drew figures of animals and gods on pottery and on seals. From these we can guess what animals they knew, what gods they worshipped and what sort of writing they used. Their necklaces of beads, and ornaments of gold and ivory, tell us that they loved beautiful things and knew how to make them. They used cotton for making cloth. They prayed to a Divine Mother and to a god who was very much like Shiva. They knew how to write although we do not yet know how to read what they wrote. —SHEILA DHAR

MOHENJO DARO, AN ANCIENT CITY IN INDIA

The most striking of the few large buildings is the great bath in the citadel area of Mohenjo Daro. This is an oblong bathing pool 39×23 feet in area and 8 feet deep, constructed of beautiful brickwork made watertight with bitumen. It could be drained by an opening in one corner and was surrounded by a cloister, onto which opened a number of small rooms. Like the "tank" of a Hindu temple, it probably had a religious purpose, and the cells may have been the homes of priests. The special attention paid by the people of the Harappa culture to cleanliness is hardly due to the fact that they had notions of hygiene in advance of those of other civilizations of their time, but indicates that, like the later Hindus, they had a strong belief in the purificatory effects of water from a ritual point of view. —A. L. Basham

The first paragraph is obviously written for young readers; the second, for the more mature, more knowledgeable reader. The choice of words and the choice of details have been carefully chosen for the specific audience for whom the writer is writing.

2. **A good writer knows his purpose for writing.** In determining the purpose for his composition, the good writer will decide whether he wishes to *entertain* his readers, *describe* something for them, or *explain* something to them. This decision is important because it will set the *tone* and *mood* for the entire composition.

Is your composition going to be humorous? sad? serious? Do you want your reader to laugh? to cry? to be moved by the beauty or ugliness of a scene you are describing? to think seriously about the idea you are presenting? Once this decision is made, you should be ready to begin organizing your ideas for the next step in writing your composition.

Exercises
Deciding on the Audience and the Purpose

A. Decide upon the audience for your composition.

B. Decide upon the purpose for writing your composition.

Part 5
Planning the Composition

You must know exactly where you are going and you must organize your composition into some form of logical order so that your reader can follow your ideas. Planning your composition is a necessary step in writing. Without preliminary planning, your composition could easily become nothing more than a series of disorganized ideas that ramble on to nowhere.

Writing Down Ideas

You may already have some ideas concerning points you wish to include as you begin to plan your composition. Jot them down on a sheet of paper or on 3 × 5 cards as they come to you. If you use a card for each idea, you will find that the next step in organizing your ideas will be much easier.

As you continue to read and study your subject, be sure to add further ideas and information from that research to your list. Your finished list might look something like this:

THE ORIGINS OF JAZZ

clapping and dancing
Congo Square
Ragtime
military bands
drums played by slaves
spirituals
the brass band
work songs
plantation cries
the blues
field "hollers"
the beat
French quadrilles
syncopation

If you have put your ideas on cards, you will, of course, have a card for each statement. You will also note that, at the moment, the above list has no organization to it. Our purpose here is simply to get down as many ideas as possible as we read.

Exercise
Writing Down Ideas

Make a list, or a series of cards, containing as many ideas related to your subject as you can think of.

Grouping Your Ideas

After you have completed your list of ideas, your next step is to organize those ideas in relation to each other; that is, to group similar ideas with other similar ideas.

In order to clarify this point, let's continue with our composition on American music which we have now narrowed to "The Origins of Jazz."

From our study of jazz, we will have learned that jazz developed from three basic roots: the beat, the brass bands, and the blues. Let's make a heading for each of these:

    I.   The Beat

    II.   The Brass Bands

    III. The Blues

These three major ideas will be our primary concern. Our next step is to list all the rest of our ideas under the appropriate headings:

    I.   The Beat

             clapping and dancing
             Congo Square
             drums played by slaves

    II.   The Brass Bands

             Ragtime
             military bands
             French quadrilles
             syncopation

III.   The Blues

> spirituals
> work songs
> plantation cries
> field "hollers"

If you have written your ideas on cards, all you need to do is to reorganize them into a logical order.

Exercises
Grouping Your Ideas

A. Following is a list of "ideas." Decide which of these ideas should be general headings. Then list the remaining ideas under their appropriate headings.

1. provide adequate street lighting
2. pedestrians injure themselves
3. they cross streets diagonally
4. they cross streets in the middle of the block
5. they walk with their backs to traffic on the highway
6. pedestrian lives can be saved
7. they step into traffic from parked cars
8. provide traffic lights for pedestrians
9. they step from behind parked cars
10. give traffic tickets to pedestrians
11. they cross against lights
12. they don't watch for traffic

B. Follow the directions for Exercise A above.

1. service to society
2. description of career
3. specific attitudes
4. income
5. qualifications needed
6. personal satisfaction
7. physical and personal qualities
8. rewards of this career

9. opportunities
10. kinds of work involved
11. education and other training
12. places where such work is done

c. Using the ideas you have been gathering from your reading on your own subject, organize your ideas into related groups.

Making a Working Outline

Making a **working outline** is the final step in organizing your ideas.

Because you now have all your ideas in related groups, this final step is not at all difficult. You are merely going to delete those ideas which are of little importance and reorganize your ideas into a logical order. By a logical order, we mean an order that is easy for your reader to follow. Unfortunately, there is no simple, one-two-three order for a composition. Each composition presents an organizational problem of its own.

Organizing Ideas in Chronological Order. The simplest and most natural order is *chronological*; that is, placing the ideas in order of time—first things first.

I.   The Beat

        drums played by slaves
        clapping and dancing

II. The Brass Band

        military bands
        French quadrilles
        Ragtime

III. The Blues

        work songs
        field "hollers"
        plantation cries
        spirituals

You will note that in our outline we have dropped "Congo Square" and "syncopation" because they are less important ideas.

Organizing Ideas in Order of Importance. We may also organize our ideas in *order of importance;* that is, from the least important to the most important:

THE DEAD WATERFOWL

I. The Threat
    loss of wildlife
    loss of water supplies

II. The Causes
    accidental seepage of industrial waste
    accidental collisions of oil tankers
    deliberate piping of industrial wastes directly
        into water
    deliberate flushing of tankers' oil compartments
        on the high seas

III. The Remedy
    informal individual and collective action
    formal national and international legislation

In this example, the writer is concerned about the death of wild waterfowl, but the important idea is the remedy for these deaths, so that idea comes at the end of the outline.

As you can see, the outline works as a guide to help you keep your ideas moving in a logical direction. Eventually, you will need to learn how to write a formal outline; but for the moment, you will find the informal outline a useful tool in helping you to write a composition.

Exercises
Making a Working Outline

A. Following are three lists of "ideas." Rearrange each of the lists into an informal outline, using whatever order seems best for the subject.

A. MARKET GARDENING

1. selling the products
2. selecting seed
3. planting
4. preparing the soil
5. deciding what to plant
6. gathering the products
7. cultivating
8. preparing the products for market

B. TENNIS IS A GOOD GAME FOR STUDENTS

1. increase in mental alertness
2. relaxation from study
3. joy of competition
4. citizenship
5. stimulation of bodily functions
6. health
7. pleasure
8. development of regard for others
9. development of cooperation

C. AUTOMOBILES SHOULD BE BANNED FROM OUR CITIES

1. because people prefer to drive automobiles, cleaner public transportation facilities suffer
2. the automobile is the major source of air pollution
3. cities are supposed to serve the needs of people, not the cars they drive
4. cities are strangling to death in an attempt to accommodate both people and their automobiles
5. automobiles contribute to such things as noise pollution
6. large cities cannot afford to allow operation of automobiles in crowded urban centers
7. automobiles are an inefficient means of moving large numbers of people in and out of cities
8. new freeways remove more land from residential, business, and recreational use

9. the automobile should be banned from crowded city
   areas because it is a nuisance and a health hazard
10. many automobiles carry only one driver

B. Organize your list of ideas for your own subject into a working outline containing three major headings.

Part 6
Organizing and Writing the Composition

A major part of your work is now finished. Your topic has been selected, your audience and purpose have been decided on, and your information has been organized into a logical pattern of development. You are now ready to organize and begin writing your composition.

The Organization of the Composition

When we defined the composition earlier, we said: "A composition is a group of closely related paragraphs dealing with a single topic or idea. Usually, one paragraph, called the thesis paragraph, states the main idea of the composition. All the other paragraphs must be related to this thesis paragraph. These other paragraphs further explain or support the main idea." To this definition, we now need to add: "A good composition always contains a *beginning*, a *middle*, and an *end*."

You have already completed the organization of the *middle* of your composition, so all you need to add to the final organization of your composition is the beginning and the end. When that is completed, the final organization of your paper will look like this:

   I.   The Thesis Paragraph

II.   The Body

      A. Supporting information   The information

      B. Supporting information   in your working

      C. Supporting information   outline.

III.   The Concluson

The Thesis Paragraph

The thesis paragraph of your composition serves two very important functions and must, therefore, be written with great care. First, a good thesis paragraph catches the reader's attention. Second, it gives the reader an idea as to what the composition is about. For this reason, a good writer avoids such dull and uninteresting statements as these:

1. In this paper, I am going to tell you about the origins of jazz.

2. Hang-gliding is an exciting sport.

3. There are three important reasons why automobiles should be banned from our cities.

There is nothing here to catch the reader's attention, nothing to make him want to read further. It is true that the statements tell us what the compositions are going to be about, but how lacking in interest they are in comparison with the following:

1

The roots of American jazz were planted long before this century was born. These roots were the beat, the music of the brass bands and the blues—three roots which eventually joined together to form the most American of music—Jazz!

2

"What am I doing here?" The surge of panic raced through my body as I felt the wind begin to tug at the contraption strapped to my arms. "I could break a leg, an arm. I could be killed!" But at that moment, the full pressure of the wind caught at the hang-glider's sail, and I was lifted upward, upward, held aloft by only the rising currents of air.

3

The automobile has got to go! We have reached a point in the history of our cities where we can no longer allow this primitive mode of transportation to eat up our land, pollute our atmosphere, and press our citizens into financial ruin.

In each of these thesis paragraphs, not only has the writer given an indication of what his composition will be about, but he has done so in a manner that catches the reader's attention.

There are many ways to approach the writing of the thesis paragraph. Two of the most effective are the following:

1. THE DIRECT APPEAL

If you like riddles, try this one: What do teeth fillings, engagement rings, eyeglasses, and toasters have in common with gasoline, fiber-glass curtains, synthetic fertilizers, and the catalytic converters in most 1976 automobiles? Answer: All of these products rely on one of earth's most expensive and least publicized metals—platinum. —RONALD SCHILLER

How hard should you work? The obvious answer is another question: What do you want from life? But even that isn't the whole answer. Some people labor long and diligently, never making progress, while others seem to coast along in their jobs, reaping promotions and raises. Still others achieve success by working so hard that they sacrifice leisure, family life and sometimes sanity. —CAROLINE DONNELLY

2. THE PERSONAL APPROACH

The time was June 1941 and the place was Vilna, a city in the northeastern corner of Poland. I was ten years old and took it quite for granted that all over the globe people tended their gardens on such a morning as this. Wars and bombs stopped at the garden gates, happened on the far side of garden walls. —ESTER HAUTZIG

Halloweens I have always considered wilder and richer and more important than even Christmas morn. The dark and lovely memories leap back at me as I see once again my ghostly relatives, and the lurks and things that creaked stairs or sang softly in the hinges when you opened a door. —RAY BRADBURY

Whatever approach to the writing of your thesis paragraph you use, remember that its purpose is *to attract your reader, to give your reader an indication of what your subject is,* and *to limit the subject matter of your composition.*

Exercises
The Thesis

A. Read the following opening statements and decide which ones have definite reader appeal. Rewrite those that are lacking in appeal. You may use more than one sentence in your revision if you wish.

1. Habits are first cobwebs, then cables.
2. This composition is about learning to ski.
3. My kid sister is a difficult person to live with.
4. Nobody goes to the hardware store for a loaf of bread.
5. I would like to tell you about an interesting trip I took to Chicago.
6. Today we need all the help we can get in sifting food facts from food fads.
7. Say "New Orleans" to somebody who has been there, and you get a most predictable response: "Ah, the food."
8. Jerusalem is as important as it is unique.
9. Our camping trip turned out to be an exciting experience.
10. My teacher has asked me to write a paper about censorship.
11. The first time I met Joe Benton, I thought he was a great guy; now I think he's crazy.

12. My father works in a local filling station.

13. My friend Andrea is very intelligent.

14. Accidental swallowing of tabs and rings from soft-drink cans can be a serious problem.

15. It is a picture that has haunted me for months.

B. Write two different thesis paragraphs for your own composition, one using the direct appeal, and one using the personal approach. Read your paragraphs in class. In discussion with your classmates and your teacher, decide which one you will use as the thesis statement for your composition. Revise if necessary.

The Body

The major part of the composition is the **body.** It is here that the ideas indicated in the thesis paragraph are further developed or explained. As an example, let's follow through with the composition on "The Origins of Jazz" to see how the ideas are expanded.

The thesis paragraph said:

> The roots of American Jazz were planted long before this century was born. These roots were the beat, the music of the brass bands, and the blues—three roots which eventually joined together to form that most American of music—Jazz!

The thesis paragraph indicates that we will discuss the beat, the music of the brass bands, and the blues. If you recall our working outline for this composition, you remember that we had indicated that the body of our paper would be concerned with these three ideas. As we expand, now, upon these three ideas, the body of our paper will look like this:

> The beat, the first root of jazz, began with the varied rhythms of African slaves in New Orleans. Each Sunday these slaves would gather on Congo Square for a celebration, a *bamboula*. There they recalled the rhythms of their home-

land, rhythms passed down from parent to child. As some of the musicians beat their intricate rhythms on drums of many sizes, others would dance and clap. Thus, the beat was born.

The second root of jazz was also planted in New Orleans. Through its years as a French colony, this city on the Delta had heard the strident music of the military brass band, and had danced to the rhythms of French quadrilles played by some of these same bands at evening *soirées*. These sounds and rhythms they combined with the beat of the Congo drums into a music of their own, a syncopated form of melody which became known as "rag" or "Ragtime." This music was also played by small brass bands made up of the descendants of those earlier slaves who had established the "beat" in Congo Square.

No one knows who first made up the blues. It is fairly certain, however, that its roots were firmly planted in the work songs, the plantation cries, the field "hollers," and the spirituals heard and sung by the early slaves as they gave vent to their loneliness, frustration, and sorrow.

From this example, you can also see two important points concerning the body of the composition:

1. **The composition is always divided into paragraphs.** The division of the composition into paragraphs has a psychological effect upon the reader. Often, if he sees a page covered with writing, with no blank space to relieve the monotony of that page, he may not read any further.

Because each paragraph contains a new idea, the indentation of the paragraph indicates to the reader that he is moving to the next point of development, or the next point of information in the composition.

2. **Each paragraph of the composition usually begins with a topic sentence.** Just as the thesis statement of the composition indicates what the composition is about, the topic sentence, as you know from your previous study, gives an indication as to what the paragraph will be about.

To clarify these ideas, let's analyze another example.

When the earth was young, the beasts roamed the world. One was a snake of many colors. The snake was a sight to behold, for the Creator had endowed him with beauty. The creatures admired him. Never had they seen so many colors on any one animal.

The snake's beauty brought him fame in the animal kingdom. With fame came the friendship of all the animals. The animals complimented him until, one day, he thought more highly of himself than all others. He became boastful, claiming to be the King of Beauty.

The animals were tolerant, but not the Creator. Upon hearing the boasts, the Creator sent a warning message to the snake to cease his boasting, but the snake would not listen, and kept on boasting. The Creator was angered and was determined to put an end to the silly snake's boasts. He sent a great white eagle to seize the snake and fly with him into the sky, then drop him.

The great bird flew to the earth, seized the snake and flew high into the sky, then released him. The snake dropped toward earth. The snake pleaded for his life, and the Creator took pity, but was determined to punish him. The Creator sent the eagle once more to place on the earth the snake unharmed.

Once more safe on the earth, the snake discovered he no longer was beautiful. So angered was he that he developed the venom of hate. The ungrateful snake lifted his head to curse the Creator, only to see his coat of many colors in a bow across the sky. Now the beauty of the colors was to be enjoyed by everyone and not just one.

Thus, after every rainfall the rainbow comes out to remind the snake of his fall to earth, leaving behind him his coat of many colors. —GLENDA CELESTINE

From a psychological point of view, the composition appeals to the eye. It is broken up into short paragraphs with enough blank space to indicate to the reader that he is not going to lose himself in long, involved ideas.

The thesis paragraph indicates that the composition is going to be about a beautiful snake of many colors.

Each paragraph in the body begins with a topic sentence that indicates what the paragraph will be about:

1. The snake's beauty brought him fame in the animal kingdom.

2. The animals were tolerant, but not the Creator.

3. The great bird flew to the earth, seized the snake and flew high into the sky, then released him.

4. Once more safe on the earth, the snake discovered he no longer was beautiful.

The supporting details in each paragraph are directly related to the topic sentence, and each paragraph is directly related to the thesis paragraph. Thus, the composition is well written, is well organized, and has a feeling of *unity*.

Achieving Unity in the Composition

The good writer makes use of **transitional devices** in order to give a composition a feeling of unity—a feeling that everything is tied together and is not merely a series of isolated ideas. These devices tie the ideas of the composition together by referring both to the idea that precedes and the idea that follows.

Transitional Devices

There are six basic transitional devices that the writer should learn to use:

1. **Using a Word That Indicates Time.** Such words include the following:

first	before	meanwhile	until
next	after	in the meantime	finally
then	afterwards	eventually	today

A special type of Japanese wrestling is called *sumo*. Sumo is probably Japan's oldest sport. It began hundreds of years ago as a part of a Shinto religious ceremony. Some Shinto shrines had special buildings built for sumo matches, held to honor the gods. In the year 858, it is said, the two sons of the emperor wrestled to see who would succeed to the throne.

Today sumo is so popular that tournaments are held every year in the large cities. Thousands go to the huge stadiums to watch the matches. Others view them on television. The sumo wrestlers are tall and heavy, sometimes weighing 300 pounds. Each wrestler wears only a ring about his waist and a loin cloth. The place where they perform is a circle that measures 15 feet across. —LEE W. FARNSWORTH

2. Using a Word That Shows the Relationship Between Ideas. Such words include the following:

and	since	moreover
also	therefore	similarly
because	besides	unless

For the individual American, the main advantage of the metric system will be its simplicity. Instead of the fifty-five measurement units of the English system, the metric system has only three. These are meters, grams, and liters.

Calculations will be simpler because all multiples are powers of 10. There will be no more pound-and-ounce perplexity. Simply move the decimal point.

3. Using a Word That Shows an Opposite Point of View. Such words include the following:

but	while	on the other hand
however	although	in contrast

Over the years, oil and natural gas gradually replaced coal as the major fuels for homes and industry. Gas and oil were cheaper. They were also more convenient.

Today, however, America is faced with an energy dilemma. Our supplies of gas and oil are dwindling. We now import more than 40 percent of the oil we need, and the need for imports continues to increase.

4. Using a Word That Repeats a Word Used Earlier

Almost everybody daydreams. But what do such dreams indicate about a person? And how do one person's dreams differ from another person's?

Science is just beginning to probe the deeper meanings of daydreams, yet it has come up with some startling preliminary findings. —DOROTHY BRANT WARWICK

5. Using a Synonym for a Word Used Earlier

It's hard to find another city in the country that is so prosperous and problem-solving. In recent years, most U.S. cities have been suffering acute ills. Not Houston.

The city's racial minorities—28 percent black and 12 percent Latin—are relatively serene, satisfied that they are at least in the city's mainstream. . . . —NOEL F. BUSCH

6. Using a Pronoun That Refers to a Word Used Earlier

After the Flyers' upset Cup victory, four games to two, two million Philadelphians cheered a motorcade taking their heroes to Independence Hall. Along the route signs read: "Bobby Clarke for Mayor."

In the eyes of his teammates, he already occupies a higher office. "Clarkie is our leader," declares Bernie Parent, the Flyers' superb goalie. —DAVID McDONALD

The use of these devices will help you tie your ideas together into a unified, smoothly-flowing composition.

Exercises
The Body

A. Study the following pairs of paragraphs carefully. Identify the transitional device, or devices, that each writer has used to tie the paragraphs together.

1

After I returned from India, I entered into a correspondence with Ved, whose letters were surprisingly mature for a boy in his teens. They were clearly the work of a resourceful mind. What impressed me particularly was his supple use of the English language.

I met Ved for the first time in the spring of 1952. He came to our home with his father, then in the United States as a visiting Fulbright professor. There was nothing about Ved that suggested a handicapped person. He used no cane. He had no seeing-eye dog. He didn't wait for people to lead him from one place to another. Not once did his father take him by the hand. Yet he moved about easily. —NORMAN COUSINS

2

Pavlov discovered he couldn't make dogs salivate on signal until he put them in artificial, controlled environments. By controlling space, sound, temperature and food, he made them respond to his slightest signal.

Disney made the same discovery. "Control" was his favorite word. He controlled every stage in the production and "total marketing" of his films. He developed the "wrap-around screen," which was an effort at total environment. His studio was a rigidly controlled environment and served as the prototype for Disneyland. —EDMUND CARPENTER

3

To come all that way, rifle in hand, with two thousand people marching at my heels, and then to trail feebly away, having done nothing—no, that was impossible. The crowd would laugh at me. And my whole life, every white man's life in the East, was one long struggle not to be laughed at.

But I did not want to shoot the elephant. I watched him beating his bunch of grass against his knees, with that preoccupied grandmotherly air that elephants have. It seemed to me that it would be murder to shoot him. At that age I was not squeamish about killing animals, but I had never shot an elephant and never wanted to. —GEORGE ORWELL

4

Marget was both my first love and hurt. I met her when she joined our sixth-grade class.

She stood before the class, her blue, frightened eyes sweeping back and forth across the room until they came to rest on my face. From that very first day we became friends— Marget, just fresh from Sweden, and I, a sixth-generation American. —CARRIE A. YOUNG

5

The heat pressed down on me, as if suddenly in league with gravity. My pack sagged. And then all at once, a thread of clear water was sparkling on bare rock. I walked up beside it with light and springing step. The thread broadened. Half a mile, and I camped in the shade of some green creekside bushes. Soon I was stretched out cool and naked on my sleeping bag.

The little creek, still less than a foot wide, bubbled and babbled past so close that I could reach out whenever I wanted to and scoop up a cupful of cool drinking water. All I could see was green foliage and a hint of glaring rock beyond. That, and the sparkling creek and the oddly humped, blue-gray rock over which it flowed. —COLIN FLETCHER

6

During my three years as Executive Director of the National Congress of American Indians it was a rare day when some white didn't visit my office and proudly proclaim that he or she was of Indian descent.

Cherokee was the most popular tribe of their choice and many people placed the Cherokee anywhere from Maine to Washington State. Mohawk, Sioux, and Chippewa were next in popularity. —VINE DELORIA

7

Buried in the homemade cakes the family loves, lost among the stitches of patches, sunk in the suds of the week's wash, are incalculable skilled services.

But just as slaves were in the service of individual masters, so are housewives bound to the service of individual families. That it devolves upon a mother to tend her children during helpless infancy and childhood—or at any rate to see that they are tended by someone—is undeniable. But only a psychology of slavery can put women at the service of grown men.
—EDITH M. STERN

8

The Concorde, loudest airplane in the world, hits 117.9 EPNdB on take-off. That means 117.9 Effective Perceived Noise Decibels.

Maude, taking off on CBS the Monday night I measured her with my sound meter, registered no higher than 60, and cruised at 57. But she hit that peak-60 five different times during her half hour on the air, squeezing in six screams and six arguments along the way.

Maude's figures may not look bad against Concorde's until you learn that many experts assume that a comfortable sound-strength level is 55 decibels or under. When you converse normally, you are in the 45–50 decibel range. Above 55, sound can begin to annoy. Add 10 decibels to 55, and the human ear begins to perceive this increase as a doubling of loudness.
—MAX J. FRIEDMAN

B. Complete the body of your own composition, making certain that you have used appropriate transitional devices to tie the paragraphs together. Make certain that each paragraph is directly related to your thesis statement.

Reread your composition. Revise where necessary.

The Conclusion

After you have finished writing the body of your composition, your final step is to write the conclusion. The concluding paragraph ties all the ideas together and indicates to the reader that you are finished.

For example, we might end our composition on "The Origins of Jazz" in this manner:

> Eventually, interest in the blues grew until it joined with the beat and the music of the brass bands. From this union, a new and completely American form of music was born—Jazz!

You will notice that our conclusion *repeats* some of the ideas from our thesis paragraph.

In "Message in the Sky," you may recall, the writer ended her composition in this manner:

> Thus, after every rainfall the rainbow comes out to remind the snake of his fall to earth, leaving behind him his coat of many colors.

In this short, concluding statement, the writer has effectively *summarized* her story.

Let's look at another effective ending:

> What of the heroic horseman who aroused the Minutemen on that April night? Henry Wadsworth Longfellow lifted him from a footnote of history to a place in American poetic literature with a ballad that includes these words:
>
> So through the night rode Paul Revere;
> A cry of defiance and not of fear,
> A voice in the darkness, a knock at the door,
> And a word that shall echo forevermore!

This writer has chosen an appropriate stanza of poetry that indicates "finish" to the composition.

Exercises
The Conclusion

A. Write the concluding paragraph of your own composition. Be sure that it ties in well with the rest of your paper.

B. Revise your entire paper where necessary.

Chapter 6

Types of Compositions

Just as there are several types of paragraphs, there are several types of compositions. Because you are already familiar with descriptive, explanatory, and narrative paragraphs, we will now expand those paragraph types into descriptive, explanatory, and narrative compositions. This will not be difficult because many of the skills you have learned in writing the three types of paragraphs, and in organizing the composition as a whole, also apply to these three types of compositions.

Part 1

The Descriptive Composition

Description is seldom used alone as the basis for an entire composition. Rather, it is usually used in conjunction with other types of writing. However, there are times when a writer may be so deeply moved by a scene, an incident, or a situation that he can communicate his feelings only through pure description. Therefore, he writes a descriptive composition.

In writing this type of composition, here are several points you should be familiar with:

1. point of view
2. unity
3. coherence
4. emphasis

Point of View

From your study of the descriptive paragraph, you are already familiar with one aspect of point of view—*the physical*. If you recall, we said that in writing the descriptive paragraph, your details should follow some logical order. That is, "You may describe your scene from side to side, from bottom to top (or the reverse), or from near to far (or the reverse). You may use other methods of organization, provided you include key words to indicate to your reader that you are changing directions." This is what we mean by "physical point of view."

In addition, once you have chosen your physical point of view, your description should include only those details that can be sensed from that given point. For example, if you are standing on a high cliff overlooking a mountain valley, you will get only a general impression, and there will be some things you cannot hear, see, touch, taste, or smell from that vantage point. The scene would be quite different from what it would be on the floor of the valley, so this must also be taken into consideration when deciding upon the physical point of view.

The other aspect of point of view is *mental*. If, for example, as you look at the mountain valley, the sky is dark; heavy, black clouds are forming on the horizon; the wind is moaning faintly through the pines, and thunder crashes over the distant peaks, you may feel sad, depressed. This is your *mental point of view* at the moment, and will be reflected in your composition.

On the other hand, the morning sun may be shining down into the valley; the sky may be a cloudless blue. In the distance you hear the rhythmic clatter of a woodpecker, and catch a hint of lingering pine scent. All this may combine to make you feel happy, carefree, even excited. This is your mental point of view at the moment, and will be reflected in your composition.

Thus, while the physical point of view will remain fairly stable, the mental point of view will vary according to mood and the individual.

Unity

The purpose in writing the descriptive composition is to create *a single, unified impression* in the mind of the reader. This is done by having a definite point of view, by choosing your details carefully, and by making sure that each sentence in each paragraph relates to the topic sentence and that each paragraph relates back to the thesis paragraph.

One point here may need further clarification—*choosing your details carefully*. This is an important point, not only in the writing of the descriptive composition, but in all writing.

Choosing your details carefully means choosing those details that are important, and then describing them with *precise* words. As an example, look at the following statements:

1. The bird sang in the tree.
2. The mourning dove grieved in the old pine.

The first statement is too vague, too general, too lacking in precision; while the second statement is precise in its identification of the bird and the tree, and also precise in the use of the verb.

Another example:

1. The elephant moved down the ramp.
2. The huge elephant lumbered down the ramp.

The addition of an appropriate adjective, and the choice of a strong, precise verb create a much clearer image in the second statement than in the first.

Coherence

Coherence, or clarity, in description is achieved through the logical arrangement of ideas, as previously discussed under "point of view."

Emphasis

Emphasis in description is achieved (1) by placing the details in a logical order, (2) by *emphasizing* those details that are important and de-emphasizing details of lesser importance.

In describing a scene, the writer often chooses a *center of interest*—an unusual mountain, a unique building, an interesting play of light or color—and groups his ideas around it. The central image will dominate the scene and all other details will be described in relation to it.

Now, in order to see how all these techniques work when put together, let's analyze the following composition:

It is not yet 4:30 and the sun is setting behind the low ridge to the west. The last, long light climbs from the valley's frosted pasture grass up the gray trunks of the naked maples and seems to pause on the hilltops to the east. Then it is gone. Twilight, the glow of November evening, possesses the day.

At first there is the bright shadowless light, a sunless daylight in which the growing moon, halfway up the eastern sky, is only a ghost. Then the glow comes, a rosy suffusion so subtle it could be a reflection of the maple leaves at the roadside or the bronze-red grass in the neglected meadow. The air seems to thin and brighten, and the chill diminishes distances. The world comes close, the familiar world of this place called home.

The glow fades. Dusk creeps in, unhurried but insistent, and the clarity of vision dims. In its place is a deceptive clarity of hearing. The farm dog barking just down the road sounds no closer than a truck shifting gears on a hill a mile away. The rustle of leathery leaves in an oak not ten feet away seems as far off as the hooting of the barred owl across the valley. And time somehow has lost its dimensions. It is evening and it is autumn, and the moon has begun to glow. The scuffle of leaves at the roadside just ahead could be a noontime cat or a midnight fox. Or the evening breeze.

Sunset, twilight, dusk, darkness, all by six o'clock on a mid-November evening, late autumn's summary of serenity.
—THE NEW YORK TIMES

The writer's physical point of view is at the edge of a valley; his mental point of view is one of serenity, of peace.

The single, unified impression is one of serenity. Unity is achieved through a stable physical point of view and the careful choice of precise details. Notice the carefully chosen words, such as "The last, long light climbs from the valley's frosted pasture grass"; "the growing moon, halfway up the eastern sky, is only a ghost"; "Dusk creeps in, unhurried, but insistent"; and "The rustle of leathery leaves in an oak." All of these images add to a unified impression of serenity.

Each paragraph relates back to the thesis paragraph concerning the setting sun and the coming of "the last, long light."

Coherence is achieved through the use of a logical arrangement, this time chronological, in which the writer describes the order of sunset, twilight, dusk, and darkness.

Emphasis is achieved by grouping all the minor details in relation to *light*. It is the changing light, reflecting the oncoming night, that is the dominant or central image in the composition, a light through which all other objects are seen and heard.

Careful attention to these techniques will greatly improve your ability to write the descriptive composition.

Exercise
Writing a Description

Following the techniques we have already discussed in writing the composition, write a descriptive composition of five paragraphs.

Because the descriptive composition is highly personal, you will not need to research your subject. In choosing your subject, however, remember to choose one that will interest both you and your readers. Then remember the following steps:

1. Limit your subject.
2. Decide on your audience and your purpose.
3. Jot down your ideas.
4. Group your ideas.
5. Organize your ideas into a working outline.
6. Decide on your point of view, both physical and mental.
7. Write your composition, being sure to include the thesis statement, the body, and the conclusion.
8. Check to make sure that all ideas are related to each other and to the thesis statement.
9. Make sure that your composition has unity, coherence, and emphasis.
10. Check to be sure that you have used strong verbs and precise details.
11. Revise carefully where necessary.

Part 2
The Explanatory Composition

Just as the explanatory paragraph *explains*, so does the explanatory composition. Like the explanatory paragraph, the explanatory composition uses facts or statistics, specific examples, incidents or anecdotes, and comparison or contrast.

Because, in the previous chapter, you went through the steps of organizing and writing an explanatory composition, we will not cover that information again. We want only to emphasize the fact that the explanatory composition must have an interesting thesis paragraph, a body which supports or expands that paragraph, and an interesting conclusion. Like the descriptive composition, it must also have unity, coherence, and emphasis.

As a matter of review, let's see how Neil Armstrong, the first man on the moon, used these techniques.

WHAT AMERICA MEANS TO ME

America means opportunity. It started that way. The early settlers came to the new world for the opportunity to worship in keeping with their conscience, and to build a future on the strength of their own initiative and hard work.

The new land was bountiful—and seemingly unlimited. Over the decades, the immigrants poured in, bringing their talents and their traditions as gifts to this country: John Audubon, Irving Berlin, Samuel Gompers, Albert Einstein, Arturo Toscanini, Thomas Mann, Alexander Graham Bell, Andrew Carnegie, Igor Sikorsky, Felix Frankfurter, to name but a few. They discovered a new life with freedom to achieve their individual goals.

Today, for immigrants and natives alike, America remains a land of opportunity. Today's citizens, however, are surrounded by a forest of restrictions that would have confounded their forefathers. The manufacturer must equip his plant to conform to environmental standards, the farmer is limited in his use of pesticides, the user of public roads must be licensed and operate his vehicle in conformance with a myriad of traffic regulations. Over the years, personal freedom has often given way to public safety.

The erosion of personal freedom has been accompanied by some decline in opportunity. Nevertheless, new challenges to our creativity always seem to arise: curing cancer, turning arid wastelands into fertile fields, extracting energy from wind and tide.

One opportunity of enormous import has emerged during recent years. Few developments in history have so excited the citizenry as has the exploration of space. It is far too early to know the extent of our use of the vast expanse beyond Earth, but it is clear that the new vistas will reveal new goals and perhaps new understanding of human destiny.

A great nation will look to the future, not just for its own citizens, but for all humanity. The understanding of the universe beyond our home planet is fundamental to that future. America has provided the opportunity for that understanding.

If we break this composition down into a working outline, it looks like this:

I. THESIS: America means opportunity.

II. BODY:

A. The new land was bountiful—and seemingly unlimited.

B. Today, for immigrants and natives alike, America remains a land of opportunity.

C. The erosion of personal freedom has been accompanied by some decline in opportunity.

D. One opportunity of enormous import has emerged during recent years.

III. CONCLUSION: A great nation will look to the future, not just for its own citizens, but for all humanity.

Mr. Armstrong begins his thesis paragraph with a personal definition: "America means opportunity." You can assume then, that the body of the paper will be concerned with "opportunity." And, if you look at the topic sentences in the body, they all, with the exception of the first one, contain the word "opportunity."

The organization of the paper is chronological. It begins with a discussion of the past in the thesis paragraph and the first paragraph of the body; moves to a discussion of the present in the third, fourth, and fifth paragraphs; and moves to the future in the conclusion.

Mr. Armstrong also uses several different devices in organizing the individual paragraphs. The thesis paragraph begins with a personal definition followed by a general fact. The second paragraph lists specific examples. Paragraph three uses contrast, as does paragraph four. Paragraph five uses a specific fact. The conclusion not only makes a general concluding statement, but also uses the words "America has provided the opportunity," which re-echoes the thesis statement, "America means opportunity."

Mr. Armstrong's most obvious transitional device is, of course, the repetition of the word *opportunity*, which helps to give his composition unity, coherence, and emphasis.

Exercise
Writing an Explanatory Composition

On page 116, you were asked to study to list of topic examples, then to make a list of ten topics of your own. You were also asked to keep that list for future reference.

Refer to your list at this time. Study it; then choose a topic from it to serve as the basis for an explanatory composition.

In writing this composition, be sure you follow all the necessary steps in limiting your subject, organizing your ideas, and writing your paper.

Part 3
The Narrative Composition

You recall, of course, that the narrative paragraph describes an event; in other words, it tells a story. So does the narrative composition. But because the narrative composition is longer, we can devote more attention to such details as *character, setting,* and *conflict*.

By **character,** we mean "the people." Who are the people in the narrative? What are they like? What are they doing? What do they want?

By **setting,** we mean "the place." Where does the narrative take place? What is it like? Does it have any effect on the characters?

By **conflict,** we mean "the struggle" or "the problem." This is usually brought about because of something the character, or characters, want. There are four basic types of conflict:

THE INDIVIDUAL AGAINST A SUPERNATURAL FORCE: the struggle against God, or the gods (as in the ancient myths and legends) or, as seen more recently in books and movies, the struggle against the devil.

THE INDIVIDUAL AGAINST NATURE: the struggle to survive such acts of nature as a flood, an earthquake, a hurricane—any of the natural catastrophes that might destroy human life. This would also include the struggle against beasts, reptiles, insects, and so on.

THE INDIVIDUAL AGAINST SOCIETY: the struggle against social forces of justice or injustice, against prejudices, against the loss of individual freedom, and so on. This also includes the struggle of one individual against another individual.

THE INDIVIDUAL AGAINST HIMSELF: the struggle within the mind or conscience of an individual as he or she attempts to make a personal decision.

Let's look at an example of a narrative composition.

HUMORESQUE

Beatrice, with three syllables, lives diagonally across the street from where I live and directly across from the plot I call my garden. Beatrice thinks she can play the piano. She sits in a room with three huge mirrors, and nods to the other members of her piano quartet; they nod back at her and the room. My house and my garden are flooded, inundated, drowned in a golden honey gravy of romantic (used in the popular sense) music.

"Painting the Clouds with Sunshine" becomes "Every Cloud Must Have a Silver Lining" becomes something about a "golden daybreak" becomes "Love Is a Many-Splendored Thing" becomes "He Can Make the Sun," or whatever it's called, all with the same three-beat bottom hand, and each one pouncing, without a thought of key or transition, into the next. One can pull weeds to this music, or dust for aphids, or squash Japanese beetles, and never once break the incessant dignity, the overwhelming dignity of one, two, three/ one, two, three/ one, two three.

The key of C: Theme and variations for one piano and three mirrors. Etude for white keys and leave the black ones be. Music for weeding, spraying, and waltzing in rubber boots, too. Also lawnmowing music. When Beatrice begins with "Painting the Clouds," her husband, ordinarily a mild enough man, slips from the house and begins cutting his lawn with a power mower. Now and then the tone-deaf, gasoline-engine machine comes between the music and my garden, but not often. Beatrice may or may not know about me and my garden. Once, I had to go inside the house to get a drink of water and she got stalled on "He Can Make the Sun" or whatever it is, until I got back at work.

After the religious songs, quote/unquote, there is always a thunderous pause, as though she had taken a look outside to see the world she had charmed and seen instead that the sun had walked out on her and that it was too dark to mow any longer (or weed or dust). Then, as though in a whisper, as though the mirror had fallen, comes the single, child voice of an early piano lesson before the bass notes had overcome it—the fragile, quiet, tiptoe melody of "Humoresque."

Always the same. I pick up my hoe and other tools, always the same way, and walk slowly to the garage. Her husband goes back into the house; perhaps he says something to Beatrice, pushing the piano bench back under the piano, about how beautiful the sunset was. —FRED MOECKEL

There are three characters in this narrative—the major character, "Beatrice, with three syllables," and two minor characters, Beatrice's husband, and the narrator.

The setting is on the street where Beatrice and the narrator live diagonally across from each other. The setting does have some effect upon the minor character of the narrator inasmuch as it is his proximity to Beatrice's house that causes his problem.

The conflict here is a rather subtle, or understated, one. It is a silent conflict with Beatrice—the struggle of the husband and the narrator to "survive" Beatrice's piano playing.

Unity, in this narrative, is achieved by the writer's concern for Beatrice and her music. Not once does he deviate from Beatrice and her piano playing.

Coherence is achieved by the organization of the ideas. Again, they all focus on Beatrice and her music and are tied together with appropriate transitional devices.

Emphasis is achieved by the writer's unrelenting focus upon Beatrice and her music. Presumably, Beatrice is a complex, many-sided individual, but the purpose of this narrative is not to reveal the whole of Beatrice's personality. It is her dreadful piano music with which the writer is concerned, and it is that music which is emphasized in this narrative.

Exercise
Writing a Narrative

On page 113, you were asked to study a list of topic examples, then to make a list of ten topics of your own. You were also asked to keep that list for future reference.

Refer to your list at this time. Study it; then choose a topic from it to serve as the basis for a narrative composition.

In writing this composition, be sure you follow all the necessary steps in limiting your subject, organizing your ideas, and writing your paper. Remember to revise where necessary.

Before leaving this chapter on the writing of the composition, we would like to make an important final statement. Good writing is always the result of conscious effort, and conscious attention to detail and organization. It is not an easy task.

Good writing carries with it its own rewards. There is the personal satisfaction in a job well done. There is also the knowledge that if you have communicated something of yourself to your readers with clarity and understanding, then, perhaps, we can all understand each other a little better. Only when we can communicate with such clarity and understanding can we communicate at all.

Chapter 7

Writing
Letters

Letters! Every day over two hundred million pieces of first-class mail are handled by the United States Postal Service. People are mailing get-well notes, love letters, birthday cards, business letters, and many other kinds of communications. Children are writing letters home from camp, innocently telling of possible cases of plague and food poisoning. Grandmothers are desperately writing their grandchildren, hoping for a peanut butter-stained response. College students are writing home for money. Families and friends are arguing, apologizing, and "chatting" across many miles.

How about you? Every time you're faced with a letter to write, do you make excuses, find other things you have to do, and finally telephone instead? If so, you're not completely alone. The problem is usually that you don't know what to write, and exactly how to start. You can put the words down on paper, but they don't sound right. If your letters seem like recorded messages, if you're uncertain as to how to go about writing different types of letters, if you'd like to get a message to someone without paying a long distance telephone bill, then read on.

Part 1

Addressing the Envelope

Let's start with the simplest part of letter-writing first—the envelope. Probably the worst thing that could happen to a letter you've painstakingly written is that it isn't delivered. Hundreds of thousands of letters end up in the Dead Letter Office in Washington, D.C. The usual problem is an incorrect address, which can be easily avoided. Double-check to be certain you haven't inverted any numbers in the address. Don't forget the ZIP code. This is a five-digit code that identifies a small area within a city or state, and enables the post office to sort mail much more efficiently and rapidly. The ZIP should immediately follow the state in addresses. If you don't know the ZIP, and can't find it in your telephone directory, call your post office. They have a complete ZIP code listing for every community in the United States and will be happy to help you.

Always put your return address on the envelope.

Envelopes come in many different sizes and colors. The two most-used sizes are $9\frac{1}{2}'' \times 4''$ and $6\frac{1}{2}'' \times 3\frac{1}{2}''$. When sending a business letter, you should always use a white $9\frac{1}{2}'' \times 4''$ envelope.

Ms. Betty Sergeant
1429 Oakridge Road
Ft. Worth TX 76135

Mr. Larry Spenser
341 Queen Avenue
Yakima WA 98902

If you are writing a specific person or department within a large company, you will use four lines for the address.

Ms. Betty Sergeant
1429 Oakridge Road
Ft. Worth TX 76135

> Mr. Larry Spenser
> A + G Electronics Company
> 341 Queen Avenue
> Yakima WA 98902

When addressing the small, square envelope that is usually included with invitations, note cards, etc., you may put your return address on the flap on the back of the envelope, with the receiver's name and address centered on the front.

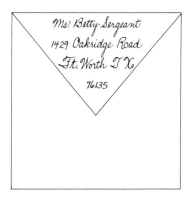

Ms. Betty Sergeant
1429 Oakridge Road
Ft. Worth TX
76135

Mr. Larry Spenser
341 Queen Avenue
Yakima WA 98902

Caution: Be sure to check the back of any envelope before addressing it. You might have it upside down!

Did you notice the abbreviations of the names of states on the examples? These may be used in addressing envelopes, but you *must* use the ZIP code with them. When you use these abbreviations, you do not need to separate the city and state with a comma. However, if you don't use these abbreviations you must place a comma between the city and state.

Mr. Larry Spenser
341 Queen Avenue
Yakima WA 98902

Mr. Larry Spenser
341 Queen Avenue
Yakima, Washington 98902

Here is a list of the approved abbreviations as issued by the United States Postal Service:

Abbreviations of State Names

Alabama	AL	Montana	MT
Alaska	AK	Nebraska	NE
Arizona	AZ	Nevada	NV
Arkansas	AR	New Hampshire	NH
American Samoa	AS	New Jersey	NJ
California	CA	New Mexico	NM
Canal Zone	CZ	New York	NY
Colorado	CO	North Carolina	NC
Connecticut	CT	North Dakota	ND
Delaware	DE	Ohio	OH
District of Columbia	DC	Oklahoma	OK
Florida	FL	Oregon	OR
Georgia	GA	Pennsylvania	PA
Guam	GU	Puerto Rico	PR
Hawaii	HI	Rhode Island	RI
Idaho	ID	South Carolina	SC
Illinois	IL	South Dakota	SD
Indiana	IN	Tennessee	TN
Iowa	IA	Trust Territories	TT
Kansas	KS	Texas	TX
Kentucky	KY	Utah	UT
Louisiana	LA	Vermont	VT
Maine	ME	Virginia	VA
Maryland	MD	Virgin Islands	VI
Massachusetts	MA	Washington	WA
Michigan	MI	West Virginia	WV
Minnesota	MN	Wisconsin	WI
Mississippi	MS	Wyoming	WY
Missouri	MO		

Exercises
Addressing Envelopes

A. Put each of the addresses below in proper three or four-line form as it should appear on an envelope. Capitalize, abbreviate, and punctuate correctly.

1. 462 zane avenue philadelphia pennsylvania 19111
   mrs. jill erikson

2. washington d c 20013 national geographic society
   melvin m payne post office box 2895

3. 111 west washington street chicago illinois 60602
   chicago title insurance company

4. salt lake city utah 84104 appliance department 1133 glendale
   drive gibson's discount center

5. mr. john johnson oklahoma city oklahoma 1462 longridge
   road 73115

B. Draw four "envelopes" on a plain piece of paper. Three of the envelopes should measure $9\frac{1}{2}'' \times 4''$, and one $5'' \times 5''$. Now pick three of the choices below and with the aid of a telephone directory write the addresses correctly on the envelopes. Address the $5'' \times 5''$ envelope to your best friend. Don't forget to include your return address.

1. Anyone whose last name is Smith
2. The service department of an automobile agency
3. Your favorite disc jockey
4. An employment agency
5. The sportswear department of a department store
6. A television station

Now that you're an expert at addressing envelopes, you can begin to study the different types of letters to put inside them. The form for an envelope doesn't change; it's the same for any letter.

Part 2

Writing Informal Notes

Whenever you've written a short letter thanking a relative for a gift or expressing your appreciation for a weekend visit, you've used a form of letter known as an **informal note.**

These notes all have one thing in common. They're short. They could be referred to as "people-pleasers" because they definitely impress the receiver. You might have been less than completely delighted with the complete dental care kit your aunt sent you for Christmas, but they will be pleased to receive your letter of thanks. Remember, there's always next year!

Informal notes have a definite form:

Date

August 30, 1977

Salutation

Dear Uncle Fred and Aunt Fran,

    You never told me you had ESP—how else could you have known I've been craving that particular album? It's great! I've played it at least twenty times, and Mom says that next time you send an album to me, she'd   Body *appreciate your enclosing a pair of earplugs for her.*

    Thanks so much for the perfect gift. I hope you can visit sometime and hear it for yourselves—before I wear it out!

Closing   *Love,*

Signature   *Jennie*

The first part of the form of an informal note is the **date.** Remember to leave a margin between the end of the date and the right side of the paper.

The second item is the **salutation.** This is usually very simple, addressing the person you're writing. Always use a comma after the salutation. Next is the **body** of the letter, or the message. The **closing** can be one of many, depending on the relationship. *Sincerely, Affectionately, Lovingly, Happily,* and *Thankfully* are some of the choices. Always capitalize the closing and use a comma after it.

As you can see, a casual language style is fine. Write naturally, the way you would normally speak to the person you're writing.

There are other varieties of the informal note. Apologies, congratulations, invitations, and R.S.V.P.'s are the most common. Of these, only the R.S.V.P. might require some explanation.

> *July 27, 1977*
>
> *Dear Jim,*
>   *You are invited to attend my birthday dinner on August 16. It will be held at the Sundance Room of the Hotel Towers at 7:30 p.m.*
>   *I'm looking forward to seeing you.*
>
>   *Sincerely,*
>   *Mary Barnes*
>
> *R.S.V.P.*

R.S.V.P. is an abbreviation for a French phrase meaning "please respond." It is necessary for the sender to have an exact count of the attending guests before the party. Unless you want to appear "uninformed," you must reply. You write a brief note stating your intention to attend or not.

August 1, 1977

Dear Mary,
    I would love to attend your birthday dinner, but will be unable to as we are planning a vacation and will be out of town on August 16.
    Have a very happy birthday!
        Sincerely,
        Jim Harris

August 1, 1977

Dear Mary,
    Thank you so much for the invitation to your birthday dinner. I'd be delighted to attend.

        Sincerely,
        Jim Harris

Exercise
Writing Informal Notes

Choose two of the following and write the appropriate notes on plain paper. On the back draw an envelope for each and address it correctly.

1. Write a note thanking a friend for the fantastic party he gave last Saturday.

2. Write your friend's mother apologizing for dropping a full bowl of punch on her new white carpet.

3. Write a note of congratulations to a friend who has moved from your neighborhood. You have just learned that he or she won a cash prize in a contest. You determine the contest.

4. Write a note thanking a relative for something—the only problem is, you don't have any idea what the item is!

5. Write an invitation to a party, using R.S.V.P. Exchange your invitation with another student and write a reply.

6. Write a note to a friend's mother or father for something very nice the person did for you. You decide the reason.

7. Write a note to a cheerleader at your school apologizing for tackling her during the last game.

8. Write a note congratulating your dog for passing obedience school.

Part 3
Writing Friendly Letters

These letters seem to be going down in popularity as your long-distance telephone bills go up. Haven't you tearfully said goodbye to a friend, promising to write, and then put it off until you didn't know what to write or where to start? It happens to everyone, and it's too bad. Through this type of letter, friendships endure over many years and more miles. This should be an easy letter to write, as you're communicating with someone you know very well—someone who has shared many experiences with you. Just keep sharing experiences—only now through letters. The language is informal, just as you would speak to the person.

There is a little more involved in the form of a friendly letter than in informal notes. Below is an example. Once you learn the parts of a friendly letter, you'll have to concentrate only on writing the body of the letter itself.

Heading

162 New Road
Raleigh, North Carolina 27608
July 16, 1977

Salutation

Dear Jess,

Body

_____

_____

_____

_____

Love, **Closing**

Jill **Signature**

The **heading** is written in three lines. The first line consists of your street address. The second line contains the city, state and ZIP. The third line is the date of the letter. Don't abbreviate on the date line.

The **salutation** can be as casual as you'd like in a friendly letter. The only two rules are to capitalize the first word and any other nouns, and to use a comma following the salutation.

Dear Sue,   *Hi Slim,*

Howdy Friend,   *Hello Good Buddy,*

The **closing** is usually kept simple: *Love, Sincerely, Always,* etc. The first word is the only one capitalized. You can use your originality and the closeness of the friendship for something more appropriate for the particular person you're writing.

Lovingly yours,   *Still waiting,*

Always here,   *Frustrated,*

The most important part of any letter is the **body.** Let's hope you haven't received or been guilty of sending a disaster like the following:

---

162 New Road
Raleigh NC 27608
July 16, 1977

Dear Jess,

Your letter arrived yesterday and I'm happy to hear about all the great things you've been doing.

As usual, things around here aren't very exciting. The weather's been hot for so long I can't remember what "cool" means.

Everyone here says to say "hi".

There's not much more to write. Wish you were here so we could have a good talk. Write soon.

Love,

Jill

Not only is Jill's letter not going to win any writing awards, but she'll also be lucky if she doesn't lose a friend. All that's needed to turn dull paragraphs into interesting ones is detail. If the person you're writing were with you, what would you say? In all probability you wouldn't sound like the letter above. Here are a few points to remember when writing a friendly letter:

1. Make comments on the letter you've received.
2. Avoid using "I" constantly.
3. Write one or two detailed paragraphs regarding events and people. They will be much more interesting than a series of one-sentence statements.
4. Ask questions. Then the person has something to write back about.

With a little more time and thought, Jill might have written two opening paragraphs like this:

Maybe this letter should be written in special ink so you can read it underwater—don't you ever get waterlogged? From the sound of things you're either in training for the Olympics or trying to get a role in the next "Jaws." You're way out of my class now—unless they've started giving medals for floating in a tube. Couldn't you manage to compete in a meet around here?

Things here are not too exciting—and that's an understatement! It's been so hot for so long that everyone's dragging. I've been lying around the yard or the house most of the time. But you know my Mom—if I'm not "doing something" I can't possibly be happy. So she keeps finding things for me to "do." Clean out your closet. Change the water. Straighten your dresser. Change the water! Run to the store. Change the water!! I'm beginning to feel as if I've got a hose growing out of my right arm! The lawn's so soaked now we could grow rice! Next summer a job is a necessity—only with my luck it would probably be watering lawns.

Detail, along with conversational writing, can make a letter come to life. Choose one of the next three statements in Jill's letter on page 169 and rewrite it in a detailed paragraph. Make it interesting. Be prepared to exchange your paragraph with a classmate, or read it aloud to the class.

Exercise
Writing Friendly Letters

One of your best friends has moved out of the city. Write a friendly letter detailing three events that have taken place since he or she left. You can use actual events or choose from the list below.

1. Your school team lost a close game for the state basketball championship.
2. A good friend (?) just stole your steady.
3. You're positive someone tried to break into your house when your parents were out.
4. Your new puppy is methodically eating his way through the house—couch, chairs, carpets, shoes.

Part 4
Writing Business Letters

Over ten thousand business letters are processed for each friendly letter or informal note that is written. With odds like that, the business letter has to be an important letter to master. The term "business" means that the letters have a definite purpose to accomplish, not that they're written only by and for business firms.

There are two main skills to master in writing a business letter: (1) Use the proper form. (2) Be brief and specific.

Use the Proper Form. There are two basic forms for business letters: **block form** and **modified block form.**

Block Form   (used only when the letter is typewritten)

Heading

416 Paxton Road
Rochester, New York 14617
April 23, 1977

Inside Address

Sales Department
Stereophonics, Inc.
231 Garrison
Boston, Massachusetts 02116

Salutation

Ladies and Gentlemen:

_____
_____
_____   Body

_____
_____

Sincerely,   Closing

José Martinez

José Martinez   Signature

Note: Always use plain white 8½″ × 11″ paper for business letters, whether you handwrite or type them.

Modified Block Form

Heading

416 Paxton Road
Rochester, New York 14617
April 23, 1977

Inside Address

Sales Department
Stereophonics, Inc.
231 Garrison
Boston, Massachusetts 02116

Salutation

Dear Sir or Madam:

_____

_____

_____ Body

_____

_____

Sincerely,   Closing

José Martinez

José Martinez   Signature

You're already familiar with the heading of a letter. It's the same as that used for writing friendly letters.

The one section that has been added is the **inside address.** It's important to have the name and address of the person or department you're writing to on the face of the letter. Occasionally a letter is opened by mistake and the envelope misplaced; if this happens, the name and address are still clearly visible. The inside address is usually four lines on a business letter, as you'll be writing to a specific person or department within a company. Leave a space between the inside address and the salutation.

The salutation varies, depending upon the first line of the inside address. If you are writing to a company or department within a company, use one of the following:

```
Dear Sir or Madam:
Gentlemen:
```

If you are writing to a particular person, but don't know his name (such as the Personnel Manager, President, or General Manager), you should use *Dear Sir*:

The form for writing to someone whose name you know is quite simple:

```
Dear Mr. Brown:
Dear Ms. Allred:     (if her marital status is unknown)
Dear Miss Allred:
Dear Mrs. Allred:    (if her marital status is known)
```

Only the first word and any proper nouns are capitalized in the salutation, and it is always followed by a colon. A space is left between the salutation and the body of the letter.

A blank space is left between the body of the letter and the closing. Only the first word of the closing is capitalized, and it is always followed by a comma.

```
Sincerely,
Very truly yours,
Respectfully yours,
```

You type or print your name four spaces below the closing, then write your signature in the space between. This assures that the reader can still identify your name, even if you have a fancy, illegible signature.

Make a Carbon Copy. Whenever you write a business letter you should make a carbon copy for yourself. Then you will know just what you wrote or ordered in case you don't receive an immediate reply. To use carbon paper, first place a piece of plain paper on your desk. Then place a sheet of carbon paper on top of it. The "shiny" or carbon side of the paper should be face down, so you'll get a copy. Now place another piece of plain paper on top and you're ready to write. (To avoid slippage, you can paper clip the three pieces together.) When you write, be certain you use the type of carbon paper that is made for pen or pencil. Typewriter keys exert much more pressure on the carbon paper than a person's hand.

Fold the Letter Correctly. Folding a business letter correctly is sometimes a problem. You want only two folds in your paper when using a standard 9½″ × 4″ envelope. Starting at the bottom of the paper, fold it into thirds toward the top. Usually you'll find that after the first fold is completed, only the inside address and heading will be visible to you. When properly folded, the letter will easily fit into the envelope, and can readily be taken out by the receiver.

First Fold	Second Fold	Complete

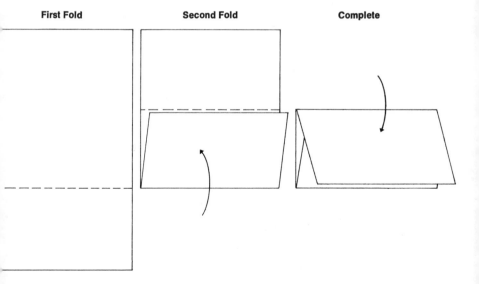

Exercises
Using Proper Form

A. Below is an example of a business letter in modified block form. There are errors in capitalization, punctuation and spacing. Correct the errors by rewriting the letter on a plain sheet of paper.

Jan. 14, 1977
1452 Balboa Drive
Pensacola Florida, 32506

General supply Company
sales mgr.
462 acacia avenue
Palo Alto Calif. 94306

Dear Sir or Madam,

    Regarding the order I placed with you on December 15, ———————————————————
——————————————————————————
——————————————————————————
——————————————————————————

Very Truly Yours

Thomas A. O'Leary

Thomas A. O'Leary

B. Using correct form, write a letter of your own with a local company as the addressee. You do not have to write the body of the letter.

Be Brief and Specific. When you write a business letter you include only what is absolutely necessary, and no more. State the purpose of the letter and then stop. Use only those details that are vital to accomplish your purpose.

1942 Griffin Road
Indianapolis, Indiana 46227
June 14, 1977

West Hills Pro Shop
571 Moon Clinton Road
Coraopolis, Pennsylvania 15108

Dear Sir or Madam:

Please send me the following items which appeared in your advertisement in the June issue of Travel and Leisure.

1 pr.	Foot-Joy Golf Shoes	Size 11D	Black	$ 48.00
2	Canvas Sunday Bags		@$19.00	38.00
1	Model M-20 Lynx Putter			25.00
			Total	$111.00

Enclosed is a money order for $111.00. The advertisement states that prices include postage and insurance.

Yours truly,

Scott Andersen

Scott Andersen

Whenever you place an order, be sure you have a complete description or a model number. Include sizes, colors, and the number of items desired. Check the charge for postage. In some instances the buyer will pay for postage and this amount must be included with the order. Any errors on your part will result in a delay in delivery, or in receiving unwanted merchandise. It's much easier to double-check an order than to return merchandise. Keep a carbon copy in case any mix-ups occur.

Exercise
Being Brief and Specific

Clip an advertisement from a magazine, or choose one of the groups below and write an order letter. Total the order and add any postage that is necessary. On the back of the order draw an envelope and address it correctly.

1. Columbia House, 1400 North Fruitridge Ave., Terre Haute, Indiana 47808

   1 8-track cartridge No. 259788 *Kiss Alive* $7.98
   1 record No. 263517 *Captain & Tennille* $6.98
   1 two-record set No. 260349 *The Osmonds* $9.98
   Postage $.75

2. Walter Drake & Sons, 4085 Drake Building, Colorado Springs, Colorado 80940—Advertisement in August issue of *Better Homes and Gardens*

   No. S717—two sets of 1,000 name labels @ $1.00 per set
   No. S854—one set of personalized pencils @ $.89 per set
   No. S6066—two full-page magnifiers @ $1.98 each
   Postage and handling—$.40

3. Sea Horses, Box 342096, Coral Gables, Florida 33134
   Advertisement in July issue of *Boy's Life*

   3 live sea horse kits   @ $ 2.98
   2 custom aquariums @ $ 5.98
   1 deluxe aquarium $10.95

   Air mail postage paid by advertiser—live delivery guaranteed

Types of Business Letters

The three main types of business letters are these:

1. **Requests for Information.** Perhaps you've been thinking about buying some specialized stereo equipment. You could write a business letter requesting information regarding additional speakers.

2. **Letters of Order.** You'd order your stereo equipment through a business letter if you were unable to purchase it locally.

3. **Letters of Complaint.** If your speaker didn't operate when you received it, you'd write a business letter to complain. The ability to write this type of letter is invaluable.

Requests for Information. Letters which request information must be as specific as possible. Also, since you are really asking the receiver to take time to reply, you must always check for politeness.

1315 Summer Road
Trenton, New Jersey 08618
May 15, 1977

Chamber of Commerce
Zuni
New Mexico 87327

Dear Sir or Madam:

As a class assignment, I am working on a paper dealing with the Indians of New Mexico, and particularly the Zuni tribe. Any information or addresses you could provide would be appreciated.

I am particularly interested in the culture of the Zuni Indians today as compared with the culture of the 1800's.

Very truly yours,
Susan Campbell

Special Note for Typists: If any of your business letters are extremely short you may double-space for the sake of appearance. If you do double-space, be consistent with the prescribed form.

Exercise
Writing a Request for Information

1. Write a letter to a chamber of commerce asking for information about their city. Be specific as to why you need this information: you are planning to move to that city; you are interested in vacationing there; or you have been given that particular area to research as a class assignment.

2. Write a college or university requesting information regarding tuition costs. State your major field of interest: law, medicine, computer science, etc.

3. Write a company in your area asking for information about summer employment. Let them know your age, qualifications, and previous experience.

4. In groups, plan the "ideal" vacation to an exotic spot. Write the various letters necessary for transportation, hotels, and tours. Then plan the vacation with the information you receive.

Letters of Complaint. Have you ever purchased something that fell apart, didn't work, or was a disappointment? Write a letter of complaint! This is not a "gripe" letter; it's written to let a store or company know that there is a problem and you would like it taken care of. Most companies are interested in hearing from you. If you're not happy with a purchase you probably won't buy that brand again, or maybe you'll shop at a different store. This is of great concern to the seller. After all, he wants you to keep buying that particular product or coming to his store. So don't just sit around and tell your friends what a rotten deal you got; let the proper people know you're unhappy. You'll be surprised at the response you'll receive.

Avoid the temptation to be sarcastic, angry, or vulgar. This will not accomplish your purpose; it will merely make you look pretty sad. Let the store or company know when and where you purchased the item and exactly what is wrong with it. Volunteer to mail the item if they would like to inspect it. A manufacturer can tell rapidly if the problem was his fault or yours.

631 Inca Lane
St. Paul, Minnesota 55112
October 6, 1977

Public Relations Department
Woolcraft, Inc.
1300 West Fremont Place
St. Louis, Missouri 63142

Gentlemen:

In September I purchased one of your new "Ski-Sno" sweaters from a local department store. After wearing it twice, I washed it according to the directions on the label. While it is still soft and the colors are as bright as when it was brand-new, it is now several sizes smaller. Needless to say, I am very disappointed.

I would be happy to send the sweater directly to you, as there has obviously been some oversight in your washing instructions. I would appreciate an explanation.

Sincerely,

Elsa Johnson
Elsa Johnson

Perhaps your problem is closer to home than Elsa's. After many futile phone calls to a local company, you might find it easier to state your problem in a letter.

123 La Clede Avenue
Memphis, Tennessee 38126
August 31, 1977

General Manager
Sutton's Department Store
432 Oak Street
Memphis, Tennessee 38142

Dear Sir:

In June I purchased a pair of water skis in your Sporting Goods Department. These skis are model no. 143 and the price was $26.95, on sale. I used my parents' charge account, number 47727, for this purchase. Enclosed is a copy of the sales receipt.

The July statement which we received shows a charge in the amount of $269.50. Upon calling the Billing Department, I was informed that this was a computer error and would be corrected. The August statement has a past-due charge of $2,695.00. Is there some way you can communicate with the computer and correct this error?

Your earliest attention to this problem would be greatly appreciated.

Very truly yours,
Benjamin Erickson
Benjamin Erickson

Exercise
Writing a Letter of Complaint

Write a letter of complaint regarding one of the following problems.

1. The new jeans you purchased fell apart after three wearings. (Write to the manufacturing company.)

2. You ordered a CB antenna through the mail, but received an aquarium. (Write a hobby shop.)

3. The records you ordered from your club were warped when delivered. (Write a record club.)

4. The live sea horses you ordered through the mail weren't. (Write a pet shop.)

5. Four weeks ago you ordered $28.70 in supplies for a science project. You haven't received them and it's now too late to complete your project. Explain the problem and ask for a refund. (Write a hobby shop.)

Knowing Where and Whom To Write

You can spend a great deal of time writing the "perfect" letter, addressing it correctly, and still not receive a response. It's frustrating, but curable. The usual problem is that you haven't directed the letter to a specific person or department. There are many different departments within each large company which have different purposes. A request for employment would go one place and a complaint another. There are special sections to handle orders, service calls, parts, etc. If the address on your letter is simply to the company, it might take a week or more for it to find its way to the proper person who can respond.

Exercises
Knowing Where and Whom to Write

A. Using the list provided, where would you send a letter dealing with each of the following problems?

1. Employment information
2. Ordering parts
3. Requesting information regarding the operation of a product
4. Asking if a store carries a specific brand of swimwear
5. Being charged twice for the same item

Personnel Department	Sportswear Department
Accounting Department	Service Department
Parts Department	

B. How many different departments does a large store in your area contain? Can you list the different departments within a large corporation such as the telephone company? Write them down, then look in a telephone directory to see how close you are.

If your particular problem is one that originated with the manufacturer and not the store where you made the purchase, then you should write directly to the manufacturer. The address is usually on the label attached to the product. If not, you can obtain the necessary information through your local store. There's a special department which will pay particular attention to your letter and is interested in hearing from you. This department is referred to as Public Relations. They'd like to hear from you because they want to keep you happy. One important thing to bear in mind is that you don't have to have a complaint to write a business letter. If you've been thoroughly happy with one particular product, let the manufacturer know. After all, we all appreciate a nice comment now and then.

Happy letter writing!

Chapter 8

Improving Your Sentences

You may already know how to write sentences that are grammatically correct. You may know how to express a complete thought by means of a subject, a verb, and modifiers. Is there anything more you should learn about writing sentences? Frequently, there is.

Your sentences may be correct grammatically, yet fail to do the job. *The job of a sentence is to say something—to convey facts, ideas and feelings.* Some of your sentences may say too little. Others may say too much. Still others may be unsatisfactory because their meaning is not clear.

This chapter will help you improve your sentences. It gives examples of unsatisfactory sentences and shows you how to go about revising them. It then supplies additional sentences for you to revise on your own.

Almost all of the sentences you will work with in this chapter were written by high school students. They did not have a chance to revise what they had written. You will be doing the revising for them.

This chapter is a challenge to you to think clearly and to write clearly.

Part 1
Avoiding Empty Sentences

The purpose of a sentence is to say something. Unfortunately, words may be put into sentence form and still not say anything. Such a sentence is called an **empty sentence.**

There are two kinds of empty sentences:

1. Sentences that merely repeat an idea and end up where they started.

2. Sentences that make a statement they fail to support with a fact, a reason, or an example.

Sentences That Repeat an Idea

Notice the repetition of an idea in the following sentences:

FAULTY   He had no friends, and because of this he was always alone.

REVISED   He had no friends.
(Omit the second clause. It merely repeats the idea *He had no friends.*)

FAULTY   I have a minor *crisis* in my life, and to me it presents a *problem.*
(Since *crisis* and *problem* are similar, use only one. Omit the second clause entirely.)

REVISED   I have a minor crisis in my life.

Sometimes a whole sentence is repeated. This repetitious style is boring and monotonous to read.

FAULTY   My father *complains* that I'm always on the phone, no matter what the time of day. His *complaint* is that I don't give anyone else a chance to use it.

REVISED	My father complains that no one else has a chance to use the phone because I'm on it all day. (Expressing the idea of *complaint* once is sufficient. The father's complaint has two parts: (1) *I'm always on the phone,* and (2) *I don't give anyone else a chance to use it.* Combine these two ideas as in the revision above.)
FAULTY	From my earliest days I have been an avid reader. I suppose I inherited this love of books from my mother. *She also loves to read.*
REVISED	From my earliest days I have been an avid reader. I suppose I inherited this love of books from my mother. (The second sentence indicates the mother's love of reading in her love of books. *She also loves to read* is unnecessary repetition.)
FAULTY	I asked Tom to stop at my house *for a Coke* and *to meet my mother.* After he *met my mother,* we went into the kitchen and *had a Coke.*
REVISED	Tom accepted my invitation to stop at my house for for a Coke and to meet my mother.

Two suggestions will help you avoid this writing fault: (1) read aloud what you have written, and (2) revise.

Exercise
Revising Sentences That Repeat an Idea

Revise the following sentences:

Suggestions:

1. Look for repeated words in the same sentence.
2. Look for repeated ideas in the same sentence.
3. Look for sentences that repeat an idea already expressed.
4. Omit the repetitions wherever possible.
5. Combine two sentences into one, if necessary.

6. Realize that there is more than one way to revise these sentences.

1. Many people are interested in chess because it is a very interesting game.
2. The movie was boring, and I found it very dull.
3. Of course, you can't go on a hike without food. Who would ever dream of going on a hike without food?
4. Dad can't understand why I have to call my friends when I get home from school. He claims that I see my friends all day long in school, so I don't have to phone them as soon as I reach home.
5. At this point I usually burst into a torrent of tears. Mom and Dad usually know the right words to comfort me, however, for I soon feel better and begin to be a little more cheerful.
6. Have you ever watched television in a crowd? If you haven't watched it in a crowd, you can't imagine what it is like to watch television with three hundred people.
7. On Sunday we are going on a trip for the day. I am sure we will have a good time if the weather permits. There are seven of us going on the trip, and everyone is praying that we will have a wonderful day for our trip.
8. When I was small, I was rather spoiled. It wasn't because I was an only child, because I had two brothers. I think it was because I was the only girl and the only granddaughter. You see, all my cousins were boys.
9. In our high school, at every lunch period, there is a long cafeteria line. In the cafeteria we can purchase ice cream, candy, pretzels, hot food, and so on. To purchase these items, we must stand in a line.
10. If you have ever been to the zoo, you know what a great time you can have there. The zoo is a place to visit again and again. At the zoo there is always something new, wonderful, and educational to see.

Sentences That Contain Unsupported Statements

A kind of emptiness in writing results from statements that are not supported by reasons, facts, or examples. The reader is left with the question "Why?" in his mind.

Try to find the unsupported statement in this group:

> Chess is becoming popular with people of all ages. Even young children play it. I think it would be good for everyone to learn the game.

The unsupported statement is not difficult to find. Look for the sentence that involves an opinion. *Why* would it be good for everyone to learn chess?

Exercise
Revising Unsupported Statements

Revise the following selections:

Suggestions:

1. Locate the statement that needs support.
2. Ask "Why?" Then add whatever reasons or facts you think are necessary.

1. You can get a good laugh from practical jokes played in school. They can relieve the monotony of lessons. However, school is not the place for practical jokes.

2. There are more good job opportunities for minorities now because more good jobs are opening up.

3. Detroit is making a lot of small cars now. I think that is very good. I like these small cars and hope to own one in a few years.

4. Some people are talking about making the school year longer. This would be a mistake. The school year is long enough as it is.

5. I want to get a part-time job this year. I could work at least two hours after school each day. My parents do not approve of the idea.

6. For a long time American cars got bigger and bigger. Then foreign cars came into the picture. Now American companies are making little cars. I think these cars will soon drive the big cars off the market.

7. According to the state law, you have to be eighteen before you can get a decent job. I think this is very bad.
I think the law should be changed.

8. Every year a million Americans go to Europe. How many of those people have traveled around this country? Everyone ought to see his own country before going to Europe.

9. I always cheer for the Steelers (or Bears or Jets) because they are my favorite team.

10. The movie rating system ought to be changed because it isn't effective the way it is.

Part 2
Avoiding Padded Sentences

Some sentences contain padding like *the fact that* and *the reason is*. Others contain clauses that could easily be reduced to phrases without any damage to the thought. Although such padding may not always be considered incorrect, it often clutters the sentences and prevents writers from expressing their ideas clearly and concisely.

Taking Out the Padding

Phrases that puff up a sentence with unnecessary words get in the way of the meaning of the sentence. Trying to get to the meaning can be like trying to find a path that is overgrown with weeds.

Some of the padding it is better to avoid are the following:

"FACT" EXPRESSIONS	"WHAT" EXPRESSIONS
because of the fact that	what I mean is
owing to the fact that	what I believe is
due to the fact that	what I want is
on account of the fact that	

OTHER EXPRESSIONS TO AVOID

the point is   the reason is   the thing is

Sentences are smoother and simpler when unnecessary words are omitted.

PADDED	My family did not go to the shore *on account of the fact that* there was a storm.
REVISED	My family did not go to the shore *because* there was a storm.

PADDED	*What I mean is* that his ideas of summer camp are not realistic.
REVISED	His ideas of summer camp are not realistic.

PADDED	*The reason* I washed my father's car *was* that he hinted that it was dirty.
REVISED	I washed my father's car *because* he hinted that it was dirty.

PADDED	*What I want is* to go to Baltimore to see my grandparents if I don't get a job.
REVISED	I want to go to Baltimore to see my grandparents if I don't get a job.

PADDED	I know *that* if I study hard *that* I can get a scholarship.
REVISED	I know that if I study hard I can get a scholarship. *Or*, I know that I can get a scholarship if I study hard.

Reducing Clauses to Phrases

Clauses that begin with *who is* and *which is* can sometimes be simplified to phrases or to words in apposition. If these clauses are nonrestrictive (see Handbook, Section 11.12), they can be reduced to phrases or appositives or, in some cases, compound verbs.

LENGTHY	We admired the lights at the airport, *which is across the bay*.

REVISED	We admired the lights at the airport *across the bay*. (A clause has been reduced to a phrase.)
LENGTHY	Her latest movie, *which is a modern Western,* has been nominated for an Oscar.
REVISED	Her latest movie, *a modern Western,* has been nominated for an Oscar. (A clause has been reduced to an appositive.)
LENGTHY	The swimming meet, *which was the most exciting event of the year,* attracted crowds of students.
REVISED	The swimming meet, *the most exciting event of the year,* attracted crowds of students. (A clause has been reduced to an appositive.) *Or,*
	The swimming meet was the most exciting event of the year and attracted crowds of students. (A clause has been reduced to a compound verb.)

Exercises
Revising Padded Sentences

A. Revise these sentences by reducing and simplifying them.

Suggestions:

1. Look for "fact" expressions, "what'" expressions, and other padding.
2. Look for *who* or *which* clauses that can be simplified.
3. Eliminate as many unnecessary words as possible.
4. Realize that there is more than one way to revise these sentences.

1. What Jim wants is to be a football coach.

2. The thing that nobody could understand was Ann's fear.

3. You must admit that even if you don't admire him that he plays well.

4. The Eiffel Tower, which is located in Paris, is a symbol of France.

5. On account of the fact that she had learned to bowl during the summer, Debbie wanted to join the school team.

6. We immediately called Mrs. Vincent, who is our lawyer, to ask for advice.

7. Due to the fact that the fog was dense, the two ships collided.

8. What I believe is that you succeed largely because of your own efforts.

9. The point is that the study of French has many values.

10. Howie, who is our class clown, wore a T-shirt which had a formal black tie and ruffles printed on it.

B. Revise these sentences:

1. The reason that we took the car through the car wash was that it was covered with tree spray.

2. The rocks, which extend out into the bay, are dangerous at low tide.

3. The reason that Venice is fascinating is that many of its streets are all water.

4. Whenever it happens to rain hard, our cellar fills up with water and becomes a lake.

5. Many ruins in Rome are visible to tourists on account of the fact that much excavating has been done.

6. What I couldn't help hearing all night was the drone of the planes.

7. I knew that if I had to change the typewriter ribbon that I would create a hopeless tangle.

8. The fountain of Trevi, which is in Rome, is connected with a legend about coins.

9. What we finally did about our rehearsals was hold them in Mr. Steiner's garage.

10. I bought this ring in a novelty store, which is on Walnut Street.

Part 3
Avoiding Overloaded Sentences

Long sentences containing a number of ideas, usually connected loosely by *and*'s, are confusing and ineffective. They give the reader a whole series of ideas to sort out without any clue as to their relationship to each other. Such sentences violate the principle that a sentence usually contains *one* central thought. It is better to break them into shorter sentences.

LENGTHY I went into the building *and* I waited for the elevator in the lobby *and* when it didn't come I had to walk up eight flights of stairs.

REVISED I went into the lobby of the building and waited for the elevator. When it didn't come, I had to walk up eight flights of stairs.

LENGTHY Horrible faces glared at me from the shelves in the costume shop. All of them were contorted *and* most of them were scarred, *and* they were a deathly gray with a greenish cast, *and* their eyes looked like black holes.

REVISED Horrible faces glared at me from the shelves in the costume shop. All of them were contorted and most of them were scarred. The faces were a deathly gray with a greenish cast. Their eyes looked like black holes.

Exercise
Revising Overloaded Sentences

Revise these sentences:

Suggestions:

1. Separate each sentence into two or three shorter ones.
2. Reduce the number of *and's*.

1. In my frenzied rush to get the patient's tray, I failed to notice the sign on the door and I walked in and I noticed the woman was very pale and suddenly I realized I was in an isolation room.

2. The picnic was a great success and we all started to gather our various belongings and then we started bounding over the sleek, gleaming rails of the tracks which were in front of my home and I tripped over one of the rotted ties and fell into a puddle of oil and I cried because my father had forbidden me to go to the picnic in the first place.

3. One of the Atlanta Braves came up and reached first base on an error, and a sacrifice fly advanced him to second base, and the first Brave hit of the game drove him home.

4. Beany Malone's father was the editor of the newspaper and he was told to go to the South for a rest, and Mrs. Malone had to go with him and Beany was left to take care of a motherless household.

5. It was a hot summer day in June and the family was sitting on the patio and no one said a word, for the heat was terrific and everyone was exhausted.

6. There was nothing in Eric's pocket but a small hole, and Eric's eyes filled with tears and he bit his lip and the three boys searched the street but there was no penny to be found.

7. I always wanted to play tennis, so I decided to try my luck and bought a racket and a can of balls and talked my father into teaching me the fine points of the game, but I spent most of my time looking for the ball and I became so discouraged that I went back to playing pingpong.

8. Nancy and I went downtown last night and we went shopping for a dress and Nancy bought a beautiful yellow one, and although I intended to buy a green one, I bought a pretty blue dress, and when I came home with the dress, my mother said, "Not another blue one!"

9. The little boy was sturdy and browned by the sun and his blue eyes looked mischievously at a world that was full of interesting things to do, and he decided that the first thing was to race down the driveway on his bicycle while he yelled like Tarzan.

10. My brother has a 1976 Ford Granada with whitewall tires, a stereo, and a CB radio, and he washes his car at least once a day.

11. Debbie got a white Schwinn bike for her birthday, and it is a Sting Ray model and it has a floral print saddle seat.

12. Dad lost his wallet last Saturday with all his credit cards in it, but, luckily for him, it was returned yesterday by a neighbor who found it in the street outside our house.

Part 4

Writing Sentences That Make Sense

Sometimes students write sentences that do not make complete sense because they shift from what they started to say to something else. In between, the main idea has become confused or lost. They may also write quickly and carelessly and fail to check what they have written. The result is a hodgepodge, and situations like these occur:

1. A verb has no subject.
2. A prepositional phrase is used as a subject.
3. A faulty comparison is made.
4. Single words, necessary to complete the meaning, are left out.

Making Sure That the Verb Has a Subject

Study the following examples:

FAULTY   If you constantly practice is a help in becoming a better dancer.
(There is no subject for the verb *is*.)

REVISED   Constant practice helps you to become a better dancer.

FAULTY   His character was very weak and never did the right thing.
(There is no subject for the verb *did*.)

REVISED   His character was very weak, and *he* never did
           the right thing.

By re-reading and revising what you have written, you can frequently eliminate this problem.

Avoiding the Use of a Prepositional Phrase as the Subject

Study the following examples:

FAULTY   By setting up observation posts near volcanoes
          and detecting eruptions early can save many lives.

          (A prepositional phrase is used incorrectly as
          the subject of *can save*.)

REVISED   *Setting* up observation posts near volcanoes and
          detecting eruptions early can save many lives.

          (The italicized words are acceptable subjects
          for *can save*.)

Avoiding Faulty Comparisons

A special kind of senseless sentence is one in which there is a faulty comparison or one in which two things not equal are made equal.

FAULTY   *Studying biology* in high school is very different
          from *college*.

          (*Studying biology* should not be compared with
          college.)

REVISED   *Studying biology* in high school is very different
          from *studying it* in college.

FAULTY	The requirements for the job are an engineer and at least one year of experience.
	(An *engineer* is a person and does not equal the word *requirements*.)
REVISED	The requirements for the job call for an engineer with at least one year of experience.

Sentences that have pieces missing are like puzzles that do not form a complete picture because an important part is left out. Re-reading and revising can straighten out the confusion.

Making Sure That Necessary Words Are Included

The omission of a single word can make a sentence meaningless. This kind of carelessness can be avoided by re-reading and revising your work.

FAULTY	The little Swiss family find themselves comfortably situated as conditions will permit.
	(The word *as* has been left out.)
REVISED	The little Swiss family find themselves *as* comfortably situated as conditions will permit.
FAULTY	Elizabeth Barrett, an invalid for many years, knew what she wanted to do but was afraid of her father to attempt it.
REVISED	Elizabeth Barrett, an invalid for many years, knew what she wanted to do but was *too* afraid of her father to attempt it.

Exercises
Revising Sentences That Do Not Make Sense

A. Revise the ten sentences on the next page.

Suggestions:

1. Make sure that every verb has a subject.
2. Make sure that a prepositional phrase is not used as a subject.
3. Correct the faulty comparisons.
4. Make sure that necessary words have been included.

1. The cost of running a small car is less than a big car.

2. The real test of Donna's personality was her older sister.

3. The easier a subject is and the higher marks you can get with little work does not mean you should choose it.

4. To anyone who observes life and the game of football will soon detect many similarities.

5. The only real problem I find I wear out the rug by dancing.

6. Paula's fever has broken and is now feeling much better.

7. You could tell by my expression the anguish I was through.

8. Andy's explanation of scuba diving is clearer than high-diving.

9. By applying for a summer job early is the best way to be hired.

10. The faster the car goes is not the best reason for buying it.

B. Revise the following sentences:

1. Playing football in college is much different from high school.

2. The way I check a person is how he acts.

3. The more you have to do and the less time makes you work harder.

4. Some hobbies are so that you can make money out of them.

5. Going to college or a job is a question every student must face.

6. I burned the hamburgers is why we finally went to McDonald's.

7. Because it's a white dog with black spots all over it is why I'm sure it's a Dalmatian.

8. Any fad that Jerry hears about, he follows it.

9. Radio commercials don't bother me as much as TV.

10. You tell a good friend what he wants to hear is not always the kindest thing to do.

Part 5
Varying Your Sentence Beginnings

The usual order of the sentence in English is:

SUBJECT + VERB + ⎡ OBJECT (AND MODIFIERS)
⎢ or
⎣ PREDICATE WORD (AND MODIFIERS)

You are interested in making your writing lively and effective. You want people to *want* to read what you have to say. One way to achieve this effectiveness is to vary the beginnings of your sentences, to give them a new look by inverting the order of their parts. You must be careful not to overwork this plan because inverted order often has a dramatic quality that could be out of place in certain kinds of writing. Use it to intensify a situation or an idea, or to momentarily slow down the pace of your writing.

Ways to Vary Your Sentence Beginnings

1. **Put an adverb before the subject.**

USUAL ORDER   Butch inched his way *cautiously* to the deserted house.

(adverb)
INVERTED   *Cautiously*, Butch inched his way to the deserted house.

USUAL ORDER   She stopped *abruptly* and stared at him.

(adverb)
INVERTED   *Abruptly*, she stopped and stared at him.

2. Put the verb or direct object before the subject.

USUAL ORDER   The *torrents* of rain *poured* down.

                         (verb)   **(subject)**
INVERTED   Down *poured* the *torrents* of rain.

USUAL ORDER   *Anchorage was* twenty miles ahead of us.

                                        (verb)   **(subject)**
INVERTED   Twenty miles ahead of us *was Anchorage.*

USUAL ORDER   *I* could not tolerate an *insult* like that.

                        (object)   **(subject)**
INVERTED   An *insult* like that *I* could not tolerate.

USUAL ORDER   *I* can recall certain *songs* without difficulty.

                       (object) (subject)
INVERTED   Certain *songs I* can recall without difficulty.

3. Begin the sentence with a prepositional phrase, a participial phrase, or an infinitive phrase. Be sure the phrase modifies the proper word.

USUAL ORDER   Nothing is more beautiful *to me* than a snowstorm.

(prepositional phrase)
INVERTED   *To me,* nothing is more beautiful than a snowstorm.

USUAL ORDER   I waited alone *for ten minutes.*

(prepositional phrase)
INVERTED   *For ten minutes* I waited alone.

USUAL ORDER   James led her into the hall, *taking her gently by the hand.*

(participial phrase)
INVERTED   *Taking her gently by the hand,* James led her into the hall.

USUAL ORDER	We headed for the dude ranch, *excited about our unusual vacation.*
	(participial phrase)
INVERTED	*Excited about our unusual vacation,* we headed for the dude ranch.
USUAL ORDER	Tom went to the library *to get information about satellites.*
	(infinitive phrase)
INVERTED	*To get information about satellites,* Tom went to the library.
USUAL ORDER	Dick must pass a physical examination *to be eligible for the team.*
	(infinitive phrase)
INVERTED	*To be eligible for the team,* Dick must pass a physical examination.

4. **Begin the sentence with a subordinate clause.**

USUAL ORDER	Dave's father was at the airport to meet the boys *when they got off the plane.*
	(subordinate clause)
INVERTED	*When the boys got off the plane,* Dave's father was there to meet them.
USUAL ORDER	I felt like a millionaire *as I boarded the ship for France*
	(subordinate clause)
INVERTED	*As I boarded the ship for France,* I felt like a millionaire.

Exercises
Varying Your Sentence Beginnings

A. Rewrite the following sentences, varying the positions of the words or word groups in italics.

You may have more than one effective arrangement. Say the sentences out loud to help you decide which arrangement sounds better.

1. We tried not to show our excitement *as we sat on the stage listening to the speaker.*
2. The clock *finally* struck ten.
3. It is spring *once more.*
4. The combo settled down and played good music *after the audience left.*
5. He looked uncomfortable and unhappy, *dressed in his best suit.*
6. The plow was tossing up huge mounds of snow *in the corners of the parking lot.*
7. Nothing will happen *unless I make the first move.*
8. The driver was *suddenly* blinded by a flash of light.
9. I picked up a Super 8 movie camera *at a garage sale.*
10. The frightened men hurried *out into the rain.*
11. I went to the rink *every day* and finally learned to skate.
12. I lost my interest in snowmobiling *after the accident.*
13. Paul buried himself in his work *to fight against his fear.*
14. We sold everything from fish tanks to snow tires *at our garage sale.*
15. *The tenor sax* is one of the instruments Leo plays.

B. Rewrite each sentence below. Change the position of words so that you have an effective variation to the sentence.

1. My pen ran dry in the middle of the test.
2. The swirling, muddy torrent came down, dragging tents and equipment with it.
3. Still we had no coach for the team.
4. Peter sold his stamp collection reluctantly.
5. A young woman sat in one corner, clutching her small baby.
6. My dad gave me my first driving lesson after I reminded him that the car was insured.
7. She went off to the fitting room, carrying three new dresses.
8. Joe's problem grew heavier as he shuffled down Main Street.

9. The police questioned the suspect for eight hours.
10. The treasure, strangely beautiful, was all mine.
11. Dick hurried to the locker room as soon as the game was over.
12. I cannot tell how long it took me to reach home.
13. Andy kept on eating pizza even though he knew he was gaining too much weight.
14. Greg's face lit up like a candle when he smiled.
15. Mom climbs the walls when our Siamese cat climbs the curtains.

Review Exercises
Revising Sentences with Various Problems

A. Revise the following sentences. They contain various problems you have dealt with in this chapter.

1. I know that if I try that I can get into college.
2. The pen that has the red felt tip leaks.
3. Each time, I went through a routine that was different.
4. The reception on Dad's stereo is better than my radio.
5. My speech did not go over well due to the fact that I was nervous.
6. What I sometimes really wish is people wouldn't behave like sheep.
7. Mr. Russo is completely bald is probably the reason he always wears a cap.
8. The photos of the surface of Mars look just like the Painted Desert of Arizona.
9. I got sick on account of the fact that I ate too many tacos.
10. Make my bed, clean up my room, but put away my barbell is the only thing I forget to do.

B. Revise the following:

1. Television lets you sit back and let a machine think for you. You don't do any of the thinking yourself.
2. When you think about it, you realize that death is something that happens to everyone, but most of the time you think it will happen only to other people and that it will never happen to you.

3. In Switzerland, only the men can vote. No women are allowed to vote at all.

4. Bill has his CB license, and he is talking all the time with everybody under the sun, and in case you want to talk to him yourself, his handle is "Cookie Monster."

5. Capital Records has started a big campaign to bring back the Beatles, which were its most popular singing group, and young people are flocking to record stores to buy the re-released records and put the old Beatle songs back on the charts.

6. A girl from our high school has just been admitted to West Point, and to be admitted she had to be nominated by a U.S. Congressman and, of course, to have good grades and a good all-round record.

7. Last weekend a car smashed into the back of our camper and shook us up, and fortunately nothing was damaged except our bike carrier which was at the back.

8. How to load an Instamatic camera is the thing I have trouble doing.

9. The little chestnut foal, which was born yesterday morning and is still a bit unsteady on his legs, has beautiful soft eyes and is never more than a step away from his mother, who is very protective.

10. By brother says the Beatle lyrics stun him, and that they have phrases like "yellow matter custard jumping from a dead dog's eye," and he says people are always trying to figure out their real meaning, but the Beatles say there is no meaning.

Chapter 9

Using the Library

Learning to use library resources efficiently and quickly will be of great practical value not only for your work in English but for all your studies. In high school you will do research in literature, history, science, and other subjects. You will find the library an indispensable tool.

Before you can make efficient use of the library, however, you will have to know how books are classified and arranged on the shelves, and how to find them by using the card catalog. And you should be familiar with a wide variety of reference works, so that you will be able to find easily the best available information on any subject.

Suppose, for example, that you were asked to write a brief biographical sketch of Mark Twain. Would you read a short biography, or read entries on Twain in *Twentieth Century Authors* and a large encyclopedia? What other sources could you use? If you know what resources the library has, you will be able to answer these questions immediately.

This chapter will give you the basic information you need to make the best use of the library.

Part 1

How Books Are Classified and Arranged

It is important for you to understand the classification and arrangement of books in a library. Knowing how and where books are placed will enable you to find any book you need.

The Classification of Books

Fiction. Novels and short-story collections are usually arranged in alphabetical order by author. For example, if you want to read the American classic *The Pearl,* by John Steinbeck, you would first look for the section in the library which has shelves reserved for FICTION. Then you would look for books which have authors whose last names begin with S and find the book in its alphabetical position. If the book is not there, someone else has borrowed it, or a browser has carelessly returned it to the wrong position. You would be wise to check part of the shelf to see if the book has been returned out of alphabetical order. If you do not find the book and you need it soon, fill out a reserve card (a postcard mailed to you when the book has been returned to the library) which the librarian will give you.

Nonfiction. Most libraries classify nonfiction books according to the Dewey Decimal System. This system, which is named for its originator, the American librarian Melvil Dewey, classifies all books by number in ten major categories:

000–099	**General Works**	(encyclopedias, handbooks, almanacs, etc.)
100–199	**Philosophy**	(includes psychology, ethics, etc.)
200–299	**Religion**	(the Bible, theology, mythology)

300–399	**Social Science**	(sociology, economics, government, education, law, folklore)
400–499	**Language**	(languages, grammars, dictionaries)
500–599	**Science**	(mathematics, chemistry, physics, biology, etc.)
600–699	**Useful Arts**	(farming, cooking, sewing, nursing, engineering, radio, television, gardening, industries, inventions)
700–799	**Fine Arts**	(music, paintir.g, drawing, acting, photography, games, sports, amusements)
800–899	**Literature**	(poetry, plays, essays)
900–999	**History**	(biography, travel, geography)

As you can see from the major categories of the Dewey Decimal System, each discipline has a classification number. For example, all science books have a number between 500 and 599, and all history books have a number between 900 and 999. The system becomes more detailed as each of these major groups is subdivided. The table below shows how the subdividing works in the literature category (800–899):

800–899   Literature

810 American literature	810 American literature
820 English literature	811 Poetry
830 German literature	812 Drama
840 French literature	813 Fiction
850 Italian literature	814 Essays
860 Spanish literature	815 Speeches
870 Latin literature (classic)	816 Letters
880 Greek literature (classic)	817 Satire and Humor
890 Other literatures	818 Miscellany
	819 Canadian-English Literature

Arrangement of Books on the Shelves

You will see at a glance that books are arranged on the shelves numerically in order of classification. Most libraries mark their shelves prominently with the numbers indicating the books to be found in each particular section. Within each classification, books are arranged alphabetically by authors' last names.

Biography. The Dewey Decimal System division for Biography is 920. However, large libraries will often place biographies in a separate section because of the large number of these books. In this case they will have a "B" on the spine of the book and on the catalog card. If you are looking for a particular biography and are unable to locate the 920 division, ask the librarian for assistance.

Reference Books. Reference books of particular types or on specific subjects are also shelved together, often with the letter R above the classification number.

Exercises
How Books Are Classified and Arranged

A. In which major division would the following information be located?

1. Plays for high school productions
2. How to plant a vegetable garden
3. A comparison of Greek and Roman gods
4. "Killer" bees
5. Motocross racing
6. Recessions and depressions in the United States
7. Macramé
8. Rules for playing lacrosse
9. How to say "no" in any country
10. Operating a CB radio.

B. Using the Dewey Decimal System listed on pages 210 and 211, assign the correct classification number to each of the following books:

1. *Voices of the Rainbow: Contemporary Poetry by American Indians,* ed. Kenneth Rosen.
2. *Great Religions of the World,* ed. Merle Severy.
3. *America,* by Alistair Cooke.
4. *Metric Power,* by Richard Deming.
5. *A History of American Painting,* by Ian Bennett.
6. *Dolphins,* by Jacques Cousteau and P. Diolé.
7. *Planning the Perfect Garden,* ed. Good Housekeeping.
8. *A Treasury of Afro-American Folklore,* ed. Harold Courlander.
9. *The Art of Printmaking,* by E. Rhein.
10. *Clarence Darrow: A One-Man Play,* by David W. Rintels.

Part 2
Using the Card Catalog

To determine whether the library has a book you want and where to find it, use the **card catalog.** The card catalog is a cabinet of small drawers or file trays containing alphabetically arranged cards. Each card bears the title of a book which the library has on its shelves. The card also carries the classification number, or as librarians say, **call number** in the upper left-hand corner. (See the illustration on the next page.)

To find your book, write down the call number on a slip of paper. If it is a literature book—for example, *Selected Poems* by Langston Hughes—the call number will be in the 800 range. Specifically, American poetry will be found in 811.

Go to the section of shelves marked 811, and you will find your book alphabetically placed among those authors' last names that begin with *H.* The same call number you originally found on the catalog card will be imprinted on the spine of the book near the bottom.

There are usually three cards for the same book in the card catalog: the *author card,* the *title card,* and the *subject card.*

The Author Card. Perhaps you are writing a paper about a modern-day sports figure, or you are simply interested in reading the story of an athlete. O. J. Simpson, one of football's greatest, is the topic of a book by Larry Fox. You will find the author card in the card catalog, and it will look like this:

796.33   **Fox, Larry**

          The O. J. Simpson story: born to
          run; introduction by Weeb Ewbank.
          Dodd, Mead, © 1974.
          173p., illus.

                    ◯

Author cards for all books by one author will be filed together alphabetically according to title. Notice also that books *about* the author are filed *behind* his author cards.

The Title Card. Suppose you do not know the author's name, but do know the title of the book about O. J. Simpson. Look in the card catalog for a card bearing the title at the top as follows:

796.33   **The O. J. Simpson story: born to run**

          Fox, Larry

          The O. J. Simpson story: born to
          run; introduction by Weeb Ewbank.
          Dodd, Mead, © 1974.
          173p., illus.
                    ◯

The place of the title card in the catalog is determined by the first letter of the first word in the title. (A, *An*, and *The* do not count as first words.)

The Subject Card. You may not know whether a book has been written about O. J. Simpson. However, because he is an outstanding football player, you suspect that there may be a book about him. If you look through the cards cataloged under the subject Football, you will find the following:

796.33   **FOOTBALL**

Fox, Larry
      The O. J. Simpson story: born to
run; introduction by Weeb Ewbank.
Dodd, Mead, © 1974.
      173p., illus.

      ◯

Subject cards are most useful when you want information on a specific topic from a variety of sources. Cards for all books on a particular subject are cataloged together. The subject card may also indicate whether a book has chapters on a single aspect of the topic you are interested in. And the publication date on the card will help you find the most up-to-date book on your subject.

Catalog Card Information

Notice that all three types of catalog cards (author, title, subject) give the same information. This information includes:

1. The call number.
2. The title, author, publisher, and date of publication.

3. The number of pages, and a notation on whether the book has illustrations, maps, tables, or other features.

Often the catalog card will also provide:

4. A brief description of the nature and scope of the book. (This will help you decide whether the book will be useful to you.)
5. A listing of other catalog cards for the book.

Cross Reference Cards

Occasionally, in looking up a subject, you will find a card that reads *See* or *See also*. The "See" card refers you to another subject heading in the catalog which will give you the information you want. Let's say you want a book on television commercials, and you find a card that reads:

```
Television commercials
            see
Television advertising




                    ◯
```

It means that the library catalogs all books on television commercials under the heading of television advertising.

The "See also" card refers you to other subjects closely related to the one you are interested in. This card may be helpful to you in making sure that your research on a particular topic is complete. A "See also" card will look like this:

```
Biology

    see also
Natural history
Physiology
Psychobiology
Variation (Biology)
Vitalism
Zoology

    See also headings beginning
with the word Biological
```

Guide Cards

Besides the catalog cards, you will find guide cards in the cabinet trays. These are blank except for the guide word (general subject heading) on a tab that projects above the other cards. Guide cards aid you in finding other catalog cards quickly. For example, if you want books on cartooning, you will find them easily by means of alphabetically arranged guide cards such as the following:

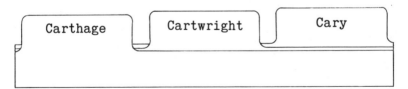

Exercises
Using the Card Catalog

A. The drawing at the top of the next page represents the first   six trays of a card catalog. The items at the right name authors, titles, and subjects that would be filed in these trays. Copy the list at the right on a separate sheet of paper, and write 1, 2, 3, 4, 5 or 6 in the blanks to show in which trays you would find the items listed.

1—	**A—Boat**
2—	**Bog—Cist**
3—	**City—Deep**
4—	**Den—Ebony**
5—	**Eco—Fed**
6—	**Fil—From**

___ *A Doll's House*
___ Charles Dickens
___ *The Call of the Wild*
___ *The Art of Walt Disney*
___ Backgammon
___ E. E. Cummings
___ Frisbees
___ *The Bermuda Triangle Mystery—Solved*
___ Backpacking
___ *A Christmas Carol*

B. Use the card catalog in your public library to find the title, author, call number, and publication date of the following books. Number your paper from 1 to 10 and write the answers.

1. A book by Ray Bradbury
2. A book about Harry S. Truman
3. A book on consumerism
4. A book on Renaissance art
5. A book by Agatha Christie
6. An anthology containing poems by Robert Frost, Emily Dickinson, and Carl Sandburg.
7. A book with information on immigration to the U.S.
8. A book with plays by Eugene O'Neill and Thornton Wilder
9. A book by Harper Lee
10. A book about cross-country skiing

C. What subject cards would give you information about the following topics? Discuss your answers in class.

1. "Peanuts" cartoons
2. Repairing minibikes
3. Developing photographs
4. Beer can collecting
5. How films are made
6. The origin of the Olympics
7. The first astronauts
8. Popular music of today's youth
9. Fashions of today's youth
10. The first television program

D. Using the card catalog, list the title, author, call number, and publication date of all books about two of the following people:

1. Eleanor Roosevelt
2. Henry Kissinger
3. Mark Twain
4. Gwendolyn Brooks
5. Pablo Picasso

6. Billie Jean King
7. James Baldwin
8. Walt Whitman
9. Beverly Sills
10. Ernest Hemingway

Part 3
Using Reference Works

One of the best ways to get information is to consult a reference work. Suppose your teacher were to ask you to write a brief biographical sketch of the American writer John Steinbeck. One good source would be *Twentieth Century Authors*, by Kunitz and Haycraft. It may be found in the reference room of most libraries. Know the various types of reference works and where they are kept in your school and public library.

Reference works are tools, and like tools, should be used in definite ways. Most reference works have prefaces which describe how information is arranged, show sample entries, and explain the symbols and abbreviations used in the book. Before using any reference work for the first time, you would be wise to at least skim the preface.

Nine basic types of reference works are described in this part.

1. Dictionaries. The most widely used reference books in the library are the general dictionaries. They may be classified in three major types. The first is the unabridged (complete) dictionary containing more than 500,000 words. Secondly, there are abridged (shorter) editions, commonly called "desk" or "collegiate" dictionaries. The third group are pocket-sized; they are convenient for checking the spelling of ordinary words, but too limited for high school and college use.

Here is a list of reliable dictionaries for your use:

Another group of dictionaries are those dealing with certain aspects of the English language: synonyms and antonyms, rhymes, slang, Americanisms, etymology, and so forth. Finally, there are special-purpose dictionaries which deal exclusively with music, medicine, biography, and many other subjects. The list below is by no means complete, but it provides good source material for you. You may check your school and community library as to the availability of specific-subject dictionaries.

Harvard Dictionary of Music
Mathews' Dictionary of Americanisms
The New Roget's Thesaurus in Dictionary Form
The Oxford Dictionary of English Etymology
Roget's International Thesaurus
Webster's Biographical Dictionary
Wood's Unabridged Rhyming Dictionary

2. Encyclopedias. These are collections of articles, alphabetically arranged, on nearly every known subject. Guide letters on the spine of each volume and guide words at the top of the pages aid you in finding information. It is best, however, to first check the general index when looking for information. It may list several good sources. For up-to-date information on a topic, check the yearbook which many encyclopedias issue. (A word of caution: When you write essays and reports, you must put all material taken verbatim from encyclopedias and all other sources in quotes.) The following arc some of the most reliable encyclopedias:

GENERAL ENCYCLOPEDIAS

Collier's Encyclopedia (24 volumes)
Compton's Encyclopedia (26 volumes)
Encyclopaedia Britannica (29 volumes)
Encyclopedia Americana (30 volumes)
World Book Encyclopedia (22 volumes)

The library has many special-purpose encyclopedias dealing with a wide variety of subjects. These encyclopedias are located in the library's reference room or area.

ENCYCLOPEDIAS ON SPECIFIC SUBJECTS

The Baseball Encyclopedia
The Concise Encyclopedia of Archaeology
*The Concise Encyclopedia of English and American
    Poets and Poetry*
The Concise Encyclopedia of Modern Drama
Encyclopaedia of Occultism
Encyclopaedia of Religion

The Encyclopedia of American Facts and Dates
Encyclopedia of Animal Care
Encyclopedia of Auto Racing Greats
Encyclopedia of Careers and Vocational Guidance
The Encyclopedia of Chemistry
Encyclopedia of Gardening
Encyclopedia of World Art (15 volumes)
Grzimek's Animal Life Encyclopedia (13 volumes)
The Illustrated Encyclopedia of Aviation and Space
The Illustrated Encyclopedia of World Coins
The International Encyclopedia of Cooking
International Encyclopedia of Social Sciences (17 volumes)
LaRousse Encyclopedia of Mythology
McGraw-Hill Encyclopedia of World Biography (12 volumes)
McGraw-Hill Encyclopedia of World Drama (4 volumes)
The Mammals of America
The New Columbia Encyclopedia
The Pictorial Encyclopedia of Birds
Universal Encyclopedia of Mathematics

3. Almanacs and Yearbooks. Published annually, almanacs and yearbooks are most useful sources of facts and statistics on current events, as well as matters of historical record in government, economics, population, sports, and other fields:

Guinness Book of World Records
Information Please Almanac, Atlas and Yearbook
Statesman's Yearbook
Statistical Abstract of the United States
Women's Rights Almanac
World Almanac and Book of Facts

4. Biographical References. There are brief biographical notations in dictionaries and longer biographical articles in encyclopedias. Often, however, a better source is one of the specialized works listed below:

American Men and Women of Science
The Book of Presidents
Current Biography

Dictionary of American Biography
Dictionary of National Biography
The International Who's Who
Twentieth Century Authors
Who's Who
Who's Who in America
Who's Who in the East (and Eastern Canada)
Who's Who in the Midwest
Who's Who in the South and Southwest
Who's Who in the West
Who's Who in American Women

5. Books About Authors. Six good reference works are the
following:

American Authors 1600–1900
British Authors of the Nineteenth Century
Contemporary Authors
Twentieth Century Authors
Twentieth Century Authors: First Supplement
Writers at Work

6. Literary Reference Books. The following are valuable reference books on the history of literature, on quotations and
proverbs, and for locating poems and stories, and for finding
information about writers:

Bartlett's Familiar Quotations
Contemporary Poets
Cyclopedia of Literary Characters
A Dictionary of Literature in the English Language
Encyclopedia of World Drama
Granger's Index to Poetry
A Literary History of England
A Literary History of the United States
Mencken's *A New Dictionary of Quotations*
The Oxford Companion to American Literature
The Oxford Companion to English Literature
The Oxford Companion to the Theater
Poetry Handbook

Twentieth Century Authors
World Authors

7. Pamphlets, Handbooks, and Catalogs. Many libraries have pamphlets, handbooks, booklets, and clippings on a variety of subjects including vocations, travel, census data, and program schedules. They also have a collection of college catalogs. All of these are kept in a set of file cabinets called the **vertical file.** This file can be an invaluable source to you when writing a report or looking for information on careers.

8. Atlases. We usually think of an atlas mainly as a book of maps, but it contains interesting data on a number of subjects. The excellent *National Geographic Atlas of the World,* for example, lists some of the following topics in its table of contents: "Great Moments in Geography," "Global Statistics," and sections on population, temperatures, oceans, and place names. Below is a list of other widely used atlases:

> *Atlas of World History*
> *Atlas of World Wildlife*
> *The Britannica Atlas*
> *Collier's World Atlas and Gazetteer*
> *Goode's World Atlas*
> *Grosset World Atlas*
> *The International Atlas from Rand McNally*
> *The Times Atlas of the World*
> *Webster's Atlas with Zip Code Directory*

9. Magazines. The *Readers' Guide to Periodical Literature* lists the titles of articles, stories, and poems published during the preceding month in more than 100 leading magazines. It is issued twice a month from September through June and once a month in July and August. An entire year's issues are bound in one hardcover volume at the end of the year. Articles are listed alphabetically under *subject* and *author* (and *titles* when necessary). You will find the *Readers' Guide* invaluable when looking for articles on a subject for a composition.

The following excerpt from the *Readers' Guide* illustrates how articles are listed:

DEFECTORS, Political
Korchnoi's complaint; case of chess master, V. Korchnoi.
R. Carroll and F. Endt. il por Newsweek 88:38 Ag 9 '76
Schoolboy and the paraplegic; defection of S. Nemtsanov
and I. Szelenyi to Canada. il por Newsweek 88:45 Ag 16 '76
DEFENSE manpower commission. |See United States—De-
fense manpower commission.| **"see" cross**
DEFORD, Frank   **reference**
High wide and handsome. il Sports Illus 45:14-17 Ag 2 '76
|In a strike zone of his own.| il pors Sports Illus 45: 28-9 +   **title of article**
Jl 26 '76
Nadia awed ya. il pors   Sports Illus   45:28-31 Ag 2 '76
Twelve quiet men on a rampage. il|Sports Illus|45:33-5 Ag 9 '76   **name of magazine**
DEGAETANI, Jan
DeGaetani's Ives: up to all expectations. R. P. Morgan por
Hi Fi 26:84 Ag '76*
DELANEY, Patricia A.   **volume number**
Registration/certification. Parks & Rec [11] |:78-9|Jl '76   **page reference**
DELANEY, Paul
Something that had to be done.   Nation 223:78-82 Jl 31 '76
DELURY, Bernard Edward
World of work—world of education; address, April 28, 1976.
Vital Speeches 42:594-7|Jl 15 '76| **date of magazine**
DEMOCRACY
Two centuries of liberal democracy; excerpts from address.
W. H. Goetzmann. por Intellect 105:12 Jl '76
DEMOCRATIC party
Democratic ticket. Commonweal 103:483-4 Jl 30 '76
Preserving unity: no easy task. |il| U.S. News 81:20 Jl 26 '76   **illustrated article**
Unified or pacified? New Repub 175:5-6 Jl 31 '76
|DENIM| **subject entry**
Jeans: how to get the kind you want. il Good H 183:60 Ag '76
DENNIS, Lloyd B.
Charitable contributions: address. May 26, 1976. Vital Speeches
42:597-602   Jl 15 '76
|DENNIS, Robert T.| **author entry**
Planning for how many people? BioScience 26:127 Jl '76
DENNISON, David Mathias
Obituary
Phys Today 29:71 Jl '76 H. R. Crane and K. T. Hecht
DENTAL instruments and apparatus
|See also
Dental supplies industry| **"see also"**
DENTAL supplies industry   **cross reference**
Bright, white future for dental suppliers. J. Madrick. Bus W
p 102 Ag 16 '76
DENTISTRY
Cosmetic dentistry. C. Duhé. Am Home 79:8-9+ Ag '76

Exercises
Using Reference Works

A. Find information on one of the following subjects by using the general index of three different encyclopedias available in your school or public libraries. Write a brief report on the topic. At the end of your report tell which encyclopedia was most useful and why.

The Middle Ages	Greek Mythology
The Globe Theatre	Aberdeen Angus cattle
Ellis Island	The Metric System
The Roaring Twenties	The Structure of a Cell
The Opera	Great American humorists

B. Using the dictionaries available in your library, write answers to the following questions. Write the title of the dictionary used after each answer. Do not use the same dictionary twice.

1. Define the word *crepuscular* and use it in a sentence.
2. What is the origin of the American word *gerrymander?*
3. List four synonyms for the word *product.*
4. List three antonyms for the word *delightful.*
5. List fifteen words that rhyme with *kind.*
6. Define the word *antediluvian.* Discuss its origin and use it in a sentence.
7. List three synonyms for the word *devote* and define each of them.
8. Define the word *nepotism* and use it in a sentence.

C. Use the current issue of the *World Almanac* to answer the following questions:

1. When was the Smithsonian Institution established?
2. What is the principal form of religion in Japan?
3. What happened on the evening of May 4, 1886, in Chicago?
4. What team won the Stanley Cup in hockey last year?
5. Where are the following national parks located?

Bryce Canyon	Rocky Mountain
Everglades	Mammoth Cave
Yosemite	Acadia

D. Use the *Readers' Guide* to answer the following:

1. Turn to the "Key to Abbreviations" and write the meaning of the following symbols used in the *Readers' Guide:*

bibliog	v	Je	Mr	pub	abr	Jl
O	il	rev	no	bi-m	ed	ja

2. List the titles of three articles on each of three subjects of current international importance. (List titles, authors, magazines, page numbers, and dates.)

3. Following the directions above, make a list of articles about a prominent person who interests you.

E. Using the special-purpose dictionaries, encyclopedias, and biographical and literary reference works noted in this chapter, find answers to the following questions. Write the name of the reference work you used after each answer.

1. Who are the authors of the following passages and from what works are they taken?

"Hog butcher for the world, Tool maker, stacker of wheat, Player with railroads and the nation's freighthandler; . . ."

"I'm Nobody! Who are you? Are you—Nobody—too?"

2. What reference works contain information on the following:

Susan B. Anthony	William Shakespeare
Carl Sandburg	Gerald R. Ford
Helen Keller	Clarence Darrow

3. What literary reference work includes a discussion of *Tom Sawyer?*

4. What are pelagic animals?

5. Name four works by the conductor-composer Leonard Bernstein.

6. In what year did the Russian author, Alexsandr I. Solzhenitsyn, win the Nobel Prize?

7. Who was Crispus Attucks, and what did he do?

8. What great American president lived at Monticello, and where is it located?

Chapter 10

Giving a Talk

There is one assignment that seems to strike fear into the heart of most students and turns the biggest and bravest into a mass of quivering bones and quavering voices. That assignment is, "Next week you will present an oral report to the class." For some unknown reason, talking in class is enjoyable only when it's not allowed. The student who can rattle on for forty minutes to the friend at the next desk about the lunchroom antics can't think of anything at all to say about World War II.

This is not an isolated problem. Ninety percent of all high school students share it. However, the problem can be overcome by acquiring a few skills involved in delivering an effective talk. Once you've mastered these skills, you will not only be able to speak effectively and knowledgeably, you might even enjoy speaking to a group. Some of us will always shake inside, but with a little practice no one else will even notice.

Part 1

Informal Talks

Let's deal first with those instances that come up quite often in your school years and require some oral presentation, but are not formal talks. At this point it's doubtful that you'll be asked to stand up and tell the class what you did on your vacation, and you've graduated from show-and-tell, but there are other types of oral presentations in which you'll be involved.

Preparation

While the amount of preparation involved for an informal talk isn't lengthy, you must do some background work. In most instances you won't be speaking for more than a minute or two, so it's easy to write out the talk. For brief announcements you'll find that notes are adequate, but make sure you do some amount of preparation. Your personality alone won't carry you through this assignment. You must know what you're going to say and how you're going to say it. *Always* practice reading your material aloud. What looks good on paper is sometimes difficult to read orally.

Presentation

This is the part you dread—standing there with all those grinning faces staring at you. You're certain everyone can see your knees knocking, and you seem to have no control whatsoever over your once-steady voice. Don't despair. There are some strategies you can employ to overcome your fears. First, until you feel very comfortable speaking before a group, don't try to make eye contact. That is, don't look directly at anyone in the audience. Instead, choose a spot just above their heads and move your eyes slowly around the group. It will seem to your audience that you're looking directly at each of them.

Good posture is another strategy. You must appear relaxed, even though you feel as if every one of your joints is welded together. Don't pose; just stand easily. Putting one foot slightly ahead of the other, or adopting a little wider stance than usual, will help you maintain your balance. Don't be afraid to move. If your instructor permits, make your first few presentations from the safety of a podium or desk. As you gain self-confidence—and you will—you can dispense with these aids. Try to speak without notes in your hand; more than likely they'll be shaking too badly for you to read, anyway.

The most important principle of presentation is to be well prepared. If you know exactly what you're going to say, it will be much easier. Practicing with a tape recorder can be very helpful, as we seldom actually "hear" ourselves. Hearing yourself can help you overcome repetition, vary the pitch of your voice, and slow your delivery. For some reason, everyone is inclined to speed up when giving a talk. It's a little like listening to a 45 record played at 78 rpm.

Mainly, relax and try to enjoy yourself!

Types of Informal Talks

Making Announcements

The simplest informal talk is the announcement, but no matter how short or how simple it seems, you must remember the following points:

> **What** is happening?
> **Where** is it happening?
> **When** is it happening?
> **Why** should the listeners be interested?

Always repeat *where* and *when*. There are those who don't listen to the beginning of an announcement but become interested about halfway through. They need to hear *where* and *when* repeated at the conclusion. Speak distinctly and clearly. Don't rush. Emphasize the important points.

There are times when you'll be asked to make an announcement concerning something that has already taken place, much like a newscast. This talk will be a little longer and will require a little more preparation. Again, you must tell your audience *what* happened, *where* it happened and *when* it happened. In this newscast you may also need to deal with *why* it happened or *how* it happened. Make some notes so that you won't leave out an important fact, and so that you can keep your presentation flowing smoothly without long pauses.

Exercises
Making Announcements

A. Make an announcement to the class regarding one of the events below, or announce something else that is going on at your school or in your community. So that this will seem more like an actual announcement, do not face the class when giving it. Stand behind the class or behind a screen so the audience is not looking at you. After three or four announcements have been given, see how many *what*'s, *where*'s, *when*'s, and *why*'s the class can remember. Listening is as important a skill as speaking!

an athletic event	an Honor Awards assembly
a school-sponsored movie	tryouts for cheerleaders
a club meeting	a skateboard competition
school elections	a procrastinators' party

B. Prepare and present a sixty-second newscast regarding something that has happened recently at school, or a fictitious happening. It could also be a sportscast, reporting on an athletic event. Keep your audience's attention with your voice. Again, don't face the audience, but deliver your newscast from the back of the classroom or behind a screen.

Giving Directions

Have you ever stopped someone on the first day of school to ask the location of a classroom? Isn't it amazing how few people can really help you? The reply is usually as follows:

> Just go down this hall and then turn by the water fountain (there are three) and then keep going past the type room (you have no idea where the type room is) and then turn at the next corner (which way?) and you'll find it.

With directions like these, you may not find the class for days. When giving directions, use accurate details, be as clear as possible, and never back up to correct yourself. Instead, start over again and be sure you're being understood.

> Go down this hall toward the front of the building. Turn right at the second water fountain. At the next corner turn left and the room will be the third one on your left.

This is still complicated for a new student, but at least you have a chance to be in the right part of the building. Of course, if you ask for directions you have to be a good listener.

Exercises
Giving Directions

A. Choose a specific place with which the other students are familiar. It can be in the school building, close to the grounds, or in your community. Without identifying the place, give students specific directions for getting there. When you've finished, see how many know the exact place.

B. Each member of the class is to give directions on how to draw a certain figure. It could be a stick figure, or a geometric figure of some kind using squares, triangles, rectangles or circles, such as a house or barn. This is a difficult assignment because you have to go over the figure time and again yourself while planning this talk, so keep it simple.

The class members can try following the directions as you're speaking, but they cannot ask questions. You'll know if they understand by the expressions on their faces. When you've finished, see how many students actually drew the figure. Was the problem in the directions? Was it that those who didn't draw the correct figure weren't listening closely? Try to analyze the problem.

Giving a Demonstration Talk

Did you ever try to tell someone how to tie his shoes? It's impossible! Try sitting on your hands and telling a friend how to swing a baseball bat or how to do a simple exercise. There are some instances when it's absolutely necessary to demonstrate what you mean. Of course, as you're demonstrating you're also giving oral instructions. This type of direction-giving sounds easy, but your thinking must be extremely well organized. What seems easy and uncomplicated to you can be sheer frustration to someone else.

Exercise
Giving a Demonstration Talk

Give a demonstration talk to the class. You might show how to do one of the following:

swing a golf club	bake a cake or pie
repot a plant	groom a dog
work with macramé	change a bicycle tire
plant a terrarium	build a bird house
prepare a Caesar salad	handle a rod and reel
hook a rug	arrange flowers
make a candle	fundamentals of frisbee
make a collage	

Doing Commercials

Does a future as a salesperson appeal to you? How would you like to perform in a commercial on television? Being able to sell a product to the public may be valuable; after all, you sometimes have to "sell" yourselves to teachers, friends, and employers. You might want to sell the idea of an open-book test to a particularly demanding instructor, convince your parents that a backpack family vacation trip would be better than visiting relatives in a big city, or try promoting a band trip to the summer Olympics to the school administration. Selling can involve more than products; it can also involve ideas. The specific criteria are that you must be sincere, persuasive, and above all, enthusiastic. The salesman who starts his pitch with, "I don't suppose you'd be interested in . . ." won't get too far.

Exercise
Doing a Commercial

Sell a fictitous product to the class in a one-minute commercial. Don't use any product that's currently on the market; devise your own. It might be a breath freshener that solves the problem by completely sealing your mouth, or a wrinkle cream for those who want to look older. Be original!

Making Introductions

The chances are good that at some time you'll be asked to introduce someone. It might be to a class, a club, an organization, or some other group with which you're involved. This will require more than, "This is Anita Rivera, president of the ninth grade." First you must get some background information on the person to give to the audience. Who is she? What has she done? Why is she here? Try to find some interesting or amusing incident to lighten your introduction. Be careful, though: everyone must be amused; *no one* must ever be embarrassed.

Exercises
Making Introductions

A. Choose a well known person and write an introduction that could have been used at some time in his or her life, or could be used today. You decide the occasion and the circumstances.

B. Choose a character from a book, movie, or television series and introduce him or her to the class.

C. Introduce one of your classmates.

Part 2
Formal Talks

Formal talks are delivered to a specific group, for a specific purpose, on a specific topic. They are lengthier than informal talks and require more thought, time, and preparation. You will first have to organize them completely on paper, and then spend some time rehearsing out loud for the best possible effect. This sounds complicated, but taken one step at a time it becomes a routine process at which you'll be adept in no time.

What is the reason for discussing formal talks rather than oral reports? It does seem that you're asked to give many oral reports in school, and few formal talks. Oral reports and talks do differ in some respects, but an oral report can always be turned into a formal talk. Reports often tend to be dry and dull, simply because you prepared them as written reports and gave little thought to the fact that they were to be presented orally. Being able to turn your report into an informative formal talk can bring instant results in the form of audience interest and higher grades.

Preparation. Every talk will require six steps:

1. Select your topic.
2. Define your purpose.
3. Select your theme.
4. Gather your material.
5. Organize your material.
6. Deliver your talk.

Select Your Topic

There are times when you will be given a specific topic to speak on. This makes it easier, as you can proceed with the next step immediately. However, more often than not you'll simply be asked to talk to a certain group about ecology, current events, today's school, or some other general subject. You'll have to make the decision as to the final topic. Don't hesitate to choose a topic you know little about if you have time to research it. Your new interest will add enthusiasm and liveliness to your talk.

Choose a topic you are sure will interest your audience. Here are a few things to be aware of:

The unusual appeals to everyone.

The familiar has value; but be sure to furnish some new sidelights on any familiar topic, or it will be dull.

The factual is sometimes useful, but it can also be dull. Avoid using facts already known to your audience.

Remember one thing: There are no uninteresting subjects. There are just uninterested people. If you are really interested in the topic, that interest will be contagious to your audience.

Exercises
Selecting a Topic

A. Choose three of the following occasions and decide on a topic for each.

1. You're a class officer and must prepare a talk for the opening assembly.

2. Your scout troop has asked you to deliver a talk for the awards banquet.

3. Your class has decided that you're the one to deliver a talk to a group of Senior Citizens.

4. You're to give a talk to the PTA or PTSA concerning an issue of importance to the students.

5. You're to give a talk to your geography class regarding some section of the United States.

6. It's getting close to a particular holiday, and you've been asked to talk about a custom.

7. You're captain of the team and have to give a talk after the final game.

8. A sixth-grade teacher has asked you to give a talk to his or her class.

Before you can even begin to deal with the actual talk, however, you must be aware of the one vital concern to any speaker: the audience. Consider their age, background, economic level and education. Be aware of what brings them into this one setting to listen to a talk. Know that they must be able to relate to what you're saying on an individual level. For example, a talk given to a group of elementary children would differ considerably from a talk given to the faculty of your school. You might change your topic somewhat if you were giving it before a group of parents rather than to the football team.

Plan your talk so you will get the attention of your audience. Make it interesting, so they will listen and respond. Speak to them knowledgeably and give them something to think about. By the time you deliver your talk you'll have as much information on the topic as anyone in the room, so you're the expert.

B. What would you title each of the following talks if you were asked to present it to (1) a sixth-grade class, (2) a group of parents, (3) your class, and (4) a club or organization to which you belong?

voting	drug addiction
teenage drivers	school drop-outs
vandalism	

Define Your Purpose

There are three major purposes that cover almost any talk you will be asked to give: to inform, to persuade, to entertain. You must decide which of these three your talk involves.

To inform

This is the type of talk you are asked to give more than any other. Most class reports are supposed to be informative. The low grades you sometimes receive are for those that didn't meet the requirements. You simply want your audience to understand or appreciate what you are telling them. Talks to inform might describe the advantages of belonging to a school club, explain the brake system of a car, or report on a book.

To persuade

To be successful, this kind of talk should lead to some change in the listener's point of view, attitude, or course of action. Talks to persuade, for example, may appeal for the election of a candidate, try to enlist support for some school or charitable activity, or try to prevent a course of action that you think unwise.

To entertain

In this kind of talk you simply want your audience to enjoy what you say. A talk to entertain might be an after-dinner speech, an account of a humorous or embarrassing experience, or a between-the-acts speech by a master of ceremonies.

Of course, any one of these talks does not exclude aspects of the others. An informative talk, for example, should contain something entertaining. A talk aiming to persuade would not get far without information to support its points.

Exercise
Defining Your Purpose

How many formal talks have you listened to in the past month? Write down the occasions, the topics, the audience, and the purposes of the talks. Were they effective? If not, briefly state why you think the speaker failed in his purpose. Limit yourself to five different talks.

Select a Theme

Your theme is the main idea you want to get across to your audience. At first you should write it down in full sentence form:

Violent crimes are increasing rapidly in our community.
Strip mining will destroy the natural environment.
We should organize a procrastinators club.

Your theme sentence is the key to your entire talk. Everything you say should support this theme in some way. You may wish to use your theme sentence in your talk, either early in the talk, or at the end, or both. It should not be used as a title.

Exercise
Selecting a Theme

Using your class as an audience, select a topic for a talk you will prepare and give. Decide the purpose and state the theme. Do no more on it at the present time.

Gather Your Material

In gathering material for your talk, look for ideas, details, illustrations, facts, figures and quotations. Some of your material will come from firsthand experience; some you will obtain from the experience of others. Try to deal with personal experience whenever possible. It's much more interesting to listen to someone speak about survival who has actually been on a survival trip, rather than just researched it. You can expand on your personal experience through reading and talking to others, but your talk will bear more weight if you can actually speak with the authority of one who has been there.

This does not mean you must deal exclusively with personal experiences. In that case, few of us would ever give talks. You must also rely on reading for more information. Here are some guidelines:

1. **Read for specific purposes.** For a talk, your purposes will be to gather facts, details, and illustrations to develop your central idea.

2. **Read for the main points.** Don't get lost in the forest of words.

3. **Evaluate the material you read.** Don't accept all ideas just because they're in print. Is the material useful to you? Is it up-to-date? Is it authoritative?

4. **Make the material your own.** Except for direct quotations, summarize and condense what you want to use. And one important point: Put it in your words. Word-for-word copying is plagiarism, for which you could be severely penalized.

Your library will be an indispensible asset in gathering your material. Unless you are contrasting ancient practices with modern ones, you will be dealing mainly with the vertical files and the *Readers' Guide to Periodical Literature.* This guide is an alphabetical index of contemporary magazine articles, so your information can be as current as possible.

Take notes on any reading you do. If you interview someone in the field, be sure to take notes during the interview. Notes are the backbone of any good talk, so take more than you need. You can always throw the surplus away.

Exercise
Gathering Material

Using 4″ × 6″ cards, take notes on everything you might include in a talk on the topic you have chosen.

Organize Your Material

At this point you have much more material than you can possibly use. You must now organize it so you'll end up with a coherent, logical talk. The only way to achieve this purpose is to divide your material into three parts: *the introduction, the body,* and *the conclusion.*

The Introduction

The introduction is used to gain attention and interest. It must be forceful. Many times you will hear a speaker use an anecdote as a means of gaining attention. An anecdote also relaxes an audience and gains their cooperation. You might use the introduction to explain the title of your talk, or state your theme. You could also refer to any background information here. Below is the introduction of a talk given by Will Rogers, an American humorist, to the alumni of Columbia University.

> President Butler paid me a compliment a while ago in mentioning my name in his introductory remarks, and he put me ahead of the Columbia graduates. I am glad he did that, because I got the worst of it last week. The Prince of Wales last week, in speaking of the sights of America, mentioned the Woolworth Building, the subway, the slaughterhouse, Will Rogers, and the Ford Factory. He could at least have put me ahead of the hogs.

The Body

The body of the talk is the "meat." This is the part of the talk that must inform, entertain, or persuade your audience. After drawing them in with your introduction, you now give them the facts and information to support your theme. You should be aware of the amount of time your total talk will take. The body of the talk should take at least twice as much time as the total of the introduction and conclusion. Here are some guidelines for organizing the body of your talk:

1. **Determine your major points.** The amount of time you have allotted for your talk will determine how many major points you wish to cover. You would be wise to outline your talk so you can be sure that your points are actually major ones and that they are in a logical, coherent order. Use your notes to sort out your major points.

2. **Develop your major points.** After you have decided exactly what major points you are going to cover, use the information from your notes to develop those points. You will develop each point in exactly the same way you develop each paragraph in a composition. The theme of your talk, along with the purpose, will determine your use of facts, statistics, details, illustrations, descriptions, anecdotes, personal experience, or a combination of these.

3. **Build your talk toward a climax.** To build your talk toward a climax, you will want to present your ideas in order of their importance. In some cases you will have to present your ideas in a logical time sequence. A outline will help you see immediately if your ideas are well ordered, if each of them is specifically related to your theme, and if each of them is fully developed.

The Conclusion

The conclusion is a summary of the main points of your talk. When preparing a persuasive talk, you might want to appeal to or challenge the audience in the conclusion. In an informative talk a quotation or illustration could appropriately conclude your talk. This is a good place to repeat your theme, bearing in mind the purpose of your talk. The purpose of Will Rogers' talk was to entertain. Here is the conclusion of that talk:

> There are more students in this university than there are in any other in the world. It is the foremost university. There are thirty-two hundred courses. You spend your first two years deciding what courses to take, the next two years finding the building that these courses are given in, and the rest of your life wishing you had taken another course. And they have this wonderful society called the Alumni Association, a bunch of men who have gone to school and, after they have come out, formed a society to tell the school how to run it.

A successful talk should conform to the rules for good speech-making. The introduction attracts attention; the body holds that attention and gains consideration; the conclusion summarizes briefly. Sufficient detail, and reference to authority, make the talk compelling. Ideas are presented in a logical manner so that any listener can follow them and understand the talk.

Exercise
Organizing Your Material

Using the material you have gathered, organize it in outline form into the three divisions: introduction, body, and conclusion. Then write your talk.

Deliver Your Talk

The effective presentation of a formal talk is no easy task. The "ideal" speaker would stand easily and comfortably, words flowing from his or her mouth in beautifully modulated tones. Unfortunately, we're not all that professional. But it's not impossible to give the same impression if you work at it. Here are some guidelines.

1. **Rehearse your talk aloud many times.** You'll finally get to the point where it docs flow easily.

2. **Take advantage of a tape recorder to listen to your delivery.** Be critical. If something doesn't sound right, try it again with emphasis on a different word or phrase. If it still doesn't sound right, rework your ideas into smoother sentences. Perhaps your sentences don't seem to flow smoothly from one idea to another. If they don't, revise your sentences so they say exactly what you want them to say. Check also to see if each idea actually does flow out of the one preceding it. Maybe an idea is in the wrong place.

3. **Choose a method of delivery that's comfortable for you.** If you prefer to memorize the entire talk, do it. If you'd feel more comfortable referring to notes, have them in an inconspicuous spot. Don't just read the talk. You'll be so engrossed in the paper that any personal contact with the audience

will be lost, and they'll feel left out. You want an audience involved, not isolated. For your first experience use a podium; it promotes feelings of security and authority, and makes it easier not to worry about the lower half of your body. But don't lean on it or drape yourself over it. You want your audience to focus on your talk, not your posture.

Exercise
Delivering a Talk

Deliver your talk to the class.

Congratulations! You have just given a formal speech!

Handbook

A detailed Table of Contents of the Handbook appears in the front of this book.

How To Use the Handbook

This Handbook is your reference book. In it the concepts of grammar and usage are organized so that you can study them efficiently and refer to them quickly. To use the Handbook well, you should first leaf through it to become familiar with its organization and contents. Note especially the following:

Organization of the Handbook

Grammar (Sections 1–5) Sections 1–5 provide a comprehensive treatment of English grammar. They give the rules and explanations for grammatical questions you want answered.

Usage (Sections 6–9) Sections 6–9 are a guide to English usage. When you are puzzled about which form of a word to use in your writing, turn to the appropriate part of these sections.

Forms and constructions marked STANDARD are accepted as standard usage—the kind of usage that is appropriate at all times and in all places. Forms and constructions marked NONSTANDARD are not accepted everywhere. While they may go unnoticed on the playground or in the locker room, in many other situations they mark the user as careless or untrained in the English language.

Capitalization (Section 10)

Punctuation (Sections 11–14)

Spelling (Sections 15–16)

Good Manuscript Form (Section 17)

Throughout the Handbook are many exercises that test your understanding of the concepts explained. These exercises are the first steps in putting what you learn here to practical use. The next steps are in your own writing and speaking.

1.0 The Classification of Words

Traditionally, the words in our language have been classified into eight large groups, called parts of speech. Here are the eight groups:

nouns	adjectives	conjunctions
pronouns	adverbs	interjections
verbs	prepositions	

In the twentieth century, however, language scholars have developed a different system of classifying words and of describing how our language works. These scholars, called linguists, believe that their system is more accurate than the older system. You will learn about this new system in Section 5 of this Handbook.

Understanding both the older system and the newer system, and how they differ, will give you a deeper understanding of how our language works.

We have chosen to begin with the traditional system described in Sections 1–4 for two reasons:

1. It is the system which, according to research, the majority of schools are using today.

2. It is the system with which you are expected to be familiar if you take the Scholastic Aptitude Test or any other college entrance examination.

1.1 The Noun

Certain words in the language are used as labels with which we identify people and things.

A noun is the name of a person, place, or thing.

Things named by nouns may be visible, such as *hats, buildings,* and *books.* Things may be items that we perceive with our other senses: *odors, sounds, tastes.* Other things are abstract and not observed through the five senses: *beliefs, ideas, wishes,* and so on.

PERSONS	PLACES	THINGS
Benjamin Franklin	Boston	baseball
lawyer	cellar	charity
priest	country	Buddhism

A **common noun** is the name of a whole group of persons, places, or things. It is a name that is common to the whole group: *stone, glass, minister, building.*

A **proper noun** is the name of an individual person, place, or thing.

A proper noun always begins with a capital letter.

COMMON NOUNS	PROPER NOUNS
desk	John F. Kennedy
schedule	Golden Gate Bridge
encyclopedia	Africa
custom	Jordan Marsh Company
night	Israel

As the above list shows, a noun may consist of more than one word. Each word in a proper noun is capitalized.

Any word that can be immediately preceded by *the* is a noun: *the* bridge, *the* George Washington Bridge, *the* language. Many proper nouns, but not all of them, can be preceded by *the: the Milwaukee Zoo, the Hyatt House,* but not *the* Abraham Lincoln or *the* France.

Exercise A: Find all the nouns in the following sentences.

1. The announcer said that the plane for Minneapolis would leave in thirty minutes.

2. Dr. Cooper was in college with my father.

3. John wanted to change the ribbon on his typewriter, but the ribbon would not cooperate.

4. There was a scream of skidding tires and then a metallic thud, followed by the sound of splintered glass.

5. Bob and his brother crossed the continent in their old car last summer.

6. The boys drove through the desert at night and slept in the daytime.

7. Helen is president of the class, and her sister is secretary.

8. Al wrote a paper about Babe Didrikson and her life in sports.

9. Half of the people in the world can neither read nor write.

10. There is a fine exhibition of paintings by Thomas Hart Benton at the Cleveland Public Library.

Exercise B: Decide which are common nouns and which are proper nouns. Write the proper nouns, beginning each with a capital letter.

1. german, science, language, english
2. lake, lake erie, mountain, mount everest
3. park, joshua national monument, gulf, cape cod
4. village, fairfield township, country, saint paul
5. labor, labor day, good friday, birthday
6. secretary, governor brown, senator kennedy, mayor
7. judge, justice douglas, police, detective bryant
8. uncle harry, bridge, rittenhouse square, boston common
9. cathedral, rabbi, saint patrick's cathedral, church
10. college, dartmouth college, university, jefferson high school.

1.2 The Pronoun

Since it would be awkward and cumbersome to repeat the name of a person or thing every time we wish to refer to it, we use other words in place of names. These words are pronouns. They may be used in a sentence in any way that a noun is used.

A pronoun is a word used in place of a noun.

The noun for which the pronoun stands and to which it refers is its **antecedent.**

> *Sue* had changed *her* dress. (*Sue* is antecedent of *her*.)
>
> The *players* changed *their* jerseys. (*players* is antecedent of *their*.)

Sometimes the antecedent of a pronoun appears in a preceding sentence.

> The fishermen cheered as *they* entered the harbor. *They* had not seen *it* for a month, and *they* longed for home. (*They* in each sentence refers to the antecedent *fishermen; it* refers to *harbor*.)

Indefinite pronouns do not often refer to any specific noun. The indefinite pronoun itself may be the antecedent of a personal pronoun.

> The *students* were jubilant. *Some* lifted the coach on their shoulders. (The antecedent of the indefinite pronoun *Some* is *students*.)
>
> Has *anyone* lost *his* hat? (The antecedent of *his* is the indefinite pronoun *anyone*.)

There are six kinds of pronouns:

personal pronouns	demonstrative pronouns
compound personal pronouns	interrogative pronouns
indefinite pronouns	relative pronouns

Personal Pronouns

Pronouns used in place of persons' names are called **personal pronouns.** They permit us to identify the person speaking, the person spoken to, and the person spoken about. Personal pronouns are also used to refer to things.

First person (the person speaking)
   I, me, my, mine, we, us, our, ours

Second Person (the person spoken to)
   you, your, yours

Third Person (the person or thing spoken about)
   he, she, it, they
   his, hers, its, their, theirs
   him, her, them

Personal pronouns change their form, or spelling, for different uses in sentences. This change of form is called the **case** of pronouns. There are three cases: *nominative, possessive,* and *objective.* Personal pronouns also change their form to show the difference between singular (one) and plural (more than one). This change of form is called the **number** of pronouns.

The following table shows the forms of the three *persons,* for the three *cases,* and for the *number* of all of the personal pronouns.

Personal Pronouns

Singular

	NOMINATIVE	POSSESSIVE	OBJECTIVE
FIRST PERSON:	I	my, mine	me
SECOND PERSON:	you	your, yours	you
THIRD PERSON:	he, she, it	his, her, hers, its	him, her, it

Plural

	NOMINATIVE	POSSESSIVE	OBJECTIVE
FIRST PERSON:	we	our, ours	us
SECOND PERSON:	you	your, yours	you
THIRD PERSON:	they	their, theirs	them

Third person pronouns that refer to male persons are in the **masculine gender.** Those that refer to female persons are in the **feminine gender.** Pronouns that refer to things are in the **neuter gender.**

Here are some important things to remember about pronouns:

The pronoun *it* is called a personal pronoun even though it refers to things more often than to persons.

Countries, ships, and airplanes are sometimes referred to by the feminine pronouns, *she, her, hers.* Animals may be referred to by *it* and *its* or by *he, his, she, her, hers,* depending on the sex of the animal.

The words *mine, yours, hers, ours,* and *theirs* are always used as pronouns. The words *my, your, its, our,* and *their* are always used as modifiers before nouns. They are **possessive pronouns.** *His* may be used either as a pronoun or as a modifier.

This hat is *mine.* (pronoun)
There is *my* record. (modifier)
The victory is *theirs.* (pronoun)
It was a gift from my mother to *his.* (pronoun)
We celebrated *her* anniversary. (modifier)

Compound Personal Pronouns

A **compound personal pronoun** is formed by adding *-self* or *-selves* to certain of the personal pronouns, as follows:

FIRST PERSON:	myself, ourselves
SECOND PERSON:	yourself, yourselves
THIRD PERSON:	himself, herself, itself, oneself, themselves

There are no other acceptable compound personal pronouns. Never say *hisself* or *theirselves.*

Compound personal pronouns are used *intensively* for emphasis or *reflexively* to refer to a preceding noun or pronoun.

The President *himself* welcomed the ambassador. (intensive)

Dawn treated *herself* to a soda. (reflexive)

Exercise A: In the following sentences find the personal pronouns. Find the antecedent of each pronoun.

1. The doctor told the boys that they could use his boat.
2. Bob, your father wants you to call for him.
3. Helen and Karen finished the test first. They found it quite easy.
4. The long run brought the crowd to its feet.
5. Jane has her own ideas, but the family does not agree with them.
6. The *Viking 2* spacecraft made its way to the northern hemisphere of Mars.
7. The boys cooked their meals in the open and made their beds of pine boughs.
8. When Jim's power mower broke, the neighbors let him use theirs.
9. Betty has a driver's license, but she doesn't have it with her.
10. The police found the car, but they couldn't move it.

Exercise B: Supply an acceptable compound personal pronoun in each of these sentences. Find the antecedent for each compound personal pronoun.

1. The doctor (_____) helped Mrs. Brown into the car.
2. The students have no one but (_____) to blame.
3. Jane (_____) answered the telephone.
4. You girls can see the evil results for (_____).
5. Jack blames (_____) for the accident.
6. Harry, you will have to solve this problem (_____).
7. The boys cleaned up the kitchen by (_____).
8. The president of the company (_____) replied to our criticism.

Indefinite Pronouns

Some pronouns, such as *anyone* and *anything,* do not refer to a definite person or thing. They are called **indefinite pronouns.** Normally, indefinite pronouns do not have antecedents.

SINGULAR INDEFINITE PRONOUNS

another	anything	either	everything	no one
anybody	one	everyone	neither	someone
anyone	each	everybody	nobody	somebody

PLURAL INDEFINITE PRONOUNS

both   many   few   several

The pronouns *all, some, any,* and *none* may be singular or plural, depending upon their meaning in the sentence.

All of the candy *has* been sold. (singular)
All of the skiers *have* returned. (plural)

Some of the money *is* counterfeit. (singular)
Some of the voters *were* angry. (plural)

None of the cider *is* sour. (singular)
None of the doors *were* locked. (plural)

Has any of the coffee spilled? (singular)
Were any of the movies good? (plural)

Demonstrative Pronouns

The words *this, that, these,* and *those* are used to point out which one or which ones are meant. Since they point to, or demonstrate, what is meant, they are called **demonstrative pronouns.** They always refer to a definite person or thing, but the words they refer to may come later.

This is the *camera* I won. (*camera* is the word referred to.)

On his wall were several Picasso *prints. These* had been given to him by his uncle. (*prints* is the word referred to by *These.*)

Note: The demonstrative pronouns *this, that, these,* and *those* may also be used as adjectives: *this hat, those curtains.*

Interrogative Pronouns

The pronouns *who, whose, whom, which,* and *what* are used to ask questions. When used in this way, they are **interrogative pronouns.**

      Who took the pretzels?   *What* is the time?
      Whom did you want?   *Which* do you like?

      The shoes aren't mine. *Whose* are they?

Relative Pronouns

The words *who, whose, whom, which,* and *that* are sometimes used to introduce an adjective clause. They relate the clause to some other word in the sentence. When used in this way, they are called **relative pronouns.**

A relative pronoun is used to introduce a relative clause. It also has a use within the relative clause. See Section 3.6.

Exercise: List the pronouns in these sentences. Tell what kind each pronoun is.

1. Someone had dropped her purse into the pool.
2. What have you done to make Mike feel so good?
3. This is the kind of problem that baffles me.
4. Is this the face that launched a thousand ships?
5. Have you had anything to eat?
6. Which of these coats is yours?
7. Neither of the girls could find anything to say.
8. Nobody knew the answer to the question.
9. That is the best course for anyone to follow.
10. Several of our students have won valuable scholarships.

1.3 The Verb

Every sentence must contain a word that tells what is happening. This word is the verb.

A verb is a word that tells of an action or state of being.

Grammatically, the verb is the most important word in the sentence. If you can find the verb and manage it properly, many of your grammar and usage problems will be solved.

Most verbs change their form (their sound or spelling) to show past time and present time. They are the only words to do so. This fact can help you decide which word in the sentence is the verb.

The commuter trains *were* rarely on time. (past)
The commuter trains *are* rarely on time. (present)

The Smiths *loved* Arizona. (past)
The Smiths *love* Arizona. (present)

Most verbs also change their form to show the difference between singular and plural in the third person.

Joe *finds* country music entertaining. (third person singular)
Sue and Marcella *find* rock absorbing. (third person plural)

Action Verbs

The action asserted by an action verb may be visible, physical action, or it may be invisible action.

Fred *knocked* on the door. (visible)
The car *skidded*. (visible)
Tony *rocked* the boat. (visible)
Jane *wanted* a new cat. (not visible)
The ambassador *hoped* to save face. (not visible)
Joe *liked* the movie. (not visible)

Linking Verbs

A few verbs, such as *be*, link the subject to a noun, to a pronoun or to an adjective. Hence they are called **linking verbs.**

>Ron *is* vice-president.   Sherman *seems* gloomy.

The most common linking verb is *be* with its forms *am, are, is, was, were, been, being.*

Other linking verbs are *appear, become, seem, look, sound, grow, feel, smell, taste, remain,* and *stay.*

>The children *appeared* sleepy.   The radio *sounds* awful.
>The sky *became* threatening.   The crowd *grew* restive.
>Sheila *seemed* annoyed.   The mayor *feels* confident.
>The prospects *look* good.   The forest *smelled* dank.
>The victory *tasted* sweet to the new coach.
>The weather *remained* unchanged for two months.
>The flagpole *stayed* upright throughout the storm.

Some linking verbs may also be used as action verbs.

>We *looked* into the cage.   Paul *sounded* the gong.
>Linda *tasted* the waffles.   The cat *smelled* the lobster.
>We *grew* all our own vegetables last year.
>Tammy *felt* the bump on Annelinde's head.

Main Verbs and Auxiliaries

Many verbs consist of more than one word. They consist of a **main verb** and one or more helping verbs or **auxiliaries.** The last word in the phrase is the main verb.

There are three verbs that can be used either as main verbs or as auxiliaries. Here are their forms:

DO	HAVE	BE		
do	has	is	was	be
does	have	am	were	been
did	had	are		being

AS MAIN VERB	AS AUXILIARY
He will *do* the work.	We *do* enjoy having you here.
Have you the strength?	They *have* lost it.
The marks *were* good.	The waters *were* receding.

The most frequently used auxiliaries are the forms of *be* and *have*. The most common of the other auxiliaries are the following:

must	may	shall	could	would
might	can	will	should	

AUXILIARY	MAIN VERB	VERB
has	had	has had
had	been	had been
was	doing	was doing
had	done	had done
could have	gone	could have gone
might have been	seen	might have been seen
is being	improved	is being improved

Often the parts of a verb are separated by a modifier or modifiers that are not part of the verb.

We *had* certainly *known* it.   It *had* just *stopped* snowing.

Exercise A: Find the verb in each of these sentences. Include all the words that make up the verb. Do not include any word that separates an auxiliary from a main verb.

1. The lighthouse keeper had never seen such a storm.
2. When will the next pollutant be banned?
3. The truck driver was completely blinded by the flash.
4. Our people have always had enough to eat.
5. The new school will almost surely be ready by fall.
6. The new law has been poorly enforced.
7. Do you and your brother have enough blankets?
8. The freighter had apparently run aground in the fog.

9. The park benches had been freshly painted.
10. The swimmers were obviously nearing exhaustion.
11. The fog was now rapidly lifting from the field.
12. No one has ever returned from that desert.
13. The flaws can easily be seen under a magnifying glass.
14. Have you really been trying your hardest?
15. The oxygen supply in the submarine was slowly being exhausted.

Exercise B: Find each verb and tell whether it is an action verb or a linking verb.

1. Everyone sat quietly during the speech.
2. Alice smelled smoke in the cellar.
3. The study hall remained quiet for the rest of the hour.
4. The proposal for a student discount sounded good.
5. Suddenly, the twelve o'clock whistle sounded.
6. For two hours we lay under the boat.
7. Helen felt her way down the dark steps.
8. The coach seemed uneasy about something.
9. After the conference, we all felt better.
10. The boys left the building immediately after school.
11. We looked everywhere for the keys.
12. The influenza epidemic appeared without warning.
13. Stan looks unhappy.
14. The house appears empty.
15. On the way to Boston, the team seemed unusually quiet.

The Principal Parts

The principal parts of a verb are those from which all forms of the verb are made. They are (1) the *present infinitive* (usually called simply the *present*); (2) the *past*; and (3) the *past participle*.

A **regular verb** is one that forms its past and past participle by adding *-ed* or *-d* to the present.

PRESENT	PAST	PAST PARTICIPLE
talk	talk*ed*	talk*ed*
dazzle	dazzle*d*	dazzle*d*
arrive	arrive*d*	arrive*d*

An **irregular verb** is one that does not form its past and past participle by adding *-ed* or *-d* to the present. See Section 9.1 for usage of irregular verbs.

PRESENT	PAST	PAST PARTICIPLE
burst	burst	burst
sing	sang	sung
freeze	froze	frozen

The **present participle** of a verb is formed by adding *-ing* to the present form:

     come—coming   run—running   walk—walking

The Progressive Forms

The **progressive forms** of the verb are used to show on-going action. They are formed by using the forms of *be* with the present participle:

She *is running.*	Rob *has been sleeping.*
We *are going.*	The water *had been running.*
The cars *were stalling.*	We *must be going.*
Someone *will be arriving.*	They *might have been shouting.*

The Emphatic Forms

Special emphasis is given to a statement by using *do, does,* or *did* with the present form of the verb. These are examples of **emphatic forms.**

    I *did enjoy* your speech.
    We *do like* the new cottage.
    Horace *does seem* pleased.

Transitive and Intransitive Verbs

A **transitive verb** carries over the action from the subject to the object of the verb. An **intransitive verb** expresses an action that is complete in itself; it does not carry action over to an object.

TRANSITIVE	INTRANSITIVE
Mark *completed* the **application.**	Mr. Jones *died.*
My neighbor *raises* **avocados.**	The motor *sputtered.*
José *entered* the **subway.**	The doctor finally *came.*
Maria *bought* the **scarf.**	The plan *succeeded.*

Many verbs may be transitive in one sentence and intransitive in another.

INTRANSITIVE	TRANSITIVE
Everyone *applauded.*	Everyone *applauded* **John Denver.**
Are you *selling?*	*Are* you *selling* your **home?**
Mr. Berra *called.*	Mr. Berra *called* the **lawyer.**

The Active and Passive Voice

When the subject performs the action expressed in the verb, the verb is in the **active voice.** When the subject receives the action of the verb, the verb is in the **passive voice.** The passive voice is formed by using some form of *be* with the past participle of the verb.

ACTIVE: Jeanne *threw* the *ball* out-of-bounds.
PASSIVE: The ball *was thrown* out-of-bounds.

ACTIVE: Fritz *is carving* the *turkey.*
PASSIVE: The turkey *is being carved* by Fritz.

A transitive verb can be put into the passive voice because it has an object that receives the action of the verb. The object of the active verb becomes the subject in the passive form.

In a sentence containing an intransitive verb, there is no word that receives the action of the verb. For this reason no intransitive verb can be put into the passive voice.

Arthur Miller *wrote* the introduction. (active)
The introduction *was written* by Arthur Miller. (passive)
Tracy Childs, the secretary, *read* the minutes. (active)
The minutes *were read* by Tracy Childs, the
    secretary. (passive)

Exercise A: Find the verb and tell whether it is active or passive.

1. The lights had been turned down.
2. We have been invited to the symphony concert.
3. My sister has already picked a career.
4. The next batter was hit by a pitched ball.
5. Many New York school children do not understand English.
6. Several of the games were played at night.
7. A new school will be constructed here.
8. The speaker told of her adventures in Africa.
9. More than 100 elements have been discovered.
10. Jack has bought a new book about sports cars.

Exercise B: Change the active verbs to passive and the passive verbs to active.

1. The class president introduced the speaker.
2. Only Woodbridge has equaled our record.
3. The freshman class decorated the gym.
4. The influenza shots were given by the school doctor.
5. The game was ruined by the rain.
6. The officer warned Pat to drive more slowly.
7. A flat tire delayed the team bus.
8. The citrus fruit was destroyed by frost.

Exercise C: Find the verbs. Tell whether they are transitive or intransitive.

1. The band uniforms finally arrived just before Christmas.

2. The trainer stepped into the cage of the wounded leopard.

3. The sophomore class has a very good attendance record.

4. Greg walked unsteadily to the front of the stage and swallowed hard.

5. The author tells of his childhood on a Wyoming ranch.

6. Our team played over its head in the first half.

7. Once a circus horse literally stuck his right hind foot into his mouth.

8. Helen enjoys responsibility.

9. The murderer does not appear until the second act.

10. All cars have safety belts as standard equipment.

Exercise D: Find the verbs. Decide whether they are progressive or emphatic forms.

1. What has Karen been doing this summer?

2. The punishment does seem a bit severe.

3. Has anyone been doing anything about decorations for the party?

4. Astronomers do not really know if there is life on Mars.

5. We are now exploring new energy sources.

6. The principal did not approve the student council's plan.

7. Many scientists have been working on a cure for cancer.

8. We have been hoping for a new school for years.

Tense

Most verbs change their forms to tell present, past, and future time. **Tense** means "time." There are three simple tenses and three perfect tenses for each verb. They are formed as follows:

1. **Present tense.** The present tense is formed from the present or simple form of the verb.

The present forms of verbs usually tell of something that exists at the present moment.

> The mailman *is* at the door. (right now)
> The jacket *feels* too tight. (at this moment)

The simple or present forms of verbs, however, are not always used to tell of actions that are going on at the moment. We do not say, "I read." We are more likely to use the **progressive form** "I am reading" or the **emphatic form** "I do read." An exception is the use of the present to describe on-going sports events:

> Madlock *slides* and Bench *tags* him out.

The present forms of verbs are used to tell of repeated or regular and habitual action.

> We *go* to band practice on Thursday evenings.
> The factory *closes* at five o'clock.

The present forms of verbs are also used to tell of something that is generally true at all times.

> All politicians *need* a base of power.
> The sun *rises* in the east.
> Dr. Joyce Brothers *writes* about human behavior.

The **historical present tense** is used to tell of some action or condition in the past as though it were occurring in the present:

> The captain *orders*, "Abandon ship!" as the great vessel *lists* dangerously to starboard, its decks ablaze.

2. **Past tense.** Past time is usually told by the past tense, which is the second principal part of the verb: We *talked, they ran, nobody stirred.* Continuing past action is shown by the **past progressive:** We *were having* a good time.

3. **Future tense.** Future time is shown by using *shall* or *will* with the present form of the verb: We *shall arrive, you will hear, I will listen.*

Future time may be shown by the present tense together with an adverb or phrase that tells time. Future time may also be shown by the use of a form of *be* with *going to* or *about to.*

> We *get* the grades *tomorrow.* (*tomorrow* is an adverb telling time.)
> I *am going to* resign in January.

The bull *is about to* enter the ring.

The planes *are grounded until further notice.* (*until further notice* is an adverb phrase telling time.)

4. **Present perfect tense.** The present perfect tense is formed by using *has* or *have* with the past participle (third principal part) of the verb. This tense is used to refer to some indefinite time in the past.

The mayor *has promised* his support.

I *have* often *written* letters to the editor.

The present perfect is also used to show action that began in the past and continues into the present.

We *have worked* here for ten years. (We still work here.)

We *have been debating* long enough. (present perfect progressive)

5. **Past perfect tense.** The past perfect tense is formed by using *had* with the past participle (third principal part) of the verb. The past perfect tense tells of an action completed in the past before some other action.

EARLIER	LATER
We *had finished* the harvesting	before the storm *broke.*
George *had been* pessimistic	until the acceptance notice *came.*
We *had been waiting* an hour	before the President *arrived.*

6. **Future perfect tense.** The future perfect tense is formed by using *will have* or *shall have* with the past participle of the verb (third principal part). This tense is used to tell of one time completed in the future *before* some other time in the future.

Before the season *ends,* the Mets *will have won* eighty games.

When the campaign *is* over, he *will have made* 150 speeches.

Note: The first verb in the present tense indicates far future action. The second verb indicates future action *before* the action of the first verb.

Conjugation of *Save*

Conjugation is a presentation of the various forms of a verb. Usually, verbs are conjugated in the order shown here:

Principal Parts: save, saved, saved   **Present Participle:** saving
Present Infinitive: to save   **Perfect Infinitive:** to have saved

Present Tense

FIRST PERSON:	I save	we save
SECOND PERSON:	you save	you save
THIRD PERSON:	he, she, it saves	they save

PRESENT PROGRESSIVE: I am saving, you are saving, etc.
PRESENT EMPHATIC: I do save, you do save, he does save, etc.

Past Tense

FIRST PERSON:	I saved	we saved
SECOND PERSON:	you saved	you saved
THIRD PERSON:	he, she, it saved	they saved

PAST PROGRESSIVE: I was saving, you were saving, etc.
PAST EMPHATIC: I did save, you did save, etc.

Future Tense

FIRST PERSON:	I shall (will) save	we shall (will) save
SECOND PERSON:	you will save	you will save
THIRD PERSON:	he, she, it will save	they will save

FUTURE PROGRESSIVE: I shall be saving, you will be saving, etc.

Present Perfect Tense

FIRST PERSON:	I have saved	we have saved
SECOND PERSON:	you have saved	you have saved
THIRD PERSON:	he, she, it has saved	they have saved

PRESENT PERFECT PROGRESSIVE: I have been saving, you have been saving, he has been saving, etc.

Past Perfect Tense

FIRST PERSON: I had saved   we had saved
SECOND PERSON: you had saved   you had saved
THIRD PERSON: he, she, it had saved   they had saved

PAST PERFECT PROGRESSIVE: I had been saving, you had been saving, he had been saving, etc.

Future Perfect Tense

FIRST PERSON: I shall have saved   we shall have saved
SECOND PERSON: you will have saved   you will have saved
THIRD PERSON: he, she, it will have saved they will have saved

FUTURE PERFECT PROGRESSIVE: I shall have been saving, etc.

Exercise: Find each verb and tell its tense.

1. We do not know the answer.
2. The workers handled the explosives carefully.
3. Mary always seems restless.
4. At the side of the road stood two state police cars.
5. The crew of the *Mary Jane* had vanished.
6. Will the new offices have air-conditioning?
7. Amateur rock-collectors are finding many valuable gems.
8. By 1980, the world population will have grown to nearly four billion.
9. The car had been behaving oddly on hills.
10. There have been lighthouses on our coasts since 1716.
11. Sue had lived in Duluth as a child.
12. The President now serves only two terms.

13. By eight o'clock tomorrow morning, the rocket will have passed the moon.
14. The band was playing as we entered the hall.
15. The Chicago Symphony returned yesterday from Europe where it had played to enthusiastic audiences.

Mood

The mood of a verb shows the writer's attitude about the actuality of a happening. The **indicative mood,** which we use most of the time, indicates that we are talking or writing about a fact. That is, we are speaking of something that has happened, is happening, or definitely will happen.

The **subjunctive mood** is used to express only wishes, commands, and conditions that are doubtful or contrary to fact. The forms of the subjunctive mood are like those of the present tense of the indicative mood, except in the third person where the *s* ending is omitted.

INDICATIVE: He *uses* safety belts—even for short drives.
SUBJUNCTIVE: We asked that he *use* safety belts—even for short drives.
SUBJUNCTIVE: He asked that we *use* safety belts—even for short drives.

The subjunctive form of the verb *be* is a special case. With this verb, the form in the present tense for all persons and numbers is *be.*

Mary asked that the order *be* cancelled.
Phil moved that the amendment *be* accepted.

The past subjunctive form of the verb *to be* is *were.*

If I *were* President, I would limit spending.
I wish I *were* going to Europe this summer.
If I *were* you, I would study harder.

The **imperative mood** is used to express a command, a directive, or a request. The imperative mood has only one tense—the present—and only one person—the second.

> *Take* your sister with you.   Please *call* me.
> *Find* all your errors.   *Be* quick.

1.4 The Adjective

To express our point of view fully or to make our meaning clear and definite, we do not rely on nouns and verbs alone. We use other kinds of words to describe or limit or qualify the meaning. We call these words modifiers.

An adjective is a word that modifies a noun or pronoun.

Adjectives are used to tell *which one, what kind, how many,* or *how much* about nouns and pronouns.

> WHICH ONE: this, that, these, those
> WHAT KIND: large, sweet, dull, beautiful
> HOW MANY: some, all, several, six, seven
> HOW MUCH: little, much, plentiful

The Articles

The word *the* is called a **definite article** because it is usually, though not always, used to refer to a definite or specific thing or person.

The words *a* and *an* are called **indefinite articles** because they refer to no particular thing or person. A is used before words beginning with consonant sounds. *An* is used before words beginning with vowel sounds. The sound, not the spelling, makes the difference.

> They went to *an* auction every Saturday.
> It was *a* historic meeting.
> The bus was *an* hour late.
> It was *a* heated argument.

Proper Adjectives

A **proper adjective** is one formed from a proper noun. The proper adjective is always capitalized.

NOUN	ADJECTIVE	NOUN	ADJECTIVE
Ireland	Irish	East	Eastern
France	French	Shakespeare	Shakespearean
Canada	Canadian	India	Indian
Australia	Australian	Democrat	Democratic

Predicate Adjectives

An adjective is frequently separated from the noun or pronoun it modifies by a linking verb.

Karen seems *sleepy*. (separated)
We were *exhausted*. (separated)

An adjective in the predicate that modifies the subject is a predicate adjective.

Exercise: Find each adjective and tell which word it modifies. Ignore the articles.

1. The old house had been empty for several years.
2. The second team played during the last quarter.
3. The new coach seems determined and competent.
4. The old elephant was suffering from a bad toothache.
5. The enormous jet cannot land at a small airport.
6. A magnetic field surrounds the entire earth.
7. The new atomic submarines are spacious and comfortable.
8. The water in this lake tastes salty.
9. Many young Americans are making important scientific discoveries.
10. The two men in the other car seemed angry.
11. Most European students can speak the English language.
12. This little book contains some big ideas.
13. A cold wind drove the deep snow into huge drifts.

14. Some small economy cars are neither small nor economical.
15. This new arrangement will be better for all of us.

Adjectives in Comparisons

Persons and things are compared as to various qualities. The comparison is made by use of two different forms of adjectives. The **comparative** form of the adjective is formed in two ways:

1. All adjectives of one syllable and a few adjectives with two syllables add -er.

warm—warmer   loose—looser   funny—funnier

2. Most adjectives with two syllables and all adjectives with more than two syllables use *more* to form the comparative.

mature—more mature   optimistic—more optimistic
careful—more careful   ambitious—more ambitious

The **superlative** form of the adjective is formed by adding -est or by using *most*. Adjectives that form the comparative with -er form the superlative with -est. Those that form the comparative with *more* form the superlative with *most*.

COMPARATIVE	SUPERLATIVE
warmer	warmest
funnier	funniest
more mature	most mature
more ambitious	most ambitious

Irregular Comparisons

We form the comparative and superlative of some adjectives by changing the words themselves.

	COMPARATIVE	SUPERLATIVE
good	better	best
well	better	best

bad	worse	worst
ill	worse	worst
little	less *or* lesser	least
much	more	most
many	more	most
far	farther *or* further	farthest *or* furthest

Exercise: Find the adjectives and tell whether they are in comparative form or superlative form.

1. We gave our best performance on Friday.
2. Tokyo is now bigger than New York.
3. The pen is mightier than the sword.
4. The zebra is the most vicious of the animals in the zoo.
5. Jack was the most unhappy boy on the team.
6. Fruit is more plentiful than ever before.
7. Which is harder, calculus or algebra?
8. Where can I find a larger dictionary?
9. That was the worst mistake I ever made.
10. The largest crowds in history witnessed the World Series.

1.5 The Adverb

Nouns and pronouns are modified by adjectives. Other parts of speech are modified by adverbs.

An adverb modifies a verb, an adjective, or another adverb.

MODIFYING A VERB: Barnes answered *angrily*.
MODIFYING AN ADJECTIVE: It was a *most* enjoyable trip.
MODIFYING AN ADVERB: They moved *rather* cautiously.

Adverbs tell *where, when, how,* or *to what extent:*

WHERE: The family is *inside*.
WHEN: I'll bring you the present *soon*.
HOW: The storm struck *swiftly*.
TO WHAT EXTENT: He did not *fully* understand the question.

Many adverbs are formed by adding -*ly* to an adjective: *cautious—cautiously, quick—quickly, soft—softly, wise—wisely*. However, not all modifiers ending in -*ly* are adverbs. The following, for example, are adjectives: *lively, homely, friendly, lovely, kindly*.

Some words may be either adjectives or adverbs.

ADJECTIVE	ADVERB
a *fast* game	Run *fast*.
a *slow* trot	Drive *slow*.
a *high* building	The bird flew *high*.

Many adverbs do not end in -*ly*. The negatives *no, not,* and *never* are almost always adverbs. Many time-words, such as *now, ever, almost, soon,* are always adverbs.

Directive Adverbs

Adverbs that tell *where* (place or direction) about the verb are called **directive adverbs.** They normally follow the verb they modify.

We searched *near* and *far*.	The sign fell *down*.
They are waiting *outside*.	The conductor walked *in*.

Many of these directive adverbs are combined with verbs to make idioms: *give out, give up, give in, give off*. An idiom is a group of words with a meaning different from the literal meanings of the words taken individually.

Position of Adverbs

A directive adverb normally follows the verb it modifies. An adverb modifying an adjective or another adverb usually comes immediately before the word it modifies. Other adverbs may be shifted from one place in the sentence to another.

DIRECTIVE:	The elevator went *up*.
ADVERB MODIFYING MODIFIER:	It was a *very* common name.
OTHER ADVERBS:	*Suddenly*, he turned and ran.
	He *suddenly* turned and ran.

Adverbs in Comparisons

Like adjectives, adverbs are used in comparisons. The comparative and the superlative are formed as follows:

1. Adverbs of one syllable add *-er*.

> The sun shone *brighter* yesterday.
> The assignment took *longer* than usual.

2. Most adverbs ending in *-ly* form the comparative with *more*.

> The second round of talks ended *more fruitfully*.
> I walked into the baby's room *more quietly*.

3. The superlative form of the adverb is formed with *-est* or *most*. Adverbs that form the comparative with *-er* form the superlative with *-est*. Those that use *more* for the comparative use *most* for the superlative.

COMPARATIVE	SUPERLATIVE
brighter	brightest
longer	longest
more fruitfully	most fruitfully
more quietly	most quietly

Note: See Section 1.4 for irregular comparisons of adjectives. Some of the words listed there as adjectives may also be used as adverbs and are compared in the same way.

Exercise A: Find each adverb and tell which word or words it modifies.

1. The bus almost always arrives late.
2. The entire class worked hard and successfully on the project.

3. The car usually starts easily on cold mornings.
4. The streets have become rather crowded recently.
5. The auditorium was soon completely filled.
6. The heart of nearly every large city is deteriorating.
7. The doctor gave orders quietly and confidently.
8. Polio is sometimes rather difficult to diagnose.
9. Lately, the summers have been extremely hot.
10. There goes Dr. Harrison now.

Exercise B: Find the adverbs and list the word or words they modify.

1. The doctor approached the sick tiger carefully.
2. Carlotta wrote for the tickets yesterday.
3. By noon the boys had almost finished the signs.
4. The plane's fuel supply was now nearly exhausted.
5. David raised his hand eagerly.
6. We had often explored the cave before.
7. Geologists have recently discovered oil below the Sahara.
8. The football field was almost completely flooded.
9. On Sunday, Helen's condition suddenly became worse.
10. Come in quietly and leave your boots outside.

1.6 The Preposition

The words in an English sentence do not occur in haphazard order. They are arranged in precise patterns in order to convey meaning. The words that go together are joined or linked in a variety of ways. One means of linking words is the **preposition.**

There are seventeen one-syllable prepositions in English.* They are used to show the following relationships.

LOCATION: at, by, in, on, near
DIRECTION: to, from, down, off, through, out, past, up
ASSOCIATION: of, for, with, like

* The word *but* may be used as a preposition with the meaning of *except*.

There are also certain two-syllable prepositions.

about	along	below	during
above	among	beneath	except
across	around	beside	inside
after	before	between	outside
against	behind	beyond	over
			under

A number of prepositions have been formed by combining some of the one-syllable prepositions:

into	upon	without
onto	within	throughout

Compound prepositions have been formed by combining a modifier with a preposition or by grouping prepositions, as follows:

according to	out of	on account of	aside from
prior to	owing to	instead of	by means of
in front of	subsequent to	because of	as to

Objects of Prepositions. A preposition never appears alone. It is always used with a word or group of words that are called its **object.**

A preposition relates its object to some other word in the sentence.

The object of a preposition usually follows the preposition. The only exception occurs in a sentence or clause introduced by an interrogative pronoun or a relative pronoun.

The President walked briskly *into* the *hall.*
The President walked briskly *from* the *hall.*
Whom did you write the letter *to?*
The police did not know *whom* the shot was meant *for.*
Whose party did you go *to?*

The object of a preposition may be a single word or a group of words.

WORD: The box fell behind the *refrigerator*.
WORD: The fox dashed over the *hills*.
WORD: In *writing*, clarity is prized.

WORD GROUP: After *leaving school*, Chet joined the Navy.
WORD GROUP: Before *signing the contract*, read it carefully.
WORD GROUP: Give the package to *whoever answers the door*.

Exercise: Find the prepositions and their objects.

1. The truck was stopped at the border and searched for arms.
2. During the centuries, the continents have been drifting apart.
3. Booth jumped to the stage and screamed at the astonished audience.
4. For many years, there has been bad feeling between the two towns.
5. After the game, the crowd rushed for the goal posts.
6. According to the morning paper, there will be no school on Friday.
7. Everyone but John had seen the car approaching.
8. Beyond the city limits there is no rule against fireworks.
9. All but one of the trees died during the winter.
10. To whom is the announcement addressed?
11. Karen felt better after talking with the coach.
12. Apart from the cost, there is no objection to the proposal.

1.7 The Conjunction

Another kind of word used to tie the parts of a sentence together is a conjunction.

A conjunction is a word which connects words, phrases or clauses.

There are three kinds of conjunctions: coordinating conjunctions, correlative conjunctions, and subordinating conjunctions.

Coordinating Conjunctions

There are three conjunctions used only to connect like sentence parts. They are called **coordinating conjunctions** because they tie together things of the same kind or order. These coordinating conjunctions are *and, but,* and *or.*

The roads were covered with snow *and* sleet.
(connects nouns)
The train was fast *and* comfortable. (connects adjectives)
The traffic moved slowly *but* steadily. (connects adverbs)
The rocket shot off the pad *and* into the air.
(connects prepositional phrases)
We could take a walk *or* go for a swim. (connects predicates)
The weather report said "rain," *but* the sun is shining brightly.
(connects clauses)

For is used as a coordinating conjunction only between clauses. *Nor* is used as a coordinating conjunction only when it is preceded by another negative word.

The Senator ended her *speech, for* it was clear the
bill would pass.
The migrant workers have *no* organization, *nor* do they
have leaders.
Betty did *not* have her skis, *nor* did she have her skates.

Correlative Conjunctions

A few conjunctions are used in pairs: *not only . . . but (also); either . . . or; neither . . . nor; both . . . and; whether . . . or.* Such conjunctions are called **correlative conjunctions.**

Some cats are *not only* independent *but* aloof.
Both Tim *and* his brother made the team.
Neither the mayor *nor* his aide would comment on the report.
We must decide *whether* to stand firm *or* compromise.

Subordinating Conjunctions

Words used to introduce adverb clauses are called **subordinating conjunctions.** These words not only introduce the subordinate clause but link it to the main clause. Their chief function is to make clear exactly what is the relation between the two clauses. The chief relations they show are *time, place, cause, result, exception, condition,* and *alternative.* The most common subordinating conjunctions are these:

after	as though	provided	till	whenever
although	because	since	unless	where
as	before	so that	until	wherever
as if	if	than	whatever	while
as long as	in order that	though	when	

Conjunctive Adverbs

Certain adverbs are used to join main clauses. When so used, they are called **conjunctive adverbs.** A conjunctive adverb is preceded by a semicolon and followed by a comma. The most common conjunctive adverbs are these:

accordingly	hence	nevertheless	therefore
consequently	however	otherwise	yet
furthermore	moreover	also	

Exercise A: Find the conjunctions and conjunctive adverbs. Tell what kind each joining word is.

1. Neither the speeches nor the music was very exciting.
2. Both the Japanese and the Italian delegates opposed the investigation.
3. The search party worked quickly and carefully.
4. We must either sell more subscriptions or give up the paper.
5. The policeman beckoned us forward, but we could not move.
6. Although the odds were against him, Washington drove forward.

7. We were not at home when the package arrived.

8. The evidence sounded convincing; nonetheless, we believed Northrop innocent.

9. The dictionary is a valuable tool; however, not all dictionaries agree.

10. When the planes flew over, the sub was lying silently 300 feet down.

11. Think of us whenever you play the record.

12. We must leave at once; otherwise, we will be late.

13. You may have the car, provided you pay for the gas.

14. The outfielders wear glasses so that the sun won't blind them.

15. Wave after wave engulfed the tower, but the light kept on shining.

Exercise B: Find the conjunctions in the following sentences. Tell what kind of words or word groups they join.

1. The test was difficult but fair.

2. We wanted to watch the game, but our television set was broken.

3. John Adams and Thomas Jefferson died on the same day in 1825.

4. Germanium is a rare but useful metal.

5. The burglars went down the alley, into the basement, and up the stairs.

6. The women and children were the first into the lifeboats.

7. Sophomores may take either biology or general science.

8. You will enjoy both *Old Yeller* and *The Home Place* by Gipson.

1.8 The Interjection

An interjection is a word or group of words interjected, or thrown, into the sentence. It is usually followed by an exclamation point.

An interjection is a word or word group used to express surprise or other emotion. It has no grammatical relation to other words in the sentence.

Ouch! Oh! Ah! For heaven's sakes! Hurrah! Great! Congratulations!

1.9 Words Used in Different Ways

Some words, such as *is, believe, see,* are always verbs. The personal pronouns *I, me,* etc., are always personal pronouns. Many words, however, may be used in sentences in different ways.

> He would never forget the great Chicago *Fire.* (noun)
> Among the chief duties of a ranger is *fire* patrol. (adjective)
> The alumni wanted to *fire* the coach. (verb)
> The howling dogs came *near.* (adverb)
> He asked to be seated *near* Alice. (preposition)

Noun or Adjective?

A word used to name a person, place, or thing is a noun. The same word may be used before another noun to tell "what kind." When so used, it is an adjective.

> *Jazz* has come of age in America's concert halls. (noun)
> Would you call Billie Holiday a *jazz* singer? (adjective)
> *Plastic* is now used in making most toys. (noun)
> They bought their daughter a *plastic* swimming
>   pool. (adjective)

Adjective or Pronoun?

A demonstrative pronoun—*this, that, these,* and *those*—may also be used as an adjective. If the word is used alone in place of a noun, it is a pronoun. If used before a noun to tell "which one," it is an adjective.

> *This* is my Uncle Jim. (pronoun)
> *These* are Ted's gloves. (pronoun)
> *That* composition is excellent. (adjective
>   modifying *composition*)
> *Those* hamburgers are really good. (adjective
>   modifying *hamburgers*)

In a similar way the words *what, which,* and *whose* may be used alone as pronouns or before nouns as adjectives.

> *What* should I say? (pronoun)
> *What* street is this? (adjective modifying *street*)
> *Which* is your painting? (pronoun)
> *Which* train do I take? (adjective modifying *train*)
> *Whose* can it be? (pronoun)
> *Whose* plan was accepted? (adjective modifying *plan*)

The words *your, my, our, his, her, their* are forms of the personal pronouns used to show possession. Used in this way, they perform the job of adjectives. The words *mine, yours, hers, ours* and *theirs* are always pronouns. The word *his* may be used either as a pronoun or an adjective. See Section 1.2.

> The yellow slicker is *hers*. (pronoun)
> The new Volkswagen is *his*. (pronoun)
> That is *his* Uncle Charlie. (adjective use)

Adjective or Adverb?

Several words have the same form whether used as adjectives or adverbs. To tell whether a word is used as an adjective or as an adverb, determine what other word in the sentence it goes with, or modifies. This is a matter of sense, which you can get from the meaning. If it modifies a verb, it is used as an adverb. If it modifies a noun or pronoun, it is used as an adjective. If it tells *how, when, where,* or *how much,* it is an adverb. If it tells *what kind,* it is an adjective.

The plane flew *low*. (adverb telling *where* about *flew*)
The song ended on a *low* note. (adjective telling *what kind* about *note*)

Adverb or Preposition?

A number of words may be used either as prepositions or as adverbs. If the word is followed by a noun or pronoun, it is probably a preposition. The noun or pronoun is its object. If the word in question is not followed by a noun or pronoun, it is probably an adverb. If the word can be moved to another position, it is an adverb.

Sue threw *out* her old bathing suit.
Sue threw her old bathing suit *out*.
    (In both sentences *out* is an adverb. It can be moved without changing the meaning.)
The parakeet flew *out* the window.
    (*out* cannot be moved; it is a preposition.)
The sundial had been knocked *down*. (adverb)
Will you all please stand *up*? (adverb)
Whom are you searching *for*? (*Whom* is object of the preposition *for*.)

Exercise A: Determine how the italicized word is used in each sentence.

1. A special plane stood waiting *for* the President.
2. It was difficult to make a decision, *for* there were too few facts.
3. We started out with our packs full of food, cooking utensils, clothes, chocolate bars—everything *but* soap.
4. We telephoned on Saturday morning, *but* the office was closed.
5. *After* his accident, Harry drove with great caution.
6. *After* the doors had been closed, the judge rose to speak.
7. Are *these* your books?

8. *These* lucky discoveries have greatly benefited mankind.
9. *What* college does your brother attend?
10. *What* are you going to read for your report?
11. The clock is *slow*; it always runs *slow*.
12. The *brick* wall was crumbling.
13. Please take the dog *outside*.
14. *Inside* the house, everything was in disorder.
15. We stood on the balcony watching the sun go *down*.

Exercise B: Determine how the italicized word is used in each sentence.

1. The *pull* of sun and moon on the earth creates tides.
2. *Which* is the problem that bothered you?
3. The wind blew *hard* all night long.
4. At the North Pole, the sea is very *deep*.
5. The scientists are boring *deep* into the earth's crust.
6. There will be no *afternoon* games next year.
7. The sun came out late in the *afternoon*.
8. My uncle has a very *fast* boat.
9. Unfortunately, he cannot run the boat *fast* on the narrow river.
10. *This* paper is easy to read; *that* is not.
11. The fireplace was made of *brick*.
12. The *brick* wall was crumbling.
13. The builder tore into the windows and *bricked* up the opening.
14. The opossum was hanging head down from a lower *branch*.
15. Before long, Edison's new company *branched* out into new fields.

1.10   Verbals

There are a number of highly useful words in English that are difficult to classify. These are **infinitives, participles,** and **gerunds.** They are called verbals because all of them are formed from verbs. Like verbs they may all be completed by objects or predicate words. Like verbs they may all be modified by adverbs.

1.11 The Infinitive

Usually, but not always, the infinitive is preceded by *to*, which is called the "sign of the infinitive." The kinds of infinitives are as follows:

ACTIVE PRESENT: to honor
PASSIVE PRESENT: to be honored
ACTIVE PERFECT: to have honored
PASSIVE PERFECT: to have been honored

The infinitive may appear without the word *to:*

No one saw Fred *leave*.
She did not dare *call* her dentist.

The infinitive may be used as a noun. It may be subject or object of the verb, a predicate noun, or an appositive.

To win was not the only reason for playing the game.
  (subject of *was*)
My little brother always wants *to argue*. (object of *wants*)
Sherry's ambition is *to act*. (predicate noun)
The mayor's proposal, *to cut* the budget, was
  rejected. (appositive)

The infinitive may also be used as a modifier. Used as an adjective, it may modify nouns and pronouns.

Cape Cod is the place *to see*.
The Dodgers are the team *to beat*.

As an adverb, the infinitive may modify adverbs, adjectives, or verbs.

The suit was easy *to clean*. (modifying the adjective *easy*)
Bob came too early *to see her*. (*to see her* modifies the
  adverb *early*)
They went *to see* Macbeth. (modifying the verb *went*)

The Infinitive Phrase. An infinitive itself may have modifiers. It may also have a subject, an object, or a predicate word. An **infinitive phrase** consists of the infinitive together with its modifiers, its subject, object, or predicate word.

The infinitive may be modified by adverbs, phrases, or clauses. These modifiers are part of the infinitive phrase.

> To *speak* confidently requires poise.
> (*confidently* modifies *To speak*.)
> To *survive* in the nuclear age, we must disarm.
> (The phrase *in the nuclear age* modifies *To survive*.)
> The teacher said to *read* widely if I want to go to college.
> (The clause *if I want to go to college* modifies *to read*.)

The infinitive may have a direct object, an indirect object, or a predicate word. These words, completing the meaning of the infinitive, are part of the infinitive phrase.

> To *start* the *motor*, first turn on the ignition.
> (*motor* is the direct object of *To start*.)
> We voted *to offer him* the *nomination*.
> (*him* is the indirect object and *nomination* is the direct object of *to offer*.)
> Connie asked *to be team manager*.
> (*team manager* is a predicate noun after *to be*.)
> The solution to the problem ought *to be easy*.
> (*easy* is a predicate adjective after *to be*.)

The infinitive may have a subject. The subject always follows the main verb and comes directly before the infinitive. Since it follows the main verb and is in the objective case, it is sometimes mistaken for an object of the main verb. The subject of the infinitive is part of the infinitive phrase. In the following examples, the entire phrase is the direct object of the verb.

> The commander ordered *them to charge*.
> The editor urged *his readers to vote*.
> Andy asked *Phil to drive*.

Note: If the main verb is a linking verb (a form of *be, appear, seem*, etc.), the noun following it is a predicate noun. If a predicate noun is followed by an infinitive, the infinitive modifies the noun.

Sarah is the person to *ask*.   These are the sentences *to study*.

Exercise A: Find the complete infinitive phrase in each sentence.

1. The children are really trying to help.
2. The plan is to survey the bottom of the oceans.
3. Althea decided to accept the challenge.
4. I want to work on the problem slowly and carefully.
5. The giant radio antenna is designed to pick up sounds far out in space.
6. It was an honor to be invited to the dinner.
7. Everyone thinks he wants to be told the truth.
8. The last question was supposed to have had two parts.
9. We were glad to have been invited.
10. The lock appears to have been broken.
11. To gain admission to the Air Academy, you must be recommended.
12. The tourists asked to be given fuller directions.
13. The class voted to end the party at midnight.
14. We stayed up late to hear the election returns.
15. It takes patience, practice, and stamina to be a writer.

Exercise B: Find the complete infinitive phrase in each sentence.

1. We ought to leave now.
2. It would be a good idea to telephone home.
3. Your parents should be told that you are going to be late.
4. The propeller seems to be broken.
5. The cables appear to have been cut deliberately.
6. A raccoon always tries to wash its food.
7. Before taking action, we want to be sure of the facts.
8. The author of the play rose to take a bow.
9. To get a better view, Lucy stretched on her tiptoes.
10. It is better to be forewarned than to be surprised.

1.12 The Gerund

The gerund is a verbal noun that always ends in *-ing*. It is used in the sentence as a noun and in almost every way that a noun can be used.

> *Debating* is Fred's favorite school activity. (subject of the verb)
> Linda likes *skating* and *skiing*. (object of the verb)
> Before *writing*, be sure of your facts. (object of the preposition)

The Gerund Phrase. A gerund may be modified by adjectives or adverbs. It may be completed by objects or predicate words. A **gerund phrase** consists of the gerund together with its modifiers, objects, or predicate words.

The gerund may be modified by single adjectives and adverbs or by phrases and by clauses.

> *Proper lighting* is necessary for studying.
> (*Proper* is an adjective modifying *lighting*.)
> Hal likes *walking briskly*.
> (*briskly* is an adverb modifying *walking*.)
> *Playing without adequate practice* demoralizes a team.
> (*without adequate practice* is a phrase modifying *Playing*.)
> *Swimming after eating a meal* is dangerous.
> (*after eating a meal* is a phrase modifying *Swimming*.)

Gerunds may be completed by objects or predicate words. These words are part of the gerund phrase.

> *Being president* of the group is an honor.
> (*president* is a predicate noun completing *Being*.)
> *Giving Phil those books* changed his whole life.
> (*Phil* is the indirect object and *books* is the direct object of *Giving*.)

Exercise: Find the gerund or the complete gerund phrase in each of the following sentences.

1. Walking is not considered exercise by anyone under fifty.
2. Making a speech was torture for Thomas Jefferson.
3. Some people enjoy standing in line.
4. Quick thinking saved the ship from disaster.
5. Tom saved money by painting the house himself.
6. Before raking leaves, decide what you will do with them.
7. Making new friends is something you can learn.
8. Spending more than you earn is an easy way to anxiety.
9. By backing down the hill, Sue got the car started.
10. Before leaving the city, we took one more subway ride.
11. Studying is a lot like boxing; you have to be on your toes.
12. We cannot avoid making decisions.
13. Some people invite eavesdropping by talking too loud.
14. The constant dripping of water will erode the hardest of stones.
15. After waiting patiently for an hour, Bill left the office.

1.13   The Participle

There are several forms of the participle, all widely used.

PRESENT PARTICIPLE:	following
PAST PARTICIPLE:	followed
PERFECT PARTICIPLE:	having followed
PASSIVE PERFECT PARTICIPLE:	having been followed

The present participle always ends in *-ing*. The past participle is the third principal part of the verb, and its endings are various. (See Section 1.3.)

The participle is always used as an adjective to modify a noun or a pronoun. In the following examples, the arrow indicates the word modified by the participle.

Smiling, Laura accepted the award.

Elated, the class arrived in Washington.

Having been accepted, Arthur looked forward to college.

The Participial Phrase. A participle may be modified by single adverbs or by phrases and clauses. The participle may also be completed by objects or predicate words. A **participial phrase** consists of the participle together with its modifiers, objects, or predicate words.

When a participle is modified by an adverb, a phrase, or a clause, these modifiers are part of the participial phrase.

Mo͞ving closer, we could see the tiger's teeth.
(*closer* is an adverb modifying *Moving*.)

W͞alking in pairs, the elephants lumbered into the ring.
(*in pairs* is a phrase modifying *Walking*.)

When a participle is completed by objects or predicate words, these words are part of the participial phrase. In the examples below, the arrow indicates the word modified by the participial phrase.

Having passed the test, Bob heaved a sigh of relief.
(*test* is the direct object of *Having passed*.)

Chet bent over his physics book, looking perplexed.
(*Perplexed* is a predicate adjective completing *looking*.)

Giving the first mate the charts, the ship captain scanned the radar.
(*First mate* is the indirect object and *charts* is the direct object of *Giving*.)

Exercise: Find the complete participial phrase and show which word it modifies.

1. There was something moving in the shadows.
2. Running at great speed, Lee broke the one-mile record.
3. The runner, trying for a double, was out at second base.
4. Working fast, Julia remodeled the hat in a few hours.
5. Surrounded by enemy ships, Drake decided to force the fighting.

6. Early the next morning, the prospectors arrived in San Francisco, loaded with gold nuggets.

7. Having been defeated twice, Purdue could not win the championship.

8. Outdistancing her guard, Jane raced down the court, scoring easily.

9. With somber faces, the miners arrived at the surface, carrying their injured friend.

10. The little boat, careening wildly, drove right into the judges' launch.

11. The old cobbler, stricken with grief, remained in his shop for days.

12. Struck by a sudden thought, Sally turned back to her locker.

13. Having twice won the prize, Hal gained . permanent possession.

14. The boys ran out onto the field, determined to make a good showing.

15. The old sign, worn and battered by wind and rain, was almost illegible.

2.0   The Parts of a Sentence

Single words in English are used widely to convey meaning. The words *stop, danger, poison,* for example, express full meaning to the reader. In general, however, meaning is expressed in English by groups of words acting together: *in the morning, playing tight end, Laura laughed.*

These groups of words are neither spoken nor written in haphazard order. In the English sentence there are fixed patterns into which words are placed to express meaning. These patterns are learned in childhood. They are learned because they are the chief means by which the child can express his feelings and get what he wants.

A knowledge of what these sentence patterns are and of how they work is essential for effective use of language in adult life.

2.1   The Sentence

Sentences are used to make statements and to ask questions. To be understood, they must express a complete thought, a complete idea, or a complete question.

A group of words must express a complete thought or it is not a sentence. We begin the study of the sentence with a partial definition:

A sentence is a group of words that expresses a complete thought.

INCOMPLETE	The man in the white suit (What about him?)
COMPLETE	The man in the white suit sells ice cream.
INCOMPLETE	Howard Cosell, the ABC sports announcer (Does what?)
COMPLETE	Howard Cosell, the ABC sports announcer, uses colorful language.
INCOMPLETE	Crossing the road (Who did what?)
COMPLETE	Crossing the road, he helped the lady change her tire.

Exercise A: Which of the following groups of words are sentences?

1. Immediately recognizing the danger
2. Nobody panicked
3. Like most small boys on a roller-coaster
4. Waited for the rain to stop
5. Phil answering our call
6. Quito, Ecuador, practically on the equator
7. This is an entirely new approach
8. Some highlights of his career
9. His remarks influenced the campaign
10. An ice-skating rink in the park
11. The easiest way out
12. Quadraphonic sound at home in your living room
13. There is ample evidence to prove the statement
14. Changes will certainly have to be made
15. Over the bridge to the main highway

Exercise B: Which of the following groups of words are sentences?

1. Actually, he was not at all surprised
2. No clear-cut plan or ready-made formula
3. Never spoke to us or even noticed us
4. They scraped and painted the walls
5. Disappearing in the fog
6. Always asking questions
7. Still trying to discourage the plan

8. Too much emphasis was placed on the commercial
9. The change in population throughout the country
10. Coming to a sudden stop in the middle of the intersection
11. The traffic officer waved furiously
12. Coming into the brightly lighted entrance hall
13. Renowned for its excellent service and cuisine
14. There at the pier was the glamorous cruise ship
15. Instead, he dictated a sharp reprimand

2.2 Kinds of Sentences

Sentences may be classified as to structure* or as to the purpose of the speaker or writer. There are four principal purposes served by sentences, as described below.

1. The **declarative sentence** is used to make a statement. The statement may be one of fact, wish, intent, or feeling.

The Swedes and Norwegians are descendants of the Vikings.
I would like to be a nuclear physicist.

2. The **imperative sentence** is used to state a command, request, or direction. The subject is always *You.* When the subject is not expressed, as is usually the case, it is understood to be *You.*

(You) Please turn off the light.
(You) Speak to the landlord tomorrow.
(You) Take your first right at the traffic light.

3. The **interrogative sentence** is used to ask a question. It is always followed by a question mark.

How much does it cost?
Who wrote *Gone with the Wind?*
What does "ecumenical" mean?

---

* For classification of sentences by form or structure, see Section 3.0.

4. An **exclamatory sentence** is used to express strong feeling. It is always followed by an exclamation point.

What a game it was!   How happy we were!

Exercise: What kind of sentence is each of the following?

1. Can anyone explain this problem?
2. Brasilia is the capital of Brazil.
3. Throw away those dirty old sneakers.
4. For a person of his age, he had a poverty-stricken vocabulary.
5. Please step aside and let the passengers off.
6. Oh, look at that magnificent rainbow!
7. What TV program shall I tune in?
8. Her remark was quite uncalled for.
9. What a day it was to go sailing!
10. Latin is far from being an extinct language.

2.3 Subject and Predicate

There are two parts in every complete sentence. (1) The **subject** is the person, thing, or idea about which something is said. (2) The **predicate** is the idea expressed about the subject.

Every sentence contains a subject and a predicate.
The subject of the sentence is the person or thing about which something is said.
The predicate tells something or asks something about the subject of the sentence.

The word *predicate* means "to proclaim, declare, preach, or affirm." The predicate of a sentence therefore "proclaims, declares, preaches, or affirms" something about the subject.

We may say that a sentence is a group of words that tells something (*predicate*) about a person or thing (*subject*). Our definition of a sentence may now be expanded:

A sentence is a group of words expressing a complete thought by means of a subject and a predicate.

SUBJECT	PREDICATE
Dogs	bark.
The dogs in the street	bark at passing fire engines.
Light	shines.
The light at Kennedy's grave	shines as a beacon of courage.

2.4 The Simple Predicate

In every predicate, however long, the most important word—the key word—is the **verb**.* In fact, the verb is the key word in the sentence. Sentences may be constructed without nouns, pronouns, or other parts of speech; but, without a verb, there can be no sentence.

The simple predicate of the sentence is the verb.

The verb may be a phrase consisting of more than one word: *have gone, might have gone, is running, had been running.* The words making up the verb may be interrupted by a modifier. Such a modifier is not part of the verb.

> *were* soon *found*   *had* just *left*
> *was* never *finished*   *had* almost *toppled*

The simple predicate, which we shall hereafter call the *verb*, may be compound. The word *compound* means "having more than one part of the same kind". The parts of a compound verb are joined together by a conjunction (*and, or, neither-nor*, etc.).

> She **sang** well *and* **danced** beautifully.
> The motor **sputtered, coughed,** *and* **stopped.**
> You **can** *either* **go** or **stay.**

---

* The **complete predicate** consists of the verb, its modifiers, and complements. The **complete subject** consists of the simple subject and its modifiers.

2.5 The Simple Subject

Every verb has a subject. It is the word or the words that answer *who?* or *what?* before the verb.

Harry called yesterday.	One of the ships sank.
Verb: called	*Verb*: sank
Who called?: Harry	*What sank?*: One
Subject: Harry	*Subject*: One

The **simple subject** is the subject of the verb.

The subject of the verb may be compound. The parts of a
compound subject are normally joined by a conjunction.

> The **brain** *and* **spinal cord** are parts of the central
> nervous system.
>
> A **quartet** by Haydn *and* a **quintet** by Mozart were played
> at the concert.
>
> *Either* **Sadowsky** *or* **Fisher** will start at quarterback.

Exercise: Find the verb and its subject.

1. The rocket orbits at an altitude of one thousand miles
and spins around the earth once every two hours.

2. Streams and rivers overflowed and flooded the valley.

3. All the club members stayed late and helped to decorate
the hall.

4. Imported pure silks and domestic cottons are on display
at Kessler's.

5. The old dog rose slowly, stretched, and then shook himself.

6. Oranges, grapes, and boxes of candy filled the attractive
bon voyage basket.

7. Neither she nor her friend showed up at our party.

8. At the noise, the pigeons took off and flew over into the trees.

9. He changed his seat twice, fidgeted, and then left the hall.

10. The chill and the dampness of the old house depressed us.

11. Either evaporated milk or cream may be used.

12. Unjust punishment and excessive flogging turned the
officers and crew against Captain Bligh.

2.6 Subjects in Unusual Positions

In most sentences the subject appears before the verb. This subject-verb order is the normal pattern of English sentences. In many sentences, however, this order is reversed.

Questions. In most questions the subject appears between the words making up the verb phrase.

VERB	SUBJECT	VERB
Did	you	ask?
Have	you	eaten?
Can	you	go?
Could	you	have gone?

In most questions beginning with interrogative words such as *where, when, why, how, how much,* the subject falls between the parts of the verb. In questions beginning with *who* or *what,* the verb may follow the subject in normal order:

Who shouted?   What fell?

Sentences Beginning *There* and *Here*. Many sentences begin with *There* or *Here* immediately followed by some form of *be: There is, There was, There will be, Here is, Here were,* and so on. In these sentences *Here* and *There* are introductory words used to get the sentence started. They are never the subject of the verb. In this kind of sentence, the subject follows the verb.

Here is a new idea. (*idea* is the subject.)
There were eight puppies in the litter. (*puppies* is the subject).
There will be a rehearsal Saturday. (*rehearsal* is the subject.)

Note: Not all sentences beginning with *Here* and *There* follow the above pattern: *Here we can pitch our tent. Here he comes. There he goes.* In these sentences, *Here* and *There* are adverbs modifying the verb.

Sentences in Inverted Order. For emphasis or for variety of style, the subject is sometimes placed after the verb.

> Standing next to President Carter was *Cyrus Vance*.
> On the top of the mountain was a lookout *post*.
> Onto the runway roared the sleek *jet*.

Finding the Subject of the Verb. To find the subject of the verb in any sentence, find the verb first. Then ask *who?* or *what?* before it. If the sentence is not in normal word order, change it to normal order, and the subject will become clear.

> INVERTED   From the cellar came a low whine.
> NORMAL   A low whine came from the cellar.

Exercise A: Find the verb and its subject.

1. From the top balcony came many "bravos."
2. How much money did you lose?
3. Could you have seen the show from the back row?
4. Here are the missing keys.
5. Over the treetops rose the full moon.
6. Along the hedge crept the cat.
7. There was not a house in sight.
8. Should I have telephoned so early?
9. There might have been a serious accident.
10. Through the tall grasses leaped the kangaroo.

Exercise B: Find the verb and its subject.

1. Out of the night came the hoot of an owl.
2. There on the wet grass lay my lost scarf.
3. At the end of the parade came the sanitation trucks.
4. Did you ever see such a huge crowd?
5. Have you never heard the cry of the loon?
6. Out of the fog came the warning sound of the bell buoy.
7. Where else can you enjoy such beautiful scenery?
8. There will be a fire drill tomorrow.
9. For every participant there was a prize.
10. When will your brother hear about his bar examination?

2.7 The Direct Object

In many sentences the action verb carries action over from the subject to some other word. It serves to tie these words together. The word to which the action is carried from the subject is the **direct object.**

Sometimes the direct object tells what receives the action of the verb. Sometimes it tells the result of the action.

RECEIVER OF THE ACTION	Frank baited the hook. (baited what?)
RESULT OF ACTION	Frank caught a fish. (caught what?)
RECEIVER OF ACTION	The lawyer took the case. (took what?)
RESULT OF ACTION	The lawyer won the case. (won what?)

Action verbs that carry over the action from subject to object are called **transitive verbs.** Action verbs that are not followed by direct objects are called **intransitive.** Some verbs may be transitive in one sentence and intransitive in another.

The fans *were cheering* Roger Staubach. (transitive)
The fans *were cheering.* (intransitive)

In some so-called action verbs, the action is not visible, nor otherwise evident. However, the verb does carry the thought from subject to object, tying them together.

Beth *has* high ideals. (has what?)
George *understands* Italian. (understands what?)
Ruth *wants* a snowmobile. (wants what?)

The direct object is a word or group of words to which the verb carries over the action from the subject.

The direct object may be a word, a phrase, or a clause.

They asked *to see her.* (phrase)
Terry enjoyed *going to clambakes.* (phrase)
I'll do *what you say.* (clause)

The direct object may be compound.

> I lost my *hat* and *coat*. (lost what?)
> They wanted to *swim* and *to play golf*. (wanted what?)

A word that completes the meaning of the verb is called a **complement.** The direct object is one kind of complement.

Direct Object or Adverb? To find the direct object, ask *what?* after the verb. A direct object tells *what* after the verb. An adverb following an action verb tells *how, when, where,* or *how much* about the verb.

> The dog loves the *postman.* (what)
> The ball traveled *far.* (where)
> The troops marched *triumphantly.* (how)

2.8 The Indirect Object

The indirect object of the verb tells to or for whom, or to or for what, something is done.

> We gave *Karen* the award. (*to* Karen)
> Joe made his *brother* a sandwich. (*for* his brother)

A verb has an indirect object only if it also has a direct object. Find the direct objects in the examples above.

The indirect object may be compound: I told *Jim* and *Bob* the truth.

The words *to* and *for* are never placed before the indirect object. When followed by a noun or pronoun, *to* and *for* are prepositions. The noun or pronoun following the preposition is its object.

> Alec gave *Lisa* a sweater. (*Lisa* is the indirect object.)
> Alec gave a sweater to *Lisa.* (*Lisa* is the object of
>   the preposition.)
> My grandmother made *me* a pie. (*me* is the indirect object.)
> My grandmother made a pie for *me.* (*me* is the object of
>   the preposition.)

Exercise: Find both the direct and indirect objects.

1. Jack sent Bob a card from Hawaii.
2. The principal gave the Student Council his advice.
3. The speaker told us his experiences in New Guinea.
4. The committee offered Ward the job.
5. The contract guarantees you a month of vacation.
6. A passing motorist offered the boys a lift.
7. The guide showed the visitors several of Jefferson's inventions.
8. Diana sends you her best wishes.
9. Navy planes brought the party badly needed supplies.
10. Dad wrote the mayor a letter of apology.
11. The President awarded the ship a unit citation.
12. The explorers bid the island a happy farewell.

2.9 Predicate Words

The linking verb links its subject to a word in the predicate. The word in the predicate, so linked, is called a **predicate word.** The subject may be linked to a **predicate noun,** a **predicate pronoun,** or a **predicate adjective.**

My favorite holiday is Christmas. (predicate noun)

The motor scooter is his. (predicate pronoun)

The quarterback felt confident. (predicate adjective)

A word that completes the meaning of a verb is called a **complement.** Predicate words complete the meaning of linking verbs, and since they refer to the subject, they are called **subject complements.**

Diagraming. The simple sentence with an action verb is diagramed as follows:

We sang.   We sang songs.

We	sang

We	sang	songs

We sang songs enthusiastically.

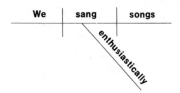

Note: The single-word modifier goes on a slant line below the word it modifies.

The simple sentence with a linking verb is diagramed as follows:

George seems well.   Mary is secretary.

Note: The line following the linking verb slants toward the subject.

The action verb with the indirect object is diagramed as follows:

My aunt sent me a sweater.

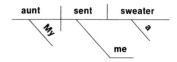

Exercise A: Find the predicate words.

1. This may be our last chance.
2. The new high school looks very modern.
3. Ann seems quite happy at college.
4. The stadium was nearly full of spectators.

5. Harry will probably be our next class president.
6. This is an unusual opportunity.
7. The demolished car was a depressing sight.
8. Bob's plans for the party sound exciting.
9. The captain of the ship is an old friend of ours.
10. Karen is clearly the best player on the team.

Exercise B: Make five columns. Head them *Subject, Verb, Direct Object, Indirect Object,* and *Predicate Word*. Place those parts of the following sentences in the proper columns.

1. The commander gave the men a stern warning.
2. We now have a permanent settlement at the South Pole.
3. Before we left, the guide showed us his collection of guns.
4. At the icy turn, four cars piled up in a single crash.
5. Jim read the directions carefully.
6. The new jets are sensitive to weather conditions.
7. Ghost towns appear all through the mining country.
8. In 1907 two men rowed a boat across the Atlantic.
9. In the first airplane race, one plane was chased by an eagle.
10. Dr. Johnson wrote an excuse for Bob.
11. The rebels appear confident of success.
12. The shop has made us a new table.
13. The leaders of the expedition are scientists and military officers.
14. New sources of power, new materials, and wonderful new machines will greatly change our physical lives in the next ten years.
15. In the last quarter, Deerfield scored two touchdowns and a field goal.

2.10   Compound Parts of Sentences

Subjects, objects, and verbs may all be compound. That is, they may consist of more than one part *of the same kind*. The parts are joined by a conjunction.

COMPOUND SUBJECT	*Time* and *Stereo Review* are Jerry's favorite magazines.
COMPOUND VERB	The plane *climbed* and *dived.*
COMPOUND DIRECT OBJECT	We want *air* and *sunlight.*
COMPOUND INDIRECT OBJECT	Pam gave *Joe* and *Bob* the directions.
COMPOUND OBJECT OF PREPOSITION	We drove steadily through the heavy *rain* and *sleet.*
COMPOUND PREDICATE WORD	We felt *warm* and *cozy.*
COMPOUND PREDICATE	The police *halted the bus* and *questioned all of the riders.*

Diagraming. Compound sentence parts are diagramed as follows:

Al and Sue (*compound subject*) sat and listened (*compound verb*)

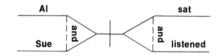

The teacher gave Louis and Josie (*compound indirect object*) the books and records (*compound direct object*).

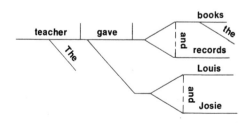

The speeches of the governor and the mayor (*compound object of the preposition*) were brief but informative (*compound predicate adjective*).

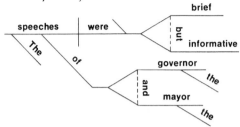

The critics praised the acting but disliked the play (*compound predicate*).

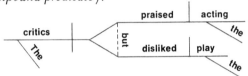

Exercise: Make five columns. Head them *Subject, Verb, Direct Object, Predicate Word,* and *Predicate.* Find the compound parts of the following sentences, and write these parts in the proper columns.

1. The plane struck the runway and bounced high in the air.
2. The airplane patrols and ground search parties sought the missing elephant for three weeks.
3. Judy sounds tired and unhappy.
4. Bernstein led the orchestra and also played the piano.
5. You will need your school record and letters of recommendation.
6. The uniforms were bright and colorful.
7. The passengers and the crew were bickering with each other.
8. Above the clouds, the sky was a brilliant blue and gold.
9. Fame and fortune are perishable.
10. The police arrived and looked around.

11. We want loyalty, sympathy, and patience from friends.
12. Tugs, fireboats, and ocean liners welcomed the gallant little ship.

2.11   The Phrase

A phrase is a group of words without a subject and a verb, used as one part of speech.

A phrase is used as one part of speech. A **verb phrase** is two or more words used as a verb: *could go, might have gone.* A **noun phrase** is two or more words used as a noun: *Pan American Highway, John Hancock Building.*

2.12   The Prepositional Phrase

The prepositional phrase consists of the preposition, its object, and modifiers of the object.

> *Behind the ramshackle red barn* was an old workhorse.
> The children ran *through the whirling lawn sprinkler.*

The object of a preposition is always a noun, a pronoun, or a group of words used as a noun.

> Esther went reluctantly *to* the concert. (*concert* is the object of *to.*)
> The dog went everywhere *with* him. (*him* is the object of *with.*)
> *After* calling the Coast Guard, we resumed the search. (*calling the Coast Guard* is a gerund phrase, used as a noun. It is the object of *After.*)
> Give the letter *to* whoever answers the door. (*whoever answers the door* is a noun clause, the object of *to.*)

The prepositional phrase is a modifier. It is used either as an adjective or as an adverb. A prepositional phrase that modifies a noun or pronoun is an **adjective phrase;** that is, it is a phrase used as an adjective.

> George is the student *with the most potential.* (*with the most potential* modifies the noun *student.*)

> The energy *of an atom* is tremendous. (*of an atom* modifies *energy.*)

> The treaty *between the two nations* was signed in Geneva. (*between the two nations* modifies *treaty.*)

An adjective phrase always comes immediately after the noun or pronoun it modifies.

A prepositional phrase that modifies a verb, an adjective, or an adverb is an **adverb phrase.** That is, it is a phrase used as an adverb to tell *how, how much, when,* or *where* about the word it modifies.

> Hank put the stereo speakers *on the bookcase.* (*on the bookcase* tells *where* about the verb *put.*)

> The movie was successful *beyond all expectations.* (*beyond all expectations* tells *how much* about the adjective *successful.*)

> The hunters rose early *in the morning.* (*in the morning* tells *when* about the adverb *early.*)

When two or more prepositional phrases follow each other in succession, they may modify the same word, or one phrase may modify the object in the preceding phrase.

> They arrived *at the airport on time.* (Both phrases modify *arrived; at the airport* tells *where* and *on time* tells *when* about the verb.)

> Cape Horn is *at the southernmost tip of South America.* (*at the southernmost tip* modifies *is; of South America* modifies *tip.* It tells *which* tip.

Diagraming. Prepositional phrases are diagramed as follows:

Eric painted a portrait *of the President.* (adjective phrase)

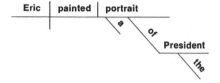

The guests left early *in the morning.* (adverb phrase)

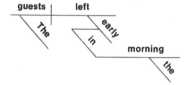

The key was stuck *in the door.* (adverb phrase)

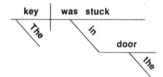

The stack *of books on the porch* got soaked.

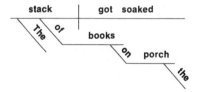

Exercise A: Write each prepositional phrase and the word or words it modifies.

1. In the late afternoon we had our first customer.
2. There was a spontaneous burst of applause.
3. John had once been lost on the Yukon River for three days.
4. The jewels had been hidden in a box of rubbish.
5. You can work at the museum after school.
6. The sudden illness of the leading lady forced a change in our plans.
7. For twenty years the man in the iron mask captured everyone's imagination.
8. Before a holiday, a feeling of excitement pervades the school.
9. A cloud of smoke appeared on the horizon.
10. For two hours Dale clung to the rock with his fingertips.

Exercise B: Write each prepositional phrase and the word or words it modifies.

1. Early in the morning we arrived at the lake.
2. There was a strange cry in the middle of the night.
3. The radio towers were visible for a distance of ten miles.
4. Below the North Pole, the sea has a depth of nearly three miles.
5. At the South Pole there is a solid mass of ice.
6. During the storm, the waves hurled heavy rocks onto the shore.
7. Ilona went shopping with her mother in the afternoon.
8. A crowd of angry people gathered outside the store.
9. Before the railroads, settlers traveled along the rivers.
10. For years the Pennsylvania Canal towed its boats over the mountains.

2.13   The Infinitive Phrase*

Usually the **infinitive phrase** begins with *to*. The phrase con-

* See also Section 1.11.

sists of *to*, the infinitive, its complements and its modifiers. If the infinitive has a subject, that is also part of the phrase.

> I tried *to write better.* (The infinitive phrase is the object of the verb *tried.*)

> Jane was careful *to check her answers twice.* (The infinitive phrase modifies the adjective *careful.*)

> We want *to play softball on Sunday afternoon.* (The infinitive phrase is the object of the verb *want.*)

Diagraming. The infinitive phrase is diagramed as follows:

We want to have a beach party soon.

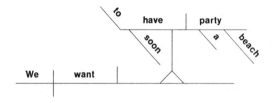

To get a summer job was not easy.

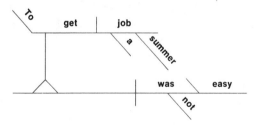

Exercise: Find the infinitive phrases in the sentences below.

1. As soon as he arrived, Jackson made plans to leave.
2. In this election, Don is sure to win.
3. Matt decided to read *Sounder* for his report.
4. Congressmen like to get letters from the voters.
5. To pay his debts, Thomas Jefferson had to sell his library.

6. The Todds are trying to rent their house for the summer.
7. Three people volunteered to change Lynn's tire.
8. People crowded the stadiums to watch Babe Ruth.
9. The Chicago Symphony Orchestra has a reputation to maintain.
10. To open the garage door, you push this button.

2.14   The Participial Phrase

The **participial phrase** usually begins with the participle. The phrase consists of the participle, its modifiers, and its complements. The modifiers and complements may themselves be phrases and clauses.

We stood in line for three hours, *hoping to get tickets.*
(The participial phrase modifies the pronoun *we.* The infinitive phrase *to get tickets* is the object of the participle *hoping.*)

Angered by poor pay and long hours, the employees decided to strike. (The participial phrase modifies *employees.*)

Knowing what the candidates said, you can vote wisely. (The participial phrase modifies *you.* The noun clause *what the candidates said* is the object of the participle *Knowing.*)

Diagraming. The participle and the participial phrase are diagramed as follows:

Purring softly, the kitten lay down.

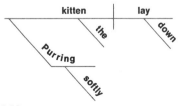

* See also Section 1.13.

Sailing his boat brilliantly, Jeff won the race.

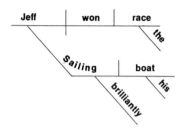

Exercise: Find the participial phrases. Tell the word each phrase modifies. Do not overlook phrases made from past participles and present participles.

1. Arriving in Philadelphia, Franklin looked for a job.
2. Having finished his required work, Jeff began an investigation of his own.
3. Lincoln entered the capital at night, disguised in strange clothing.
4. Alarmed by the condition of his men, the general ordered a retreat.
5. Appearing before the committee, Charles admitted his guilt.
6. Both men, wilting under the hot sun, played a slow game.
7. The girls came into the house, carrying a mysterious package.
8. Woodrow Wilson went to bed, convinced that he had lost the election.
9. Lynn limped out onto the court, determined to finish the game.
10. The men driving the tractors have a dangerous job.
11. The audience grew restless, waiting for the show to begin.
12. The player scoring the most points loses the game.
13. The notice posted on the bulletin board gives the examination schedule.
14. Two nurses, having finished their work, left the ward.
15. Seared by the drought, the farms looked lifeless.

2.15 The Gerund Phrase*

The **gerund phrase** consists of the gerund, which always ends in -*ing,* and the modifiers and complements of the gerund. The modifiers themselves may be phrases. The gerund phrase is always used as a noun.

> *Buying a new house* is a harrowing job. (The gerund phrase is the subject of the verb *is.*)
> We liked *picnicking on the island.* (The gerund phrase is the object of *liked.*)
> After *training intensively,* the guerillas were ready for battle. (The gerund phrase is the object of the preposition *After.*)

Diagraming. The gerund and the gerund phrase are diagramed as follows:

Hiking is his favorite sport.

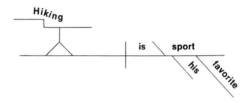

Fine passing won the game.

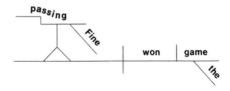

---

* See also Section 1.12.

We disliked taking the test.

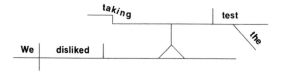

After trudging through the snow, we relaxed.

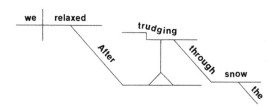

Exercise A: Find the gerund or gerund phrase in each of the following sentences:

1. Cooking is a hobby of many famous men.
2. Several football coaches enjoy painting in their spare hours.
3. By careful shopping you can make your money go farther.
4. Courteous driving saves lives.
5. After studying, Mike took a long walk.
6. We enjoyed hearing your speech.
7. The joy of the journey is not in arriving but in being on the way.
8. Don't bame Sarah for losing the game.
9. Before going to bed, Mrs. Harris turned on the radio.
10. Sleeping late on Saturdays is a great luxury.
11. Turn off the water before closing the camp.
12. Most of the class have stopped reading comic books.
13. Concentration is most important in playing chess.
14. Climbing the fence is forbidden.
15. Watching the clock is hard work.

Exercise B: Identify the verbals (see Sections 1.10–1.13).

1. Sitting on our roof, we watched the strange light in the sky.
2. Wounded by English ships, the Armada sailed north to its destruction.
3. Anyone can learn to fly a plane by taking a course of lessons.
4. Lost in his thoughts, Perry stepped right over a wallet lying on the sidewalk.
5. Jane stayed behind, hoping to talk to her teacher.
6. Exxon has started to mine the oil and minerals off the coast of Louisiana.
7. We are hoping to see many old friends at the reunion.
8. After landing in Richmond, we had to wait two hours for the next plane.
9. Finding new sources of water is essential if our cities are to survive.
10. Paul expected to pay his expenses by working after school.

2.16   The Appositive Phrase

An appositive is a word placed after another word to explain or identify it.

The Police Chief, *Alden Fisher,* spoke to the youth group.
John Keats, *the English poet,* wrote "Ode on a Grecian Urn."

The appositive always appears after the word it explains or identifies. It is always a noun or pronoun, and the word that it explains is also always a noun or pronoun.

An **appositive phrase** consists of the appositive and its modifiers, which themselves may be phrases.

Phil's cat, *an old tiger named "George,"* is missing.
(The appositive phrase identifies *cat.* The adjective *old* and the participial phrase *named "George"* modify *tiger.*)

The Donnellys bought the house, *a split-level ranch model with a swimming pool.* (The italicized words are the appositive phrase, identifying *house*. The adjectives *split-level* and *ranch* modify the appositive *model*, as does the adjective phrase *with a swimming pool*.)

Diagraming. The appositive is diagramed as follows:

Mary Alvarez, the new secretary, comes from Spain.

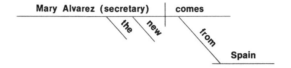

2.17 Diagraming the Simple Sentence

Meaning is conveyed in English by word-groups arranged in definite order in the sentence. Diagraming will help you see which words go together and how they are arranged.

The base of the simple sentence is composed of subject-verb-complement. These words are placed on the base line of the diagram. The indirect object is placed below the verb.

| Subject | Action Verb | Direct Object |

Indirect Object

The introductory word *There* or *Here* is placed above the base line. The subject of an imperative sentence, *you* (understood), is placed in parentheses. Note the slant line after the linking verb.

There

| Subject | Linking Verb \ Predicate Word |

(You) | Verb | Direct Object

A single-word modifier is placed on a slant line below the word it modifies. An adverb modifying an adjective or adverb is placed as shown below.

The prepositional phrase is attached to the word it modifies, as follows:

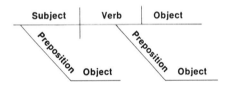

The participial phrase is shown as follows:

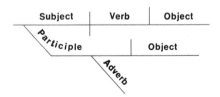

The gerund phrase is placed above the base line unless it is the object of a preposition.

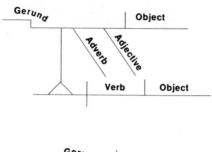

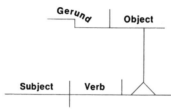

The infinitive phrase is shown in this way:

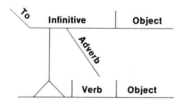

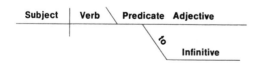

3.0 Sentence and Clause

We have seen (Section 2.2) that sentences can be classified according to the purpose of the speaker: *declarative, imperative, interrogative,* and *exclamatory.* This classification is helpful in problems of punctuation.

For help in writing better sentences, there is another, more useful classification. This is the classification by form. There are three basic forms of sentences: the *simple sentence,* the *compound sentence,* and the *complex sentence.* A fourth kind, the *compound-complex sentence,* is a combination of other forms.

3.1 The Simple Sentence

A simple sentence contains only one subject and predicate. Both the subject and the predicate may be compound.

You will recall that *compound* means having two or more similar parts.

> COMPOUND SUBJECT   The *producer* and the *playwright* argued about script changes. (The producer argued; the playwright argued.)

> COMPOUND VERB   Shakespeare *wrote* and *produced* his own plays. (Shakespeare wrote; Shakespeare produced.)

COMPOUND PREDICATE   Harry *fished all day* and *caught nothing.* (Harry fished; Harry caught.)

COMPOUND SUBJECT AND COMPOUND PREDICATE   Both *Mayor Flynn* and the *city council attended the hearings* and *defended the proposals.* (Mayor Flynn and the city council attended; Mayor Flynn and the city council defended.)

All of the preceding sentences are simple sentences. In these sentences both parts of a compound subject go with the same verb. Or both parts of a compound verb have the same subject. In all of these sentences there is only one subject-verb connection.

For contrast, note that in the following sentence the first subject goes with the first verb while the second subject goes with the second verb. There are two subject-verb connections. This is not a simple sentence:

The *visitors played* tennis; their host *took* a nap.

The Compound Predicate. The compound predicate is worth special attention because it is most useful in writing clear, smooth sentences.

The compound predicate consists of two verbs having the same subject. At least one of the verbs has a complement.

The heavy snowfall *stalled buses* and *grounded planes.*
The champion *waved* and *boarded* the *jet.*

Exercise: Identify the compound parts in the following sentences. Look for compound subjects, compound verbs, and compound predicates.

1. Both the manager and his assistant were injured in the crash.
2. The batter jumped back from the plate and fell to the ground.
3. The committee will hire an orchestra and arrange for decorations.
4. At midnight, Dr. Schweitzer put down his book and turned out the light.

5. Experts examined the old paintings and declared them priceless.

6. Hamilton and Washington wrote the Farewell Address together.

7. The general suddenly looked up and spoke to one of the soldiers.

8. Bells, sirens, and whistles joined in a deafening welcome.

9. The bus skidded and whined to a stop, inches from the huge hole.

10. Thomas Jefferson mounted his horse and rode through the snow alone to his beloved home at Monticello.

3.2 The Compound Sentence

The compound sentence consists of two or more simple sentences put together.

The parts of a compound sentence are put together: (1) with a comma and a coordinating conjunction (*and, but, or, for, nor*); (2) with a semicolon.

> Chris likes all outdoor sports, *but* she enjoys backpacking the most.
>
> The Revolutionary War had been won, *but* the thirteen states were still far from united.
>
> You can take five hours by bus, *or* you can get there in an hour by plane.
>
> He had known Carter well, *for* he had been his campaign manager.
>
> Charlie could not play the guitar, *nor* could he sing.
>
> Sally missed Prince terribly; he had been her first pet.
>
> George watched the line intently; he expected the tuna to strike.

Conjunctive adverbs (*then, however, moreover, hence, consequently, therefore,* etc.) are also used to join the parts of a compound sentence. The conjunctive adverb is preceded by a semicolon.

They went to the stadium; *however,* the game had been
rained out.

He qualified in the Olympic trials; *then* he won a
gold medal.

Jane's dress was hopelessly shrunk; *therefore,* she threw
it out.

Diagraming. The compound sentence is diagramed on two
parallel base lines as follows:

The car was nearly full, but we piled in.

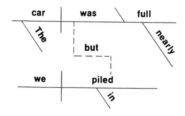

The boys grilled the steaks; the girls made the salad.

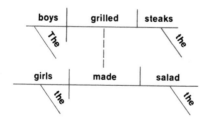

Compound Sentences and Compound Predicates. In the compound predicate every verb has the same subject. In the compound sentence, each verb has a different subject. This difference
can be seen readily in diagrams.

SIMPLE SENTENCE WITH COMPOUND PREDICATE:

Anne completed three applications and mailed them.

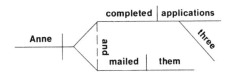

COMPOUND SENTENCE:

Anne completed three applications, and her brother mailed them.

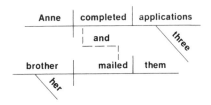

Exercise: Decide which of these sentences are compound and which are simple. In the simple sentences identify all compound predicates.

1. The house was small, but the grounds were spacious.

2. You can start French this year or wait until next year.

3. The huge rocket left the launching pad and vanished into the upper sky.

4. Leonardo painted only a few pictures, but they are all masterpieces.

5. Our library is small; however, it has a good collection of reference books.

6. We can take a train tonight or fly to Detroit in the morning.

7. The class visited the Museum of Modern Art and spent hours studying the new paintings.

8. Cliff was not happy as a successful businessman; he had wanted to be a doctor.

9. The moon turns on its axis every 28 days and therefore always presents the same face to the earth.

10. Two small moons circle the planet Mars; they are thought to be hollow.

11. New machines used in industry not only reduce back-breaking labor but produce more in less time.

12. There are probably rich mineral deposits at the South Pole, but they lie under hundreds of feet of ice.

13. Thousands of students attend college but do not stay to graduate.

14. After the death of a football player, Centerville dropped the game and did not start it again until last year.

15. The hotel room was luxurious, but we couldn't open the windows or turn off the lights.

16. Expecting a long-distance call, Kay sat by the telephone all evening and drove everyone else away.

3.3 The Clause

A clause is a group of words containing a verb and its subject.

According to this definition, a simple sentence is a clause. Indeed, the simple sentence is sometimes defined as consisting of one main clause. However, we shall find it simpler to use the word *clause* to name a *part* of a sentence.

Each part of a compound sentence has its own verb and subject. These parts of the compound sentence are therefore clauses.

Each clause in a compound sentence can be lifted out and written separately as a simple sentence.

A clause that can stand by itself as a sentence is a main clause.

We have defined a compound sentence as consisting of two or more simple sentences put together. We can now also define it as consisting of two main clauses.

A clause that cannot stand by itself as a sentence is a subordinate clause.

When he asked me . . . (What happened?)

If you don't vote . . . (Then what?)

While you were away . . . (What?)

Phrase or Clause? A clause has a subject and a verb. A phrase does not.

She saw Jack *playing in the band.* (phrase)

She met Jack *when he was playing in the band.* (clause)

The box *of jewels* had been stolen. (phrase)

The box *that contained the jewels* had been stolen. (clause)

Exercise: Are the italicized words in each sentence a phrase or a clause?

1. *To photograph the ocean bottom,* two women descended in a metal sphere.
2. It was hard to believe *that we would not see the coach again.*
3. Herb started off down the road, *rolling the tire ahead of him.*
4. We had arranged *to meet at the information desk.*
5. Is this the prize *for which you have been working so hard?*
6. We could not see *who was at the door.*
7. *After leaving high school,* Mary will go to a business school.
8. Scientists are hopeful now *of finding a cure for cancer.*
9. The men were losing weight, *for they had been too tired to eat properly.*
10. *Moving carefully under the ice,* the submarine inched its way to safety.

3.4 The Complex Sentence

The complex sentence consists of one main clause and one or more subordinate clauses.

In a complex sentence, the subordinate clause is used as a modifier. The subordinate clause modifies a word in the main clause.

When you leave, shut the door. (clause modifies *shut.*)

If he drops out of high school, he will regret it later on. (clause modifies *will regret.*)

This is the book *that you want.* (clause modifies *book.*)

In each example above, the main clause can stand as a sentence by itself: *Shut the door, He will regret it later on, This is the book.*

The subordinate clauses, however, cannot stand alone because their meaning is incomplete.

When you leave . . . (What then?)
If he drops out of high school . . . (What will happen?)
that you want . . . (What is it?)

Exercise A: Indicate whether each sentence below is simple, compound, or complex.

1. Stamp collecting is a fascinating hobby that may also be profitable.
2. The fight against tuberculosis is growing harder because the germs have become resistant to the new drugs.
3. Scientists searching for new medicines have found valuable drugs used by native tribes.
4. Puerto Rico is called a commonwealth, but just what is a commonwealth?
5. The young man ordered a rose plant for his mother-in-law, but the mail-order company sent her a horse collar.

6. During the long winter at the South Pole, the sun does not shine for six months.

7. Marysville won the toss and elected to kick.

8. On the second floor of the Philadelphia house where the Senate was meeting, Jefferson pieced together the bones of a prehistoric monster.

9. The plane taxied out into the takeoff position, started down the runway, and suddenly slid to a complete stop.

10. Everyone stopped talking when the doctor entered the room.

Exercise B: Find the subordinate clause in each sentence below.

1. This is the turn where the accident occurred.

2. It was the statement that lost Blaine the election.

3. Do you know who sent the flowers?

4. Turn off the lights before you come to bed.

5. Unless the rain stops, the game will be postponed.

6. Who knows where Carl is living?

7. Prices of farm products fell after the Erie Canal started operations.

8. Mr. Bruce is the man who bought our house.

9. What will we do if the power fails?

10. When there is a heavy snowfall in the city, everything seems to stop.

3.5 The Compound-Complex Sentence

A compound-complex sentence consists of two or more main clauses and one or more subordinate clauses.

The main clauses are joined by a coordinating conjunction (preceded by a comma), a conjunctive adverb (preceded by a semicolon), or by a semicolon alone. The subordinate clause modifies a word in one of the main clauses.

MAIN CLAUSE	MAIN CLAUSE	SUBORDINATE CLAUSE
It was night, and	Joe heard the cry of a loon	that nested by the lake.

MAIN CLAUSE   MAIN CLAUSE   SUBORDINATE CLAUSE

I will come, and I will bring my friend if he has the day off.

3.6 The Adjective Clause

The single-word adjective, the adjective phrase, and the adjective clause are used in the same way. They modify a noun or pronoun.

An adjective clause is a subordinate clause used to modify a noun or pronoun in the main clause.

Introductory Words. A majority of the adjective clauses in modern writing begin with an introductory word. There is a growing tendency, however, to use adjective clauses with no introductory word.

> This is the town *where Lincoln was born.* (*where* is an
>   introductory word.)
> This is the time *when jonquils bloom.* (*when* is an
>   introductory word.
>
> There is the suit *I need.* (no introductory word.)
> There is the suit *that I need.* (*that* is an introductory word.)
>
> The boat *you wanted* is out of stock. (no introductory word.)
> The boat *that you wanted* is out of stock. (*that* is an
>   introductory word.)

In the first two examples above, the introductory words *where* and *when* are both used within the subordinate clause as modifiers of the verb: *was born* **where;** *bloom* **when.**

Relative Pronouns. The pronouns *who, whose, whom, which,* and *that* are used to introduce adjective clauses. Used in this way they refer to a word in the main clause and are used in place of that word. That word is the antecedent of the pronoun. It is also the word modified by the adjective clause.

Phil is the one *who got the most votes.*
(*one* is the antecedent of *who* and is modified by
the adjective clause.)
There goes the man *whose son is an astronaut.*
(*man* is the antecedent of *whose* and is modified
by the adjective clause.)
Relative humidity is the amount of water vapor *which the*
air contains.
(*vapor* is the antecedent of *which* and is modified by
the adjective clause.)

An adjective clause introduced by a relative pronoun is sometimes called a relative clause.

The relative pronoun has two functions. It introduces the
clause, and it is used as a sentence-part within the clause.

Is this the book *that you want?*
(*that* is the direct object of *want.*)
Tina is the girl *whom he asked* to my party.
(*whom* is the direct object of *asked.*)
The letter *to which you refer* has been lost.
(*which* is the object of the preposition to.)
Madame Sadat is a public figure *who shrugs off criticism.*
(*who* is the subject of *shrugs.*)

Diagraming. The adjective clause is joined to the word it
modifies in the main clause. A dotted line leads from this word
to the introductory word. Note that the relative pronoun is
placed to show its use in the sentence.

The route that they took went through Washington.

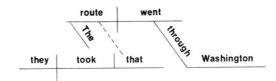

This is the spot where the plane crashed.

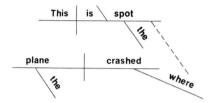

Exercise: Find each adjective clause and the word it modifies.

1. August is the month when you can see falling stars.
2. Is this the record you brought yesterday?
3. Dorothy Hamill is the American figure skater who won the gold medal.
4. This is the spot where the first state capitol stood.
5. Professor Morrison is the person to whom we wrote.
6. The aerial photographs showed buildings which no one had ever seen.
7. The energy you are using came originally from the sun.
8. We need leaders who are honest and fearless.
9. This is the book of which I was speaking.
10. Scientists have invented a light that does not produce heat.
11. The trip we are planning will take us all through the West.
12. One high school, which has only 900 students, bought 10,000 paperbacks last year.
13. Do you have all the money you need for the Washington trip?
14. The books that we ordered in September finally arrived in November.
15. The lady to whom you spoke is the director of our museum.

3.7 The Adverb Clause

The single-word adverb, the adverb phrase, and the adverb clause are all used in the same way. They are used to modify verbs, adjectives, and adverbs.

An adverb clause is a subordinate clause used to modify a verb, adjective, or adverb in the main clause.*

Adverb clauses tell *when, where, why, how, to what extent,* and *how much* about the word they modify.

ADVERB CLAUSES MODIFYING VERBS

They **put** the stop sign *where few could see it.* (where)
When the bell rings, everyone **takes** a coffee break. (when)
The Senator **talked** *as if he would run for Vice-president.* (how)
We **left** the beach *because we were surrounded by radios.* (why)

ADVERB CLAUSES MODIFYING ADJECTIVES

Winter seems twice as **long** *as it used to be.* (how much)

Kevin is as **funny** *as his uncle is.* (to what extent)

ADVERB CLAUSE MODIFYING AN ADVERB

Mary worked **harder** *than her sisters did.* (how much)

Subordinating Conjunctions. Every adverb clause is introduced by a subordinating conjunction. The function of this word is to show how two clauses are related. By use of the subordinating conjunction, one clause is made to tell *how, why, when, where to what extent,* or *how much* about another.

When a subordinating conjunction is placed before a clause, the clause can no longer stand alone.

Your grades are only average. *(complete)*
If your grades are only average . . . *(incomplete)*
Since your grades are only average . . . *(incomplete)*

* Some authorities suggest that an introductory adverb clause may modify an entire main clause rather than a single word in it.

The football season is over. *(complete)*
When the football season is over . . . *(incomplete)*
Until the football season is over . . . *(incomplete)*

A subordinating conjunction may be placed before either of two main clauses to tie it to the other. Which clause is subordinate depends upon the meaning the writer wants to express.

Although Mary bakes delicious bread, her cakes are failures.
Although Mary's cakes are failures, she bakes delicious bread.

Because few people had signed up, the trip had been delayed.
Few people had signed up, *because* the trip had been delayed.

Subordinating conjunctions can be used to show a great variety of relationships between main ideas. The careful choice of conjunctions will enable you to express your ideas clearly and exactly.

TIME:	as, after, before, since, until, when, whenever, while
CAUSE OR REASON:	because, since
COMPARISON:	as, as much as, than
CONDITION:	if, although, though, unless, provided
PURPOSE:	so that, in order that

Note how the meaning changes with the change in conjunctions in these sentences.

While he gave the speech, he seemed confident.
Before he gave the speech, he seemed confident.
After he gave the speech, he seemed confident.

Elliptical Clauses. The word *elliptical* comes from *ellipsis*, which means "omission of a word." An **elliptical clause** is one from which words have been omitted.

While he is milking the cows, he sings folk songs.
While milking the cows, he sings folk songs.
When she is watching television, she knits.
When watching television, she knits.

Diagraming. The adverb clause is diagramed on a separate line:

When the car stopped, we lurched forward.

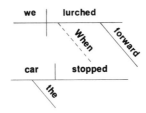

Exercise: Find each adverb clause and the word it modifies.

1. When the girls returned to Paris, they sold their car.
2. As soon as the snow starts falling, the snowplows go out.
3. Whenever there is an accident, a crowd gathers.
4. The people on the island are isolated until the spring thaws come.
5. Unless more funds are raised, the school will have no library.
6. Since this was his first meeting, Bob said very little.
7. You can return the lamp if you don't like it.
8. When the judge entered, everyone in the courtroom stood up.
9. While the car was being repaired, we walked down the road.
10. There was no light, no sound, no movement as we approached the house.

3.8 The Noun Clause

A noun clause is a subordinate clause used as a noun.

The noun clause may be used as subject or direct object of the verb, as a predicate noun, as object of a preposition, or as an appositive.

> Officer Taylor asked *where the accident occurred.*
> Angela did not agree with *what José had said.* (object of preposition)

Mother vetoed my suggestion *that we go to the fair.* (appositive)

Who began the war is not certain. (subject)

What I'd like to know is *how this dishwasher works.* (predicate noun)

Introductory Words. As the examples above clearly show, noun clauses may be introduced by some of the same words that introduce adverb clauses: *when, where.* Used in noun clauses, these words are not regarded as subordinating conjunctions. They are merely introductory words, used as adverbs within the noun clause.

Similarly, noun clauses may be introduced by the same words used to introduce relative clauses: *who, whose, whom, which, that, when, where.* Used in noun clauses, these words are not regarded as relative pronouns, but they may serve as subjects or objects within the noun clause.

Terry knows **where** *Henry is.* (noun clause as the direct object of *knows*)

We went **where** *we could swim.* (adverb clause modifying *went*)

Are you the one **who** *called me?* (adjective clause modifying *one*)

Who *sent this package* is a mystery. (noun clause as the subject of *is*)

Many noun clauses are written without any introductory word. Every direct quotation preceded by words such as *he said, I replied, Bob asked* is a noun clause without the introductory word. Every indirect quotation is a noun clause preceded by the introductory word.

She said *that the answer is wrong.* (noun clause as the object of *said*)

She said, *"The answer is wrong."* (noun clause as the object of *said*)

Diagraming. The noun clause is diagramed as shown below. Note that the use of the noun clause determines its position in the diagram.

I know that they are going.

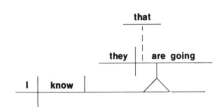

We have a job for whoever is qualified.

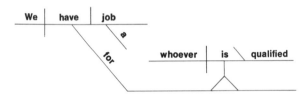

Exercise: Identify each noun clause. Tell how it is used in the sentence.

1. Barbara would not tell us where she had been.
2. What the man really wanted was a mystery to us.
3. Fred was apologetic for what he had said.
4. The doctor said that Marion could get up tomorrow.
5. Do you know who invented the microscope?
6. We had no idea of what might happen.
7. The police know who wrote the threatening letters.
8. Who will win the game is anyone's guess.
9. Everyone knew that the test would be difficult.
10. We thought the day would never end.
11. What happened to the missing man was never discovered.
12. The department will be grateful for whatever you can do.
13. You can't get what you want without making an effort.
14. We did not know Jim had such powers of concentration.

3.9 The Sentence Redefined

We are now ready to complete the definition of a sentence that we started in Sections 2.1 and 2.3. We may begin by noting once again the differences between phrases, clauses, and sentences.

A **phrase** is a group of words used within a sentence as a single part of speech. A phrase may be used as a noun, a verb, an adjective, or an adverb. It does *not* contain a subject or verb.

A **clause** is a group of words which contains a subject and its verb. It may be used within the sentence as a noun, an adjective, or an adverb.

PHRASE: Walking by the lake . . .

CLAUSE: When we were walking by the lake . . .

A main clause can stand by itself as a sentence. A subordinate clause cannot stand by itself.

MAIN CLAUSE   MAIN CLAUSE

The well was dry, and there was no sign of rain.

The well was dry. *(complete)*
There was no sign of rain. *(complete)*

SUBORDINATE CLAUSE   MAIN CLAUSE

Although the well was dry, there was no sign of rain.

There was no sign of rain. *(complete)*
Although the well was dry . . . *(incomplete)*

Clauses and phrases are sentence parts. The sentence itself is not part of any other grammatical construction. (The paragraph is not a grammatical construction.) Our complete definition of a sentence then is in three parts:

A sentence is a group of words that

1. **expresses a complete thought,**
2. **contains a subject and verb,**
3. **is not part of any other grammatical construction.**

4.0 Complete Sentences

Uncompleted sentences are more often a problem in writing than in speaking. If you use an uncompleted sentence in speaking with someone face-to-face, he or she can interrupt and ask you what you mean. In writing, you usually do not have a second chance.

The sentence is the best means you have for getting your meaning across to someone else in writing. Through study and practice, you can learn to write effective and forceful sentences. To write effectively, however, you must learn to avoid two kinds of sentence error: (1) the sentence fragment, and (2) the run-on sentence. Both of these errors cause confusion for the reader.

4.1 Fragments Resulting from Incomplete Thought

An uncompleted sentence is called a **sentence fragment.** It is only a part, or fragment of a sentence.

You can think much faster than you can write. Many of your sentence errors, if you make them, happen because your mind has raced on ahead of your hand. You have started to write a second thought before you have finished writing the first. Or, perhaps in haste, you have left out a key word necessary for a complete sentence. Suppose you intended to say something like this:

> In 1939, Ike was a colonel. After war broke out, he soon became commander of American forces in Europe. He later led all Allied forces.

In the hurry to get on with your writing, however, what you put down was something like this:

> In 1939, Ike was a colonel. After he soon became commander of American forces in Europe. He later led all Allied forces.

The second group of words is not a sentence. It causes confusion. The reader may suppose that you meant to say that Ike was a colonel after he became commander of American forces in Europe.

Exercise A: Find the sentence fragments. Add the words needed to make each fragment a sentence.

1. Then came Tom. Wearing a wide-brimmed hat and a false mustache
2. His intention to double the homework assignments
3. When we reached the top of the last hill
4. Most of the great books available in inexpensive paperbacks
5. Mr. Wallace, one of the oldest residents in the city
6. The huge trucks rolling along the nation's highways all through the night
7. Finally, in a corner of the garage, the missing wrenches
8. Nothing in the newspapers about the robbery
9. There is a reward. Anyone who finds the valuable bracelet
10. After working hard all day, a little relaxation

Exercise B: Three of the following groups of words are sentences. The rest are fragments. Find the fragments and add words needed to make them sentences.

1. Ghost towns all across the country
2. Pithole, Pennsylvania, one of the most famous

3. It flourished for a brief ten years
4. For a time, 20,000 people in the town
5. Everyone left quickly when the oil wells dried up
6. Elsewhere ghost towns in timber country
7. Modern ghost towns in the iron-mining regions of Minnesota
8. The most famous of all in the mining sections of the West
9. Houses full of furniture and offices with papers in the desks
10. Wherever people mined and the resources gave out, there are ghost towns

4.2 Fragments Resulting from Incorrect Punctuation

The first word of a sentence begins with a capital letter. The sentence is closed by a punctuation mark: *period, question mark,* or *exclamation mark.* A great many sentence fragments are written simply because the writer inserts a period and a capital letter too soon. This error is sometimes called a **period fault.**

FRAGMENT	*Before accepting the invitation.* He called his wife.
SENTENCE	Before accepting the invitation, he called his wife.
FRAGMENT	The team was still in the huddle. *When time ran out.*
SENTENCE	The team was still in the huddle when time ran out.
FRAGMENT	*At the beginning of this century.* Motoring was an adventure.
SENTENCE	At the beginning of this century, motoring was an adventure.

Exercise: Find the fragments. Correct them by changing the punctuation or by adding the words needed to make a sentence.

1. When the sky clouded up. I was sure there would be no picnic.

2. Once again the sirens wailed. Another bad accident on the highway.

3. Grace has been interested in music. For many years.

4. We arrived late. The banquet already started.

5. When the speaker came in. He explained he had been lost.

6. Wherever you see a stake. Drive in one of these iron posts.

7. We had finished the experiment. Cleaning up the lab table.

8. You will have no trouble. If you follow these directions.

9. The truck had slid into the ditch. Scattering eggs for a hundred feet.

10. No one really knows what he can do. Until he tries.

4.3 Phrases as Fragments

You know that a phrase is a group of words that does not contain a verb and its subject. A phrase, therefore, cannot be a sentence by itself. It is a *part* of a sentence.

You are not likely to mistake a prepositional phrase for a complete sentence. If you write a long prepositional phrase or a series of phrases as a sentence, it is probably because you have punctuated incorrectly.

FRAGMENT   *In the first place*. He has had no experience
in public office.

SENTENCE   In the first place, he has had no experience
in public office.

You are more likely to mistake a verbal phrase for a complete sentence. This error occurs because verbals look like verbs and function somewhat like verbs. Like verbs, they may be modified by adverbs. They may be followed by objects or predicate words. They are not complete verbs, however, and they cannot be used as the main verb of a sentence.

The most troublesome verbals are those that end in *-ing*. All gerunds and present participles end in *-ing*. You will avoid many sentence errors if you will remember this fact:

No word ending in *-ing* can be a verb unless it is a one-syllable word like *sing, ring,* or *bring.*

If an *-ing* word is preceded by *is, are, was,* or some other form of *be,* the two words together are a verb.

PARTICIPLE	COMPLETE VERB
reading	is reading
running	had been running
studying	were studying

A long infinitive phrase may sometimes be mistaken for a complete sentence. Such a phrase sounds like a sentence since it often has everything that a sentence requires except a subject.

INCORRECT	Ray has a plan. To go to Greece next year.
CORRECT	Ray has a plan. His scheme is to go to Greece next year.
INCORRECT	Kevin was overjoyed. To be one of the top contenders for a National Merit Scholarship.
CORRECT	Kevin was overjoyed to be one of the top contenders for a National Merit Scholarship.

An appositive phrase is sometimes written incorrectly as a complete sentence. Although it may seem like a sentence, it always lacks a verb.

FRAGMENT	Vida Blue, *the great Oakland pitcher.*
SENTENCE	Vida Blue is the great *Oakland pitcher.*
SENTENCE	Vida Blue, the great Oakland pitcher, signed his contract.
FRAGMENT	The rocket, *the heaviest ever launched.*
SENTENCE	The rocket, the heaviest ever launched, roared toward the moon.

Exercise: Rewrite the groups of words beside each number below to make a complete sentence. You may need to add words in some instances.

1. Ralph arranged with the band leader. To play an extra hour.

2. The leader of the expedition. A scientist of wide experience.

3. Studying the ocean as a source of food and minerals.

4. We had seen the program before. A fascinating explanation of what sound waves can do.

5. Jane delighted with the chance to visit Hawaii.

6. Sally and her mother busy making plans for the wedding.

7. Pete has a great ambition. To become a surgeon.

8. The newspaper story, an unfair statement of what happened.

9. The two books, one a true story and the other a fictional account of Frémont's expedition.

10. The *Mary Deare* found drifting with no crew aboard.

11. The need for more food for the world's population mounting daily.

12. The boy told his story. Expecting no one to believe him.

13. The class adviser arranged for a bus. To take the group to the contest.

14. The unhappy motorist searching his pockets for his license.

15. The book an account of how the Spanish Armada was defeated.

4.4 Clauses as Fragments

A subordinate clause cannot stand alone as a sentence. See Section 3.3. A sentence may be changed into a subordinate clause by having a subordinating conjunction placed before it.

SENTENCE   We were paddling the canoes upstream.

SUBORDINATE CLAUSE   As we were paddling the canoes upstream . . .

Writers sometimes mistakenly place a period before or after a subordinate clause as though it were a sentence.

INCORRECT   When we saw the Indians. We leaped on our horses.

CORRECT   When we saw the Indians, we leaped on our horses.

INCORRECT   Rosalie was excited. Because she was going
to Colorado.

CORRECT   Rosalie was excited because she was going
to Colorado.

Exercise: Rewrite the word groups below to eliminate the fragments.

1. Beth is the only one. Who knew the answers.
2. The trapper stayed in the mountains. Until the first snowfall.
3. She took the old painting. Since nobody else wanted it.
4. Although the book is unusually long. It is worth reading.
5. There will be a big celebration in Pittsburgh. When the Pirates win the pennant.
6. Linda is studying forestry. Because she likes outdoor life.
7. Preparing a report on the rock collection which we had started the year before.
8. Ruth decided to buy the red coat. Even though her mother disliked it.
9. We will be glad to see you. Whenever you can come.
10. In the camp, the explorers found food. Which had been left by the Ellsworth party ten years before.

Review Exercise: In this exercise you will find examples of many kinds of fragments. Change them into sentences.

1. Thomas Jefferson wrote the Declaration of Independence. At the age of thirty-three.
2. A mother rhinoceros always keeps her baby ahead of her. As she walks along.
3. India has over two hundred languages. And many religions.
4. My library at home contains many paperbacks. Also books with beautiful, gold-tooled leather covers.
5. Ernest Hemingway wrote "The Killers." One of the most famous short stories of our time.
6. In a full orchestra, there are four families of instruments. Stringed instruments, woodwinds, brasses, and percussion instruments.

7. He is one of those overly cautious people. Always raising objections.

8. Northern Canada is a vast Arctic waste. Has a few natives, many caribou, and numerous fur-bearing animals.

9. The needle of a compass always points north. Because it is attracted by a center of magnetic force near the North Pole.

10. Edison's first electric light burned for forty hours. The average life of a 100-watt bulb today over 750 hours.

4.5 Run-on Sentences

A **run-on sentence** is two or more sentences written as though they were one sentence. That is, the writer fails to use a period or other end mark at the end of each sentence.

RUN-ON	Danny went hunting last month he shot a bear.
CORRECT	Danny went hunting last month. He shot a bear.
RUN-ON	Pedro went to the clinic he had cut his arm.
CORRECT	Pedro went to the clinic. He had cut his arm.

The most common run-on sentence error is the joining of two sentences by a comma. This error is called the **comma fault.**

COMMA FAULT	The club held a car wash, it was a great success.
CORRECT	The club held a car wash. It was a great success.
COMMA FAULT	The critic read the book, he then wrote a review.
CORRECT	The critic read the book. He then wrote a review.

In all of the foregoing examples, notice that the two sentences are closely related and that the second sentence begins with a personal pronoun: *it, he, she.* Watch for situations like these in your own writing and avoid the comma fault.

4.6 Avoiding the Run-on Sentence

There is no objection to joining two or more closely related statements into one sentence. In fact, it is often better to join them than to write them separately. There are three ways in which closely related sentences can be joined to make a compound sentence: (1) with a comma and a coordinating conjunction; (2) with a semicolon; (3) with a semicolon and a conjunctive adverb.

RUN-ON Neal has two choices. He can play college football, he can sign with the Yankees.

CORRECT Neal has two choices. He can play college football, or he can sign with the Yankees.

RUN-ON Churchill led England through the agonizing war years, then he was defeated in the first postwar election.

CORRECT Churchill led England through the agonizing war years; then he was defeated in the first postwar election.

RUN-ON The demonstration was orderly, consequently, the mayor heard our plea.

CORRECT The demonstration was orderly; consequently, the mayor heard our plea.

Note: When a conjunctive adverb such as *consequently, however, moreover, therefore,* and *nevertheless* introduces a second main clause, it is preceded by a semicolon. Usually, it is followed by a comma.

Exercise A: Correct each of the following run-on sentences in one of these ways: (1) by using a period and a capital letter; (2) by using a semicolon; or (3) by using a comma and *and, but,* or *or.*

1. We flew to Idaho Falls, then we took a bus to the lake.
2. Andy tries to practice the flute every day, however, he doesn't always have time.
3. The Browns have a new car, it is a Mercedes.

4. Cooking the turkey takes several hours, it has to be started in the morning.

5. Howard University is small, nevertheless, it has an excellent faculty.

6. The station was crowded, we nearly missed our train.

7. It isn't a new dress, I wore it to the Christmas party.

8. Pat hasn't called, he must be lost.

9. The dog had saved the family's lives, however, they had to get rid of him.

10. Dad painted the chairs, they look very nice.

11. Mark is color-blind, therefore, his wife always buys his ties.

12. You take the general course first, then you can specialize.

13. The fog was very heavy, no planes left the airport.

14. Leona started to cross the street, then the light changed.

15. Jim hesitated too long, consequently, he missed his chance.

Exercise B: The first part of a sentence is given on each line below. Add a second main clause, starting it with the word in parentheses. If the word is a conjunctive adverb, place a semicolon before it and a comma after it. If the word is a personal pronoun, use a semicolon or use a comma with a coordinating conjunction.

1. The deer started to cross the road (then)

2. The author of the article is Woody Allen (he)

3. We were not expecting you today (however)

4. The road was strewn with heavy branches (it)

5. The boys had had plenty of time to study (nonetheless)

6. Jan and Sylvia were late to class (they)

7. The driver had simply been going too fast (moreover)

8. The town's population has been declining (consequently)

9. Eve will be married next summer (she)

10. Willy could scarcely lift the package (it)

11. First you send for an application blank (then)

12. We are rapidly exhausting some of our natural resources (for example)

13. Most words have more than one meaning (therefore)

14. You have seen this book before (it)

15. In the clear desert air, the mountains look very close (they)

Exercise C: Copy this paragraph, correcting the run-on sentences.

None of us could believe that Harry was guilty, he had never been known to do anything dishonest. He had always been careful to give customers the exact change, yet he was now charged with pilfering the cash register at his checkout counter. The manager himself usually picked up the extra cash twice a day, however, on Thursday he waited until the store closed. He put Harry's cash in a separate bag, then he locked it up in the safe. When he counted it the next morning, it was ten dollars short. He accused Harry of pocketing the money, however, Harry denied the charge. He thought for a while, then he asked to count the money. The manager agreed, he stood beside Harry while he counted. Harry went through each stack of bills slowly, he found the ten dollars. Two ten-dollar bills had stuck together. The manager and his assistant apologized, they even let Harry pick up the cash from the checkout counters the next week to show that they trusted him.

5.0 The New Grammar of English

The fundamentals of grammar which you have studied since you were in grade school were first developed during the eighteenth century. At that time, Latin was widely known and admired by all educated people. Therefore, when scholars began to describe how the English language worked, they described it in terms of Latin. They emphasized characteristics of English that are like Latin and ignored aspects which did not fit the Latin model.

During the past fifty years, however, language study has been in ferment. Linguists—scientists who study language—have come to believe that each language must be described in its own terms—that you cannot mold the English language in a Latin form. During recent years, linguists have been developing a new description of English which they feel is more complete and accurate than the traditional grammar. Although a systematic grammar which all will agree upon has not yet been completed, much of the research has been fascinating. Many scholars feel it will revolutionize English grammar.

This section will give you an opportunity to see what linguists are doing—to look at your language in new ways.

5.1 The Form Classes

Linguists believe that the most useful way to classify English words is to examine their behavior when put together in sentences. Linguists look for similarities and differences in the ways that words work together and place words that behave alike in the same group. For example, consider the following groups of words:

> The movie was remarkable.
> The sunset was remarkable.
> The speech was remarkable.

Movie, sunset, and *speech* are very different words in sound and meaning, but their behavior in sentences is similar: they all fit between *The* and *was remarkable* and form an English sentence.

Now let us try some other words in the same position:

> The eagerly was remarkable.
> The interesting was remarkable.
> The supermarket was remarkable.
> The seemed was remarkable.

Of these groups of words, only the third is an English sentence. The other groups are not English: we cannot imagine a speaker of English ever using *eagerly* or *interesting* or *seemed* in this way. We say, then, that *movie, sunset, speech,* and *supermarket* all belong to the same group, because they behave in the same way. *Eagerly, interesting,* and *seemed,* however, obviously do not belong to this group, because they behave differently.

Suppose that we now substitute these unclassified words for *remarkable:*

> The movie was remarkable.
> The movie was eagerly.
> The movie was interesting.
> The movie was seemed.

From these substitutions we can see that *interesting* and *remarkable* behave in the same way; therefore, we can place them in the same group.

Now let us try still another substitution:

> The movie was remarkable.
> The movie eagerly remarkable.
> The movie seemed remarkable.

Seemed behaves like *was*, and consequently belongs to the same group. *Eagerly*, as we have seen, behaves differently from any of the other words we have considered.

By comparing the behavior of words in this way, linguists have discovered that almost all English words can be classified in four large groups—**nouns, verbs, adjectives,** and **adverbs.** These groups are often referred to as **form classes,** because, to a certain extent, words can be placed in one class or another according to the ways they change form when used in sentences.

The small number of English words—less than three hundred —that cannot be placed in any of the form classes are called **structure words** and are divided into several **structure groups.** We will discuss the differences between structure words and form class words and describe some of the structure groups in Section 5.2.

In the remainder of this section, we will consider the signals used in English sentences to show the form class to which a word belongs.

Nouns

Linguists often use a selection of writing or a recording of speech as sample material for their investigations. In our discussion of the signals that show us which words are nouns, we will refer frequently to the following sample:

> The <u>students</u> wanted a new <u>uniform</u> for the band, because the <u>buttons</u> on the old <u>uniforms</u> had lost their <u>shine</u>. They said that the <u>school's</u> <u>reputation</u> was at stake.

The underlined words in the sample above are all nouns. What signals show that these words are used as nouns?

Signal Number 1: Nouns have more than one form. Notice that one noun in the sample has two forms: *uniform* and *uniforms.* Most nouns have a plural form ending in -s which shows that the word refers to more than one. Six nouns in the sample are singular in form; three are plural.

SINGULAR		PLURAL
uniform	school's	students
band	reputation	buttons
shine	stake	uniforms

Another form change that is characteristic of nouns is the possessive ending -'s. There is one instance of this form in the sample: *school's.* Both singular and plural nouns have possessive forms:

SINGULAR	POSSESSIVE	PLURAL	POSSESSIVE
school	school's	schools	schools'
student	student's	students	students'
band	band's	bands	bands'

Notice in the examples above that the possessive forms and the plural form sound exactly the same when spoken. In writing, we use the apostrophe to indicate which form is being used.

Signal Number 2: Nouns are often preceded, or "marked," by a group of structure words called determiners. Of the nine nouns included in the sample, seven are marked by determiners:

the students	*the* old uniforms
a new uniform	*their* shine
the band	*the* school's
the buttons	

When we see a determiner in a sentence, we know that a noun will follow. The noun may come directly after its determiner: *the students, the buttons;* or other words—modifiers of the noun—

may come between: *a new uniform, the old uniforms.*

The most frequently used determiners are *the, a,* and *an.* Many other words, however, perform the same function. Here is a partial list:

my	his	more	some	this
your	her	several	any	that
our	its	both	either	these
their	no	every	neither	those

The, a, an, and the words in the first column above are always determiners. The other words in the list sometimes perform other functions in sentences. For example:

Several parents are coming.
Several are coming.

Neither driver was to blame.
Neither was to blame.

In the first sentence in each group above, *several* and *neither* are determiners, because they are used to mark nouns. In the second sentence in each group, they function as pronouns. This multiple use of the same word is very common in English. We usually cannot classify a word that appears by itself; we must first see how it behaves when used in a sentence.

Signal Number 3: Nouns are marked by the positions they fill in sentences. For example, the position before the verb as subject is commonly filled by a noun. Three nouns in the sample fill this position:

students is the subject of *wanted*
buttons is the subject of *had lost*
reputation is the subject of *was*

Another common noun position is after the verb as object. Two nouns in the sample function as objects:

uniform is the object of *wanted*
shine is the object of *had lost*

Still another noun position is after a preposition. Three nouns in the sample function as objects of prepositions:

> *band* is the object of *for*
> *uniforms* is the object of *on*
> *stake* is the object of *at*

There are two special kinds of words that should be mentioned in connection with nouns.

Proper nouns are the names of specific people, places, or things. They fill the same positions in sentences that regular nouns do, but they are not marked by determiners in the same way. Some proper nouns—words like *Paul, Mrs. Conway, Oregon, Boston*—do not occur with determiners. We never say "the Paul," "several Oregons," or "every Boston." Other proper nouns always occur with the determiner *the*. Words like *the Great Plains, the United States, the Pacific* ordinarily do not occur without *the* and are seldom used with any other determiner.

Pronouns are words like *I, you, he, she, it, they,* and their various forms. As we saw on page 109, many of the words listed as determiners can also function as pronouns. Although these words do not change form as nouns do or occur with determiners, it is convenient to place them in the same class as nouns because they fill the same positions in sentences.

Exercise A: Point out the nouns in the following sentences. How can you tell that these words are nouns?

1. The conductor lectured on the instruments of the orchestra.
2. That girl's father is a famous European acrobat.
3. Cheerfulness is the best policy before a test.
4. Men's shoes are on the second floor; children's shoes can be found in the basement.
5. He became a hewer of wood and a drawer of water.

Exercise B: Fill each blank in the sentences on the next page with a determiner. Use as many different determiners as you can. You will find that some determiners cannot be used in a particular blank. Try to explain what it is about the noun or the rest of the sentence that prevents their use.

1. _____ mother baked _____ kinds of cookies for _____ birthday.
2. _____ cat hurt _____ paw playing on _____ cinders _____ morning.
3. Please tell him to send _____ copies to _____ members of _____ committee.
4. _____ restaurant serves you _____ food for _____ money.
5. _____ students are going to _____ mountains for _____ vacation; others prefer _____ beach.

Exercise C: If we want to know whether a particular word can be used as a noun, we can find out by seeing whether it will work in a noun position. For example, any word that fits in one of the blanks below can be used as a noun:

The _____ is remarkable.
We admired their _____ .

Since we can say "The garden is remarkable" and "We admired their cheerfulness," we know that *garden* and *cheerfulness* can be used as nouns. Make a list of fifteen more words that can be used as nouns by seeing which words will fit in one of the blanks above.

Verbs

The underlined words in the following sample are all verbs. What signals in the sentences show us that these words are used as verbs?

Paul <u>plays</u> a good game of golf. He has been <u>playing</u> every Saturday since he <u>broke</u> his tennis racket. His father can <u>play</u> only on Sunday, because he must <u>work</u> on Saturday. Paul's mother has never <u>played</u> golf; she <u>prefers</u> tennis.

Signal Number 1: Verbs have more than one form. One of the verbs in the sample has four different forms: *play, plays, playing,* and *played.* The majority of verbs change form in this way.

There are, however, a considerable number of verbs, including some of those we use most frequently, that change form in a different way. These irregular verbs have *-s* and *-ing* forms just as regular verbs do, but they have a wide variety of forms instead of the regular *-ed* ending. The most common irregular verbs and their various form changes are listed and classified on pages 173–179 of the Handbook.

Signal Number 2: Like nouns, verbs are often preceded by structure words. Four of the seven verbs in the sample are marked in this way:

> *has been* playing   *must* work
> *can* only play   *has* never played

The italicized words in the phrases above are members of a group of structure words called **auxiliaries.** Auxiliaries regularly come before verbs in sentences. Thus they help us to tell which words are verbs in much the way that determiners mark which words are nouns. Like determiners, auxiliaries do not always come directly before the words they mark. Sometimes adverbs —such as *never* and *only* in the phrases above—come between.

Here is a list of words that are frequently used as auxiliaries:

can	could	must	is/am/are/was/were
may	might	ought to	be/being/been
shall	should	used to	do/does/did
will	would	have to/has to	have/has/had
		had to/having to	get/gets/got/getting

These auxiliaries combine with each other and with verbs in a great variety of ways to form **verb phrases** such as the following:

may be played	used to have to play
would have been broken	did get broken
must have preferred	ought to have preferred

The words in the last column of the list of auxiliaries above may also occur in sentences as verbs. For example, in the first sentence of each of the following pairs, the italicized word is used as an auxiliary; in the second sentence in each pair, it is used as a verb:

> She *is* working hard.
> She *is* a hard worker.
>
> He *did* study for the test.
> He *did* well on the test.
>
> She may *be* going.
> She may *be* late.
>
> Our team may *get* beaten next week.
> Our team should *get* new uniforms.
>
> He *has* grown several varieties of cucumbers.
> He *has* several varieties of cucumbers.

Thus, when these words precede verbs in sentences, they are used as auxiliaries. When they occur by themselves or as the last word in a verb phrase, they are used as verbs.

Signal Number 3: Verbs occur regularly in certain positions. We identify them from these positions when other signals are absent. The most common verb position is after the noun that serves as its subject. All the verbs in the sample fill this position.

Verbs fill a different position in sentences that express a command or a request. They occur either at the beginning or following a structure word like *please* or *let's*.

> *Walk* a little faster   Let's *see* if he is home.
> *Hold* that line.   Please *call* back in an hour.

In sentences such as these, the verb is usually not marked by form changes or auxiliaries. We must identify it from its position.

Exercise A: Point out the verbs in the following sentences. What signals tell you that these words are verbs?

1. Every student must swim fifty yards before he or she can be graduated from our school.

2. Mrs. Jones used to have a house on Elm Street; she had to move when the new expressway was built.

3. Make three right turns and proceed on Main Street until you reach Walnut; the old water tower will be to your left.

4. Vera makes sure that the papers are flawless before she gives them to her clients.

5. Please get three bags of potato chips and bring them to the party.

Exercise B: Fill each blank in the following sentences with an auxiliary. Use as many different auxiliaries as you can. If you find that some auxiliaries cannot be used in a particular blank, try to explain what it is about the verb or the rest of the sentence that rules them out.

1. She _____ leaving tomorrow; she _____ return next week.

2. She _____ spent the whole day looking for shoes.

3. I _____ open an account at that bank.

4. You _____ gone to see him yesterday.

5. I _____ going to the beach tomorrow; you _____ come with me.

6. Those houses _____ painted only last week.

7. Many people _____ not have good telephone manners.

8. She _____ go if she _____ be sure that they _____ _____ waiting for her.

Exercise C: Words that can be used as verbs will work in the following blanks:

Please _____ .	Please <u>stay</u>.
Let's _____ it.	Let's <u>send</u> it.
It might _____ .	It might <u>rain</u>.

Find fifteen words that will fit in one or more of the blanks above.

Exercise D: It would be convenient if nouns were always nouns and verbs always verbs. English, however, is not that simple. Many words behave like nouns in some sentences and like verbs in others. We cannot classify these words until we see them in a sentence. For example, *film* will fit both a noun blank and a verb blank.

The film was remarkable.   Let's film it.

List ten words that can be used in both noun and verb positions.

Adjectives

The adjectives in the following sample are underlined. How can we tell that these words are used as adjectives?

That rather underlined remarkable house on the corner is much older than the others; in fact, it is thought to be the oldest residential building in the state. It has recently been restored to its original appearance as seen in old engravings. The red door and green shutters are quite characteristic of the very colorful era in which it was built.

Signal Number 1: Adjectives have more than one form. In the sample, notice that one of the adjectives has three forms: *old, older,* and *oldest.* Adjectives of one or two syllables usually change form in this way to show comparison. Adjectives of more than two syllables usually show comparison by using the structure words *more* and *most.*

old	older	oldest
red	redder	reddest
green	greener	greenest
remarkable	more remarkable	most remarkable
colorful	more colorful	most colorful

Many adverbs also show comparison in this way:

soon	sooner	soonest
eagerly	more eagerly	most eagerly

Although these form changes do not help us to tell adjectives from adverbs, they do help to separate adjectives and adverbs from nouns and verbs.

Signal Number 2: Adjectives are often preceded, or marked, by structure words.

rather remarkable	*quite* characteristic
much older	*very* colorful

The italicized words in the phrases above are members of a group of structure words called **intensifiers.** Intensifiers regularly precede adjectives in sentences and thus help to identify them.

We have already mentioned the two intensifiers used to show comparison: *more* and *most.* Other words that occur as intensifiers are *somewhat, too, less, least, really,* and *pretty.* Intensifiers are also used to mark adverbs: *too slowly, less thoroughly, pretty soon, very eagerly.*

Signal Number 3: Adjectives occur in certain positions. Since both adjectives and adverbs are marked by the form changes *-er* and *-est* and by intensifiers, we must depend upon position in a sentence to help us tell them apart. Normally, adjectives occur in one of two positions.

1. Adjectives most commonly occur before nouns as modifiers. Eight of the ten adjectives in the sample fill this position:

remarkable house	red door
oldest residential building	green shutters
original appearance	colorful era
old engravings	

However, not every word that occurs in this position is an adjective. Other kinds of modifiers may also precede a noun, particularly verbs and other nouns. Compare the modifiers in the following phrases:

ADJECTIVE	NOUN	VERB
remarkable house	apartment house	boarding house
red door	barn door	revolving door

When we are not sure whether a word preceding a noun is an adjective or another kind of modifier, we can find out by trying to use an intensifier with it. If the intensifier sounds natural, then the word is an adjective; if it does not, the word is another kind of modifier. Thus, we might say "a rather remarkable house," but we would never say "a rather apartment house" or "a rather boarding house." Similarly, we can say "a very red door," but not "a very barn door" or "a very revolving door."

2. Another important sentence position for adjectives is that following a linking verb, as *seem, become,* or the various forms of the verb *be* (*is, am, are, was, were, being, been*). Two adjectives in the sample fill this position:

LINKING VERB	ADJECTIVE
is	(much) older
are	(quite) characteristic

We will discuss this position more fully when we describe the basic sentence patterns in Section 5.3.

Exercise A: Which words in the following sentences are adjectives? How can you tell that these words are adjectives?

1. This is the hardest test I have taken this year.
2. These green apples are sweeter than the ripe apples we ate yesterday.
3. Much of that long story he told us sounds doubtful.
4. Our marching band won the blue ribbon at the state fair.
5. The weather has been quite unpredictable this year; we have had an unusually cool summer and a rather mild winter.

Exercise B: Adjectives regularly occur between a determiner and a noun and after a linking verb. We can tell which words can work as adjectives by seeing whether they will fit in both these positions. For example, we can try words in sentences like the following:

> That beautiful painting is very beautiful.
> His new television is very new.
> This unpredictable weather is quite unpredictable.

Find fifteen adjectives by constructing sentences like these.

Exercise C: The word *general* can work as either a noun or an adjective:

> The general was remarkable.
> These general directions are too general.

Try to think of five other words that can be used in both noun and adjective positions.

Adverbs

Adverbs are the most difficult of the form classes to describe. As we have seen, their form changes and their occurrence following intensifiers help us to separate them from nouns and verbs, but not from adjectives. We must therefore identify them on the basis of their positions in sentences. The most characteristic of these positions is at the end of a sentence pattern:

> She read the poem very *slowly*.
> Jimmy opened his gift *eagerly*.
> He decided that he had to walk somewhat *faster*.
> The Conways are spending the summer *abroad*.
> The milk is delivered *daily*.
> I don't see Ray very *often*.
> Why don't the new movies come *here*?
> Sandra feels that she must learn to study more *efficiently*.
> In this game you must deal the cards *counterclockwise*.
> Why didn't you ask him to come *in*?

Adverbs are, however, very flexible with respect to position. They can be found in many different places in the sentence. On the next page are a few examples:

> AT THE BEGINNING
> *Seldom* have I seen such coordination.
> *Recently* they have been living in Chicago.

BETWEEN SUBJECT AND VERB
The neighbors *above* make a lot of noise.
No one *here* can help you.

WITHIN VERB PHRASES
I can *usually* tell which questions will be on the test.
You can *always* count on him to be late.

BEFORE AN ADJECTIVE
His solution to the problem was *essentially* correct.
These two drugs are *equally* effective.

The behavior of adverbs in sentences is one of the more complicated parts of English grammar, and we cannot tell the whole story here. You will find, however, that you will be able to identify most adverbs on the basis of the positions listed here. In other cases, you will know that a word is an adverb because it does not behave like a member of any other form class or of any structure group.

How the Signals Work

In this section, we have classified words as belonging to one form class or another on the basis of (1) the ways in which the word changes form, (2) the kind of structure word that the word follows, and (3) the position that the word fills in a sentence.

A good reason for classifying words on the basis of their behavior in sentences is that this is the way speakers of English actually do classify them. We realize this when we see unfamiliar words. For example, try to classify the italicized words in the following sentences:

I *rove* a new backstay and borrowed a set of *battens*.
We can consider noise to be the sum of many
sinusoidal components.

Even if we don't know the meanings of these words, we can

still tell what form class each one belongs to. We can tell because the signals that the sentences contain show clearly that *rove* is a verb, that *battens* is a noun, and that *sinusoidal* is an adjective.

Sentences almost always contain more than enough signals for us to sort out the words into form classes. There are, however, occasional sentences in which the signals fail to mark a word clearly as belonging to one form class or another. When this happens, the sentence is ambiguous; that is, it has at least two possible meanings. For example:

> Lynn is entertaining tonight.

Entertaining may be either an adjective following the linking verb *is*, or it may be a verb following the auxiliary *is*. If we take it as an adjective, the sentence means that Lynn is amusing; if we take it as a verb, it means that Lynn is giving a party. We can make each meaning clear by adding signals:

> Lynn is very entertaining tonight.
> Lynn is entertaining several friends tonight.

Sentences that are ambiguous in this way are interesting because they demonstrate that we actually do classify words when we use language and that the way we classify them affects the meaning. In other words, all users of English automatically and unconsciously react to the signals we have analyzed in our discussion of the classification of words. They may not know the names "noun" or "verb," but they do know instinctively which words work as nouns and which work as verbs, adjectives, and adverbs. They must know this in order to speak or understand English sentences.

Exercise: Give the form class of each italicized word in the sentences below.

1. The *forecast* didn't mention *rain*, so it will, of course, *rain today*.
2. Some quite *superstitious people* will not *wear green*.

3. The children *here* are more *hospitable* than their *parents*.

4. Hal fell *backwards* into the mud and *ruined* his *new green* jacket.

5. He will *talk* to me *now*, but he *was* quite *silent then*.

6. The *dark bars* on these *spectrograms* are produced by the *formants*.

7. Since we don't *get* much *sleep* during the *week*, we *sleep* until *noon* on Saturdays.

8. You must *always* study *hard* for a *hard* test.

9. *Persons* whose books are *overdue* will be *fined*.

10. *Axons* from these *cell bodies pass inward* to the *modiolus*.

5.2 Structure Words

There are between two and three hundred words that cannot be placed in any of the form classes. They are called **structure words** and are divided into several **structure groups.**

Structure words differ from form class words in several ways. One difference is that structure words are used more frequently than form class words. We cannot write or talk very long without using structure words like *in, of, the, and, very,* and *will* over and over again. In fact, the comparatively small number of structure words supplies over one-third of the words in ordinary speech and writing.

Another difference is that the structure groups are more stable than the form classes. New form class words are developed constantly as the need for them arises (*transistor, paramedic, minicam*). At the same time, older words continually fall into disuse and disappear from the living language (*trow, yclept, prithee*). The list of structure words, however, changes very slowly; new structure words are developed very infrequently.

Structure words and form class words also differ in the kind of meaning they have. Form class words like *blue, wagon, slowly, carelessness,* and *walk* bring pictures to our minds. They refer to something in the world outside language, and we can define them by telling what they refer to. This kind of meaning is called **lexical meaning.**

Structure words, on the other hand, have no reference to the world outside language and therefore have no lexical meaning. They are used to show the relationships between form class words. We can define the meaning of structure words, not by telling what they refer to, but only by telling what they do in a sentence. For example, the word *very* has no lexical meaning; it is used to intensify the lexical meaning of the word that follows: *slowly, very slowly; blue, very blue.* This kind of meaning is called **structural meaning.** We shall have more to say about structural meaning in connection with the basic sentence patterns in Section 5.3.

We have already mentioned three of the structure groups. In our discussion of the form classes, we saw that one way to classify a word was to notice the kind of structure word that accompanied it. We found that nouns were marked by **determiners;** verbs by **auxiliaries;** and adjectives and adverbs by **intensifiers.** In the rest of this section we will describe the functions of some of the other important structure groups: prepositions, includers, relatives, question words, and conjunctions.

Prepositions are words like *in, of, outside, except, beyond, at, with,* and *after.* Prepositions combine with an object (usually a noun) to form a **prepositional phrase.** When we see a preposition, we know that its object is not functioning as part of the basic sentence pattern, such as the subject or the object of the verb, but that it is used as a modifier:

The building *on the corner* is being renovated.
Never cross *in the middle of the block.*

Includers are words like *since, whether, if, when,* and *although.* Includers introduce clauses; they show us that the noun-verb combination that follows is not a sentence pattern, but only a part of one.

I wonder *whether* he is going.
The house has been extremely quiet *since* she left.
If you don't succeed, try again.

Words like *who, which, that,* and *whom* are called **relatives.** These words make clauses part of larger structures just as includers do. They are placed in a separate group, however, because they also serve a function within the clause, such as the subject or the object of the verb:

The man **who** *lives next door* has several acres of peonies.
The last book **that** *he wrote* became a best seller.

Question words are words like *who, what, where, how,* and *when.* They are used at the beginning of a sentence to indicate that the sentence is a question:

Who told you about the meeting?
Where did I leave my mandolin?
When did you last see him?

Conjunctions are words like *and, or,* and *but.* They tie two or more similar elements together so that they operate in a sentence as a single unit. Many conjunctions have two parts: *either . . . or, both . . . and.*

My mother *and* father went to Mexico last summer, *but* they didn't visit *either* Mexico City *or* Acapulco.

In addition to the important large structure groups, there are several small groups and some individual structure words that behave in a unique way and do not fit in a group. For example, notice the different functions of the italicized words in the following sentences:

There are several robins in the yard.
To cut your own hair takes courage.
Frank said that we should *not* go, did*n't* he?
Please close the door, and *let's* get some work done.

Exercise: The structure words in the following sentences are printed in italics. Tell what structure group each structure word belongs to. When structure words do not belong to one of the seven large groups, "structure word *there*" or "structure word *not*" is sufficient classification.

1. She gave *our* problem *very* close attention.
2. She *must have* been *in a* hurry *when* she addressed *this* package.
3. *Most* students find *their* class notes *most* helpful.
4. *The* package *that* came yesterday contained *a* gift *which* astonished *my* friends.
5. *When does* he arrive, *and who is* picking him up *at the* station?
6. Madelyn looked *the* word up *and* found *that* I was correct.
7. *There* are *several* possibilities *that* we *haven't* explored.
8. *Which* twin took *the* final twice?
9. Frank wanted *to go to the* hotel *that his* father *had* recommended.
10. *Please* give *that* package *either to* Joe *or to his* mother.
11. Mrs. Moore was *very* annoyed *because* we *had* broken *her* window.
12. *As this* construction becomes obsolescent, *its* function *is* taken over *by* catenatives *and* modals *with* prescriptive *or* contingent components.

5.3   The Basic Sentence Patterns

We do not arrive at the meaning of an English sentence by adding up the meanings of its individual words. An important part of a sentence's meaning depends on the way the words are organized, that is, on the order in which the words come in the sentence. Compare the following groups of words:

> the saw bear first driver the
> the driver saw the bear first
> the bear saw the driver first

Each group contains the same words, but the meaning of the groups is very different. The first group is not organized according to English word order, and the only meaning we get from it is the meanings of the individual words. In the second and third groups, the words are organized into English sentences, and in addition to the meanings of the individual words, we get the meaning supplied by the word order. Since the two sentences are made up of exactly the same words, the difference in meaning between them is entirely due to the difference in word order.

Not all languages use word order to convey meaning. Latin, for example, depends on word endings to signal grammatical relationships.

> Agricola puellam amat.   Puellam amat agricola.
> Agricola amat puellam.   Amat agricola puellam.

The first sentence above represents the usual Latin word order; the other sentences vary in emphasis but not in basic meaning. No matter what order the words come in, the sentence means "The farmer loves the girl." The fact that *agricola* (farmer) is the subject of the sentence is signaled—not by the word order—but by the ending -*a*. Similarly, *puellam* (girl) is the object of the verb because it ends in -*am*.

In English, the subject is indicated by its position preceding the verb. The object is indicated by its position following the verb. We can change the meaning of a sentence by changing the word order:

> The farmer loves the girl.
> The girl loves the farmer.

To make the same change in meaning in a Latin sentence, however, we must change the word endings:

> Agricola amat puellam.
> Agricolam amat puella.

If we examine English sentences, looking at the different orders in which words occur, we find that the majority of English sentences are based on a few ways of putting form class words together. We call these different word orders the **basic sentence patterns.** In the rest of this section we will discuss the most important of these patterns.

Pattern One

NOUN	VERB	(ADVERB)
The fans	cheered.	
Casey	struck	out.
It	might snow.	
Both children	are sleeping.	
Mrs. Conway	is going	by bus.
That movie	ended	strangely.

Pattern One sentences consist most simply of a noun followed by a verb. Frequently the pattern is completed by an adverb or an adverbial element, such as a prepositional phrase. Verbs that occur in Pattern One sentences are called **intransitive verbs**

Pattern Two

NOUN	VERB	ADVERB
The firemen	were	in a hurry.
Mrs. Conway	will be	here.
Frank	is	on the carpet.
The snowshoes	ought to be	inside.

The verb in Pattern Two sentences is always some form of *be* (*is, am, are, was, were, be, being, been*). The adverbs and adverbial elements that occur in this pattern always refer to time or place; we never find adverbs of manner, such as *strangely, eagerly, noisily, slowly*.

Pattern Three

NOUN	VERB	ADJECTIVE
His mother	seems	very young.
Those rocks	are	treacherous.
Mrs. Conway	is	bitter.

My overcoat	has become	quite shabby.
Her story	sounded	true.
That tree	will grow	even taller.

Verbs that occur in Pattern Three sentences are called **linking verbs.** There are thousands of intransitive verbs in English, but only a few words are regularly used as linking verbs. The most important are *be* (and its various forms), *seem,* and *become.*

Pattern Four

NOUN	VERB	NOUN
His mother	is	a doctor.
Both books	have become	best sellers.
Luther	remained	my friend.
Our street	is	a thoroughfare.

Be, become, and *remain* are the verbs that usually appear in Pattern Four sentences. They are classed as linking verbs.

Pattern Five

NOUN	VERB	NOUN
The choir	sang	several selections.
The pitcher	hit	a home run.
The class	should elect	officers.
Mrs. Conway	has given	the money.
Carelessness	causes	accidents.
Our team	has to win	every game.

Pattern Four and Pattern Five sentences have the same sequence: noun-verb-noun. We can tell them apart, however, because these two patterns contain different kinds of verbs. The verbs that occur in Pattern Five form a large class called **transitive verbs.** These verbs produce sentences in which the two nouns refer to different persons or things. The linking verbs that occur in Pattern Four, on the other hand, produce sentences in which the two nouns refer to the same person or thing. In each pair of sentences below, notice how the relationship between the nouns changes when we replace a linking verb with a transitive verb:

His mother became a doctor.
His mother needed a doctor.

Frank remained my friend.
Frank snubbed my friend.

Our street is a thoroughfare.
Our street intersects a thoroughfare.

The noun following the verb in a Pattern Four sentence is called a **predicate noun;** in Pattern Five sentences, it is called a **direct object.**

Most of the thousands of transitive verbs in English occur only in Pattern Five sentences. There are, however, two small classes of transitive verbs that may occur in sentences that have two nouns following the verb. One of these groups occurs in Pattern Six sentences; the other group occurs in Pattern Seven.

Pattern Six

NOUN	VERB	NOUN	NOUN
Mrs. Conway	gave	us	the money.
He	wrote	each aunt	a postcard.
Jimmy	should tell	his parents	our plans.
His uncle	got	Frank	that job.

Pattern Seven

NOUN	VERB	NOUN	NOUN
The class	elected	Jimmy	president.
Perseverance	made	him	a millionaire.
Everyone	considers	him	a hero.
The judge	declared	the plan	a fraud.

Both Pattern Six and Pattern Seven are noun-verb-noun-noun. We can tell them apart because the verbs that occur in Pattern Six sentences are followed by nouns that refer to different persons or things. The verbs in Pattern Seven sentences are followed by nouns that refer to the same person or thing. In Pattern Six the first noun following the verb is called the **indirect object;** the second noun is the direct object. In Pattern Seven the first noun is the direct object; the second noun is called the **object complement.** With some of the verbs that occur in Pattern Seven, an adjective can replace the second noun:

> Everyone considers him heroic.
> The judge declared the plan fraudulent.

English sentences are seldom as simple as the basic sentences listed above. In order to convey meaning adequately, we usually need to expand the basic patterns by adding modifiers and more complicated constructions. But no matter how complicated or how long a sentence becomes, it will always have one of the basic patterns as a foundation.

More About Structural Meaning

The meaning of an English sentence is a combination of lexical meaning and structural meaning. The lexical meaning is contained in the form class words. The structural meaning is represented by three different elements: (1) word endings, (2) structure words, and (3) word order.

Structural meaning can be seen most clearly if it is isolated from lexical meaning. We can do this by composing sentences that contain nonsense words instead of regular form class words. For example:

> That boofical flugness has blanged many shmumps.

Since this sentence has no lexical meaning, we can see how the structural elements (word endings, structure words, and word order) work together to produce structural meaning. Thus, although we don't know what *flugness* means, the structural meaning shows us that it is a noun, that it is something that can be boofical, and that it can blang. Similarly, we can tell that *blang* is a verb and that it is something that a boofical flugness can do to shmumps. Shmumps are obviously things that can be blanged by a flugness.

In this way, structural meaning shows important relationships —even between nonsense words. Suppose we replace the nonsense words with blanks:

That _____ has _____ ed many _____ s.

We now have a sentence pattern into which we can fit many different sets of form class words:

That long wait has annoyed many customers.
That European acrobat has performed many feats.
That old car has traveled many miles.
That fat man has tried many diets.

The lexical meaning of these sentences varies a great deal. But the structural meaning is the same because the form class words in each sentence have the same relationships with each other.

Exercise A: Write five sentences that follow each of the sentence patterns listed below. Nouns that are marked with an asterisk (*) should refer to the same person or thing.

1. Noun	Verb	·Adjective	
2. Noun	Verb	Noun*	Noun*
3. Noun	Verb	(Adverb)	
4. Noun*	Verb	Noun*	
5. Noun	Verb	Noun	Noun
6. Noun	Be	Adverb	
7. Noun	Verb	Noun	

Exercise B: Substitute meaningful English words for the nonsense words in the sentences below. Then see if you can think of still another set of words that will fit the pattern of each sentence.

1. The greeb on the mumf is glibbing our glacks.
2. His plome has been greebing plooshly.
3. Bool that skillity moughly.
4. Their blang has been rackled by the glumps.
5. Where has my bloop bleemed?

6.0 Agreement of Subject and Verb

In grammar the word *agreement* means "likeness." To make two words agree is to make them alike in some respect.

A common error in American speech is the failure to make subject and verb agree (*you was, we was, he don't.*) Errors of agreement in speaking are sometimes difficult to avoid. In writing, however, these errors should be easier to avoid because the writer always has the time and opportunity to revise his work before presenting it to a reader.

6.1 Subject-Verb Agreement in Number

There are two numbers in grammar: **singular** and **plural.** A word is singular in number if it refers to one person or thing. A word is plural if it refers to more than one person or thing.

Except for *be*, English verbs show a difference between singular and plural only in the third person and only in the present tense. The third person singular present form ends in *s*.

$$\left.\begin{array}{l} \text{I} \\ \text{you} \\ \text{we} \\ \text{they} \end{array}\right\} \text{walk} \qquad \left.\begin{array}{l} \text{he} \\ \text{she} \\ \text{it} \end{array}\right\} \text{walks}$$

The verb *be* presents several special problems in agreement. First, the second person pronoun *you* is always used with the plural form of the verb: *you are, you were.* Second, the difference between singular and plural is shown in the past tense as well as in the present tense.

SINGULAR	PLURAL	PRESENT TENSE	PAST TENSE
I *was*	we *were*	I *am*	we *were*
you *were*	you *were*	you *are*	you *were*
he, she, it *was*	they *were*	he, she, it *is*	they *were*

The most common errors with *be* are *you was, we was, they was.*

A singular verb is used with a singular subject.

A plural verb is used with a plural subject.

The subject determines whether the verb is singular or plural. The verb does not agree with any other part of the sentence.

The cat (singular) *likes* liver.
The cats (plural) *like* liver.

The teacher (singular) *works* hard.
The teachers (plural) *work* hard.

Note: A verb also agrees with its subject in *person.* When there are two or more subjects that differ in person, the verb agrees with the subject nearest to it.

I *go* to the orthodontist every month.
Al *goes* to the movies every week.
Neither Fred nor I *play* chess.

6.2 Plural Words Between Subject and Verb

The verb agrees only with its subject. Occasionally a word with a different number from that of the subject occurs between the subject and the verb. This word usually has no effect upon the number of the verb even though it is closer to the verb than the subject is.

The *revolution,* led by a group of guerillas, *has* been won.
(*revolution* is the subject.)
One of her classmates *is* a guide at the United Nations.
(*One* is the subject.)
The *Congress* of the United States *is* in session.
(*Congress* is the subject.)
The *pears* on that old tree *are* not edible.
(*pears* is the subject.)

The words *with, together with, along with, as well as* are prepositions. The objects of these prepositions have no effect upon the number of the verb.

The *President,* together with his aides, *was* studying the crisis.
(*President* is the subject.)
Your *dress,* as well as your manner, *is* important.
(*dress* is the subject.)
The *singer,* along with her band, *is* on tour for six months.
(*singer* is the subject.)

Exercise: Choose the standard form of the verb for each sentence.

1. When (was, were) you at the doctor's office?
2. Is it true that one of the passengers (was, were) killed?
3. (Is, Are) the book reports due this week or next?
4. The teacher as well as the class (were, was) surprised by Betty's report.
5. The pilot, in addition to the crew, (have, has) your comfort and safety in mind.
6. The age of the huge sequoias (are, is) hard to believe.

7. The high cost of repairs always (come, comes) as a surprise.

8. The lights in the store window (is, are) turned off at midnight.

9. The decision of the umpires (were, was) hotly disputed.

10. The danger of floods on the Ohio and Allegheny rivers (has, have) been exaggerated.

11. It is now thought that Saturn as well as Mars (has, have) some form of life.

12. The scientist's report, together with the photographs, (is, are) very convincing.

13. The older members on the local school board (want, wants) to build a new school.

14. The lights in the valley down below (look, looks) like tiny jewels.

15. The captain of any of our teams (have, has) a special responsibility.

16. (Was, Were) you at home all day?

17. The aim of the talks (are, is) supposed to be arms reduction.

18. The sale of the school yearbooks (have, has) been disappointing.

6.3 Indefinite Pronouns

Some indefinite pronouns are always singular. Others are always plural. Some may be either singular or plural.

SINGULAR			PLURAL
each	everyone	anyone	several
either	everybody	someone	few
neither	no one	somebody	both
one	nobody		many

Each of the candidates *has* criticized spending.
Neither of the *buses* was full.
Everybody in the fields *was* working.
Several in this class *are* good writers.
Few in the student council *have* been re-elected.
Both of the quarterbacks *were* injured.

SINGULAR OR PLURAL

some   all   most
none   any

Some, all, most, none, and *any* are singular when they refer to a quantity. They are plural when they refer to a number of individual items.

Some of the cream *was* sour. (quantity)
Some of the buildings *were* being demolished. (number)

Most of the forest *was* saved from fire. (quantity)
Most of his friends *are* going to the movie. (number)

All of the turkey *was* eaten in two days. (quantity)
All of the English classes *are* entering the writing
    contest. (number)

Exercise: Choose the standard form of the verb for each sentence.

1. Either of these hats (suit, suits) you.
2. Most of the television programs (is, are) boring.
3. Not one of the papers (has, have) the name spelled correctly.
4. Neither of the drivers (was, were) hurt in the accident.
5. One of the violins (are, is) playing off key.
6. Each of the new cars (come, comes) equipped with safety belts.
7. (Have, Has) either of the buses left yet?
8. Obviously, one of the witnesses (were, was) not telling the truth.
9. Some of the teams (has, have) new uniforms.
10. The old houses in this block (is, are) being torn down.
11. Everyone in the stands (was, were) sure a touchdown had been scored.
12. Few in this school (know, knows) about Mr. Moore's trouble.
13. One of the boats (seem, seems) to have a leak.
14. It was reported that neither of the bridges (were, was) safe.
15. The pilot discovered that one of the engines (were, was) not working right.

16. Each of the balloons (carry, carries) scientific instruments.
17. Everyone in the pictures (is, are) grinning foolishly.
18. Neither of these patterns (is, are) what I want.
19. Several of the listeners (has, have) telephoned the studio.
20. (Has, Have) either of the candidates promised lower taxes?

6.4 Compound Subjects

Compound subjects joined by <u>and</u> are plural. *

Overloaded circuits and faulty wiring *cause* fires.

Singular words joined by <u>or, nor</u>, <u>either-or</u>, <u>neither-nor</u> to form a compound subject are singular.

Neither your grammar nor your punctuation *is* perfect.
Either Joe or Pat *has* your baseball.
Is Shirley or Olga *baby-sitting* after school?

When a singular word and a plural word are joined by <u>or</u> or <u>nor</u> to form a compound subject, the verb agrees with the subject that is nearer to it.

Neither the police nor the suspect *wants* to make a statement.
  (*suspect* is closer to the verb than *police*.)
A novel or two plays *meet* the reading requirements.
Neither the songs nor the singer *pleases* him.

Exercise: Find the errors in subject-verb agreement in these sentences. Write the sentences correctly. Two of the sentences are correct.

1. Neither the train nor the airlines run on schedule in bad weather.
2. The chairs and the table was loaded with packages.
3. Neither the gloves nor the sweater were the right size.

---

* If the words making up the compound subject are habitually used together to refer to a single thing, the subject may be used with a singular verb: *bread and butter, macaroni and cheese,* etc.

4. Either Bob or Jeff have been here.

5. The gloves and the hat is the same color.

6. The lifeguard or the swimming coach are always on duty.

7. Neither the newspapers nor the radio have reported the full story.

8. Either the meat or the potatoes is burning.

9. Both skill and constant practice go into the making of a champion.

10. Neither the doctor nor his nurse were at the office.

11. Two squirrels and a jackrabbit is all we saw.

12. Have either Mrs. Barnes or Mrs. Brown arrived yet?

13. Neither the watchman nor the policeman were really on the job.

14. Either Jack or his sister have your books.

15. Neither the audience nor the actors was aware of the trouble backstage.

6.5 Subject Following Verb

The most difficult agreement problem in speech arises when the subject follows the verb. The speaker must think ahead to the subject in order to decide whether the verb is to be singular or plural.

This problem arises in sentences beginning with *There* and *Here*. It also arises in questions beginning with *who, why, where, what, how.*

NONSTANDARD	Here's the skis for Kay.
STANDARD	Here *are* the skis for Kay.
NONSTANDARD	There's four letters for you.
STANDARD	There *are* four letters for you.
NONSTANDARD	Who's the three boys at the door?
STANDARD	Who *are* the three boys at the door?
NONSTANDARD	What's the amendments to the constitution?
STANDARD	What are the amendments to the constitution?

NONSTANDARD   From out of the blue *comes* three jets.
STANDARD   From out of the blue *come* three jets.

6.6 Predicate Words

The linking verb agrees with its subject, *not* with the predicate word.

NONSTANDARD   Hamburgers *is* his favorite food.
STANDARD   Hamburgers *are* his favorite food.

NONSTANDARD   Martha's main interest *are* horses.
STANDARD   Martha's main interest *is* horses.

NONSTANDARD   Money and power *is* his only aim.
STANDARD   Money and power *are* his only aim.

6.7 <u>Don't</u> and <u>Doesn't</u>

The word *does* and the contraction *doesn't* are used with singular nouns and with the pronouns *he, she,* and *it.* The word *do* and the contraction *don't* are used with plural nouns and with the pronouns *I, we, you,* and *they.*

DOES, DOESN'T	DO, DON'T
the law does	the laws do
he doesn't	we don't
she doesn't	you don't
it doesn't	they don't

Exercise: Choose the standard form from the two in parentheses.

1. (Where's, Where are) the stack of papers I put on the desk?
2. (Don't, Doesn't) the wind sound wild tonight?
3. (Here's, Here are) the books you lent to Robin.
4. (What's, What are) the names of the mountain ranges in California?
5. It seems that there (was, were) two men named Clyde Smith.

6. Hard work and ambition (is, are) not the answer.

7. Money and power (was, were) Wilson's goal.

8. The leader of the expedition (don't, doesn't) dare to take chances.

9. Sunny days and a beautiful beach (is, are) the town's claim to fame.

10. Up the steps (move, moves) the procession.

11. (Don't, Doesn't) the bus stop at this corner?

12. Protein and fats (is, are) the great dietary need in India.

13. (There's, There are) two good motels right outside of town.

14. Down into the cave (go, goes) Cousteau and Didi.

15. The wax on the floors (make, makes) them dangerously slippery.

16. The biggest difficulty (is, are) the inexperience and indifference of the workers.

17. Through this door (passes, pass) the lawmakers of our nation.

18. The expedition's task (were, was) to establish a base camp and to begin scientific observations.

19. (Where's, Where are) the men who are coming to help us?

20. (What are, What's) the weather predictions for this week?

6.8 Collective Nouns

A collective noun names a group of people or things: *committee, flock, team, herd, crowd.*

When the writer refers to a group acting together as one unit, the collective noun is used with a singular verb. When the writer refers to the individuals in the group acting separately, one by one, the collective noun is used with a plural verb.

> The team *was* the best in the history of the school.
> (united action)
> The team *were* putting on their uniforms. (separate actions)
>
> The council *is* in emergency session. (united action)
> The council *were* debating the proposals. (separate actions)

Once the writer decides whether the collective noun is a unit or a group of individuals, he must abide by his choice. Later in the same sentence he may not use a verb or pronoun of different number.

<dl>
<dt>NONSTANDARD</dt>
<dd>The Senate has (singular) changed their (plural) rules.</dd>
<dt>STANDARD</dt>
<dd>The Senate has changed its rules.</dd>
</dl>

6.9 Nouns Plural in Form

Some nouns are plural in form but are regarded as singular in meaning. That is, they end in *s* as most plural nouns do, but they do not stand for more than one thing: *news, mumps, measles.* Therefore, they are used with a singular verb.

There are many words ending in *-ics* that may be either singular or plural: *economics, athletics, civics, politics.* These words are singular when they are used to refer to a school subject, a science, or a general practice. When singular in meaning, they are not usually preceded by *the, his, some, all* and singular modifiers.

Ethics *is* important in the study of religion and
philosophy. (singular)
The council's ethics in this matter *are*
questionable. (plural)
Politics *is* a fascinating game. (singular)
His politics *involve* only a struggle for power. (plural)
Physics *was* Donna's most difficult subject. (singular)
Athletics *was* de-emphasized after the betting
scandal. (singular)

6.10 Titles and Groups of Words

The title of a book, play, story, film, musical composition or other work of art is used with a singular verb. The name of a country is used with a singular verb. Such words, even though plural in form, refer to a single thing.

> The Philippines *is* made up of 7,083 islands and islets.
> *All the President's Men was* produced by Robert Redford.
> "War of the Worlds" *was* written by H. G. Wells.
> The United Nations *is* discussing the problem.
> Vivaldi's "The Seasons" *was* played by the Boston Symphony.

Any group of words referring to a single thing or thought is used with a singular verb.

> What we need *is* votes.   Ham and eggs *is* on the menu.

6.11   Words of Amount and Time

Words or phrases that express periods of time, fractions, weights, measurements, and amounts of money are usually regarded as singular.

> Ten dollars *is* too much to pay.
> Two-thirds of the money *has* been raised.
> Five hours *seems* a long time for that trip.
> One hundred pounds of bird seed *is* ridiculous.
> Ten yards of curtain material *was* not enough.

If a prepositional phrase with a plural object falls between the subject and the verb, the verb is singular if its subject is considered as a single thing or thought. The verb is plural if its subject is felt to be plural.

> Sixty pounds of potatoes *was* what we ordered.
> Sixty of the passengers *were* saved.

Exercise: Choose the standard form from the two forms given in parentheses.

1. On their hours off duty, the crew (was, were) not allowed to leave the ship.

2. Making their way slowly up the cliff, the relief party (was, were) nearly at the ledge.

3. Next year, civics (is, are) to be taught in the ninth grade.

4. Politics (is, are) my father's hobby.

5. What we call politics (is, are) necessary in our form of government.

6. The East Indies (was, were) a source of European wealth.

7. All that we need (is, are) time and money.

8. Two-thirds of the crop (was, were) not even harvested.

9. Two-thirds of the students (want, wants) a real weekly paper.

10. Six quarts of milk (are, is) what we ordered.

11. Athletics (is, are) taking too much of Harry's time.

12. With its new plays, the team (was, were) confident of winning.

13. Economics (was, were) once known as the dismal science.

14. At its meetings, the group (see, sees) movies.

15. The United States (has, have) started explorations beneath the earth's crust.

16. Pneumatics (deal, deals) with the properties of air and other gases.

17. Two thousand dollars (are, is) a lot to pay for a secondhand car.

18. Sixteen hours on the bus (was, were) too much for us.

19. "By the Waters of Babylon" (are, is) a thought-provoking story.

20. One of the lifeboats (have, has) sunk.

6.12   Relative Pronouns

A relative pronoun stands in place of its antecedent (the word to which it refers). If that antecedent is plural, the relative pronoun is plural. If the antecedent is singular, the relative pronoun is singular.

A relative pronoun agrees with its antecedent in number.

When a relative pronoun is used as subject of the verb in the relative clause, the number of the verb depends upon the number of the pronoun's antecedent.

> They are the *candidates* (plural) who (plural) *have*
> been elected.
>
> Fay is the *girl* (singular) who (singular) *manages* the store.
>
> King is one of those *dogs* who *are* always chasing cars.
> (*dogs* are always chasing cars.)
>
> Ms. Foss is the only *one* of the teachers who *has* a master's
> degree. (Only *one* has a master's degree.)

The problem of agreement arises in the preceding sentences because there are two words, either of which *might* be the antecedent of the relative pronoun. Usually the meaning of the sentence shows which word *is* the antecedent.

Exercise: Choose the standard form from the two forms given.

1. This is the only one of the books that (is, are) worth reading.
2. Tom is the only one in the class who (has, have) climbed Mt. Washington.
3. Anne is one of those individuals who (is, are) always finding fault.
4. Gibson is one of the members who always (listen, listens) attentively before replying.
5. Here are two new fabrics of the kind that (resist, resists) moisture.
6. He is the only one of the refugees who (speak, speaks) English fluently.
7. Joan is the one person in the group who (has, have) a good record collection.
8. There are three members of our class who (have, has) won prizes.
9. Tim is one of those persons who (seem, seems) always good-natured.
10. He is the one of our neighbors who never (fail, fails) to greet us.

7.0   Pronoun Usage

In grammar, the term *inflection* has a special meaning. It means "a change in form to show how a word is used in a sentence." Prepositions, conjunctions, and interjections do not change their form. All other parts of speech do. Usually, the change in form is just a change in spelling:

NOUN:	girl	— girl's	— girls	— girls'
VERB:	need	— needs	— needed	— needing
ADJECTIVE:	new	— newer	— newest	
ADVERB:	near	— nearer	— nearest	

Often, however, the change involves the use of a completely new word:

VERB:	do	— did	— done
PRONOUN:	I	— me	— mine

Pronouns change their form in both ways. The changes in pronouns correspond to their use in sentences. These changes are called the **cases** of pronouns. These cases are the **nominative, possessive** and **objective.**

You will recall that pronouns can be used in sentences in the following ways:

subject of the verb   object of a preposition
object of the verb   appositive
predicate pronoun   modifier

Nearly all pronouns change their form for different uses in the sentence. The indefinite pronouns have the least change. They change only when used as modifiers. As modifiers, they are in the possessive case:

POSSESSIVE

everyone — everyone's
nobody — nobody's
anyone — anyone's

The pronouns *this, that, these, those, which,* and *what* do not change their forms to indicate case. None of these has a possessive form.

The pronoun inflections are as follows:

NOMINATIVE	POSSESSIVE	OBJECTIVE
I	my, mine	me
we	our, ours	us
you	your, yours	you
he	his	him
she	her, hers	her
it	its	it
they	their, theirs	them
who	whose	whom
whoever	whosever	whomever

7.1 The Pronoun as Subject of a Verb

The nominative form of the pronoun is used as subject of a verb.

The problem of which pronoun form to use as subject arises chiefly when the subject is compound. The compound subject

may be made up of pronouns or of both nouns and pronouns.
To decide which pronoun form to use in a compound subject,
try each part of the subject by itself with the verb.

> Hal and (I, me) went to the movies.
> (Hal went; I went, *not* me went.)
> The McCarthys and (they, them) are in the club.
> (The McCarthys are; they are, *not* them are.)
> We and (they, them) tried out for the Olympics.
> (We tried; they tried, *not* them tried.)
> He and (I, me) read *Huckleberry Finn.*
> (He read; I read, *not* me read.)

The plural forms *we* and *they* sound awkward in many compounds. They can be avoided by recasting the sentence.

> AWKWARD The girls and we are going.
> BETTER   We and the girls are going.

> AWKWARD We and they planned to swim at dawn.
> BETTER   We all planned to swim at dawn.

7.2 The Predicate Pronoun

The verb *be* is a linking verb. It links the noun, pronoun, or
adjective following it to the subject. A pronoun so linked is
called a **predicate pronoun.**

The nominative pronoun form is used as a predicate pronoun.*

The problem of which form to use in a predicate pronoun
occurs primarily after the verb *be.* The rule applies to all verb
phrases built around forms of *be: could have been, can be, should
be,* etc.

> It *was* **I** whom they called.
> *Could* it *have been* **he** who won?
> It *must have been* **they** in the sports car.

* Standard usage permits the exception in both speech and writing of *It is me.*

Sometimes the nominative form sounds awkward. The awkwardness can be avoided by recasting the sentence.

AWKWARD The winners are she and Loretta.
BETTER Loretta and she are the winners.

AWKWARD It was we who found the entrance to the cave.
BETTER We are the people who found the entrance to the cave

7.3 The Pronoun as Object of a Verb

The objective pronoun form is used as direct or indirect object.

The problem of which pronoun form to use as object of the verb arises chiefly when the object is compound. The compound object may consist of pronouns or of both nouns and pronouns.

To decide which pronoun form to use in a compound object, *try each part of the object by itself with the verb.*

DIRECT OBJECT:

The principal wanted to see George and (I, me).
(see George; see me, *not* see I)
Jenny invited both (they, them) and (we, us) to the party.
(invited them, *not* invited they; invited us, *not* invited we.)
Did you ask (he, him) and (I, me) to dinner?
(ask him, *not* ask he; ask me, *not* ask I)

INDIRECT OBJECT:

The counselor gave Janet and (I, me) good advice.
(gave Janet; gave me, *not* gave I)

Exercise A: Choose the standard form from those given in parentheses.

1. Jeff and (me, I) are applying for scholarships at Northwestern.
2. The chairman invited Mrs. Dawson and (she, her) to speak to the group.

3. At the bottom of the class were Roger and (me, I).
4. How much money did Lynn and (she, her) make?
5. Give Marion and (she, her) the extra tickets.
6. Marge and (me, I) are having a party after the game.
7. The Warners and (them, they) are good friends.
8. The last on the program are Herb and (me, I).
9. The coach gave Harold and (I, me) passes to the game.
10. Was it (he, him) who answered the telephone?
11. (Her, She) and the traffic cop were having a loud argument.
12. Can you tell Beth and (me, I) where the party will be?
13. Grace and (I, me) were watching television when you called.
14. The sophomores and (us, we) are sponsoring the play together.
15. We were sure that it was (him, he) at the door.

Exercise B: Choose the standard form from those given in parentheses.

1. The bus met (he, him) and (I, me) at the station.
2. The police telephoned Gary and (they, them) right after the accident.
3. The store manager greeted (her, she) and (he, him) cordially.
4. The airlines office told (they, them) and (we, us) different stories.
5. Was it (them, they) who wrote you?
6. It might have been (us, we) in that crash.
7. The seniors scarcely noticed Betty and (I, me).
8. Why don't you let (they, them) and (we, us) take care of decorations?
9. Dad drove Karen and (me, I) into town.
10. Will you and (he, him) study together for the test?
11. It must have been (her, she) in the window.
12. If it were (him, he), I would certainly be surprised.
13. What would you do if you were (her, she)?
14. The boss gave Herb and (me, I) a rush job.
15. We met (they, them) and their parents at the theater.

7.4 The Pronoun as Object of a Preposition

The objective pronoun form is used as object of a preposition.

The problem of which pronoun form to use as object of a preposition arises only when the object is compound. The compound object may consist of pronouns or of both nouns and pronouns.

To decide which pronoun to use in a compound object of a preposition, *try each part of the object by itself with the preposition.*

> Will your aunt be going with you and (I, me)?
> (with you; with me, *not* with I)
> We had Christmas cards from (they, them) and the Clarks.
> (from them, *not* from they)
> The doctor gave virus shots to both the coaches and (we, us).
> (to us; *not* to we)

The preposition *between* causes especially noticeable errors in pronoun usage. Use only the objective pronoun forms after *between.*

> between you and him, not between you and he
> between him and me, *not* between he and I

7.5 The Pronoun Used with a Noun

In a construction such as *we girls* or *us boys*, the use of the noun determines the case form of the pronoun.

> We girls can bring the lunch.
> (girls is the subject of *can bring*; the nominative pronoun is therefore required.)
> The Kiwanis Club gave the sports equipment to us girls.
> (girls is the object of the preposition *to*; the objective pronoun is therefore required.)

To decide which pronoun form to use in a construction such as *we boys,* try the pronoun by itself with the verb or preposition.

The test was not too difficult for (we, us) boys.
(for us, *not* for we)
The policeman told (we, us) boys not to play ball in the street.
(told us, *not* told we)
(We, Us) friends must not part.
(We must not part, *not* us must not part)

Exercise A: Choose the standard form from those given in parentheses.

1. Make out the check either to Dad or (I, me).
2. At Christmas time, we had a card from Beth and (he, him).
3. It was hard for Mark and (I, me) to understand the directions.
4. There is a package for you and (she, her) at the post office.
5. Between you and (me, I), that party will never be held.
6. Stacey is going home with Grace and (he, him).
7. The time has come for (us, we) students to stand up for our rights.
8. (We, Us) Americans are the envy of the rest of the world.
9. The doctor arranged for Mrs. Barry and (he, him) to stay at the hospital.
10. There is no quarrel between (she, her) and (I, me).
11. Will you save tickets for (they, them) and (we, us)?
12. The books have been ordered for (we, us) boys.
13. (We, Us) two will have to do most of the work.
14. There were many compliments for you and (her, she).
15. There is a special practice for (we, us) flute players today.

Exercise B: Choose the standard form from those given in parentheses.

1. We had a long visit with Sue and (she, her).
2. The camp counselor asked Jay and (I, me) to help him.
3. To (we, us) newcomers, the coach gave special exercises.
4. Sarah, Lynn, and (her, she) are the committee.

5. The bad news reached Ted and (me, I) just before Christmas.
6. The usher seated Terri and (he, him) way up front.
7. For Jason, Lee, and (we, us), the party was just a lot of work.
8. There are no secrets between Sally and (I, me).
9. (We, Us) baseball fans were not surprised by the Yankees' downfall.
10. After John and (she, her) had spoken, there was a general discussion.
11. Only (us, we) three have been called to the office.
12. To Jack, Nancy, and (I, me) the decision was a great disappointment.
13. The principal warned (we, us) students to stay in the stands.
14. Just between you and (I, me), the test was really very easy.
15. The scholarship committee asked Barry and (he, him) to meet with them after school.

Exercise C: Choose the standard form from those in parentheses.

1. The mechanic advised Dick and (I, me) not to buy the car.
2. Later, (her, she) and (I, me) found the book at the public library.
3. The guide showed (he, him) and (I, me) some synthetic diamonds.
4. The Clarks and (we, us) are having Thanksgiving dinner together.
5. For (us, we) boys, the lecture on job opportunities was an eye opener.
6. Mr. David had several jobs for (us, we) three girls.
7. (Us, We) two had better get started.
8. The school has given (us, we) scholarship winners an extra day of vacation.
9. Just between you and (I, me), our chances in this game are not good.
10. We left the selection of a class ring to (she, her) and Lillian.
11. There was no mail for Jeff and (I, me).
12. Tom left ahead of Alice and (I, me).
13. (She, her) and (he, him) used to live in Duluth.
14. The girls joined Mary and (we, us) at the bowling alleys.

15. The driver asked (he, him) and (I, me) to help change the tire.
16. The uniforms fit neither (he, him) nor Brad.
17. We have had no letters from Holly or (she, her).
18. The Hanleys entertained Sue and (us, we) royally.
19. The Governor shook hands with Dad and (I, me) as we left.
20. It was a long trip for (they, them) and the children.

7.6 Pronouns in Comparisons

Sometimes a comparison is made by using a clause that begins with *than* or *as*.

> Fred is better at chess *than George is*.
> You have as many A's *as he has*.
> Marie likes me more *than she likes you*.

Sometimes the final clause in the comparison is left incomplete.

> Fred is better at chess than George (is).
> You have as many A's as he (has).

To decide which pronoun form to use in an incomplete comparison, complete the comparison.

> Herb plays the trumpet better than (I, me).
>   (Herb plays the trumpet better than I *play*.)
> Betty wrote a better composition than (I, me).
>   (Betty wrote a better composition than I *wrote*.)

7.7 Possessive Case with Gerunds

The possessive form of the pronoun is used when the pronoun immediately precedes a gerund.

All gerunds end in -*ing*, and they are all formed from verbs. The present participle also ends in -*ing*, and it, too, is formed from a verb. If the -*ing* word is used as a modifier, it is a participle.

If it is used as a noun, it is a gerund.

The possessive form of the pronoun is used before a gerund. The nominative and objective forms are used before a participle.

> We saw *him running* toward the finish line.
> (*running* is a participle modifying *him*.)

> *His running* had improved since the last track meet.
> (*running* is a gerund, the subject of the verb *had improved*.)

> They disliked *his playing* the piano at midnight.
> (*playing* is a gerund, the object of the verb *disliked*.)

> The tenants heard *him playing* the piano at midnight.
> (*playing* is a participle modifying *him*.)

7.8 The Pronoun with Infinitives

The objective form of the pronoun is used as the subject, object, or predicate pronoun of an infinitive.

> The officer told *me to stop.* (*me* is the subject of *to stop.*)
> The official asked *them to observe* the rules. (*them* is the subject of *to observe.*)
> They took *him to be me.*
> (*him* is the subject of *to be*, and *me* is the predicate pronoun following *to be.*)
> Reporters were at the airport *to question him.*
> (*him* is the object of *to question.*)
> They didn't want the winner *to be her.*
> (*her* is the predicate pronoun following *to be.*)

7.9 The Pronoun as an Appositive

The form of a pronoun used as an appositive is determined by the use of the noun to which it is in apposition.

The delegates, *Tony* and *I*, want your support.

> (*Tony* and *I* are in apposition to *delegates*, which is the subject of *want*. Therefore, the nominative form of the pronoun is required.)

For the two producers, *Kermit* and *him*, the show was a success.

> (*Kermit* and *him* are in apposition to *producers*, which is the object of the preposition *for*. Therefore, the objective form of the pronoun is required.)

We gave the children, *Toby* and *her*, new tricycles.

> (*Toby* and *her* are in apposition to *children*, which is the indirect object of *gave*. Therefore, the objective form of the pronoun is required.)

To determine which form of the pronoun to use in apposition, try the appositive by itself with the verb or preposition.

> Her admirers, Andy and (he, him), were always calling.
> (Andy and he were, *not* Andy and him were.)
> The flowers are from two of your friends, Sally and (I, me).
> (The flowers are from me, *not* from I.)

7.10 Compound Personal Pronouns

Compound personal pronouns are used only when their antecedents appear in the same sentence.

STANDARD	I carried it up the stairs myself.
STANDARD	We made lunch for ourselves.
NONSTANDARD	The hat belongs to yourself.
STANDARD	The hat belongs to you.
NONSTANDARD	The cheers were meant for ourselves.
STANDARD	The cheers were meant for us.

Exercise: Choose the standard form from those given in parentheses.

1. Bill can type much faster than (I, me).

2. Mr. Crofts was disturbed by (us, our) blowing the horn.
3. The class would rather have you for president than (he, him).
4. (Their, Them) shouting kept us awake.
5. We knew the "ghost" would turn out to be (him, he).
6. No one was more frightened than (her, she).
7. Did you hear (our, us) calling you?
8. Dad and (I, myself) will clean up the yard.
9. We gave the soloists, Jenny and (her, she), bouquets of roses.
10. We had twice as big a squad as (they, them).
11. We kept some of the strawberry shortcake for (us, ourselves).
12. The committee gave two students, Ginny and (me, I) first prizes.
13. We were expecting Mr. Bruce rather than (she, her).
14. Please return the unused cartons to Ted or (me, myself).
15. No one but (yourself, you) saw the accident.
16. I didn't like (his, him) sneaking in through the back door.
17. California played a better defensive game than (we, us).
18. We didn't expect the winner to be (he, him).
19. Write a bread-and-butter letter to your hosts, Tom and (he, him).
20. The audience was no more surprised than (them, they).

7.11 Pronouns and Antecedents

A pronoun agrees with its antecedent in number, gender, and person.

Agreement in Number. If the antecedent of a pronoun is singular, a singular pronoun is required. If the antecedent is plural, a plural pronoun is required.

The indefinite pronouns that are singular in meaning cause the greatest difficulty. The following are referred to by singular pronouns:

anybody	either	neither	somebody
anyone	everybody	nobody	someone
each	everyone	one	

Each of the boys brought *his* sleeping bag.
Everyone should make up *his* own mind.
Someone had left *his* briefcase on the bus.

Two or more singular antecedents joined by _or_ or _nor_ are referred to by a singular pronoun.

Either Bob or Hank will let us use *his* car.
Neither the cat nor the dog had eaten *its* meal.

Collective nouns may be referred to by either a singular or plural pronoun, depending upon the meaning intended.

The track team *has its* new uniforms.
The track team *have* been beaten in *their* last three outings.

The indefinite pronouns _all_, _some_, _any_, and _none_ may be referred to by either a singular or plural pronoun, depending upon the meaning intended.

All the furniture *was* in *its* best condition.

All the students *were* taking *their* last examination.

Some of the cider *has* lost *its* tang.

None of the refugee children *have* heard from *their* parents.

Note: In all of the foregoing examples, the collective nouns and indefinite pronouns are used as subjects. The number of the verb and the number of the pronoun referring to them must be the same.

NONSTANDARD	Some of the orchestra *are* playing *its* new instruments.
STANDARD	Some of the orchestra *are* playing *their* new instruments.
NONSTANDARD	None of the singers *was* making their debuts.
STANDARD	None of the singers *were* making *their* debuts.
STANDARD	None of the singers *was* making *his* debut.

Agreement in Gender. Masculine gender is indicated by *he, his, him*. Feminine gender is indicated by *she, her, hers*. Neuter gender is indicated by *it* and *its*. These pronouns must be the same gender as the word to which they refer.

> The lion had fought for *its* life. (neuter)
> The actor rehearsed *his* lines. (masculine)
> The queen was riding in *her* coach. (feminine)

When a singular pronoun must refer to both feminine and masculine antecedents, the phrase "his or her" is acceptable. It is, in fact, preferred by some people who wish to avoid what they consider to be sexist language.

> STANDARD Every student should have *his* ticket ready.
> STANDARD Every student should have *his or her* ticket ready.

Agreement in Person. A personal pronoun must be in the same person as its antecedent. The words *one, everyone,* and *everybody* are in the third person. They are referred to by *he, his, him, she, her, hers.*

> NONSTANDARD *One* should always wear *your* seat belts.
> STANDARD *One* should always wear *his* seat belts.
>
> NONSTANDARD *I* find that the baby's crying grates on *your* nerves.
> STANDARD *I* find that the baby's crying grates on *my* nerves.

Exercise A: Find and correct the errors in agreement in these sentences. Make sure that both the verb and the pronoun are correct. Three of the sentences are correct as they stand.

1. Someone had left their car in our driveway.
2. Each of the boys promised that they would come early.
3. Either Jane or Peggy left their scarf here.
4. Neither of the persons who complained would give their name.
5. Not one of the crew expected to see his home again.
6. Some of the team is wearing their new uniforms.

7. Nobody had done their homework during vacation.

8. Did either your father or grandfather change their name?

9. Neither of the witnesses admitted that they had seen the stranger.

10. Neither the principal nor the class adviser would give their approval to our plan.

11. None of the students were minding their own business.

12. Everyone on our street had decorated his house.

13. The student council has made up their mind to drop the Christmas party.

14. The majority of the class plans to buy their rings this year.

15. Everyone was doing their best to make the party a success.

Exercise B: Find and correct the errors in agreement between pronouns and antecedents in these sentences.

1. One should start early to plan your career.

2. I find that moderate exercise makes you feel better.

3. Everyone can now have your own CB radio.

4. We discovered that you could hear well even in the back seats.

5. You will find cooking easy if one follows the directions.

6. Everyone brought their own food to the picnic.

7. What happens if one's foot slips when you are driving?

8. Nobody in the club has their own equipment.

9. Everyone in class is busy working on their own project.

10. It is a mistake for anyone to try being your own lawyer.

7.12   Indefinite Reference

To avoid any confusion for the reader, every personal pronoun should refer clearly to a definite antecedent.

INDEFINITE   The yearbook is good, but *they* didn't include enough pictures of the glee club.

BETTER   The yearbook is good, but the editors didn't include enough pictures of the glee club.

INDEFINITE *It* says in the newspaper that it will
rain tomorrow.

BETTER The newspaper says that it will rain tomorrow.

INDEFINITE Harry wants to run for office because *it*
is exciting.

BETTER Harry wants to run for office because politics
is exciting.

INDEFINITE Read what *they* say about stereo components.

BETTER Read what *Consumer's Guide* says about
stereo components.

The pronoun *you* is sometimes used when it is not meant to
refer to the person spoken to. The effect is usually confusing.

INDEFINITE In that course *you* have fewer exams.

BETTER In that course there are fewer exams.

INDEFINITE From a single corn kernel *you* grow a corn plant
from twelve to fourteen feet high.

BETTER From a single corn kernel one may grow a corn
plant from twelve to fourteen feet high.

Exercise: Revise the sentences below to remove all indefinite reference of pronouns.

1. It says in the paper that the President vetoed the bill.
2. In this school, they make you study a foreign language.
3. When you work in a laboratory, they expect you to
be accurate.
4. Maureen wants to be a ski instructor because it is glamorous.
5. The exterior of the building is modern, but they ruined
its interior.
6. In Hawaii, they greet you with leis.
7. The plumber worked hard, but it still continued to leak.
8. The temperature is dropping; it may ruin the orange crop.
9. In Colonial days, they preached very long sermons.
10. As an exchange student, they expect you to represent
your country.

7.13 Ambiguous Reference

The word *ambiguous* means "having two or more possible meanings." The reference of a pronoun is ambiguous if the pronoun may refer to more than one word. This situation arises whenever a noun or pronoun falls between the pronoun and its true antecedent.

AMBIGUOUS	Take the books off the shelves and dust *them*.
BETTER	Dust the books after you take them off the shelves.
AMBIGUOUS	The hounds chased foxes until *they* were exhausted.
BETTER	The hounds chased foxes until the dogs were exhausted.
AMBIGUOUS	Before they could get the rocket off the pad, *it* had to be repaired.
BETTER	They had to repair the rocket before they could get it off the pad.
AMBIGUOUS	Vince told Joe *he* had won the prize.
BETTER	Vince had won the prize, he told Joe.

Exercise: Revise the sentences below to remove all ambiguous pronoun references.

1. Sara told Tanya that she really should try out for track.
2. When I put the candle in the holder, it broke.
3. Tom explained to Fred that his car needed to be overhauled.
4. Take the tennis rackets out of the presses and dust them.
5. I saw the picture in a magazine, but I can't find it.
6. Joan took the collar off her dress and washed it.
7. Ellen told Kay that she had made a serious mistake.
8. When the traffic officer spoke to Dad, he frowned.
9. Take the groceries out of the bags and place them on the shelf.
10. We tried hanging the picture over the bookcase, but it was too big.

8.0 Adjective and Adverb Usage

Certain adverbs are formed by adding *-ly* to adjectives, as *sweet— sweetly*. The problem then is whether to use the modifier with or without the *-ly* ending after a verb.

8.1 Adverbs with Action Verbs

When a modifier comes just before an action verb, it is always an adverb, and no problem arises. When the modifier follows the action verb, there is a temptation to use an adjective rather than an adverb.

The problem is made more difficult by the fact that many adverbs have two forms, one with and the other without the *-ly* ending.

<blockquote>Come quick!   Drive slow.   Come close.</blockquote>

All of the words used above as adverbs are also used as adjectives: a *quick* response, a *slow* horse, a *close* call, and so on.

Most of the words that may be either adjectives or adverbs are words of one syllable. Adjectives of two or more syllables almost never have the same form for the adverb.

The *noisy* tenant was scolded by the landlord. (adjective)
The dishes fell *noisily* to the floor. (adverb)

The doctor received a *sudden* call. (adjective)
The doctor was called away *suddenly*. (adverb)

After an action verb use the -ly form of the modifier if the modifier has two or more syllables.

8.2 Adjectives with Linking Verbs

Linking verbs are usually followed by adjectives rather than adverbs. The adjective is a predicate adjective and modifies the subject.

There is no problem with modifiers following the form of *be*, the most common linking verb. Most of the other linking verbs, however, may also be used as action verbs. As action verbs, they may be followed by adverbs.

The groundhog *appeared suddenly*.
(*appeared* is an action verb modified by an adverb.)

The actress *appeared nervous*.
(*appeared* is a linking verb followed by a predicate adjective.)

The baby *grew quickly*.
(*grew* is an action verb modified by an adverb.)

The lake *grew dark and ominous*.
(*grew* is a linking verb followed by predicate adjectives.)

The following verbs are linking verbs. Most of them may also be used as action verbs.

look	feel	stay	become
sound	smell	remain	seem
appear	taste	grow	

To decide whether a verb is used to link or to show action, try substituting a form of *be*. If the sentence still makes sense, the verb is a linking verb.

>The bride *seemed* (happy, happily).
>(*The bride was happily* does not make sense. *The bride was happy* makes sense; *seemed* is a linking verb here.)
>The bride *looked* (happy, happily) at the groom.
>(*was* does not make sense with either modifier; *looked* is an action verb here.)

Exercise A: Choose the standard form from those given in parentheses.

1. You can find the way (easy, easily) from here.
2. The old man seemed (unsteadily, unsteady) on his feet.
3. Larry looked very (happily, happy) in his new job.
4. It rained (steady, steadily) all day long.
5. Loretta worked at the fatiguing job as (rapid, rapidly) as she could.
6. Mary felt (uneasy, uneasily) about her mother's illness.
7. Harold found the solution to the first problem (quick, quickly) and turned to the second.
8. We thought the game was (certain, certainly) lost.
9. Your voice sounds (different, differently) over the telephone.
10. Twelve passengers in the first car were hurt (bad, badly).

Exercise B: Decide whether the italicized modifier is standard or nonstandard. If it is nonstandard, substitute the standard form.

1. You can get an office job *easier* if you can take dictation.
2. Harriet seemed *angrily* about the interruption.
3. You must drive more *careful*.
4. Dr. Sanders signs his name *differently* on every prescription.
5. Barbara felt *unhappily* about her choice.
6. The repair shop fixed the radio *perfect*.
7. It is well to skate *cautiously* on thin ice.
8. The old cottage on the dunes smelled *damply*.

9. We thought the dog was not behaving *normal*.
10. Herb studied the letter very *careful*.

8.3 *This—These; That—Those*

This and *that* modify singular words. *These* and *those* modify plural words. The words *kind*, *sort*, and *type* require a singular modifier.

NONSTANDARD	These kind are the best.
STANDARD	This kind is the best.
NONSTANDARD	These sort of gloves wear well.
STANDARD	This sort of gloves wears well.

8.4 *Them—Those*

Those may be either a pronoun or an adjective. *Them* is always a pronoun and never an adjective.

NONSTANDARD	How did you get *them* blisters?
STANDARD	How did you get *those* blisters? (adjective)

8.5 *Bad—Badly*

In standard usage, *bad* is always used after linking verbs.

He felt bad. (*not* he felt badly)
He looked bad.
The fish tastes bad.
The stereo sounds bad.

8.6 *Good—Well*

Good is used only as an adjective to modify nouns and pronouns.

Well is an adjective when it means "in good health, of good appearance, or satisfactory." *Well* is used as an adverb to modify an action verb when it means that the action was performed properly or expertly.

The Vice-President looks *well*. (adjective)
That coat looks *well* with those trousers. (adjective)
The baby walks *well* now. (adverb)

8.7 *Fewer—Less*

Fewer is used to describe things that can be counted. *Less* refers to quantity or degree.

Patricia has *fewer* headaches than she used to have.
There has been *less* rain this year than last year.
This dishwasher will give you *less* trouble than that one.

Exercise: Decide whether the italicized words are standard or nonstandard usage. Substitute a standard form for each nonstandard one.

1. There are *less* pupils studying French this year.
2. We enjoy your letters; don't stop writing *them*.
3. Be careful not to trip over *them* wires.
4. The milk tastes *badly* to me.
5. The bush grew *good* after being transplanted.
6. The team felt *badly* about Hal's injury.
7. There are *fewer* new students in school this year.
8. *Less* voters turned out than we had expected.
9. You can't buy *those* kind of candy any more.
10. Bob has all *them* power tools in his shop.
11. Mr. Jackson has looked *badly* ever since his operation.
12. Boys don't do as *good* on assembly jobs as girls.
13. We had some of *these* kind of apples last year.
14. There have been *less* traffic deaths since we put in the new stoplight.

15. Leslie isn't singing as *good* as she did last week.
16. The boys were frightened *bad* by the runaway truck.
17. You will have *less* trouble with these new tubes.
18. The school chorus did very *good* in the regional contest.

8.8 Comparative and Superlative

The comparative form is used to compare two things; the superlative is used in comparing more than two.

STANDARD   We went to see both the Giants and the Raiders, but we liked the Giants *better*. (*not* best)

STANDARD   You can have either this dress pattern or that one, but I think you will find this one *easier* to follow. (*not* easiest)

STANDARD   Of the three speakers, the Jensen brings out the bass notes *best*. (*not* better)

8.9 The Double Comparison

The comparative form of a modifier is made either by adding *-er* or by using *more*. It is nonstandard to use both.

The superlative form of a modifier is made either by adding *-est* or by using *most*. It is nonstandard to use both.

NONSTANDARD   My boat will go much more faster than yours.

STANDARD   My boat will go much faster than yours.

NONSTANDARD   You should find it more easier to do.

STANDARD   You should find it easier to do.

NONSTANDARD   It was the most fanciest house I'd ever seen.

STANDARD   It was the fanciest house I'd ever seen.

8.10 Illogical Comparisons

The word *other*, or the word *else*, is required in comparisons of an individual member with the rest of the group.

ILLOGICAL	Sylvia has won more honors than any child in school. (Sylvia is also in school.)
CLEAR	Sylvia has won more honors than any *other* child in school.
ILLOGICAL	George is as tall as anyone on the basketball squad.
CLEAR	George is as tall as anyone *else* on the basketball squad.

The words *than* or *as* are required in a compound comparison.

ILLOGICAL	Tim is as tall if not taller than Brad.
CLEAR BUT AWKWARD	Tim is as tall *as*, if not taller than, Brad
BETTER	Tim is as tall *as* Brad, if not taller.
ILLOGICAL	Sue had as many examinations to take if not more than Helen.
CLEAR	Sue had as many examinations to take *as* Helen, if not more.
ILLOGICAL	The Dodgers' chances of winning the pennant are as good if not better than the Giants'.
CLEAR	The Dodgers' chances of winning the pennant are as good *as* the Giants', if not better.

Both parts of a comparison must be stated completely if there is any chance of its being misunderstood.

CONFUSING	I miss her more than Sandra.
CLEAR	I miss her more than Sandra *does*.
CLEAR	I miss her more than *I miss* Sandra.
CONFUSING	Harvard defeated Yale worse than Dartmouth.
CLEAR	Harvard defeated Yale worse than Dartmouth *did*.
CLEAR	Harvard defeated Yale worse than *it defeated* Dartmouth.
ILLOGICAL	The population of New York is larger than London.

CLEAR   The population of New York is larger than *that of* London.

BETTER   New York has a larger population than London *has*.

Exercise: Revise the following sentences.

1. Turn the radio up a little more louder.
2. Our team is more weaker this year because of graduation.
3. Some students can study more easier with the radio turned on.
4. Harry is the tallest of the twins.
5. This was the less expensive coat of the dozen I looked at.
6. We looked at both programs, but Alistair Cooke's was the best.
7. Please open the window just a bit more wider.
8. The water is more softer now that we have the new filtration plant.
9. Our chances of winning are as good if not better than theirs.
10. The problem is less clearer to me now than before.
11. The work of a miner is more dangerous than a carpenter.
12. Sue is the smartest of that pair.
13. Joyce is as bright as any member of the committee.
14. In the 1975 World Series, the Cincinnati Reds had the best team.
15. Beth chose the longest of the two books for her report.
16. Please talk a little more softer.
17. The coach was the better of the three speakers at the banquet.
18. I respect Harry more than Chuck.
19. Our school is more than ever bigger this year.
20. Eve and Janet are both good students, but Janet is the best.

8.11   The Double Negative

A double negative occurs when a negative word is added to a statement that is already negative. The double negative is non-standard usage.

NONSTANDARD	He didn't have no soda left.
STANDARD	He didn't have any soda left.
NONSTANDARD	She didn't know nothing about the Civil War.
STANDARD	She didn't know anything about the Civil War.

Hardly or *barely*, used with a negative word, is nonstandard.

NONSTANDARD	There wasn't hardly a ticket left for the show.
STANDARD	There was hardly a ticket left for the show.
NONSTANDARD	Eric couldn't barely hit the ball.
STANDARD	Eric could barely hit the ball.

Exercise: Find the nonstandard usages and change them to standard usage. Two sentences are already standard usage.

1. The bus hadn't never been so late before.
2. There hadn't been nothing said about staying out of the water.
3. We have never had any trouble with the ignition.
4. Nobody in the audience couldn't tell what had happened.
5. The doctor hasn't said nothing that should frighten you.
6. By midnight the turkey hadn't barely begun to thaw out.
7. Bob hasn't none of his brother's charm.
8. We had barely finished cleaning up, when a new crowd entered.
9. I'm sure that nobody else couldn't have done as well.
10. We haven't had no response to our letter.

Review Exercise: These sentences cover all of the problems of adjective and adverb usage in this section. Find the nonstandard usages and change them to standard usage.

1. You can finish the job in five minutes easy.
2. The roads are slippery. Drive careful.
3. The papers had been stacked neat on the desks.
4. You will have to speak a little more louder.
5. In every pair of shoes, the right one is the biggest.
6. The score was much more closer than in last year's game.

7. In a show of great football yesterday, the best team finally won.

8. Please don't order any more of them pencils.

9. Don felt badly about forgetting his lines in the play.

10. There were less cars on the road than we had expected.

11. We stopped using those kind of helmets two years ago.

12. Be sure to clean the metal good before applying the enamel.

9.0   Verb Usage

Most of the several thousand English verbs cause no problems of usage at all. They are **regular verbs.** That is, the past tense is formed by adding *-ed* or *-d* to the present, and the past participle is the same as the past tense form:

PRESENT	PAST	PAST PARTICIPLE
talk	talk*ed*	talk*ed*
use	use*d*	use*d*
love	love*d*	love*d*

There are about sixty commonly used verbs, however, whose past forms do not follow this pattern. They are **irregular verbs.** The most commonly used verbs, *be* and *have*, not only form the past tenses irregularly but change from person to person in the present tense: *I am, you are, he is, I have, he has.*

9.1   The Past Forms

The main problem with irregular verbs is the choice between the past form and the past participle form. These are two of the **principal parts** of every verb. (See Section 1.3.) All forms of any verb are made from the principal parts. Since they are always given in the same order in dictionaries and reference books, learning them in that order will make usage choices easier.

The past tense form is used alone. The past participle form is used with forms of *be* or *have*.

Ted *went* off to college. (past)
The cookies *were* all *gone*. (past participle with form of *be*)
The bus *had* already *gone*. (past participle with form of *have*)

There are five groups of irregular verbs.

Group 1. The easiest of the irregular verbs are those that have the same form in all principal parts.

PRESENT	PAST	PAST PARTICIPLE
burst	burst	burst
cost	cost	cost
hit	hit	hit
hurt	hurt	hurt
put	put	put
set	set	set
shut	shut	shut

Group 2. A second group that causes little difficulty is composed of verbs that have the same form for the past and the past participle.

PRESENT	PAST	PAST PARTICIPLE
bring	brought	brought
catch	caught	caught
dive	dived *or* dove*	dived
fight	fought	fought
flee	fled	fled
fling	flung	flung
get	got	got *or* gotten
lead	led	led
lend	lent	lent

* Where two forms are given, both are standard usage, but the first is more common.

PRESENT	PAST	PAST PARTICIPLE
lose	lost	lost
say	said	said
shine	shone	shone
sit	sat	sat
sting	stung	stung
swing	swung	swung

Exercise A: In the sentences below, the present form of the verb is given in parentheses. Substitute either past or past participle, whichever the sentence requires.

1. One of the men had (bring) a portable television set.
2. Mr. Allen (bring) out the fact that our enrollment is declining.
3. Two of the escaping convicts were (catch) in the swamp.
4. Without awaiting an answer, John (flee) from the house.
5. Papers had been (fling) all over the lawn.
6. This purchase (lead) us ever deeper into debt.
7. We had (lend) the wheelbarrow to our neighbors.
8. How many games have we (lose) this year?
9. The light (shine) into my eyes so that I could hardly see him.
10. The divers had been badly (sting) by jellyfish.
11. The batter (swing) at the first pitch and knocked it into the stands.
12. As we passed, the men in the boat (fling) up their arms in salute.
13. Walt has (lead) the band for three years.
14. The sun had (shine) on only one day of our vacation.
15. The crane (swing) crazily out over the street.
16. Sally (lend) me a dollar to buy my lunch.

Exercise B: Choose the standard form from those in parentheses.

1. As usual, the plumber's helper has (brung, brought) the wrong tools.

2. Running at top speed, Cal reached up and (catched, caught) the ball on his fingertips.

3. The waiting sharks turned and (fleed, fled) as the ship approached.

4. Someone had (flang, flinged, flung) a burning cigarette from a car.

5. Lewis (lead, led) us up the face of the cliff.

6. Georgina has returned the wrenches that you (lended, lent) her.

7. The travelers had (losed, lost) their way in the storm.

8. The moon (shone, shined) brightly as we started across the desert.

9. The hot liquid (stang, stung) my throat.

10. When we had finished, the car (shined, shone) like new.

11. The giant crane slowly (swang, swung) the steel girders into place.

12. Barry had (catched, caught) a skunk in his trap.

Group 3. Another group of irregular verbs adds **n** or **en** to the past form to make the past participle.

PRESENT	PAST	PAST PARTICIPLE
bear	bore	borne*
beat	beat	beaten
bite	bit	bitten
break	broke	broken
choose	chose	chosen
freeze	froze	frozen
speak	spoke	spoken
steal	stole	stolen
swear	swore	sworn
tear	tore	torn
wear	wore	worn

* Note that *borne* retains the final *e*.

Exercise A: Choose the standard form from those in parentheses.

1. Fran has (born, beared, borne) the family burdens all alone.
2. The batter should be (beat, beaten) until it is smooth.
3. I thought I had (bit, bitten) into a piece of metal.
4. All previous heat records were (broken, broken) last summer.
5. Dick had already (chose, chosen) a camera for his birthday present.
6. The car door was (froze, frozen) shut.
7. At the meeting, Mr. Davis had (spoke, spoken) against driver education.
8. The boys had (stole, stolen) onto the ship during the night.
9. The men had (swore, sworn) to hold the pass or die in the attempt.
10. Two pages had been (tore, torn) out of the index.
11. Dad has (wore, worn) the same old hat for five years.
12. The natives (beared, bore) the casket to the top of the hill.
13. The little Kansas town had (born, borne) the full fury of the tornado.
14. The Giants were badly (beat, beaten) in the championship game.
15. A little boy's finger was (bit, bitten) by a big dog.
16. All of our dishes were (broke, broken) when the van turned over.
17. Mary has been (chose, chosen) to give an address at the commencement exercises.
18. With the unusually early cold, many cars were (froze, frozen.)
19. The heavy traffic has (tore, torn) up the road.
20. The rocks had been (worn, wore) down by the constant fall of the water.

Exercise B: The present form of the verb is given. Substitute past or past participle, whichever the sentence requires.

1. Betty hasn't (wear) her new suit yet.
2. The new president was (swear) into office by her father.
3. Squirrels have (steal) the food you put out for the birds.

4. I have already (speak) to the boss about a raise.

5. On the hike, Steve's ears were badly (freeze).

6. The new coach has already been (choose).

7. Hundreds of windows were (break) by the explosion.

8. When Skip delivered papers, he was (bite) twice by the same dog.

9. Jim's ankle was (break) in the first play of the game.

10. The flowers had been (beat) down by the rain.

11. The boys (bear) no resemblance to their father.

12. The wreckers (tear) down the old building in two weeks.

13. Someone has (break) the power mower.

14. Bob (swear) he had been at home all day.

15. The pond had (freeze) solid early in November.

16. The reindeer had been (steal) from the hotel's lawn.

17. The wind (tear) the door off its hinges.

18. Mrs. Alvarez has never been (beat) in an election.

19. During the night we were attacked and (bite) by mosquitoes.

20. I think Hilda has (speak) for all of us.

Group 4. Another group of irregular verbs is alike in changing the middle vowel from i in the present, to **a** in the past, and to **u** in the past participle. Memorize these seven verbs as a unit. They are the only verbs to follow this pattern.

PRESENT	PAST	PAST PARTICIPLE
begin	began	begun
drink	drank	drunk
ring	rang	rung
sing	sang	sung
sink	sank *or* sunk	sunk
spring	sprang *or* sprung	sprung
swim	swam	swum

Exercise: The present form is given in parentheses. Substitute the past or past participle, whichever the sentence requires.

1. Has the voting (begin) yet?

2. The three boys had (drink) a gallon of milk.

3. Sarah walked up the steps and (ring) the bell.
4. Has Alex ever (sing) before an audience?
5. The weighted line (sink) quickly to the bottom.
6. The dogs (spring) at each other in great fury.
7. A seventeen-year-old girl has (swim) across Lake Ontario.
8. The snow (begin) to fall shortly after midnight.
9. The rescued airman (drink) the water slowly in tiny sips.
10. Church bells (ring) across the nation when the first transcontinental railroad was completed.
11. Our relay team (swim) the race in record time.
12. The pipe was (sink) deep into the ground and anchored in cement.
13. The men (spring) to attention when the captain entered.
14. We always (sing) "Auld Lang Syne" as the New Year began.
15. By morning, we had (begin) to see our trouble in a different light.
16. Have you ever (drink) root beer with ice cream on a hot day?
17. Someone (ring) the doorbell, left this note, and departed.
18. Has the glee club ever (sing) the "Hallelujah" chorus?
19. The ship exploded suddenly and (sink) immediately.
20. The car's right front door was (spring) in the smashup.
21. Bill had (swim) halfway across the lake before anyone noticed him.
22. Marion has (begin) to recognize the value of practice.
23. The pioneers became sick when they first (drink) the alkali waters of the Western Plains.
24. The passing bell had (ring), but we stayed in our seats, fascinated.
25. Our new boys' quartet (sing) for the school assembly.

Group 5. Another group of irregular verbs is alike in making the past participle from the present form rather than from the past form.

PRESENT	PAST	PAST PARTICIPLE
blow	blew	blown
come	came	come

PRESENT	PAST	PAST PARTICIPLE
do	did	done
draw	drew	drawn
drive	drove	driven
eat	ate	eaten
fall	fell	fallen
give	gave	given
go	went	gone
grow	grew	grown
know	knew	known
ride	rode	ridden
rise	rose	risen
run	ran	run
see	saw	seen
shake	shook	shaken
slay	slew	slain
take	took	taken
throw	threw	thrown
write	wrote	written

Exercise A: Choose the standard form from those in parentheses.

1. Don sat in his car and (blowed, blew) the horn.
2. Darla (come, came) running down the driveway.
3. By noon we had already (did, done) a day's work.
4. A police car (drawed, drew) up beside the truck.
5. Mr. Cobb had (drove, driven) off to the side of the road for a nap.
6. The birds have (ate, eaten) all the seeds we put out for them.
7. The old house has (fell, fallen) into disrepair.
8. Mrs. Hanley (give, gave) Fred a ten-year loan to cover college expenses.
9. Our neighbors have (gone, went) to Miami for the winter.
10. One of my friends (grew, growed) four inches in a year.
11. We should have (know, knowed, known) that the stores would be closed today.

12. The girls had (rode, ridden) a bus all night to get back to college.

13. This successful business is (ran, run) entirely by high school students.

14. Harry just (shaked, shook) his head and said nothing.

15. After twenty years in prison, the gangster was (slew, slain) on the day he got out.

16. Jeff felt that he had been too much (took, taken) for granted.

17. The road crews (threw, throwed) sand and salt on the icy roads.

18. It's lucky we have (wrote, written) ahead for reservations.

19. Our class has (wrote, written) a theme every week this semester.

20. Someone had (throwed, thrown) papers all along the roadside.

Exercise B: The present form is given in parentheses. Substitute the past or past participle, whichever the sentence requires.

1. The ships had been (blow) far off their course in the storm.

2. People (come) from miles around to see the new reaper.

3. Dad (do) his best to discourage us from buying the old car.

4. The Rose Bowl game has always (draw) a capacity crowd.

5. When the subways were on strike, we all (drive) into town.

6. Moths had (eat) holes in my winter coat.

7. Trees and telephone poles had (fell) across the road.

8. The coach's inspiring talk (give) us all a lift.

9. Two firemen had (go) quickly into the blazing building.

10. As midnight approached, we (grow) panicky.

11. It was the worst blizzard that Rochester had ever (know).

12. The scouts had (ride) hard all night to reach the fort.

13. As we came down the hill, two deer (run) across the road.

14. By six in the evening, the Governor had (shake) hands with several hundred people.

15. Two of the convicts were (slay) trying to escape from the prison.

16. Someone has (take) down the road sign.

17. A cordon of security agents was (throw) around the building.

18. Has anything been (do) to improve the water supply?

19. Your Christmas package finally (come) in February.

20. No signs of the downed airmen were (see).

Exercise C: The present form is given. Substitute the past or past participle as the sentence may require.

1. Fortunately, the hurricane has (blow) out to sea.

2. No one has yet (come) forward to claim the wallet.

3. Jane has (do) most of the clean-up job alone.

4. The stranger had (draw) his money out of the bank and left town.

5. The snarling tiger had been (drive) into a corner of the cage.

6. We had never (eat) a better meal.

7. Six inches of snow had (fall) during the night.

8. The clerk (give) us careful instructions on operating the projector.

9. The boys have (go) to the junkyard to look for a fender.

10. An entire city had (grow) up at Pithole within a single year.

11. Fritz has never (know) how to save money.

12. During the summer, the girls had (ride) across the country on bicycles.

13. Has Mrs. Stevens ever (run) for office before?

14. The force of the blast (shake) everything for fifty miles around.

15. The local authorities have (take) every precaution for the President's safety.

16. The tractors had been (draw) up into neat lines.

17. The car had been (drive) without water.

18. The temperature has (fall) ten degrees in the last hour.

19. The judge had (give) the man a suspended sentence.

20. A dozen communities have (grow) up just beyond the city limits.

9.2 Verbs Confused as to Meaning

Three pairs of verbs are often confused because the meanings of each pair are closely related. They are related, but they are not identical. To use these verbs correctly, keep their meanings distinct.

Lie and lay. The verb *lay* means "to put or place something." The verb *lie* has eight or nine meanings, all having in common the idea of "being in a horizontal position, or to remain, or to be situated."*

Lie is always an intransitive verb. It never has an object. *Lay* is a transitive verb. It almost always has an object. The principal parts of these verbs are as follows:

PRESENT	PAST	PAST PARTICIPLE
lay	laid	laid
lie	lay	lain

Sit and set. The verb *sit* usually means "to rest with the legs bent and the back upright," but there are many other related meanings. The verb *set* means "to put or place something."

Sit is an intransitive verb; it never has an object. *Set* is a transitive verb; it almost always has an object. The principal parts are as follows:

PRESENT	PAST	PAST PARTICIPLE
sit	sat	sat
set	set	set

Rise and raise. The verb *rise* means "to go to a higher position." The verb *raise* means "to lift to a higher position."

Rise is intransitive; it never has an object. *Raise* is transitive; it almost always has an object. Things *rise* by themselves; they are *raised* by something else. The principal parts of these verbs are as follows:

---

* There is a homonym meaning "to tell an untruth." The principal parts of this verb are *lie, lied, lied.*

PRESENT	PAST	PAST PARTICIPLE
rise	rose	risen
raise	raised	raised

Note: It is very difficult to make general statements about English usage that will hold without exception. There are exceptions to the statements given above about the three pairs of verbs:

The sun *sets.* (intransitive)
The mixture will *set* in an hour. (intransitive)
Sit her up. (transitive)
The hens are *laying* well. (intransitive)

Exercise A: Choose the standard form from those in parentheses.

1. The necessary tools (lay, laid) in a neat row on the table.
2. The fruit had (laid, lain) too long in the sun.
3. The mayor (lay, laid) the cornerstone for the new city hall.
4. Please don't (lie, lay) your wet coats on the chairs.
5. All day, the men (lay, laid) hiding in the cornfield.
6. The books were (laying, lying) on the floor of the closet.
7. It is impossible for Boots to (lie, lay) still.
8. The beautiful old chest had (lain, laid) in the attic for years.
9. The company is already (lying, laying) plans for further expansion.
10. The city has (lain, laid) new storm drains along the road.
11. The old dog was (lying, laying) in the middle of the road.
12. New duties have been (lain, laid) on the branch managers this year.
13. Here in the cave the wounded trapper had (lain, laid) down to die.
14. Near the beach a new tennis court has been (lain, laid) out.
15. After the earthquake, over half the city (lay, laid) in ruins.
16. We were (lying, laying) in the shade waiting for the bus to come.
17. Plans have been (lain, laid) for a huge demonstration.
18. After dinner, you must (lie, lay) down for a rest.
19. We (lay, laid) out our equipment on the rocks to dry.
20. The revolver was found (laying, lying) in twelve feet of water.

Verb Usage

Exercise B: Choose the standard form from those in parentheses.

1. Early in the day the wind had (raised, risen).
2. The cost of living did not (raise, rise) this last year.
3. Farm prices have not (raised, risen) for several years.
4. The proposal for a new airport (rose, raised) a storm of protest.
5. When the doctor asked for volunteers, five men (rose, raised) their hands.
6. The company's business has (risen, raised) every year.
7. Tonight, the moon is (raising, rising) in the northeast.
8. The fog was (raising, rising) as we left for the airport.
9. The archaeologists (rose, raised) the heavy stone statues by ropes.
10. Will the bus fare be (risen, raised) again this year?
11. Please (rise, raise) the window a few inches more.
12. The club plans to (rise, raise) a fund to send the band to the tournament.
13. Someone was (rising, raising) a disturbance outside the hall.
14. A sigh of relief (rose, raised) from the waiting crowd.
15. It will be Bonita's duty to (rise, raise) the flag every morning.
16. The dough has not (raised, risen) yet.
17. The landlord (raised, rose) our rent again this year.
18. A month ago, no one thought to (rise, raise) his voice in protest.
19. During the past hour, the water has (risen, raised) three inches.
20. The flock of ducks (rose, raised) gracefully from the lake.

Exercise C: Choose the standard form from those in parentheses.

1. Several of the guests were (setting, sitting) on the floor.
2. Please don't (set, sit) your glass on the table.
3. The superstitious think it is bad luck to (sit, set) a hat on a bed.
4. We will be (setting, sitting) on these chairs for a long time.
5. You will find it easier to (sit, set) still as you grow older.
6. The artist (sat, set) a fresh canvas on his easel.

7. You can (sit, set) the flowers on the hall table.

8. Mr. Donovan (set, sat) two hours today for his portrait.

9. Some of the children were (sitting, setting) on the curb.

10. Herb (set, sat) his hat carefully on the back of his head.

11. I (set, sat) the brief case on the seat and promptly forgot about it.

12. How long has the coffee pot been (sitting, setting) on this burner?

13. Extra chairs were (sat, set) on the platform.

14. (Setting, Sitting) on one's heels is called *hunkering*.

15. You can (sit, set) the bag of ice outside.

16. The family (sat, set) at the airport all night, waiting for any plane.

17. The skeleton was (sitting, setting) on a chair in the front row.

18. The empty cartons were (set, sat) in the hall outside the door.

19. A warning light had been (sat, set) in the road.

20. The students were (sitting, setting) on the steps, waiting for the library to open.

10.0 Capitalization

10.1 *A.D.*, *B.C.*, *I*, *O*

Capitalize the abbreviations _A.D._ and _B.C._, the pronoun _I_, and the interjection _O_.

The abbreviations B.C. and A.D. occur only with the number of a year: 1001 B.C., A.D. 1492. The interjection O occurs in poetry, in the Bible, or in prayers or petitions: O Lord, O King, O Master.

O is quite different from the explosive interjection *oh*, which is capitalized only at the beginning of a sentence.

10.2 First Words

Capitalize the first word of a sentence, a direct quotation, and a line of poetry.

He handed her a bouquet of daisies.

"No one," she said staring widely, "has ever given me
  flowers before."

I will arise and go now, and go to Innisfree,
And a small cabin build there, of clay and wattles made;
Nine bean rows will I have there, a hive for the honey bee,
And live alone in the bee-loud glade.*

10.3 Proper Nouns and Adjectives

A **common noun** is the name of a whole group of persons, places, or things. A **proper noun** is the name of an individual person, place, or thing. A **proper adjective** is an adjective formed from a proper noun.

COMMON NOUN	PROPER NOUN	PROPER ADJECTIVE
continent	Europe	European
section	West	Western
playwright	Shakespeare	Shakespearean

Proper nouns and adjectives occur in many compound words. Capitalize only the parts of these words that are capitalized when they stand alone. Do not capitalize prefixes such as *pro-, un-, anti-* attached to proper nouns and adjectives.

un-American   pro-Leftist   anti-war

Proper nouns occur in great variety. The following rules with their illustrations will help you solve the capitalization problems that proper nouns present.

10.4 Geographical Names

In a geographical name, capitalize the first letter of each word except articles and prepositions.

* From "The Lake Isle of Innisfree" by William Butler Yeats, quoted by permission of the Macmillan Company.

The article *the* appearing before a geographical name is not part of the geographical name and is therefore not capitalized.

CONTINENTS: North America, South America, Asia

BODIES OF WATER: the Indian Ocean, Lake Ontario, the Jordan River, Strait of Belle Isle, Cape Cod Bay, the Adriatic Sea, St. George's Channel, the Gulf of Finland

LAND FORMS: the Pyrenees, the Sinai Peninsula, the Grand Canyon, the Syrian Desert, Mount Constance, the Plains of Abraham, Raton Pass

POLITICAL UNITS: the District of Columbia, the British Isles, the Commonwealth of Pennsylvania, the State of Maine, the West Indies, San Francisco, the Republic of Texas, the First Congressional District, the Union of Soviet Socialist Republics

PUBLIC AREAS: Gettysburg National Park, Fort Niagara, the Blue Grotto, Mount Rushmore

ROADS AND HIGHWAYS: Main Street, Route 447, West Side Highway, Van Buren Avenue, the Ohio Turnpike, Strawberry Lane, Savile Row, Rue de Rivoli

10.5   Common Nouns in Names

A common noun that is part of a name is capitalized. A common noun used to define or refer to a proper noun is not capitalized.

PART OF THE NAME	REFERENCE OR DEFINITION
New York State	the state of New York*
Salt Lake City	the city of Jacksonville
the Western Plains	plains in the West
the Ohio Valley	the valley of the Ohio

---

* In official documents, words like *city, state,* and *county* are capitalized when they are part of the name of a political unit: *the County of Westchester, the State of Mississippi, the City of Los Angeles.*

10.6 Words Modified by Proper Adjectives

The word modified by a proper adjective is not capitalized unless adjective and noun together are a geographical name.

GEOGRAPHICAL NAME	MODIFIED NOUN
English Channel	English accent
the Indian Ocean	Indian customs
West Germany	French dressing

Exercise: Copy the following sentences, supplying necessary capitals.

1. How many german composers can you name?
2. The explorers skirted the gulf of mexico until they came to the mississippi river.
3. There are not many english-speaking people in the indonesian republic.
4. Many of the dutch speak german and english as well as their native tongue.
5. The republic of ghana lies on the west coast of africa.
6. The amazon river almost bisects the continent of south america
7. In an old chest found in death valley, there was a copy of a new york newspaper.
8. The old roman walls may still be seen in the northern parts of great britain.
9. The state of minnesota is supposed to have 10,000 lakes.
10. For years, one part of the western plains was surrounded by texas and oklahoma, but it belonged to neither state.
11. You can now drive from new england to the midwest on throughways.
12. Glacier national park lies in the state of montana.
13. Some people believe there is a difference between the american language and english.
14. Several languages are spoken in the republic of the philippines.
15. The geographic south pole lies under a mass of ice in antarctica.

16. Travelers can now go directly from the jersey turnpike to the pennsylvania turnpike.

17. The ohio river forms part of the boundary of the state of ohio.

18. The bus goes down fifth avenue to washington square.

19. Several american textbooks have been translated into spanish for use in the schools of the commonwealth of puerto rico.

20. There are still many dutch ships steaming up the hudson river.

10.7 Directions and Sections

Capitalize names of sections of the country but not of directions of the compass.

> Cotton was king in the South.
> Cities in the Southwest are flourishing.
> It is just north of Paris.
> They flew east through the storm.
> She lives on the north side of the street.
> The lake is west of our cottage.
> The hurricane moved northward.

Capitalize proper adjectives derived from names of sections of the country. Do not capitalize adjectives derived from words indicating direction.

> an Eastern school   a southerly course
> a Western concept   an eastern route

Exercise: Copy the following sentences, supplying the necessary capitals.

1. Many factories from the north have moved into southern states.

2. The people of the southwest think of themselves as neither southern nor western.

3. Many eastern students are going to midwestern colleges.

4. The westbound flight leaves in ten minutes.

5. The southeast and the far west are the most rapidly growing sections of the country.

6. The storm is moving rapidly eastward.

7. In the Pacific there is one great current that flows eastward and another, south of it, that flows in a westerly direction.

8. The civilization of the west has much to learn from that of the east.

9. There are many points at issue in east-west relations.

10. The sunlight moves from east to west, but the prevailing winds move eastward.

11. Water shortage is becoming a serious problem in the southeast.

12. The northern papers were printing outrageous stories about the south, and southern papers retaliated in kind.

13. From Manila, Dr. Robertson will fly west to the middle east.

14. The east branch of the Delaware flows into Pennsylvania.

15. We will take the northern route on our trip to the west.

16. The western colleges are welcoming eastern students.

17. The candidate for Vice-President will probably be a westerner.

18. The birds fly south in September but return to the north in April.

19. Is it true that Atlanta lies west of New York?

20. The northern summer resorts attract many people from the south.

10.8 Languages, Races, Nationalities, and Religions

Capitalize the names of languages, races, nationalities, and religions and the adjectives formed from them.

the Caucasian race	Judaism	Protestant
the Italian heritage	Episcopalian	Irish
Hungarian	Catholic	Peruvian

10.9   Organizations and Institutions

**Capitalize important words in the names of organizations, build-
ings, firms, schools, churches, and other institutions. Do not capitalize *and* or prepositons. Capitalize an article (*a, an,* or *the*) only if
it appears as the first word in a name.**

Pittsburgh Symphony	Carlino Tile Company
Cedars of Lebanon Hospital	Taylor Allderdice High School
Church of the Martyr	Metropolitan Museum of Art
University of Illinois	United Air Lines

Note: In brand names, the common noun is not capitalized: *a
Volkswagen bus; Indian River grapefruit; Blotz toothpaste.*

Exercise: Copy the following sentences, supplying necessary capitals.
   1. The boston choral society will appear at the university
of maine.
   2. The st. louis art museum has a fine collection of
dutch paintings.
   3. The lerner string quartet will play at the library of congress.
   4. The new york public library has a fine collection of books
on buddhism.
   5. Ship the books to the richmond field high school.
   6. The hungarian people have an asiatic background.
   7. The knights of columbus have a new office near st. mary's
hospital.
   8. The pennsylvania railroad runs under the hudson river into
the pennsylvania station.
   9. A friend of mine is teaching spanish at stanford university.
   10. The anglo-african oil company is not interested in aluminum.
   11. My sister bought a secondhand chevy van.
   12. We found some colorado brook trout at tony's market.
   13. Louis served us french toast with vermont maple syrup.
   14. The junior chamber of commerce will campaign for a
new hospital.
   15. The grand army of the republic was composed of civil
war veterans.

16. Where are the offices of the american red cross?
17. We bought our sunspeed power mower at the barclay hardware store.
18. Dad knows a vice-president at the morgan guaranty trust company.
19. Our new offices are in the first national bank building.
20. The new teacher is a leader in the boy scouts of america.

10.10 Titles of Persons

Capitalize words that show rank, office, or profession, when they are used with a person's name.

Doctor Weber	Representative Walsh	Father Forbes
Sergeant Reilly	Rabbi Kahn	Captain Brooks
Private Harrison	Mayor Derrado	Judge Bentley

The titles of high officials are capitalized even when they are used without the official's name.

the President of the United States	the Prime Minister
the Secretary of State	the Governor

The prefix *ex-* and the suffix *-elect* are not capitalized when attached to titles: *ex-president Nixon,* the *Senator-elect.*

10.11 Family Relationships

Capitalize the name of a family relationship when it is used with a person's name.

Aunt Ruth	Uncle Bill
Grandma Moses	Cousin Joe

When words like *mother, father, dad,* and *mom* are used alone in place of a particular person's name, they are capitalized. When modified by a possessive pronoun, as in *your mother,* they are not capitalized. When these and other words of family relationship do not stand for a particular person, they are not capitalized.

> My Aunt Daisy bought me this sweater.
> It's too bad Cousin Lymon isn't home.
> We begged Mom to make fried chicken.
> His father will meet him at the station.
> I can't imagine having five sisters.

10.12 Titles of Books and Works of Art

Capitalize the first word and every important word in the titles of books, stories, articles, poems, films, works of art, and musical compositions.

The only words considered not important are conjunctions, articles (*a, an,* and *the*), and prepositions containing fewer than five letters. But even these are capitalized when used as the first word in a title.

A Tale of Two Cities	*Death of a Salesman*
Notes of a Native Son	"To a Waterfowl"
"A Christmas Memory"	"Bridge over Troubled Waters"

Exercise: Copy each word that requires a capital in these sentences.

1. Is uncle john inviting dad to his camp?
2. There was a radio report of the death of ex-governor brown.
3. My aunt jenny introduced colonel hawkins as our next governor.
4. Did your father hear from cousin bert?
5. The assistant attorney-general, a future president, faced the chief justice, an ex-president, and defied him.
6. The author of the monograph is justice andrew larson.
7. We learned that the governors of these states are to meet the secretary of the interior.
8. Have mother and father met judge krantz?
9. My sister gave cousin alice *webster's new world dictionary.*

10. You will find *art through the ages* a useful reference.

11. Allen wants a copy of *two years before the mast.*

12. Mark's favorite piece is "the pines of rome."

13. The meeting will be addressed by chief of police johnson.

14. The party consisted of colonel byrd, lieutenant jack, and my cousin.

15. Your mother drove us out to see grandfather brown.

10.13 The Deity

Capitalize all words referring to the Deity, the Holy Family, and to religious scriptures.

God	the Holy Ghost	Jehovah	the Torah
the Father	the Almighty	the Bible	the Talmud
the Son	the Lord	the Gospel	the Koran

Capitalize personal pronouns but not relative pronouns that refer to the Deity.

May God make His light to shine down upon you.
Praise God from whom all mercy flows.

10.14 Days, Months, Holidays

Capitalize the names of days of the week, of months, and of holidays. Do not capitalize the names of the seasons.

Wednesday	Thanksgiving	spring
August	Easter	fall

10.15 Historical Names

Capitalize the names of historical events, documents, and periods.

World War II	the Renaissance
the Constitution	the New Deal

Exercise A: Copy the words that require capitals in these sentences.

1. Elaine is reading the chapters on the late middle ages.
2. My favorite period in american history is the age of jackson.
3. Both the declaration of independence and the emancipation proclamation are greatly admired by other nations.
4. Some authorities believe that the battle of the bulge was a decisive turning point in world war II.
5. In new york, columbus day is always a holiday.
6. The prohibition era was a time of low public morals.
7. We expect to celebrate new year's eve by staying home and watching TV.
8. The convent of st. paul the apostle is the local address of the sisters of the holy ghost.
9. The romantic period began later in american literature.
10. The second continental congress lasted for five years.

Exercise B: Copy the words that require capitals in these sentences.

1. The vice-president met the french premier at national airport.
2. The social security act is administered by the department of health, education, and welfare.
3. The little group under captain siple observed christmas leave at the south pole.
4. My uncle was on an airplane carrier in the battle of midway.
5. The ex-mayor and the mayor-elect exchanged cordial greetings.
6. In an address to congress, president monroe announced the monroe doctrine.
7. The settlers rode down the ohio river on their way to the west.
8. Several french communities were founded in the midwest.
9. On the eastbound flight, we were over the rocky mountains very quickly.
10. You can buy irish linen at dayton's department store on fourth street.

11.0 End Marks and Commas

11.1 Periods at the Close of Sentences

Place a period at the close of every declarative sentence and of most imperative sentences.

A period is also used at the close of groups of words that are used as sentences even though they are not complete sentences.

> Don't get too near the fire.
> I'll never go back to that barber. Never.

11.2 Periods in Abbreviations

Place a period after every part of an abbreviation.

U. S. Grant	Ulysses Simpson Grant
Atty. Gen.	Attorney General
N. Dak.	North Dakota
P.M.	*post meridiem*

It has become the custom not to use periods in abbreviations of certain government agencies and of international organizations.

NATO	North Atlantic Treaty Organization
FBI	Federal Bureau of Investigation

UN	United Nations
UMW	United Mine Workers
FDA	Food and Drug Administration
IRS	Internal Revenue Service

11.3   Exclamation Points

Place an exclamation point after an exclamatory sentence and after an exclamation set off from a sentence.

Wow! What a hit!	That's enough!
Help! Help!	Look out!
Bravo!	We want Armstrong!

11.4   Question Marks

Place a question mark after an interrogative sentence or after a question that is not a complete sentence.

The word order in questions is sometimes the same as in declarative sentences. In speech, the speaker raises his voice at the end of the sentence to show that it is a question. In writing, the question mark performs the same function.

Does Roger ice skate?	You call this hot?
Is this the book you want?	Who made these donuts?
The date? It's the twenty-fifth.	These are yours?

Exercise: Copy these sentences, using end marks and punctuation as required for sentences and abbreviations. Use question marks only for sentences in normal interrogative form.

1. At what time does the game begin
2. Mr L V Costello left this office at 4:30 P M
3. Dr J A Larson, Jr will attend a conference in Washington, D C
4. The contract was arranged between Brightons, Ltd of England and Sweetways, Inc of New York

5. Who ruled the Mediterranean world from 100 B C to A D 200

6. Don't touch that wire

7. When the box arrives, may we open it

8. The book was written by the Reverend Thomas Powers, S J

9. The meeting was addressed by Atty Gen Edward Levi

10. Professor Marilyn Barnard, D Sc was appointed to the ICC

Uses of the Comma

11.5   Introductory Words

Introductory words such as *yes, no, well, why,* and *oh* are followed by a comma.

> Yes, I think I would like some soup.
> Well, I haven't actually finished the assignment.
> Oh, this coat belongs to you.

Adverbs such as *besides, however, anyhow, nonetheless* at the beginning of a sentence are set off by commas.

11.6   Introductory Phrases and Clauses

A participial phrase at the beginning of a sentence is followed by a comma.
A long adverbial clause at the beginning of a sentence is followed by a comma.
A succession of prepositional phrases at the beginning of a sentence is set off by a comma.

> *Hoping to be rescued,* they treaded water all night.
>   (participial phrase)
> *When the sun rose the next morning,* our sleeping bags were
>   covered with dew. (adverbial clause)
> *Under the rug at the top of the stairs,* we found Dad's keys.
>   (succession of prepositional phrases)

11.7 Transposed Words and Phrases

Words and phrases moved to the beginning of a sentence from their normal position are usually set off by a comma.

He is usually dressed in blue jeans. (normal order)
Usually, he is dressed in blue jeans. (transposed order)

There is obviously no exit to this cave. (normal order)
Obviously, there is no exit to this cave. (transposed order)

Call Serena for directions if necessary. (normal order)
If necessary, call Serena for directions. (transposed order)

Exercise: Copy the following sentences, inserting commas where necessary. Two of the sentences are correct.

1. Honestly we are not justified in complaining.
2. At the start of the campaign Mr. Anson was favored to win.
3. Well no one was more surprised at the outcome than Robbie.
4. After scoring six runs in the first inning the Mets relaxed.
5. To avoid excess nervous tension practice physical relaxation.
6. Counting on surprise Greenville passed on the first down.
7. Although the road was icy we made fairly good time.
8. With intense concentration Lynn went over her report again.
9. No there is no other way out of the valley.
10. Dropping their tools the men scrambled for safety.
11. To save some of the money is simply good sense.
12. Keeping up the morale of the men was Paul's hardest job.
13. When the tide went out we walked along the sandy beach.
14. Hard as she worked Janet could not catch up to the rest of the class.
15. Why no one warned us to shut off the water.

11.8 Appositives

An appositive is set off from the rest of the sentence by commas.

Farrell, *our quarterback*, injured his shoulder.
Mother's guest, *Mrs. Worthall*, was not amused.

11.9   Words of Direct Address

Words of direct address are set off by commas.

> *Giles*, please stop humming that song.
> So, *Dr. Jeffries*, what is your opinion?
> Would you come here a minute, *Ms. Chilton?*

11.10 Parenthetical Expressions

Words and phrases used to explain or qualify a statement are called **parenthetical expressions.** These same words and phrases may also be used as basic parts of the sentence. It is only when they are parenthetical that they are set off by commas.

> I believe our car is over there.
> Our car, *I believe*, is over there. (parenthetical)
> We hope that we'll get back in time for the meeting.
> We'll get back, *we hope*, in time for the meeting.
>   (parenthetical)

Parenthetical expressions are set off by commas.

Some expressions often used parenthetically are:

of course	as a matter of fact	for example
in fact	I believe (hope, think)	on the other hand

Conjunctive adverbs (see Section 1.7) used parenthetically within the sentence are set off by commas: *therefore, moreover, nevertheless, however, consequently,* and so on.

> The principal, *moreover*, was in favor of their plan.
> The students, *however*, did not know this.
> The rally, *consequently*, was attended by very few.

Occasionally, words like *however, therefore,* and *consequently* are used to modify a word in the sentence. As modifiers they are an essential part of the meaning of a sentence. Since they are essential, they are not set off by commas.

Pat cannot arrive on time *however* hard he tries.

The cast had performed the play the previous semester. They *therefore* needed little rehearsal.

The club's bylaws were *consequently* altered.

11.11 Dates, Addresses, Geographical Names

In dates and addresses of more than one part, set off every part after the first from the rest of the sentence.

She comes from a small town in Ohio. (one part)

I believe that East Liverpool, Ohio, is her home town. (two parts, the second set off by commas)

V-J Day was in 1945. (one part)

It was on August 14, 1945, that the fighting with Japan ended. (two parts, the second set off by commas)

All of his mail is being forwarded to 3144 Camelback Road, Phoenix, Arizona 85016, where his aunt and uncle live. (three parts, the second and third set off by commas)

Note: The day of the month and the month are one item. The name of the street and the house number are one item. The name of the state and the zip code are one item.

May 29   313 West Houston Street   Georgia 30312

Exercise: Copy these sentences, inserting the necessary commas.

1. We visited the Adams Library one of the oldest in America.

2. There is no doubt my friends that we have hard times ahead of us.

3. One field of science electronics is almost completely devoted to storing and transmitting information.

4. The damage however was less than we had expected.

5. A good man you may be sure is still hard to find.

6. Your second sentence for example is much too long.

7. The door was opened by the butler a tall man with brooding eyes.

8. The game was played as a matter of fact exactly as we planned it.

9. The library will therefore be closed on Saturday.

10. The company has moved its offices to Morristown New Jersey.

11. Reno Nevada lies farther west than Los Angeles California.

12. Our new address is 41 East Twelfth Street New York New York 10003.

13. The treaty was signed in Geneva Switzerland on December 15 1906 but it was not ratified until March 6 1908.

14. On July 5 1835 there were snowstorms in the New England states.

15. Lee was born in Evanston Illinois on December 19 1945.

16. You know gentlemen we may be on the verge of a revolution in printing.

17. This house you see is built on a rock ledge.

18. We will meet you at Canton Ohio on Wednesday January 10.

19. The entrapped miners decided therefore to make one more try.

20. It is up to you ladies and gentlemen to decide what kind of society you want to live in.

11.12 Nonrestrictive Modifiers

A clause that identifies or points out the person or thing it modifies is a **restrictive clause.** It is essential to the meaning of the sentence. It cannot be dropped out without confusing the meaning or making the meaning incomplete.

> The car *that I told you about* is parked over there.
> (The clause tells *which* car.)
> We need a car *that can seat ten.*
> (The clause tells an essential characteristic of the car needed.)

The woman *who makes her own clothes* is never shabby.
(Without the clause, the sentence has no
specific meaning.)

Restrictive clauses are not set off from the rest of the sentence by commas.

A **nonrestrictive clause** does not contain information essential to the meaning of the sentence. It presents merely added information. It can be dropped without confusing the meaning of the sentence.

Lynn, *who had been afraid that no college would accept her,* was awarded a scholarship to Berkeley.
Our cat, *who recently had kittens,* drinks a pint of milk a day.

Nonrestrictive clauses are set off by commas from the rest of the sentence.

Participial phrases that identify or point out the thing or person they modify are restrictive.

The mechanic *lying under that Ford* worked on our car.
(Without the phrase, the sentence loses its
specific meaning.)
The tag *sewn into the lining* tells whose coat it is. (The phrase identifies the tag.)

Nonrestrictive participial phrases merely add meaning. They are not essential and can be dropped without making the meaning of the sentence incomplete.

Shading my eyes, I peered across the field.
Tony, *holding aloft a huge cake,* entered the room.
The pickets, *circling in front of the store,* sang freedom songs.

Nonrestrictive participial phrases are set off from the rest of the sentence by commas. Restrictive phrases are not set off by commas.

Exercise: Number your paper 1–18. Decide whether the adjective clause or the participial phrase is restrictive or nonrestrictive. After each number write *restrictive* or *nonrestrictive.* Copy and insert commas in the sentences in which commas are needed.

1. The book reviewed on the television program has had greatly increased sales.

2. A good dictionary read with skill and understanding can be a source of pleasure.

3. This is the house that we expect to buy.

4. Mr. Salvatore who is a famous singer will train our class.

5. The train struck by the avalanche was tossed down the hillside.

6. The picture now appearing at the Tivoli stars Glenda Jackson.

7. We were delighted by the report that appeared in the papers.

8. The new toll road which will be opened Friday will save us a great deal of time.

9. Dad's office which has always been dark has been redecorated.

10. The new show which was highly praised by reviewers was a disappointment to us.

11. These are the boxes that you are to return to the store.

12. We waited until the last moment hoping you would appear.

13. The man driving the car had neither insurance nor a license.

14. The hills that you see in the distance lie in New Jersey.

15. Our neighbor who is a fine mechanic helped us repair the dishwasher.

16. The coach fearing overconfidence put the team through a hard drill.

17. The car that you just passed is a police car.

18. The room which was too small in the first place was now overcrowded.

11.13 Compound Sentences

Place a comma before the conjunction that joins two main clauses in a compound sentence.

It snowed all night, *and* the schools were closed the next day.
Craig must leave now, *or* he will miss his plane.
The bill may not pass this time, *but* you can be certain it will be passed soon.

Lucy did not remember where they had planned to meet,
nor did she know Henry's phone number.

When the clauses are quite short, the comma may be omitted.

The sun rose and we awakened.
Reynolds hit a double but Lane popped out.

11.14 Series

A **series** is a group of three or more items of the same kind.

SERIES OF NOUNS:	*Clothing, books,* and *papers* were piled on top of Kent's dresser.
SERIES OF VERBS:	The bus driver *honked, slammed* on the brakes, and *swerved* sharply to the left.
SERIES OF ADJECTIVES:	The day that we had so long awaited was *warm, sunny,* and *cloudless.*
SERIES OF PHRASES:	Groups of children were playing *behind the house, on the porch,* and *in the yard.*

Commas are used to separate the parts of a series.

No comma is required after the last item in a series. When the last two items of a series are joined by *and* or *or*, the comma is sometimes omitted. To avoid all possibility of misunderstanding, it is wise to use a comma before the conjunction.

Do not use a comma if all parts of the series are joined by *and, or,* or *nor.*

All summer Sue swam and read and lolled.
Many children will not eat turnips or carrots or spinach.

11.15 Coordinate Adjectives

Commas are placed between coordinate adjectives that modify the same noun.

The long, dull debate seemed endless.
Raging, howling winds whipped the trees.

To determine whether adjectives are coordinate, try placing an *and* between them. If it sounds natural, they are coordinate, and a comma is needed.

PROBLEM His loud whining voice made the
audience shudder.

NATURAL His loud *and* whining voice made the
audience shudder.

SOLUTION His loud, whining voice made the
audience shudder.

PROBLEM It was a dark dreary depressing day.
NATURAL It was a dark, dreary, *and* depressing day.
SOLUTION It was a dark, dreary, depressing day.

PROBLEM Our house is the big white one.
NOT NATURAL Our house is the big *and* white one.
SOLUTION Our house is the big white one.

In general, it is safe to omit the comma after numbers and adjectives of size, shape, and age.

a big round moon   five tiny wafers

Exercise: Copy these sentences, placing commas where they are needed.

1. We asked Marion to come with us but she had another engagement.
2. The lights the movements and the presents make a pretty picture.
3. We had not intended to stay overnight but the snowfall turned into a blizzard.
4. The officer asked for Bob's license looked it over and got out his notebook.
5. The doctor must come soon or he will be too late.
6. Beethoven wrote symphonies quartets concertos and sonatas.

7. Three trucks four cars and a trailer were tangled on the icy bridge.

8. Luanne found the geology course interesting practical but difficult.

9. The boss frowned tried to look severe and finally grinned.

10. The entire roll of film was either blurred dark or out of focus.

11. Harry has his pass but he cannot leave the base until tomorrow.

12. Helen entered the room walked straight to the table and called the meeting to order.

13. Strange noises were coming from the stereo from the water pipes and from the attic.

14. I could not reach the top shelf nor could I find the stepladder.

15. You had better start now or you will miss the last bus.

16. Couples were standing in the streets sitting on telephone poles and leaning out of windows.

17. A flight attendant must be cheerful alert and always pleasant.

18. We had expected to arrive by midnight but the plane could not land.

19. All roads bridges and highways into the city have been closed by the heavy snowstorm.

20. Suddenly, the commanding officer picked up a pen reached for my papers signed them and tossed them across the desk to me.

11.16 Clarity

Use a comma to separate words or phrases that might be mistakenly joined in reading.

There are three common situations in which words may be mistakenly read together. The first occurs when the conjunctions *but* and *for* are mistaken for prepositions.

CONFUSING   I liked all the speeches but one was superb.

CLEAR   I liked all the speeches, but one was superb.

| CONFUSING | Rita listened for she thought she'd heard a cry. |
| CLEAR | Rita listened, for she thought she'd heard a cry. |

A second source of confusion is a noun following a verbal phrase.

CONFUSING	Before waxing Jill swept the floor.
CLEAR	Before waxing, Jill swept the floor.
CONFUSING	To walk a cat must withdraw its nails.
CLEAR	To walk, a cat must withdraw its nails.
CONFUSING	After painting Vincent wrote his brother.
CLEAR	After painting, Vincent wrote his brother.

A third source of confusion is the word that may be either adverb, preposition, or conjunction at the beginning of the sentence.

CONFUSING	Beneath the earth looked like a quilt.
CLEAR	Beneath, the earth looked like a quilt.
CONFUSING	Outside the courtyard was in chaos.
CLEAR	Outside, the courtyard was in chaos.

11.17 Words Omitted

Use a comma when words are omitted from parallel word groups.

Anna baked a pie; Tom, some bread.
Mr. Davis makes requests; Mr. Cowan, demands.
The day became warm, and our spirits, merry.

Exercise: Copy these sentences, placing commas where necessary to avoid confusion.

1. Ms. Ellis sent four letters; Ms. Harris two dozen postcards.
2. I recognized none of the group but John had known one of the boys in summer camp.
3. Once before the stage curtain had stuck halfway up.

4. After eating Mary cleared up the kitchen.

5. Beyond the residential section extends for ten miles.

6. Inside the church was beautifully lighted.

7. Above the men were dangling ropes over the cliff.

8. None of the girls was old enough, but Sue got in to see the movie.

9. Skip set out the chairs on the porch for the guests were arriving.

10. Outside the house looked as though no one lived there.

12.0 The Semicolon, the Colon, the Dash, and Parentheses

12.1 Semicolons Between Main Clauses

A semicolon is placed between the main clauses of a compound sentence when they are not joined by a conjunction.

The clauses of a compound sentence are closely related in thought. That is the reason for joining them into one sentence rather than writing them as separate sentences.

In some sentences the semicolon is more effective in joining main clauses than one of the conjunctions. This is especially true when *and* or *but* add little meaning to the joined clauses.

Richard is good at set shots, *but* I am not.
Richard is good at set shots; I am not.
The cyclone struck with savage fury, *and* it demolished the little coastal town.
The cyclone struck with savage fury; it demolished the little coastal town.

12.2 Semicolons and Conjunctive Adverbs

A semicolon is used between main clauses joined by conjunctive adverbs or by phrases like _for example_, _in fact_, _for instance_.

Our treasury was nearly empty; *accordingly,* we began
considering various fund-raising projects.
Marge had studied Italian for three years; *yet,* when she
arrived in Florence, she found herself tongue-tied.
Many of their talents complemented each other; *for example,*
he played the piano and she sang.
Nick is well-liked; *in fact,* he is the most popular person
in the class.

Note that the conjunctive adverb or phrase is followed by a
comma in the examples above.

12.3 Semicolons Between Word Groups Containing Commas

A sentence containing a great many commas is difficult to read.
If commas precede the conjunction between main clauses, another comma at this point would lose its value as a guide to the
reader.

**A semicolon is used between main clauses joined by a conjunc-
tion if the clause before the conjunction contains commas.**

Jim had done research, taken notes, and made an outline; but
he didn't feel ready to begin writing.
We put out sandwiches, cider, potato chips, and donuts; and
still we wondered if there would be enough.

**A semicolon is used between a series of phrases if they contain
commas.**

Members of our class come from as far away as Leeds,
England; New Delhi, India; and San Juan, Puerto Rico.
Roy was in charge of the scenery; Mabel, the costumes; and
Charles, the directing of the play.
Eric called the children together; checked their hands, ears,
and faces; and told them to be back by five sharp.

Exercise: Two of the following sentences need no semicolons. For the other sentences, indicate the point at which a semicolon should replace a comma.

1. We are disappointed in the advertisement, it is too small.

2. The team went to the hospital to see Bud, he had been hurt in Saturday's game.

3. Sylvia is doing very well, in fact, she has a B + average.

4. Dictionaries do not always agree, for instance, they differ on the pronunciation of *duty*.

5. As the game entered the last quarter, Pitt scored twice and won the game handily.

6. We have a factory in Salem, Ohio, an office in Buffalo, New York, and a mill at Andover, Massachusetts.

7. Dave Rotnam won first prize, his sister Joan, second prize, and Harry Belknap, third prize.

8. Eve was surrounded by notebooks, encyclopedias, and dictionaries, but she was reading a letter from Bill.

9. The men at the South Pole rarely got mail, but they could talk to their families by radio.

10. For Christmas, I got a radio, Joan, a typewriter, and Mark, a new suit.

11. We ought to beat Hinsdale, Elmhurst, and Bensenville, but we may lose to Oak Park.

12. The building was designed by Frank Lloyd Wright, the famous American architect, but the New York critics, in their newspaper columns, attacked it savagely.

13. The electricity was off for three hours, consequently, everything in our food locker was spoiled.

14. Harry has been on the force for twenty-three years, he is almost ready to retire.

15. Ellen has a new camera, it was made in Germany.

12.4   Colons To Introduce Lists

The colon is used to throw the reader's attention forward to what follows. It is in some respects like an equal sign, saying that what follows is the explanation or equivalent of what has gone before.

A colon is used to introduce a list of items.

Usually, a colon is required when a list is preceded by the words *the following* or *as follows.* A colon is not used before a series of modifiers or complements immediately following the verb.

> Jim had been a member of the following groups: the Drama Club, the Debate Union, and the Archery Club. (list)
> The following nations were among those represented at the congress: Colombia, Bolivia, Panama, and Ecuador. (list)
> Sue uses cream in cereal, in coffee, and in tea. (series of modifiers)
> The candidate's characteristics were forthrightness, intelligence, and courage. (series of complements)

12.5   Colons with Formal Quotations

A colon is used to introduce a formal quotation.

> The president opened the meeting with these words: "We are beginning a period of expansion in which all of you will play a key role. Many of you will have added responsibilities; others will have entirely new responsibilities."

12.6   Colons Before Explanatory Statements

A colon is used between two sentences when the second explains the first. The second sentence begins with a capital letter.

> Then I knew we were in trouble: None of our boys could match the swan dive we had just seen.
> From then on we understood Ms. Gilroy: She was demanding but she was kind.

12.7   Other Uses of the Colon

A colon is used (1) after the formal salutation of a letter, (2) between hour and minute figures of clock time, (3) in Biblical references, (4) between the title and subtitle of a book, (5) between numbers referring to volume and pages of books and magazines.

Dear Sir or Madam: Matthew 1:5
Dear Mr. Berg: *The Raven: The Life of Sam Houston*
8:20 P.M.   Volume IV: pages 126–142

12.8   The Dash To Show Break in Thought

A dash is used to show an abrupt break in thought.

In dialogue, the break in thought is often caused by uncertainty or hesitancy as in the first example below.

Photosynthesis is an action—I mean it's what happens—well, it's sunlight doing something to chlorophyll.
The movie opens with a shot of the desert—oh, you've seen it.
She told me that—oh, I really shouldn't repeat it.

12.9   The Dash with Interrupters

A dash is used to set off a long explanatory statement that interrupts the thought.

They had searched everywhere—under the seats, in the aisles, in the lobby—before Dan found the keys in his pocket.
The meeting—between two men who had clashed violently only a week before—was calm and friendly.

12.10 The Dash Before a Summary

The dash is used after a series to indicate a summarizing statement.

Insufficient heating, leaky roofs, cluttered stairways, and unsanitary corridors—for all these violations of the housing code, the landlord was hauled into court.

Yellowed song sheets, framed photographs of opera stars, programs of long-past performances—these were scattered about her room.

Exercise: Copy the following sentences, inserting semicolons, colons, or dashes where necessary.

1. Beginning next January we shall handle the following foreign cars Datsun, Volvo, Volkswagen, and Mercedes.

2. The candidate's main qualifications were these twelve years' experience in the Senate, a knowledge of foreign affairs, and the ability to get votes.

3. I am looking for the source of this quotation "When you shoot at a king, you must kill him."

4. Our new text is called *Supershopper A Guide to Spending and Saving.*

5. The quotation is found in *The Oxford English Dictionary,* Vol. II page 427.

6. High school students today are more serious they expect to work hard.

7. Alice knew at least she thought she knew what was coming next.

8. It is our obligation there is no choice in the matter to pay all of Frank's expenses to the convention.

9. It's about well, it's something like I would say it's a good ten miles from here.

10. Having a lot of clothes, owning a fancy car, going to parties are these really suitable goals in life?

11. The prizes are as follows first prize, a movie camera second prize, a portable TV set third prize, a pocket-size calculator.

12. You have three jobs for today wash the car, clean up the yard, and shop for your mother.

13. The President closed with these words "With God's help, we can face the future hopefully, in full confidence that our problems can be solved."

14. Marion saw the point no one else did.

15. We shall cover the following topics in this conference planning for new products, improving customer relations, and marketing.

16. You will find the statement in *Thomas Jefferson The Man and His Times,* Volume III page 106.

17. You can take this road down but I guess the road is closed, isn't it?

18. There is a strange light a reddish light that moves very fast in the sky to the south of here.

19. All of a sudden we had already closed the door the telephone began ringing.

20. It is rather a long walk however, it is a pleasant one.

12.11 Parentheses To Enclose Supplementary or Explanatory Words

Commas, dashes, or parentheses are used to set off words that are supplementary or explanatory. Commas are used when the material set off is fairly close to the main thought of the sentence. Dashes are used to set off material more loosely connected, and parentheses are used to set off material so loosely related to the main thought that it might be made a separate sentence.

There are few occasions in high school writing when parentheses are needed. The safest course for the student is to use commas, or even dashes, to set off parenthetical matter. If the material is so distantly related as to require parentheses, the passage might better be rewritten to place the parenthetical material in a separate sentence.

COMMAS ADEQUATE:	Kate's best point, *which she saved for the end,* was that every group needs leadership.
DASHES REQUIRED:	Modern science no longer deals directly with the visible world— that is, it deals directly only with ions, atoms, electrons, and other particles that are too small to be seen.
PARENTHESES APPROPRIATE:	But on the whole, Arthur was a well-behaved little boy; a good pupil and obedient (except when he played with the scruffy boys in the street, whom his mother disliked).—Colin Wilson, *Religion and the Rebel.*
PARENTHESES AVOIDED:	But on the whole, Arthur was a well-behaved little boy and a good pupil. He was obedient except when he played with the scruffy boys in the street, whom his mother disliked.

12.12 Punctuation Within Parentheses

Commas, semicolons, and periods are placed outside the closing parenthesis. The question mark and exclamation point are placed inside if the parenthetical material is itself a question or exclamation; otherwise, outside.

Jean (not Martha) was the dancer in the orange leotards.
Leo's speech was on disarmament; Barb's on acting as a
career (her favorite subject); Jim's, on slum clearance.
I never guessed (would you have?) that the maid did it.
Sheldon spoke of his victory over Central's debaters (*his*
victory!) as if he had been a one-man team.

13.0 The Apostrophe

The apostrophe is used with nouns to show possession or owner-ship: *Aunt Lucy's summer cottage, Carl's goldfish, the lawyer's briefcase.* The apostrophe is also used to show the following:

Close relationship:	Amy's companion, someone's parents
Source or origin:	Grace's drawings, George's ability
Identifying characteristics:	the woman's attitude, Russell's gestures, Shelley's moods

13.1 The Possessive of Singular Nouns

The possessive form of a singular noun is usually made by adding an apostrophe and s ('s) to the noun.

$$dog + 's = dog's \qquad girl + 's = girl's$$
$$Tess + 's = Tess's \qquad town + 's = town's$$

When a singular noun of more than one syllable ends in *s*, the possessive *may* be formed by adding only the apostrophe.

$$Thomas + \text{'} = Thomas' \quad hostess + \text{'} = hostess'$$
$$actress + \text{'} = actress' \quad Moses + \text{'} = Moses'$$

13.2   The Possessive of Plural Nouns

If a plural noun does not end in s, add both apostrophe and s ('s) to form the possessive.

$$women + \text{'s} = women's \quad men + \text{'s} = men's$$
$$children + \text{'s} = children's \quad deer + \text{'s} = deer's$$

If a plural noun ends in s, add only the apostrophe to form the possessive.

$$animals + \text{'} = animals' \quad members + \text{'} = members'$$
$$writers + \text{'} = writers' \quad soldiers + \text{'} = soldiers'$$

Exercise: Number 1–20 on your paper. Write *correct* for each sentence in which the possessive form is correct. If the form is incorrect, write it correctly.

1. The boys bikes had been locked up in the basement.
2. This year the team's spirit is much better.
3. Ross' minibike was stolen.
4. The waitress's friends came to her defense.
5. We found Charles's books in the back of our car.
6. The regular passengers have formed a passenger's committee.
7. We have put new heaters in the salespersons' cars.
8. The ship's doctor performed the operation at sea.
9. The governors' assistants have their own meeting at the same time.
10. Stan serves at lunchtime in the teacher's lunchroom.
11. The three reporter's statements differed on important points.
12. The gentlemens' cars are ready for them.
13. Children's toys were scattered over the driveway.
14. The sailor's leaves were suddenly canceled.

15. The actors' voices were loud and harsh.
16. The watchmen's reports make no mention of a disturbance.
17. Les's garage is always open on Sunday.
18. Diplomats and soldiers alike were showered by the hostess's smile.
19. The alumni's contributions built the chapel.
20. Cathy has entered the womens' tennis tournament.

13.3 The Possessive of Compound Nouns

A **compound noun** is a noun composed of more than one word. Some compound nouns are written with hyphens between the parts.

Only the last part of a hyphenated noun shows possession.

> jack-o'-lantern + 's = jack-o'-lantern's
> sister-in-law + 's = sister-in-law's

Nouns such as *the Queen of England, the President of the United States, the Prime Minister* form the possessive by adding an apostrophe and *s* to the last word only: *the Queen of England's throne.* Often, however, an *of* phrase is less awkward.

> the throne of the Queen of England
> the home of the President of the United States
> the wife of the Prime Minister

13.4 Joint Ownership

When the names of two or more persons are used to show joint ownership, only the name of the last person mentioned is given the possessive form. Add an apostrophe or an apostrophe and s in accord with the spelling of that name.

> Boris and Ivan's uncle
> Ed and Joanne's home
> Bob and Gregory's project

The rule also applies to firm names and to names of organizations.

> Strawbridge and Clothier's location
> Cross and Hamilton Company's sales force
> the Committee on Africa's report
> Peter and Ruthie's Waffle Shop

13.5 Separate Ownership or Possession

If the names of two or more persons are used to show separate ownership, each name is given the possessive form.

> Madison's and Monroe's administrations
> Don's and Jim's grades

This construction may become awkward. It can be avoided by using an *of* phrase.

> the administrations of Madison and Monroe
> the grades of Don and Jim
> the hopes of England and France

13.6 Possessive of Indefinite Pronouns

Use an apostrophe and s to form the possessive of indefinite pronouns.

> everyone + 's = everyone's   one + 's = one's
> either + 's = either's   somebody + 's = somebody's

The apostrophe and *s* are added to the last word in forms like *someone else, anybody else, no one else:*

> somebody else's   no one else's

The apostrophe is not used to form the possessive of personal pronouns.

> NONSTANDARD your's, her's, it's, our's, their's
> STANDARD yours, hers, its, ours, theirs

13.7 Expressions of Time and Amount

When used as adjectives, words expressing time and amount are given the possessive form.

a month's time	four days' wait
a week's notice	six months' delay
a day's holiday	thirty seconds' silence
a minute's peace	ten minutes' break
a penny's worth	two centuries' tradition

Exercise: Copy the italicized words, changing them to show ownership or possession.

1. We will meet at my *brother-in-law* house.
2. *Harry* and *Paul* uniforms did not fit.
3. Who will win is *anybody* guess.
4. Mrs. Blackmar has three *week* wages coming to her.
5. You can probably find the right kind of truck at *Smith and Weston* store.
6. Because of illness I have missed three *day* work.
7. *Roger and Sons* sale starts next week.
8. *Roosevelt* and *Rockefeller* backgrounds were somewhat similar.
9. Buffalo is ten *hours* ride from my town.
10. Where is the *League of Women Voters* office?
11. An *hour* wait now may save a *day* time later.
12. There is an advertisement of *Chase and Maxwell* sale in tonight's paper.
13. Sam picked up *somebody else* books.
14. What is the *Secretary of the Treasury* salary?
15. The school is sponsoring a *mothers* and *sons* picnic.
16. Have you paid *Lord and Taylor* bill this month?
17. *Andy* and *Marge* mother is a doctor.
18. In two *month* time your leg will be as good as new.
19. *Benét* and *Twain* stories were the best-liked.
20. There is only a *moment* delay before the phone rings at the other side of the continent.

13.8 Apostrophes To Show Omissions

An apostrophe is used to show the omission of letters or figures.

the flood of '23   1923
the class of '78   1978
they're   *they are*
shouldn't   *should not*

13.9 Plurals of Letters, Words, Numbers, and Signs

An apostrophe is used to show the plurals of letters, words, numbers, and signs.

How many *r*'s are there in *embarrass?*
Her speech relies too much on *nice*'s.
I still have to dot the *i*'s and cross the *t*'s.
Frederick Lewis Allen describes the Roaring 20's in
   Only Yesterday.

Note: The plurals of letters, numbers, signs, and words used as words are always italicized in print. In manuscript and typescript they may be underlined or placed in quotation marks. (See Section 14.7.)

Exercise A: Copy the following sentences, inserting an apostrophe (and *s*) where needed. This exercise reviews all the uses of apostrophes.

1. There are too many *thats* in your sentence.
2. Perrys address has four 3s in it.
3. There should be great prosperity in the 1980s.
4. It was three oclock before we got started.
5. Its not likely that Mars or Venus is inhabited.
6. We dont know the answer to the question and we cant find it.
7. It is clear now that Dads letter wont come today.

8. Jess' short story is being submitted to *Scholastic Magazine*.
9. The womens page in the local paper gives career tips.
10. We dont yet know whos coming.
11. Is there a good mens store in town?
12. The hostess smile was reassuring when the plane began to bounce.
13. The countys highway department is in charge of snow removal.
14. The waitresses hours and wages are good at Barneys Restaurant.
15. By working overtime, we earned a weeks wages in two days time.
16. You can buy womens coats in the young ladies department.
17. Ward was always too interested in everyone else business.
18. Have you ever shopped at a farmers market?
19. Charles order must have been lost in the mail.
20. The tugs whistles set up a frightful clamor in the harbor.

Exercise B: Write the possessive singular and the possessive plural of each of the following words:

1. woman	6. lady	11. day
2. man	7. fox	12. dollar
3. class	8. city	13. company
4. salesperson	9. boss	14. mouse
5. hour	10. employee	15. bus

Exercise C: The following sentences contain errors in the use of apostrophes. Copy the sentences, correcting all errors.

1. There is a new boy's camp across the lake.
2. Do you have an account at James's and Law's store?
3. Bess' and Gladys's telephone conversations go on for hours.
4. Alice is working at Harris' and Sons' store in Milwaukee.
5. Diana Ross and The Supreme's records will never be equaled.
6. We are publishing a collection of the years' best sport stories.
7. Mr. Harris' car wont' be ready until Friday.

8. What is your father's-in-law's business?

9. Its too late to go to Bobby Holmes' party.

10. Everyone elses boat was damaged in the storm.

11. The speakers words could not be heard above the audiences' coughing.

12. The Farewell Address was both Hamilton and Washington's work.

13. Ross' friend has just bought the J. C. Little's and Company building.

14. Two weeks stay here will give you a years good health.

15. Mason's and Dixon's survey settled many territorial disputes.

14.0 Quotations

14.1 Quotation Marks are Used To Enclose a Direct Quotation

In a direct quotation, the words of the speaker are directly quoted exactly as he spoke them.

> Greg said, "The streets should be cleared for our parade."
> "The town," the mayor said, "will be yours that day."

An indirect quotation reports the meaning expressed by the speaker but does not give his exact words.

> INDIRECT Molly replied that she was always punctual.
> DIRECT   "I am always punctual," Molly replied.

Quotation marks are not used with an indirect quotation.

Exercise: Number your paper 1–10. After each number write *Direct* or *Indirect* to describe the kind of quotation in each of these sentences. Copy and correct the sentences requiring quotation marks or other punctuation.

1. The test was hard said Sally but it was fair.
2. Don replied that he had no one to blame but himself.

3. May I have a new dress for the party asked Laura.

4. Johnny said that he wanted to study advanced science.

5. The teacher asked whether anyone was ready to give his report.

6. No one would think to look in here said Mrs. Brown.

7. Ben called out we will be home early.

8. The city is not equipped to deal with a heavy snowfall the guide explained.

9. Does anyone know asked Loretta who is to be the speaker at commencement?

10. Well I think I left it on the bus but I may have left it in the store said Jean sadly.

14.2   Punctuation of Direct Quotations

Punctuation and capitals are used as follows in direct quotations:

1. **In dialogue, the first word of the quotation is capitalized.** The material quoted from another writer may begin in the middle of a sentence. If so, the first word is not capitalized.

> On January 1, 1863, Lincoln declared the slaves
> "forever free."

2. **The speakers' words are set off from the rest of the sentence.**

Note the placement of commas in these examples:

> Michael said, "Let's meet at my house next time."
> "Let's meet at my house next time," Michael said.

When the end of the quotation is also the end of the sentence, the period falls inside the quotation marks.

3. **If the quoted words are a question or an exclamation, the question mark or the exclamation point falls inside the quotation marks.**

In this situation no comma is needed.

> "May I make the poster?" Lola asked.
> "I deny everything!" the suspect cried.

4. **If the entire sentence is a question or an exclamation, the exclamation point or question mark falls outside the quotation marks.**

Did I hear you say, "Have some cookies"?
It's absurd to consider these thieves "responsible citizens"!

5. **The colon and the semicolon at the close of a quotation fall outside the quotation marks.**

The committee said that the following states contained
"pockets of poverty": Kentucky, West Virginia,
and Pennsylvania.
Read the ballad "Sir Patrick Spens"; then study its relation
to Coleridge's poem "Dejection: An Ode."

6. **Both parts of a divided quotation are enclosed in quotation marks. The first word of the second part is not capitalized unless it begins a new sentence.**

"I plan," the Governor said, "to reduce taxes this year."
"Remember this," the counselor said. "Ten hours of casual
work may be less effective than five of real concentration."

7. **In dialogue, a new paragraph and a new set of quotation marks show a change in speaker.**

"My working habits have no pattern," the author said. "Some
writers set themselves strict schedules. I don't."
"But you've written five books in five years," the interviewer
replied. "You must work very hard day after day."
"On the contrary, there are days when I spend the entire
morning putting in a comma and the afternoon
taking it out."

14.3   Quotations Within Quotations

Single quotation marks are used to enclose a quotation within a quotation.

Herb said, "Then she actually said to me, 'I hope I didn't
keep you waiting.' "

"The announcer just said, 'More snow tonight,' "
   Len reported.
Ruth said, "Then Ray looked up from the ground and said,
   'I don't think I'll do any more skiing.' "

14.4 Long Quotations

A quotation may be several paragraphs in length.

In long quotations, begin each paragraph with quotation marks. Place quotation marks at the end of the last paragraph only.

Exercise: Copy the following sentences, adding the necessary punctuation marks and capital letters.

1. Molly asked does anyone remember when the book reports are due
2. We can't decide Mother said whether to paint the house or buy a new car
3. There is no excuse for this delay said the customer we gave you our order two months ago
4. Did Captain Perry's message say we have met the enemy and they are ours
5. Look out for a pass Bill shouted
6. Did you finish your homework Sarah asked
7. Do you happen to know asked Jack where we can get another tire
8. Are you absolutely sure Burt asked that the water has been turned off
9. What can we do now asked Beth our money is all gone
10. Dave replied I am sure the officer said come ahead
11. You can be sure Mark promised that we will not forget your kindness
12. Is it too late to apply for a scholarship asked Jeff
13. I am not afraid of the dark said Harold but I'm not afraid of a little light either
14. Did you hear the coach say no new plays this week
15. Do you have my pen asked Kathy I will need it next period

14.5 Setting off Titles

The title of a book, magazine, newspaper, long pamphlet, or bulletin is usually italicized in print. In your own writing, you indicate the italics by underlining.

To distinguish the title of a *part* of a book, magazine, or newspaper, quotation marks are used.

Use quotation marks to enclose the titles of chapters and other parts of books and to enclose the titles of stories, poems, essays, articles, and short musical compositions.

> Faulkner's story "The Bear" has become as famous as his novels.
>
> The subject of "Auspex" is an incident that occurred seventy-five years before Frost wrote the poem.

14.6 Words Used in Special Ways

Words used in special ways or special senses are enclosed in quotation marks.

A writer may want to show that he is using a word as someone else has used it. The writer can make clear that he himself does not accept this use of the word by enclosing it in quotation marks.

Slang words and phrases are also enclosed in quotation marks to indicate that the writer does not accept them as standard usage.

> There are always a few people who consider it a shameful waste to give aid to "inferior nations."
>
> The agent thought Cybil's performance was "simply divine."
>
> The reporter asked the negotiators to describe what they meant by "a satisfactory solution."
>
> The congressman considered every voter his "pal"; he called every child a "cute little doll."

Note: When a comma or period immediately follows the quoted word, it falls *inside* the quotation marks. The semicolon falls *outside* the quotation marks. See the last example above.

If the quoted word appears at the end of a question or exclamation, the question mark or exclamation point falls *outside* the quotation marks: *Is this what you mean by "cool"?*

14.7   Words Used as Words

A word referred to as a word is italicized in print. In writing, the word is underlined.

> The word *very* cannot do all the work some people require of it.
> Until then, I'd never heard the word *boondoggle*.

When a word and its definition appear in the same sentence, the word is italicized, and the definition is placed in quotation marks.

> A *borzoi* is "a large Russian wolfhound."

Exercise: Copy the following sentences. Insert quotation marks where necessary. Indicate italics by underlining.

1. What does the word serendipity mean?
2. There are too many and's in your sentences.
3. You will find Benét's The Devil and Daniel Webster in your anthology.
4. There is an interesting article entitled Swimming with Right Whales in this month's National Geographic.
5. Doris always has a hard time spelling recommend.
6. The British word for elevator is lift.
7. In Canada the word is spelled colour.
8. Why are the islands called The Lesser Antilles?
9. John Denver describes nearly everything as far out.
10. What is meant by the phrase manifest destiny?

15.0 Spelling

If you have trouble with spelling, you may be consoled by the fact that other students for generations back have also had trouble. If you are interested in improving your spelling, you may be encouraged to know that many generations of poor spellers before you have learned to spell.

There is no simple way to teach you to spell. There is no easy way to learn. If you are concerned about the problem, however, there are several helpful suggestions:

1. **Proofread all your writing.** Even the ablest scholar may write "their" for "there" or "here" for "hear" in a first draft. Many apparent errors are not spelling errors at all. They are mistakes caused by carelessness and too much haste.

2. **Learn to look at the letters in a word.** Most of us have learned to read by recognizing whole words or parts of words. Spelling errors are errors in the letters that compose a word. You will find it helpful to break a word into its parts to see and to memorize the spelling of each part.

3. **Keep a list of your spelling errors.** The point is that you can spell correctly most of the words you use. Your errors fall within a narrow range. If you will concentrate on this range—provided by your list—you may show quick improvement.

4. **Practice on your own spelling problem.** There is no reason why you cannot totally eliminate spelling errors *if you want to.* One recommended procedure is to use a card pack. Print your problem words on cards in large letters. Take a card from the pack. Look at every letter and let the order of the letters sink into your mind. Pronounce each part of the word separately. Turn the card over. Write the word on a piece of paper. Turn the card over again and compare what you have written with the correct spelling.

5. **Memorize and apply the few rules of spelling given below.** Be sure you understand the rules, or your memory work will be wasted. Practice using the rules so that their use becomes automatic and you can write *bragging, reference, occurrence,* and so on, quickly.

Exercise: Divide these words into syllables. Do not be concerned as to whether they conform to the dictionary division. Just make sure that every word part has a vowel sound.

1. occurrence	7. humorous	13. italicize
2. accidentally	8. specifically	14. miniature
3. accommodate	9. necessary	15. extraordinary
4. incredible	10. disappearance	16. secretarial
5. miscellaneous	11. mimeograph	17. athletic
6. maintenance	12. immediately	18. privilege

15.1 The Final Silent e

When a suffix beginning with a vowel is added to a word ending in a silent e, the e is usually dropped.

deceive + ing = deceiving	traverse + able = traversable
structure + al = structural	dose + age = dosage
trade + ing = trading	narrate + ion = narration
relate + ion = relation	delete + ion = deletion

When the final silent <u>e</u> is preceded by <u>c</u> or <u>g</u>, the <u>e</u> is usually retained before a suffix beginning with <u>a</u> or <u>o</u>.

trace + able = traceable   courage + ous = courageous
charge + able = chargeable   outrage + ous = outrageous

When a suffix beginning with a consonant is added to a word ending in a silent <u>e</u>, the <u>e</u> is usually retained.

grace + ful = graceful   face + less = faceless
love + ly = lovely   hope + ful = hopeful

The following words are exceptions: *truly, argument, judgment, wholly, awful.*

15.2   Words Ending in <u>y</u>

When a suffix is added to a word ending in y preceded by a consonant, the y is usually changed to i.

There are two exceptions: (1) when -*ing* is added, the y does not change. (2) Some one-syllable words do not change the y: *dryness; shyness.*

happy + ness = happiness   marry + age = marriage
company + es = companies   marry + ing = marrying
carry + ed = carried   dally + ing = dallying

When a suffix is added to a word ending in <u>y</u> preceded by a vowel, the <u>y</u> usually does not change.

pray + ing = praying   destroy + er = destroyer
enjoy + ing = enjoying   coy + ness = coyness

Exceptions: day + ly = daily, gay + ly = gaily.

Exercise A: Find the misspelled words in these sentences and spell them correctly.

1. We enjoyed sailing lazyly down the bay.
2. Mrs. Howard has sent us an invitateion to meet a famous artist.

3. She has done some architectureal work that is truly admireable.
4. The negotiators made a couragous effort to achieve a peaceable settlement.
5. There has been a noticable improvement in the safety records of our high school.
6. The caravan was moveing slowly along the icey road.
7. Creative talent can always profit from guideance.
8. Despite our arguements, the judge was immoveable.
9. The statement by the next witness was wholely false.
10. The cave was incredibely dark and terribly silent.
11. The doctor is continueing an intenseive X-ray treatment.
12. The captain's judgement is useually very good.
13. On the king's sixtyeth birthday there was great merryment.
14. There was a certain hazyness about Jack's time of arrival.
15. The heavyer carriages were almost immoveable.
16. The earlyest Mayan writing is not eassly deciphered.
17. The guide was very likeable, and his stories were exciteing.
18. We climbed clumsyly up the walls of the old fortifycations.

Exercise B: Add the suffixes as shown and write the new word.

1. mystery + ous
2. relay + ing
3. body + ly
4. frenzy + ed
5. appraise + ed
6. waste + ful
7. amaze + ing
8. insure + ance
9. grease + y
10. situate + ion
11. worry + ing
12. carry + ed
13. enjoy + able
14. create + ive
15. copy + ing
16. educate + ion
17. assemble + age
18. wide + ly
19. constitute + ion
20. like + able
21. move + ment
22. change + able
23. charge + ing
24. hurry + ing
25. debate + able
26. hasty + ly
27. merry + ly
28. ease + ly
29. day + ly
30. argue + ment

15.3 The Suffixes -ness and -ly

When the suffix -ly is added to a word ending in l, both l's are retained. When -ness is added to a word ending in n, both n's are retained.

$$\text{real} + \text{ly} = \text{really} \qquad \text{plain} + \text{ness} = \text{plainness}$$
$$\text{eternal} + \text{ly} = \text{eternally} \qquad \text{mean} + \text{ness} = \text{meanness}$$

15.4 The Addition of Prefixes

When a prefix is added to a word, the spelling of the word remains the same.

$$\text{dis} + \text{approve} = \text{disapprove} \qquad \text{dis} + \text{place} = \text{displace}$$
$$\text{mis} + \text{take} = \text{mistake} \qquad \text{re} + \text{creation} = \text{recreation}$$
$$\text{im} + \text{balance} = \text{imbalance} \qquad \text{trans} + \text{plant} = \text{transplant}$$
$$\text{il} + \text{legible} = \text{illegible} \qquad \text{co} + \text{operate} = \text{cooperate}$$

15.5 Words with the "Seed" Sound

Only one English word ends in *sede: supersede.*
Three words end in *ceed: exceed, proceed, succeed.*
All other words ending in the sound of *seed* are spelled *cede: secede, accede, recede, concede, precede.*

Exercise A: Find the spelling errors in these sentences. Spell the words correctly.

1. Because of the thiness of the paper, the print shows through.
2. Despite hours of work on the project, Betty was disatisfied with the results.
3. We usualy get a heavy snow in February.
4. Leaving the door unlocked was an iresponsible act.
5. The uneveness of the lettering ruins the whole sign.
6. We recomend this restaurant; the kitchens are imaculate.
7. Finaly, the stain dissappeared.
8. The lawyer said that the question was imaterial and irelevant.
9. We were naturaly disappointed with our poor grades.
10. Several words on the ransom note were carefuly mispelled.
11. Cheating on taxes is not only ilegal but imoral.
12. Alice proceded to pack the rest of the dishes more carefully.

13. Actualy, the tests are always preceeded by a review.
14. It is unecessary to excede the speed limit.
15. The doctor conceeded that eventualy an operation would be needed.

Exercise B: Add the suffixes and prefixes as indicated. Write the new word.

1. thin + ness	6. co + operate	11. confidential + ly
2. mis + state	7. incidental + ly	12. re + examine
3. ir + relevant	8. im + mobilize	13. dis + appear
4. im + moderate	9. uneven + ness	14. cordial + ly
5. dis + satisfied	10. im + moral	15. dis + agree

15.6   Words with ie and ei

When the sound is long e (ē), the word is spelled _ie_ except after _c_.

I BEFORE E

relieve	priest	chief
believe	shield	yield
piece	brief	niece

EXCEPT AFTER C

receive	ceiling	deceit
perceive	conceive	receipt

Exceptions: either, neither, financier, weird, species, seize, leisure. You can remember these words by combining them into such a sentence as: *Neither financier seized either weird species of leisure.*

Exercise A: Correct the spelling errors in these sentences.

1. The peice in the newspaper about our play was very breif.
2. The preist sheilded the child from the attacking dog.
3. The cheif carried a handsome sheild.
4. We do not beleive that the crop yeild will be good this year.

5. The banker gave his neice a reciept for the money.

6. You can just barely percieve the spot on the cieling.

7. Conceit causes as much trouble as deciet.

8. Niether of my parents has much leisure.

9. The caretaker weilded the mop like a baseball bat.

10. It is hard to beleive that the merchant's grief is real.

11. We were releived when the cornered man yielded his gun to the police.

12. You could not concieve of a setting more wierd.

13. The old lady had a breif cry into her handkercheif.

14. The cheif engineer has a peice of iron ore on his desk.

15. We would percieve that some mischief was afoot.

Exercise B: Copy the words below, filling the blank spaces with *ie* or *ei*.

1. perc__ve
2. n__ther
3. c__ling
4. rec__pt
5. ch__f
6. f__rce
7. n__ce
8. sh__ld
9. s__ze
10. p__ce
11. gr__vance
12. hyg__ne
13. p__r
14. th__f
15. l__sure

15.7   Doubling the Final Consonant

Words of one syllable, ending in one consonant preceded by one vowel, double the final consonant before adding a suffix beginning with a vowel.

1. Words of one syllable ending in one consonant:

   treat   near   feel   loot

The rule does not apply to these one-syllable words because two vowels precede the final consonant.

2. Words of one syllable ending in one consonant preceded by one vowel:

   grab   dig   drug   slim

These words are the kind to which the rule applies.

These words double the final consonant if the suffix begins with a vowel.

grab + ing = grabbing   drug + ist = druggist
dig + er = digger   slim + est = slimmest

3. The final consonant is doubled in words of more than one syllable:
When they end in one consonant preceded by one vowel.
When they are accented on the last syllable.

re·gret′   per·mit′   de·ter′

The same syllable is accented in the new word formed by adding the suffix:

re·gret′ + ed = re·gret′ted
per·mit′ + ing = per·mit′ting
de·ter′ + ence = de·ter′rence

If the newly formed word is accented on a different syllable, the final consonant is not doubled.

re·fer′ + ence = ref′er·ence
pre·fer′ + ence = pref′er·ence

Exercise A: Copy these words, indicating with an accent mark (′) where each word is accented.

1. control
2. excel
3. limit
4. resist
5. omit
6. regret
7. allot
8. impel
9. travel
10. distill
11. forget
12. murmur
13. defer
14. benefit
15. admit
16. differ
17. infer
18. propel

Exercise B: Add the ending indicated, and write the new word.

1. control + ing
2. bat + ed
3. compel + ed
4. bed + ing
5. differ + ence
6. limit + ed
7. commit + ed
8. book + ed
9. fur + y
10. disappear + ed
11. put + ing
12. get + ing
13. plan + ing
14. prefer + ed
15. sit + ing
16. remit + ance
17. transfer + ing
18. nod + ing
19. begin + ing
20. expel + ed
21. admit + ance
22. let + ing
23. pad + ed
24. murmur + ing
25. repel + ed
26. omit + ed
27. commit + ed
28. ton + age
29. allot + ed
30. defer + ed

15.8   Words Often Confused

capital means excellent, most serious, or most important.
capitol is a building in which a state legislature meets.
the Capitol is the building in Washington, D.C., in which the United States Congress meets.

des'ert means a wilderness or dry, sandy region with sparse, scrubby vegetation.
de·sert means to abandon.
dessert (note the change in spelling) is a sweet such as cake or pie served at the end of a meal.

hear means to listen to, or take notice of.
here means in this place.

its is a word that indicates ownership.
it's is a contraction for *it is* or *it has.*

lose means to mislay or suffer the loss of something.
loose means free or not fastened.

principal describes something of chief or central importance. It also refers to the head of an elementary or high school.
principle is a basic truth, standard, or rule of behavior.

stationary means fixed or unmoving.
stationery refers to paper and envelopes used for writing letters.

there means in that place.
their means belonging to them.
they're is a contraction for *they are*.

to means toward, or in the direction of.
too means also or very.
two is the number 2.

weather refers to atmospheric conditions such as temperature or
   cloudiness.
whether helps express choice or alternative.

whose is the possessive form of who.
who's is a contraction for *who is* or *who has*.

your is the possessive form of *you*.
you're is a contraction for *you are*.

Exercise: Choose the right word from the words in parentheses.

1. For (desert, dessert) we had strawberry shortcake.
2. The Cubs' loyal fans refuse to (desert, dessert) them.
3. The cat arched (it's, its) back.
4. (It's, Its) too hot to play tennis today.
5. I was (there, their) on time.
6. They said (they're, their) names were Sam and Stan.
7. (Their, They're) always first in line.
8. I am going (weather, whether) you go or not.
9. The (weather, whether) in August is hot and humid.
10. (Whose, Who's) got the tickets?
11. (Whose, Who's) dollar is this?
12. It's (your, you're) fault as much as mine.
13. Call me by ten if (your, you're) not going.
14. I hope the Hawks don't (lose, loose) tonight's game.
15. Somehow the puppies got (loose, lose).
16. Telling a lie is against my (principals, principles).
17. Mr. Happ is (principal, principle) at Brent High School.
18. We rode our bikes (too, to) the park.
19. The soup was (too, two, to) salty.
20. The North Star is almost (stationery, stationary).

A List of Commonly Misspelled Words

abbreviate	ab-bre-vi-ate	balance	bal-ance
absence	ab-sence	bargain	bar-gain
accidentally	ac-ci-den-tal-ly	becoming	be-com-ing
accommodate	ac-com-mo-date	beginning	be-gin-ning
accompanying	ac-com-pa-ny-ing	believe	be-lieve
achievement	a-chieve-ment	benefited	ben-e-fit-ed
acknowledge	ac-know-ledge	bicycle	bi-cy-cle
acquaintance	ac-quaint-ance	biscuit	bis-cuit
across	a-cross	bookkeeper	book-keep-er
address	ad-dress	bulletin	bul-le-tin
all right	all right	bureau	bu-reau
altogether	al-to-geth-er	business	busi-ness
always	al-ways	cafeteria	caf-e-te-ri-a
amateur	am-a-teur	calendar	cal-en-dar
analyze	an-a-lyze	campaign	cam-paign
annihilate	an-ni-hi-late	candidate	can-di-date
anonymous	a-non-y-mous	cellophane	cel-lo-phane
answer	an-swer	cemetery	cem-e-ter-y
apologize	a-pol-o-gize	certain	cer-tain
appearance	ap-pear-ance	changeable	change-a-ble
appreciate	ap-pre-ci-ate	characteristic	char-ac-ter-is-tic
appropriate	ap-pro-pri-ate	colonel	colo-nel
arctic	arc-tic	colossal	co-los-sal
argument	ar-gu-ment	column	col-umn
arising	a-ris-ing	commission	com-mis-sion
arrangement	ar-range-ment	committed	com-mit-ted
ascend	as-cend	committee	com-mit-tee
assassinate	as-sas-si-nate	comparative	com-par-a-tive
associate	as-so-ci-ate	compel	com-pel
attendance	at-tend-ance	competitive	com-pet-i-tive
audience	au-di-ence	complexion	com-plex-ion
auxiliary	aux-il-ia-ry	compulsory	com-pul-so-ry
awkward	awk-ward	conscience	con-science
bachelor	bach-e-lor	conscientious	con-sci-en-tious

conscious	con-scious	eminent	em-i-nent
consensus	con-sen-sus	emphasize	em-pha-size
contemptible	con-tempt-i-ble	environment	en-vi-ron-ment
convenience	con-ven-ience	enthusiastic	en-thu-si-as-tic
corps	corps	equipped	e-quipped
correspondence	cor-re-spond-ence	especially	es-pe-cial-ly
courageous	cou-ra-geous	etiquette	et-i-quette
courteous	cour-te-ous	exaggerate	ex-ag-ger-ate
criticism	crit-i-cism	excellent	ex-cel-lent
criticize	crit-i-cize	exceptional	ex-cep-tion-al
curiosity	cu-ri-os-i-ty	exhaust	ex-haust
cylinder	cyl-in-der	exhilarate	ex-hil-a-rate
dealt	dealt	existence	ex-ist-ence
decision	de-ci-sion	expense	ex-pcnsc
definitely	def-i-nite-ly	experience	ex-pe-ri-ence
despair	de-spair	familiar	fa-mil-iar
desperate	des-per-ate	fascinating	fas-ci-nat-ing
dictionary	dic-tion-ar-y	fatigue	fa-tigue
dependent	de-pend-ent	February	Feb-ru-ar-y
descent	de-scent	feminine	fem-i-nine
description	de-scrip-tion	financial	fi-nan-cial
desirable	de-sir-a-ble	foreign	for-eign
different	dif-fer-ent	forfeit	for-feit
dining	din-ing	fourth	fourth
diphtheria	diph-the-ri-a	fragile	frag-ile
disagree	dis-a-gree	generally	gen-er-al-ly
disappear	dis-ap-pear	genius	gen-ius
disappoint	dis-ap-point	government	gov-ern-ment
discipline	dis-ci-pline	grammar	gram-mar
dissatisfied	dis-sat-is-fied	guarantee	guar-an-tee
economical	e-co-nom-i-cal	guard	guard
efficient	ef-fi-cient	gymnasium	gym-na-si-um
eighth	eighth	handkerchief	hand-ker-chief
eligible	el-i-gi-ble	height	height
eliminate	e-lim-i-nate	hindrance	hin-drance
embarrass	em-bar-rass	horizon	ho-ri-zon

humorous	hu-mor-ous	mischievous	mis-chie-vous
imaginary	im-ag-i-nar-y	missile	mis-sile
immediately	im-me-di-ate-ly	misspell	mis-spell
incidentally	in-ci-den-tal-ly	mortgage	mort-gage
inconvenience	in-con-ven-ience	municipal	mu-nic-i-pal
incredible	in-cred-i-ble	necessary	nec-es-sar-y
indefinitely	in-def-i-nite-ly	nickel	nick-el
indispensable	in-dis-pen-sa-ble	ninety	nine-ty
inevitable	in-ev-i-ta-ble	noticeable	no-tice-a-ble
infinite	in-fi-nite	nuclear	nu-cle-ar
influence	in-flu-ence	nuisance	nui-sance
inoculation	in-oc-u-la-tion	obstacle	ob-sta-cle
intelligence	in-tel-li-gence	occasionally	oc-ca-sion-al-ly
interesting	in-ter-est-ing	occur	oc-cur
irrelevant	ir-rel-e-vant	occurrence	oc-cur-rence
irresistible	ir-re-sist-i-ble	opinion	o-pin-ion
knowledge	knowl-edge	opportunity	op-por-tu-ni-ty
laboratory	lab-o-ra-to-ry	optimistic	op-ti-mis-tic
legitimate	le-git-i-mate	original	o-rig-i-nal
leisure	lei-sure	outrageous	out-ra-geous
lieutenant	lieu-ten-ant	pamphlet	pam-phlet
lightning	light-ning	parallel	par-al-lel
literacy	lit-er-a-cy	parliament	par-lia-ment
literature	lit-er-a-ture	particularly	par-tic-u-lar-ly
loneliness	lone-li-ness	pastime	pas-time
luxurious	lux-u-ri-ous	permanent	per-ma-nent
maintenance	main-te-nance	permissible	per-mis-si-ble
maneuver	ma-neu-ver	perseverance	per-se-ver-ance
marriage	mar-riage	perspiration	per-spi-ra-tion
mathematics	math-e-mat-ics	persuade	per-suade
matinee	mat-i-nee	picnicking	pic-nick-ing
medicine	med-i-cine	pleasant	pleas-ant
medieval	me-di-e-val	pneumonia	pneu-mo-ni-a
microphone	mi-cro-phone	politics	pol-i-tics
miniature	min-i-a-ture	possess	pos-sess
minimum	min-i-mum	possibility	pos-si-bil-i-ty

practice	prac-tice	specifically	spe-cif-i-cal-ly
preference	pref-er-ence	specimen	spec-i-men
prejudice	prej-u-dice	strategy	strat-e-gy
preparation	prep-a-ra-tion	strictly	strict-ly
privilege	priv-i-lege	subtle	sub-tle
probably	prob-a-bly	success	suc-cess
professor	pro-fes-sor	sufficient	suf-fi-cient
pronunciation	pro-nun-ci-a-tion	surprise	sur-prise
propeller	pro-pel-ler	syllable	syl-la-ble
prophecy	proph-e-cy	sympathy	sym-pa-thy
psychology	psy-chol-o-gy	symptom	symp-tom
pursue	pur-sue	tariff	tar-iff
quantity	quan-ti-ty	temperament	tem-per-a-ment
questionnaire	ques-tion-naire	temperature	tem-per-a-ture
realize	re-al-ize	thorough	thor-ough
recognize	rec-og-nize	throughout	through-out
recommend	rec-om-mend	together	to-geth-er
reference	ref-er-ence	tomorrow	to-mor-row
referred	re-ferred	traffic	traf-fic
rehearse	re-hearse	tragedy	trag-e-dy
reign	reign	transferred	trans-ferred
repetition	rep-e-ti-tion	truly	tru-ly
representative	rep-re-sent-a-tive	Tuesday	Tues-day
restaurant	res-tau-rant	tyranny	tyr-an-ny
rhythm	rhythm	twelfth	twelfth
ridiculous	ri-dic-u-lous	unanimous	u-nan-i-mous
sandwich	sand-wich	undoubtedly	un-doubt-ed-ly
schedule	sched-ule	unnecessary	un-nec-es-sar-y
scissors	scis-sors	vacuum	vac-u-um
secretary	sec-re-tar-y	vengeance	venge-ance
separate	sep-a-rate	vicinity	vi-cin-i-ty
sergeant	ser-geant	village	vil-lage
similar	sim-i-lar	villain	vil-lain
sincerely	sin-cere-ly	weird	weird
sophomore	soph-o-more	wholly	whol-ly
souvenir	sou-ve-nir	writing	writ-ing

16.0 The Plurals of Nouns

16.1 Regular Formation of Plurals

The plural of most nouns is formed by adding _s_.

building + s = buildings   ground + s = grounds
yard + s = yards   carrot + s = carrots

16.2 Plurals Formed with es

The plural of nouns ending in _s_, _sh_, _ch_, _x_, and _z_ is formed by adding _es_.

rash + es = rashes   birch + es = birches
bus + es = buses   box + es = boxes

16.3 Plurals of Nouns Ending in y

When a noun ends in _y_ preceded by a consonant, the plural is formed by changing the _y_ to _i_ and adding _es_.

duty   duti + es = duties
party   parti + es = parties
pantry   pantri + es = pantries

When a noun ends in _y_ preceded by a vowel, the plural is formed by adding _s_.

tray + s = trays   envoy + s = envoys
day + s = days   boy + s = boys
pulley + s = pulleys   foray + s = forays

16.4 Plural of Nouns Ending in _o_

The plural of nouns ending in _o_, preceded by a vowel, is formed by adding _s_.

studio + s = studios   radio + s = radios
rodeo + s = rodeos   ratio + s = ratios
folio + s = folios   duo + s = duos

The plural of most nouns ending in _o_, preceded by a consonant, is formed by adding _s_, but for some nouns of this class the plural is formed by adding _es_.

piano + s = pianos   auto + s = autos
solo + s = solos   alto + s = altos
credo + s = credos

tomato + es = tomatoes   echo + es = echoes
potato + es = potatoes   hero + es = heroes

There are some words ending in -o with a preceding consonant that may form the plural with either _s_ or _es_: _motto_, _mango_, _mosquito_. The safest thing to do is to memorize the few words that add -es and to consult the dictionary when in doubt about others.

16.5 Plural of Nouns Ending in _f_ or _ff_

The plural of most nouns ending in _f_ or _ff_ is formed regularly by adding _s_.

roof + s = roofs   dwarf + s = dwarfs

belief + s = beliefs   handkerchief + s = handkerchiefs
gulf + s = gulfs   staff + s = staffs

The plural of some nouns ending in _f_ or _fe_ is formed by changing the _f_ or _fe_ to _ve_ and adding _s_.

calf—calves	shelf—shelves	self—selves
elf—elves	knife—knives	wharf—wharves
half—halves	loaf—loaves	leaf—leaves

Since most of these words with irregular plurals are in common use, careful listening may help you to spell them correctly. If you are doubtful about spelling, however, look up the singular form of the word in a dictionary. If the plural of a word is irregularly formed, the plural will be given immediately after the singular.

16.6   Nouns with Irregular Plurals

The plural of some nouns is formed by a change of spelling.

foot—feet	goose—geese
man—men	mouse—mice
woman—women	ox—oxen
child—children	basis—bases
datum—data	phenomenon—phenomena
index—indices _or_ indexes	hypothesis—hypotheses

The plural and singular forms are the same for a few nouns.

sheep	corps	Chinese
deer	cattle	Portuguese

16.7   The Plural of Names

The plural of a name is formed by adding _s_ or _es_.

Albert Steele—the Steeles	Jack Amos—the Amoses
Judy Lyons—the Lyonses	Bob Sable—the Sables

16.8   The Plural of Compound Nouns

When a compound noun is written without a hyphen, the plural is formed at the end of the word.

handful + s = handfuls   teaspoonful + s = teaspoonfuls
cupful + s = cupfuls   doghouse + s = doghouses

When a compound noun is made up of a noun plus a modifier, the plural is added to the noun.

brothers-in-law (the phrase *in law* is a modifier.)
commanders-in-chief (the phrase *in chief* is a modifier.)
attorneys-general (*general* modifies *attorneys.*)
notaries public (*public* modifies *notaries.*)
hangers-on (*on* modifies *hangers.*)
bills of sale (the phrase *of sale* modifies *bills.*)

The following are exceptions: *drive-ins, stand-bys, lean-tos.*

Exercise A: Form the plural of each of the following words.

1. holiday	11. studio	21. tablespoonful
2. herd	12. county	22. father-in-law
3. glass	13. valley	23. drive-in
4. radio	14. belief	24. attorney-general
5. dash	15. potato	25. right of way
6. hero	16. handkerchief	26. chief of police
7. watch	17. grief	27. clerk of court
8. laboratory	18. hypothesis	28. Supreme Court Justice
9. lady	19. datum	29. bill of sale
10. cupful	20. basis	30. notary public

Exercise B: Find the errors in plural forms in the following sentences.

1. The economists do not have enough datums to explain what has happened.

2. There are several hypothesis to explain the twin moons of Mars.

3. We have two brother-in-laws living in Elmira.

4. Don't use more than three cupsful of flour.

5. How many leafs are missing from your book?

6. What vegetables shall we have besides potatos and tomatos?

7. There are several solos for the sopranoes.

8. There are not many home studioes big enough for two pianos.

9. After church, we stopped to chat with the Jeffrey's and the Kennedy's.

10. In yesterday's game, Rudi made two sensational catchs.

11. American prisoners have suffered cruelties in some foreign countrys.

12. The two mother-in-laws are great friends.

13. Not many countrys have only two major political partys.

14. There are too many autoes on the streets of our citys.

15. Even during routine dutys, the researchers discovered interesting phenomenons.

16. The Chineses have a very ancient civilization.

17. We need more than two notary publics in this big company.

18. Bob brought several armsful of wood into the house.

19. In the spring the cowboys drove the cattles north on the Chisholm Trail.

20. The sheeps on the range are carefully protected against wolfs.

21. These heros lost their lifes in scientific research for mankind's benefit.

22. Several hanger-ons were waiting for the partys to break up.

23. There are two boxs of matchs in the kitchen cupboard.

24. The thiefs turned out to be brother-in-laws.

25. With their knifes the workers cut big gashs in the trunks of the trees.

17.0 Good Manuscript Form

It is well established that readers will grade a paper higher if it is neat and legible than if it is messy in appearance and hard to read. Good manuscript form assures a good hearing for what you have to say. Many high schools and colleges have regular forms that students are expected to follow. Others require manuscripts to follow the form described below.

17.1 Legible Writing

Few schools require that student papers be typewritten. A typed paper, however, is easier to read than one written by hand.

If a paper is written by hand, it should be written with pen and a dark blue or black ink. An ink of any other color is not acceptable. Letters should be formed so that there is no doubt as to what they are: *a*'s and *o*'s should be distinctly different; *u*'s and *i*'s should be distinct; if *i*'s are dotted, there can be no chance of their being mistaken for *e*'s.

17.2   Margins and Spacing

Leave a margin of an inch at the top, the bottom, and the right side of each page. The left margin should be slightly wider. If a paper is typed, the left-hand margin must be carefully maintained. The right-hand margin should be approximately the same, and it should be as even as possible without an excess of hyphens to show the break in a word. It is a good rule not to permit more than two successive lines to end with a hyphen.

All typed copy should be prepared with a double space between lines. Usually five letter spaces are provided for each paragraph indentation. One space separates each word; two spaces follow the end punctuation of a sentence. If material must be deleted, it can be struck out by x's or capital M's.

17.3   Proper Labeling

Your teacher will give you instructions on the heading for your papers. Follow these instructions exactly. Usually, you will be expected to place your name at the upper right-hand corner of the first page. On a line below your name, you will place the name or number of the course, and on a third line, you will place the date.

Number each page beginning with page two. (Do not number the first page.) The number may be placed in the upper right-hand corner. To guard against loss or misplacement, you may place your name under the page number.

17.4   Placement of the Title

The title of a paper appears only on the first page. Place the title two lines below the last line of your heading, and center it. Allow two lines between the title and the first line of your copy.

Capitalize the first word and all important words in the title. See Section 10.12. If you are typing, do not capitalize every letter but only the initial letters. Do not underline the title; do not place it in quotation marks unless it is a quotation from some other source.

If a paper is longer than three or four pages, your teacher may ask you to supply a title page. This is a separate page containing the heading in the upper right-hand corner and the title centered on the page.

17.5 Preparation of Final Copy

It is almost impossible to write a paper exactly as you want it the first time. After you have written your first draft, read it over carefully. Revise and correct it. After you have completed your revision, make a final copy. Then read over this copy.

You may find that you have left out words, or you may find errors. You can insert words neatly by writing above the line where they should appear and by using a caret (∧) to show their position. You can make corrections neatly by drawing a line through a word and writing the correction above it. If more than two or three corrections per page are necessary, recopy the page.

17.6 Numbers in Writing

Numbers that can be expressed in fewer than four words are usually spelled out; longer numbers are written in figures.

They gathered *thirty-one* bushels of apples in one day.
The piggy bank yielded *thirteen* dollars.
The tickets are selling for *eight* dollars each.
The loss amounted to $4,280.

A number beginning a sentence is spelled out.

Eight hundred were suddenly made homeless by the flood.
Twenty-five minutes passed without a word from Hugh.

17.7   Figures in Writing

Figures are used to express dates, street and room numbers, telephone numbers, page numbers, decimals, and percentages.

> Shakespeare's birth date was April 23, 1564.
> Carol lives at 5457 Guarino Road.
> The English class is in room 312.
> Is your telephone number 257-4353?
> We were asked to learn the poem on page 80.
> Last week the temperature reached 101 degrees.
> Ethel had 98 percent right in the physics test.

Note: Commas are used to separate the figures in sums of money or expressions of large quantities. They are not used in dates, serial numbers, page numbers, addresses, or telephone numbers.

> RIGHT   Terry had saved $1,270 for the trip to Europe.
> RIGHT   Bernie now owns more than 100,000 stamps.
> WRONG   Washington died in 1,799.
> RIGHT   Washington died in 1799.

Exercise: Copy these sentences, correcting any errors in the writing of figures.

1. There are now two hundred thousand volumes in the public library.

2. 7 of the students in my class want to go to Penn State.

3. When we arrived in Duluth, it was twenty degrees below zero.

4. The cost of the land alone is $7,500.

5. Nearly sixty percent of high school graduates now go on to college.

6. The offices are now located at 1,741 Broadway.

7. The satellite whirled about the earth every four and three-tenths minutes.

8. New Orleans then had a population of 125,000.

9. Our room number is four twenty-six.
10. We have had 2,275 replies to our letter.
11. The telephone number here is 275–4,000.
12. The date on the flyleaf was eighteen hundred ninety seven.
13. Helen's new address is two hundred twenty East End Avenue.
14. We have room for only 700 students in the college.
15. More than 500 students are singing in the all-state chorus.

17.8   Abbreviations in Writing

Abbreviations may be used for most titles before and after proper names, for names of government agencies, and in dates.

BEFORE PROPER NAMES	Dr., Mr., Mrs., Ms., Messrs., Rev., Hon., Gov., Capt.
AFTER PROPER NAMES	Jr., Sr., D.D., Ph.D.
GOVERNMENT AGENCIES	FBI, FCC, AEC
DATES AND TIME	A.D., B.C., A.M., P.M.

There are no periods after abbreviations of government agencies.

The abbreviations of titles are acceptable only when used as part of a name. It is not acceptable to write *The secy. of the club is a dr.* The titles *Honorable and Reverend* are not abbreviated when preceded by *the: The Honorable John Ross.* They appear with the person's full name, not just the last name. Abbreviations are not appropriate for the President and Vice-President of the United States.

In ordinary writing, abbreviations are not acceptable for names of countries and states, months and days of the week, nor for words that are part of addresses or firm names.

UNACCEPTABLE	We spent a month in Ariz.
BETTER	We spent a month in Arizona.
UNACCEPTABLE	I have never been to Toronto, Ont.
BETTER	I have never been to Toronto, Ontario.

UNACCEPTABLE	Miller's play opened on Thurs., Jan. 23.
BETTER	Miller's play opened on Thursday, January 23.
UNACCEPTABLE	Pay your bill to the Bell Tel. Co.
BETTER	Pay your bill to the Bell Telephone Company.

In ordinary writing, abbreviations are not acceptable for the following: names of school courses, *page, chapter, Christmas,* and words standing for measurements such as *bu., in., hr., min., sec.*

Exercise: Correct the errors in abbreviation in the following sentences.

1. The Rev. Carl Anderson, D.D. is one of the speakers.
2. Your reservation is on Am. Airlines for next Saturday.
3. Pam is entering Mather H. S. next fall.
4. Mr. Walsh and Jas. Perrin are at a convention in Denver, Colo.
5. Bob has an appointment with Dr. Matthews on Fri. at 4 P.M.
6. Mr. Marks has just been made vice-pres. of the bank.
7. The Xmas vacation will start on Dec. 21.
8. The club secy. has really very little to do.
9. We used to live in Ill., but then we moved to Mich.
10. In northern Minnesota, I once caught a pike 16 in. long.

17.9   Italics for Titles

The word *italics* is a printer's term. It refers to a kind of type. When a writer wants the printer to set a word in italic type, he underlines it in his manuscript.

Titles of complete books and plays, of newspapers, magazines, works of art, and long musical compositions are printed in italics. The names of ships, trains, and airplanes are also printed in italics.

MANUSCRIPT FORM	I never miss the ads in the <u>Saturday Review</u>.
PRINTED FORM	I never miss the ads in the *Saturday Review*.
MANUSCRIPT FORM	Gian Carlo Menotti's best-known opera is <u>Amahl and the Night Visitors</u>.
PRINTED FORM	Gian Carlo Menotti's best-known opera is *Amahl and the Night Visitors*.
MANUSCRIPT FORM	The front page of <u>The New York Times</u> showed the President boarding <u>Air Force One</u>.
PRINTED FORM	The front page of *The New York Times* showed the President boarding *Air Force One*.

17.10 Italics for Foreign Words and Phrases

Many foreign words have become so widely used that they are now part of the English language: *chauffeur, cul-de-sac, entrepreneur.* These naturalized words are printed in regular type. Foreign words and phrases that have not become naturalized in our language are printed in italics: *cum laude, bon vivant, mirabile dictu.*

The only way to be sure whether a word or phrase of foreign origin should be printed in italics (underlined in manuscript) is to consult the dictionary.

17.11 Italics for Words, Letters, or Figures

Italics are used for words, letters, or figures referred to as such.

In printed works, words, letters, or figures referred to as such are in italics. In writing, they are underlined.

MANUSCRIPT FORM	In England, <u>either</u> is pronounced <u>eyether</u>.
PRINTED FORM	In England, *either* is pronounced *eyether*.
MANUSCRIPT FORM	Road signs have given <u>slow</u> the status of an adverb.
PRINTED FORM	Road signs have given *slow* the status of an adverb.

17.12 Italics for Emphasis

Italics (underlining) are used to give special emphasis to words or phrases.

The tendency in modern writing is to avoid the use of italics for emphasis. One reason is that italic type is considered harder to read than regular (roman) type, particularly if there is a great deal of it. Another reason is that modern writers are developing a direct, straightforward style which gives emphasis to important words without use of printing devices.

In high school writing, use italics for emphasis only to make meaning clear.

Woman's place *was* in the home; it certainly isn't today.
"Have you *ever* seen such a mess!" Mother exclaimed.

17.13 Correction Symbols and Revision

Both in high school and in college your teachers will make marginal notes on your themes and reports before returning them to you. These notes will indicate errors or awkward passages that require rewriting. The correction of errors will make you alert to their recurrence in your later writing. Practice in rephrasing awkward sentences will give you greater skill in turning out careful, clear writing that means what you want it to mean.

Many schools and colleges have their own system of briefly indicating writing faults. If your school has such a system of abbreviations, it will be made available to you. Your teachers may prefer to use the symbols listed below. These are symbols used by professional copyreaders who work for publishers. The manuscript bearing the marks is returned to the author, no matter how experienced or professional he may be, for correction and revision before the manuscript is set in type.

ab   *Abbreviation.* Either the abbreviation is not appropriate, or the abbreviation is wrong. Consult a dictionary.

agr   *Agreement.* You have made an error in agreement of subject and verb, or of pronoun and antecedent. Consult Sections 6.1 and 7.11 in your Handbook.

awk   *Awkward.* The sentence is clumsy. Rewrite it.

cap   *Capital letters.* You have omitted necessary capitals. Consult Section 10 in your Handbook.

cf   *Comma fault.* You have joined two sentences together with a comma. Change the punctuation.

dang   *Dangling construction.* You have written a verbal phrase in such a way that it does not tie up to another word in the sentence. Rewrite the sentence.

frag   *Sentence fragment.* You have placed a period after a group of words that is not a sentence. Join the fragment to an existing sentence or add words to complete the thought.

ital   *Italics.* You have omitted italics that are needed.

k   *Awkward.* See *awk* above.

lc   *Lower case.* You have mistakenly used a capital letter where a small letter is required.

ms   *Manuscript form.* You have not followed the proper manuscript form. Consult Section 17 in your Handbook.

no ¶   *No paragraph.* You have started a new paragraph too soon. Join these sentences to the preceding paragraph.

¶   *Paragraph.* Begin a new paragraph at this point.

nc   *Not clear.* Your meaning is not clear. Rewrite the passage to say what you mean.

om   *Omission.* You have left out words that are needed for clarity or smoothness of style.

p   *Punctuation.* You have made an error in punctuation. Consult Section 11 in your Handbook for sentences like the one you have improperly punctuated.

ref   *Reference.* There is an error or a weakness in the reference of pronoun to antecedent. Consult Section 7 in your Handbook.

rep   *Repetition.* You have repeated a word too often, or you have repeated something you wrote in preceding sentences.

shift   *Shift.* You have shifted point of view or tense needlessly.

sp   *Spelling.* You have misspelled a word. Consult a dictionary.

t   *Tense.* You have used the wrong tense form. Consult Section 9 in your Handbook.

tr   *Transpose.* Your meaning would be more clear if a sentence or passage were placed at another point.

wd   *Wrong word.* You have confused homonyms, or you have used a word that does not fit the meaning. Consult a dictionary.

Sources of Quoted Material

Page 12: Doubleday and Company, Inc., for selection from *The Greek Treasure* by Irving Stone. Pages 15, 18, 20: William Collins + World Publishing Company, for entries from *Webster's New World Dictionary of the American Language,* Students Edition; copyright © 1976 by William Collins + World Publishing Company, Inc. Page 19: G. P. Putnam's Sons, for entry from the *New Roget's Thesaurus in Dictionary Form* (Revised, Greatly Enlarged Edition), edited by Norman Lewis. Page 28: Harcourt Brace Jovanovich, Inc., for poem "To Look at Any Thing" from *The Living Seed* by John Moffitt; copyright © 1961 by John Moffitt. Pages 34–35: J. B. Lippincott Company for selection from *Fair Day and Another Step Begun* by Katie Letcher Lyle; copyright © 1974. Page 39: Harold Matson Company, Inc., for selection from "All Summer in a Day" from *Twice 22* by Ray Bradbury; copyright © 1954 by Ray Bradbury. Page 43: Delacorte Press for selection from *Marathon Man* by William Goldman. Pages 43–44: Harold Matson Company, Inc., for selection from "The Long Rain" from *R Is for Rocket* by Ray Bradbury; copyright © 1962 by Ray Bradbury. Page 46: Doubleday and Company, Inc., for selection from *Death Watch* by Robb White; copyright © 1972. Pages 47 and 50: Random House, Inc., for selection from *I Know Why the Caged Bird Sings* by Maya Angelou; copyright © 1969 by Maya Angelou. Page 75: Four Winds Press, for selection from *Your City Tomorrow* by D. S. Halacy. Page 83: WFMT, Inc., for selection from "Becoming a Spokesperson" by Stephen Marshall, in the *Chicago Guide,* June 1974. Page 88: The Viking Press for selection from *The Whispering Land* by Gerald Durrell; copyright © 1964 by the Viking Press. Page 89: Houghton Mifflin Company for two selections from *Farewell to Manzanar* by Jeanne Wakatsuki Houston and James Houston; copyright © 1973 by James D. Houston. Page 90: Doubleday and Company, Inc. for selection from "San Juan and Glen Canyon" from *The Sound of Mountain Water* by Wallace Stegner; copyright © 1969. Pages 90–91: Random House for selection from "A Christmas Memory" by Truman Capote, from *Selected Writings of Truman Capote,* copyright © 1956 by Truman Capote. Page 91: Peter Jones for selection from *Wheldon the Weed.* Page 94: The Viking Press for selection from *Cannery Row* by John Steinbeck; copyright © 1945 by the Viking Press. Page 98: Woman's Day Magazine for selection from "It's All in a Woman's Day"; from *Woman's Day,* October 1976; copyright © 1976 by Woman's Day Magazine. Page 100: William Morrow & Company for "Self Expression" by Ann Darr, from *St. Ann's Gut* by Ann Darr; copyright © 1971. Page 104: Thomas Y. Crowell for selection from "Through the Tunnel" by Doris Lessing; originally published in *The New Yorker,* copyright © 1955 by Doris Lessing; from *The Habit of Loving,* Thomas Y. Crowell Company, New York (copyright © 1957 by Doris Lessing). Page 105: Harper & Row Publishers, Inc., for selection from *La Raza: The Mexican American* by Stan Steiner; copyright © 1970. Pages 105–106: Random House, Inc., for selection from *I Know Why the Caged Bird Sings* by Maya Angelou; copyright © 1969 by Maya Angelou. Page 106: Harcourt Brace Jovanovich, Inc., for selection from *Walker in the City* by Alfred Kazin, copyright 1951 by Alfred Kazin. Page 110: American Education Publications, for a paragraph from *Understanding Language;* copyright © 1969 by Xerox Corporation. Pages 110–111: Sheed and Ward, Inc., for "Whistling Through Grass" from *Sneaky Feats* by Tom Ferrell and Lee Eisenberg; copyright © 1976. Pages 114–115: McCormick-Mathers Publishing Company for "Sumo Tournaments" from *The Story of Japan* by Lee W. Farnsworth; copyright, 1970. Page 122: Publication Division, Government of India, and Shelia Dhar for "Digging Up the Past" from *Children's History of India*

Index

brand names, 192
business letters, 171–184
  forms, 171–173
  parts of, 172–175, 177–178
  types of
    complaint, 179, 180–182
    order, 178, 179
    requests for information,
      179–180
but, 31, 34, 78
by, as preposition of location, 31

can, as auxiliary, 14
capital, capitol, 241
capitalization
  of A.D., B.C., I, and O, 186
  and *and*, 192
  and articles (*a, an, the*), 192
  for days, months, holidays,
    195
  for Deity, 195
  for family relationships,
    193–194
  for first word of sentence, 96
    direct quotation, line of
    poetry, 186–187, 228, 229
  for geographical names,
    187–188, 189
  for historical names, 195
  for languages, races,
    nationalities, religions,
    191
  for organizations and
    institutions, 192
  for parts of names, 188
  for proper adjectives, 26,
    187, 189, 190
  for proper nouns, 4, 187
  in salutation, closing of
    letter, 174

  for sections of country, 190
  for titles of books and works
    of art, 194
  for titles of persons, 193
caret, 254
card catalog, 213–217
case, of pronouns, 7, 145–146
  determined by noun, 150–151,
    154–155
  nominative, 145–146, 147–148
  objective, 42, 145–146, 148,
    150, 154
  possessive, 145–146, 153–154
cause and effect relationship,
  in inferring word meaning, 11
character, in narrative composition, 153
chronology
  in composition development,
    127–128
  in paragraph development,
    99, 103–105
clause
  defined, 81, 93
  as gerund modifier, 44
  as infinitive modifier, 42
  main, 81
  nonrestrictive, 193–194, 204
  restrictive, 203–204
  as sentence fragments, 99–100
  subordinate, 204, 82, 85,
clipping file, 224
closing, in letter writing, 165,
  169, 172, 173, 174
coherence, 148
collective nouns, 140–141, 157
colon
  in Biblical references, 215
  between book title and
    subtitle, 215
  for explanatory statements,
    214

compound sentence, 78–80, 102, 205–206, 211

compound subject, 53, 76–77
   agreement with verb, 137, 147

conclusion, in composition writing, 142–143

conflict, in narrative composition, 153–156

conjugation, 22–23

conjunction, 33–35, 52, 53, 123

conjunctive adverbs, 35, 78–79, 102, 201–202, 211–212

context clues
   types of, 2
   to word meaning, 2–9

continents, 188

contrast
   as context clue, 5–6
   in inferring word meaning, 12
   key words in, 6

contrast, in paragraph development, 82, 83–84, 98

coordinate adjectives, 206–207

coordinating conjunctions, 34, 78, 102

correlative conjunctions, 34

copyreading symbols, 260–261

country names, 8, 188, 256

could, as auxiliary, 14

dash
   for break in thought, 215
   for interruptions in sentence, 215
   before a summary, 216

date
   capitalization of, 202
   in letter writing, 165

days, capitalization of, 195

declarative sentence, 50, 197

definite article, 25

definition, as context clue, 2–3

Deity, capitalization of, 195

demonstrations, in speech, 233–234

demonstrative pronouns, 10–11

description, in paragraph development, 87–94

desert, dessert, 241

details
   in inferring word meaning, 10–11
   in writing, 147, 148

determiners, 108–109, 110, 122

Dewey Decimal System, 210–212

diagraming. *See* sentences, diagraming of.

dictionaries, 219–221

direct address, 201

direct object, 56–57
   gerund as, 44
   and infinitives, 42
   of participle, 46
   pronoun as, 148
   position in sentence, 109–110, 127–128

directions, verbal, 232–234

directive adverbs, 29

do, 13–14
   in emphatic forms, 16

doesn't, agreement with subject, 139

don't, agreement with subject, 139

double negative, 169–170

down, as preposition of direction, 31

each, 10, 135

ei words, 238

inverted sentence order, 54–55
irregular comparisons, of
  adjectives, 27–28
irregular verbs, 16, 173–179
it, 7, 8
italics
  for emphasis, 259
  for foreign words and
    phrases, 258
  for names of ships, trains,
    airplanes, 257–258
  for titles of books, magazines,
    long pamphlets, bulletins,
    231, 257–258
  for titles of musical
    compositions, 257–258
  for words referred to as
    words, 232
its, 7, 8, 109, 241
it's, 241
itself, 8

joint ownership, possessive
  showing, 221–222

labeling, in manuscript preparation, 253
languages, capitalization of,
  191
lay, *lie*, 182
least, as intensifier, 116
less, 116, 166
letters
  omitted, apostrophes for, 224
  used as letters, 258–259
letters, parts of
  body, 165, 169–171, 172, 173,
    177–178

closing, 165, 169, 172, 173
  date, 165
  heading, 169, 172, 173
  inside address, 172, 173, 174,
    183
  salutation, 165, 169, 172, 173,
    174
  signature, 172, 173, 174–175
letters, types of
  business, 171–183
  friendly, 167–171
  informal notes, 164–166
lexical meaning, 121–122, 129–
  130
library usage
  card catalog, 213–217
  fiction, 210
  nonfiction, 210–211. *See also*
    Dewey Decimal System.
  biography, 212
  references, 212, 219–225
  *Readers' Guide to Periodical
    Literature*, 224–225, 241
lie, *lay*, 182
like, as preposition of association, 31
linking verbs, 13, 42–43, 113
  and predicate words, 26,
    42–43, 163–164
  in sentence patterns,
    126–127
listening, training in, 36–37
lists, colons for, 213–214
literary references, 223–224
look, as linking verb, 13
loose, *lose*, 241
-ly, 163, 236–237

magazines, 224–225
main clause, 81, 83, 93, 102,
  205–206

main idea
    of composition, 110–111
    of paragraph. *See* topic
        sentence.
main idea, in inferring word
    meaning, 10
main verb, 13–14
many, 10, 135
margins, in manuscript prep-
    aration, 253
masculine gender
    for animals, 8
    of personal pronouns, 8
may, as auxiliary, 14
me, 7, 145, 146, 148
measurements, 257
might, as auxiliary, 14
mine, 7, 8
modified block form, in letter
    writing, 173
modifiers
    position in sentence, as
        determinant, 116–117
    pronouns as, 8
    varying types, 116–117
    See also adjectives, adverbs
mood, 24–25
months, capitalization of, 195
more, 27, 30, 109, 115, 116
most, 27, 30, 115, 116, 136
much, as intensifier, 116
multiple word meanings, 14–16
must, as auxiliary, 14
my, 7, 8, 38, 109
myself, 8

narrative composition, 153–156
narrative paragraph, 103–106
near, as preposition of
    location, 31
neither, 10, 109, 135

neither . . . nor, 34, 137
neuter gender
    for animals, 8
    of pronouns, 8
no, as determiner, 109
nobody, 10, 135
nominative case
    for predicate pronouns,
        147–148
    of pronouns, 7, 145–146
    for subject of verb, 146–147
none, 10, 136, 157
nonrestrictive clause, 193–194
    commas with, 204
no one, 10, 135
nor
    and antecedents, 157
    as coordinating conjunction,
        34, 78, 137, 157
not only . . . but (also), 34
note taking, for composition,
    124
notes, use of, 241, 244
noun clause, 90–92
noun phrase, 63
nouns, 4, 37
    abstract, 4
    concrete, 4
    common, 4
    as form class, 107–110
        inflected forms of, 108, 145
        marked by determiners,
            108–109
        position of, in sentence,
            109–110
    gerund as, 44
    infinitive used as, 41
    number, 108, 141
    proper, 4
number
    agreement with antecedent,
        156–157

number—*cont.*
  of indefinite pronouns, 10, 157
  of nouns, 108
  of personal pronouns, 7, 135, 139
  of relative pronouns, 143–144
  of verb (example), 22–23
numbers, spelled out, 254

O, 186
object complement, 128–129
object of infinitive, 42
  pronoun as, 148, 154
object of gerund, 44
object of participle, 46
object of preposition, 32–33, 57, 110, 150
object of verb, 17
  gerund as, 44
  infinitive as, 41
  with passive form, 17
  See also direct object.
objective case
  with infinitives, 42, 154
  of pronouns, 7, 145, 146, 148, 150
of, as preposition of association, 31
off, as preposition of association, 31
on, as preposition of location, 31
one, 10, 135, 158
oneself, 8
or
  and antecedents, 157
  as coordinating conjunction, 34, 78, 137, 157
order, letters of, 178, 179

organizations, capitalization of, 192
other, 167–168
our, 7, 8, 109
ours, 7, 8
ourselves, 8
out, as preposition of direction, 31
outline, working, 127–128
overloaded sentences, 196

padded sentences, 192–194
paragraph, 55–56, 62
  topic sentence in, 55–56, 62–64, 66–68, 71–72, 105–106, 135
  types of
  descriptive, 87–94
  explanatory, 97–99
  narrative, 103–106
paragraph, development of, 55–85
  anecdote in, 75, 80–81
  comparison in, 74–75, 82–83
  contrast in, 74–75, 83–84
  examples in, 74–75, 78–79, 97
  facts in, 75–76, 97–98
  incident in, 75, 80–81, 97
  main idea in, 55–74
  statistics in, 75–76
  unity in, 66–85
paragraph, thesis, 110–111, 130–133
parentheses, 217–28
parenthetical expressions, 201–202
participial phrase, 204, 46, 68–69, 98, 199, 204
participle, 15, 16, 17, 22, 45–46
passive voice, 17–18

touch, sense of
in descriptive paragraphs,
93–94
in understanding, 40–44
words associated with, 42
transformational grammar,
105–130
transition
devices of, in composition,
137–142
words of, 138–139
transitive verb, 17, 56, 127–128
two, to, and *too,* 242

unity, in composition writing,
137–140, 147
up, as preposition of direction, 31
us, 7

verb phrase, 52, 63, 112–113
verbal phrase, 41–42, 44, 46,
66–67, 68–69, 70–71, 97,
112–113
verbals, 40–46, 116–117
gerunds, 44
infinitives, 41–43
participle, 45–46
verbs
action, 12
agreement with subject,
132–142
auxiliary, 13–14
confusing, 182–183
conjugation of (example),
22–23
emphatic, 16
as form class, 107, 111–113
inflected forms, 112, 145

position in sentence, 113
relation to structural
words, 112–113
in sentence patterns,
126–129
intransitive, 17
irregular, 16, 173–179
linking, 13, 26, 113, 126–127
main, 13–14
mood of, 24–25
as predicate, 52, 82
progressive, 16
regular, 15–16, 172
transitive, 17, 56
voice of, 17–18
vertical file, 224, 241
very, as intensifier, 116
vocabulary
antonyms, 19
building of, 1–25
context clues in development
of, 2–9
frequently misspelled words,
243–246
inference in development of,
9–13
multiple word meanings in,
14–16
vocabulary
sense words, 31–34, 38, 42,
45, 49
synonyms, 17–19
voice, 17–18

was, 13, 126
water, capitalization of, 188
we, 7, 147
weather, whether, 242
well, good, 168
were, 13, 126

Handbook

12.0 The Semicolon, the Colon, the Dash, and Parentheses 211

13.0 The Apostrophe 219

14.0 Quotations 227